lonely planet

New Orleans

Tom Downs
John T Edge

LONELY PLANET PUBLICATIONS
Melbourne • Oakland • London • Paris

New Orleans
3rd edition – February 2003
First published – January 1997

Published by
Lonely Planet Publications Pty Ltd ABN 36 005 607 983
90 Maribyrnong St, Footscray, Victoria 3011, Australia

Lonely Planet offices
Australia Locked Bag 1, Footscray, Victoria 3011
USA 150 Linden St, Oakland, CA 94607
UK 10a Spring Place, London NW5 3BH
France 1 rue du Dahomey, 75011 Paris

Photographs
Many of the images in this guide are available for licensing from
Lonely Planet Images.
w www.lonelyplanetimages.com

Front cover photograph
The sign outside Preservation Hall, a classic place for jazz in
New Orleans (Jerry Alexander)

ISBN 1 74059 193 3

text & maps © Lonely Planet Publications Pty Ltd 2003
photos © photographers as indicated 2003

Printed by Craft Print International Ltd, Singapore

Contents – Text

PLACES TO STAY 109

PLACES TO EAT 120

ENTERTAINMENT 139

SHOPPING 150

EXCURSIONS 159

GLOSSARY 181

INDEX 184

Contents – Maps

Authors

Downs

...ing up, Tom spent a lot of time on buses. To hear him tell it, he ...ne of age aboard a SceniCruiser.' On one cross-country trip he got ... in New Orleans, checked into the Hummingbird Hotel on St ...harles Ave (rooms $45 a week), and found a job moving used office furniture. He blew his sparse income on beer and pinball and within a month was penniless and jobless. He had to pawn an acoustic guitar to pay his way back home. That was the steamy month of July in 1988, and Tom has been returning to New Orleans regularly ever since. Today he lives in Berkeley, California, with his wife, Fawn, and their offspring, Mai and Lana.

John T Edge

John T Edge writes for *GQ, Gourmet* and *Saveur* magazines, among other publications. He is a columnist for the *Oxford American*, and his commentary has aired on National Public Radio's *All Things Considered*. His work was featured in the book *Best Food Writing 2001*.

Edge has a number of books to his credit, including the James Beard Award–nominated cookbook, *A Gracious Plenty: Recipes and Recollections from the American South*, and *Southern Belly*, a mosaic-like portrait of Southern food told through profiles of people and places. He is general editor of the book series *Cornbread Nation: The Best of Southern Food Writing*. At the time of writing, he is at work on *Map of Dixie on My Tongue*, a meditation on race and food in the South, as well as the new foodways volume of the *Encyclopedia of Southern Culture*.

He holds a master's degree in Southern Studies from the University of Mississippi and is the director of the Southern Foodways Alliance, an affiliated institute of the Center for the Study of Southern Culture at the University of Mississippi, where he dedicates his time to celebrating, promoting and preserving the diverse food cultures of the American South. He lives in Oxford, Mississippi, with his son Jess and his wife, Blair Hobbs, a poet and painter.

FROM THE AUTHORS
From Tom

For Fawn, who can coo like a turtle dove and holler like Memphis Minnie. My kind of a woman. Little smooches for Maibone and Punkin.

Many folks helped me get the job done. Many thanks to Michele Posner, the commissioning editor at Lonely Planet who lined me up for this job and provided much-needed inspiration at the planning stages. China Williams, a fine Lonely Planet author in her own right, provided key fact-checking support. Hawk-eyed editor Nancy Ianni pointed out those embarrassing inconsistencies that overworked authors so often fail to see in their own writing.

As usual, New Orleanians Heidi Elizabeth Trull and Robert Florence made certain I kept my ear to the ground in all the relevant parts of town. Thanks to Sadie Gentry, Bonny Warren and Christine DeCuir for their hospitality and helpfulness. I'd also like to tip my hat to an old friend, Bob Girault, who helped on the last edition of *New Orleans.*

From John T

Thanks to Pableaux Johnson who gave me a berth in St Martinville, to Jess and Blair for giving me leave, and to all the good folks who endured conversational gambits like, 'So tell me your philosophy of po'boy architecture.'

his Book

he first edition of *New Orleans* was written by Robert Raburn. Tom Downs wrote the second edition and updated this third edition with help from John T Edge who wrote the Excursions chapter.

FROM THE PUBLISHER

This edition of *New Orleans* was produced in Lonely Planet's Melbourne office. Nancy Ianni coordinated the editing, with assistance from Kate James, Kayla Ryan and Diana Saad. The mapping was coordinated by Barbara Benson and Laurie Mikkelsen, with assistance by Herman So and Andrew Smith. The book was designed by Anna Judd, with assistance from Nick Stebbing and Larisa Baird.

Ruth Askevold designed the cover with artwork by Brendan Dempsey. Lonely Planet Images coordinated the photographs and Pepi Bluck coordinated the illustrations.

Thank you to project manager Kieran Grogan and commissioning editor Michele Posner.

Thanks

Many thanks to the following travelers who used the last edition. New Orleans and wrote to us with helpful hints, useful advice and in teresting anecdotes.

Tracey Anderson, Sola Bankole, Graeme Bell, Bart Berggren, Tanya Bok, Astrid Bremholdt, Wayne Brideaux, Daniel Brotchie, Suzanne Bundy, William Burgers, Anna Campbell, Anne Campbell, Francette Cerulli, Helen Cole, Sarah Collins, Jenny Cooney, Lucy Cooper, Angela Crowley, Margaret Cuthbert, David Deephouse, Ingo Friese, Del Greger, Amy Groth, Sven Gustafsson, Ian Henderson, Jeff Hester, Janice Hirshorn, Brigitte Hunziker, Brenton James, Lisa Johnson, Darren Kendall, Zia Asad Khan, Mary Latham, Daphnee Lavoie, Mildred Lee, Ryan Lopez, Jill Ludwig, Linda Lyon, Tamia Marg, Caitlin Massey, Caitlin and Bill Massey, Dawn McHugh, Jason McKean, Dan Milstein, Christopher Monger, Debra Mooradian, Sumi Osada, Allan Parker, Margie Politzer, Anthony Porter, Tom Ridout, Lisa Ryers, Mark Sammut, Tanya Schmalfuss, Don Smedley, Andrew Smith, Patsy Smith, Paul Steeples, Rob Stevens, Cathy Stewart, Jayne Sykes, Helma te Velde, Brian Tiernan, Helen Williamson, Alice Winkler, Anat Zohar

Foreword

ABOUT LONELY PLANET GUIDEBOOKS

The story begins with a classic travel adventure: Tony and Maureen Wheeler's 1972 journey across Europe and Asia to Australia. There was no useful information about the overland trail then, so Tony and Maureen published the first Lonely Planet guidebook to meet a growing need.

From a kitchen table, Lonely Planet has grown to become the largest independent travel publisher in the world, with offices in Melbourne (Australia), Oakland (USA), London (UK) and Paris (France).

Today Lonely Planet guidebooks cover the globe. There is an ever-growing list of books and information in a variety of media. Some things haven't changed. The main aim is still to make it possible for adventurous travellers to get out there – to explore and better understand the world.

At Lonely Planet we believe travellers can make a positive contribution to the countries they visit – if they respect their host communities and spend their money wisely. Since 1986 a percentage of the income from each book has been donated to aid projects and human rights campaigns, and, more recently, to wildlife conservation.

Although inclusion in a guidebook usually implies a recommendation we cannot list every good place. Exclusion does not necessarily imply criticism. In fact there are a number of reasons why we might exclude a place – sometimes it is simply inappropriate to encourage an influx of travellers.

UPDATES & READER FEEDBACK

Things change – prices go up, schedules change, good places go bad and bad places go bankrupt. Nothing stays the same. So, if you find things better or worse, recently opened or long-since closed, please tell us and help make the next edition even more accurate and useful.

Lonely Planet thoroughly updates each guidebook as often as possible – usually every two years, although for some destinations the gap can be longer. Between editions, up-to-date information is available in our free, monthly email bulletin *Comet* (W www.lonelyplanet.com/newsletters). You can also check out the *Thorn Tree* bulletin board and *Postcards* section of our website, which carry unverified, but fascinating, reports from travellers.

Tell us about it! We genuinely value your feedback. A well-travelled team at Lonely Planet reads and acknowledges every email and letter we receive and ensures that every morsel of information finds its way to the relevant authors, editors and cartographers.

Everyone who writes to us will find their name listed in the next edition of the appropriate guidebook. The very best contributions will be rewarded with a free guidebook.

We may edit, reproduce and incorporate your comments in Lonely Planet products such as guidebooks, websites and digital products, so let us know if you don't want your comments reproduced or your name acknowledged.

How to contact Lonely Planet:
Online: e talk2us@lonelyplanet.com.au, W www.lonelyplanet.com
Australia: Locked Bag 1, Footscray, Victoria 3011
UK: 10a Spring Place, London NW5 3BH
USA: 150 Linden St, Oakland, CA 94607

Introduction

To walk the narrow streets and passageways of the French Quarter in New Orleans is to be taken in by the corrupted romance that lingers in the air like red wine on a lover's breath. New Orleans has its mysterious charms, to be sure; it enthralls the beguiled stroller as much as a magician ensnares his audience, making each visitor feel as if something impossible is happening, and that they are the first to come along and discover it. Each block recalls its own alluring stories that deftly blend fact and fiction, and we willingly buy into all of it.

New Orleans craftily seduces its visitors. It subdues defenseless hearts with waves of sultry heat that soften lacy iron balconies until they sag overhead. It enshrouds us in dreams in the spotted shade of live oak trees and it soothes us in worn stucco courtyards. It slips voodoo potions into sweet-tasting cocktails and casually drops anecdotes about its past. It conjures alluring melodies in the background. Moist winds make fan-like palmettos slap into each other and dime-sized raindrops pelt the leaves of banana trees. The city's Caribbean colors intensify.

In time one discovers that New Orleans – liltingly articulated as 'new **or**-lee-uns' or, more lazily, as 'new **or**-luns' (drawled out as 'Nawlins' by many) – is a complex city, more so than any other in North America. It has an impractical, romantic heart and a defiant, artistic nature. Its setting, on a water-logged patch of earth beside a particularly ominous curve of the Mississippi River, defies logic. It has chosen its own loopy course through time, following the side roads and back alleys of centuries past. It explores the bad neighborhoods of each decade with one hand on the wheel, while the other twists the dial on the radio, seeking jump rhythms and deeply felt laments recorded many years ago. It skulks through time with the cunning of a viper, refining its own peculiar, slightly disturbed sensibilities, living it up as though a death sentence hangs over it. Its tragic flaws endear it to those who love it.

This enigmatic municipality has become a major tourist draw, and its decadence has become something of a commodity. Just as salacious sailors once anticipated spending shore leaves lolling in Storyville parlors, today's enthused travelers and conventioneers come to hedonistic New Orleans with thoughts of stepping out of the routines of their lives. They flood Creole restaurants, Frenchmen St bars and French Quarter jazz clubs, they lose themselves for a little while, go a little crazy, and in the morning civic workers come out to hose away the previous night's sins. Although New Orleans remains somewhat secretive and mysterious, it is sincere in welcoming visitors. It throws parties and opens up certain rooms in the house, leaving us to wonder what's hidden behind the closed doors.

Visitors are treated to no cheap sideshow, for New Orleans stamps enough of its own unique character onto everything that happens here. In a town as poor and small as New Orleans (just 500,000 residents – roughly half the number of out-of-towners who visit the city each month), tourist dollars exert a strong influence and could easily convert the city into an amusement park, distilling all that is real, vital and attractive in the Crescent City into an easily digestible, ersatz version of the real thing. In some places, this has already happened. New Orleans, showing an unsuspected pragmatism, has donated a few of its lesser limbs and organs to tourism, lest out-of-towners try to swallow the city whole. But the indelible spirit of New Orleans will not be denied, and even its tourist traps are, well, distinctly New Orleanian.

Take Bourbon St – if you aren't looking for the real pulse of the city, you just might enjoy yourself there. It's as architecturally charming as any street in the Quarter, but on Bourbon St you can drink liquor while walking from one bar to another. You can shout from the top of your lungs and still only amount to another member of the chorus.

A much better example of the New Orleans spirit is Mardi Gras, the grand spectacle that the city has brought to the New World from the Old. It is the pinnacle of the tourist calendar, as hundreds of thousands of people descend on the city to shed their puritanical ways for just a few days. Does it get out of hand? Sometimes, yes. But the spectacle is purely New Orleanian, and it is a beautiful reaffirmation of the city's identity. The city puts its pulsating heart on a platter and parades it down St Charles Ave for all to see. The locals do this purely for themselves, and they look forward to it all year long.

Perhaps an even better example of the real New Orleans is the New Orleans Jazz & Heritage Festival, which distills all of the most vital facets of the city's culture into two intense weekends. World-class musical performances are staged in circus tents rather than in nightclubs, great food is served from stalls rather than at restaurants, and thousands come to take part in this celebration of the city's virtues.

What other city can package its culture in this way and still draw enthusiastic crowds? All it takes is a compelling spirit that people can't help but fall in love with. And, of course, it doesn't hurt to possess the guile of a seducer.

When your visit is over and you're back home, alluring dreams of the city continue to haunt you. Your thoughts continually revolve back to New Orleans and the desire to return.

Facts about New Orleans

HISTORY

Among US cities, New Orleans is in so many ways an anomaly that one can't help but wonder how the city came to be the way it is. Many aspects of New Orleans' culture today suggest a profound influence left behind by the French, who colonized New Orleans for the better part of a century, and by the Spanish, who ruled during a few formative decades. It is equally significant that African culture has always held a stronger sway here than elsewhere in the US, and often with Caribbean influences. Of course, being a major capital of the South has determined many events in the city's history and contributes to its character today.

By North American standards, New Orleans is an old city, and the depth of its history is cherished by locals. Visitors can not help but sense the city's palpable past while taking an inquisitive stroll through the Vieux Carré, as the French Quarter is commonly called.

Native Americans

Nomadic Paleo-Indians were likely to have spent time in the area more than 10,000 years ago, but most evidence of their stay was destroyed by humidity, shifting river courses and rising sea levels. By 5000 BC, Archaic-period Americans were constructing a few earthen mounds, such as those at Avery Island in southern Louisiana. The following neo-American period, from 2000 to 700 BC, saw the construction of extensive earthwork structures and the first use of pottery.

The neo-Americans were replaced by a simpler culture. The Tchefuncte built small scattered settlements with circular shelters made from poles and covered with mud-caked thatch. From their large middens, we know they gathered plants and depended on clams, oysters and wild game for food. They used pottery for cooking and burial.

After 1700, Europeans documented numerous direct contacts with local tribes. Seven small tribes known collectively as the Muskogeans lived north of Lake Pontchartrain and occasionally settled along the banks of the Mississippi River. They spoke Choctaw dialects but were not members of the larger Choctaw nation. One band, the Quinapisa, attacked the expedition led by French explorer René Robert Cavelier La Salle, and later settled above New Orleans on the Mississippi River as the tribe fled an epidemic in 1718. Other tribes south of New Orleans inhabited the bayous in Barataria and the lower course of the Mississippi. Meanwhile, the colonists adopted native foods such as maize, beans, wild rice, squash and filé, a thickening agent made from sassafras leaves.

Most indigenous groups suffered as a result of European contact. Those who survived the epidemics or avoided capture by slave traders were most likely to have been absorbed by the Houma and Choctaw tribes, who were themselves moving westward in flight from English and Chickasaw slave raids. The Houma thrived in isolated coastal bayous from Terrebonne to Lafourche up until the 1940s, when oil exploration began in southern Louisiana and disturbed their way of life.

Alliances between escaped African slaves and Native Americans were common. Early French settlers also often married Native American women. Today, it is not uncommon to encounter their culturally and racially mixed descendants among the nearly 19,000 dispersed Louisianans who identify themselves as American Indian.

European Exploration

Europeans probably first saw the mouth of the Mississippi River as early as 1519, when the Spanish explorer Alonso Alvarez de Pineda is believed to have come upon it. Word of such an entryway to the heart of North America reached Europe, and several explorers attempted to find it.

Many of those who did find the Mississippi met tragic ends. The Spanish conquistador Hernando de Soto's overland expedition from Florida to the Mississippi was a grueling three-year trek through some of the most inhospitable terrain in North America. In 1542, de Soto reached the Mississippi, where his reward was a watery grave in the river's gulf-bound muddy waters. After de Soto's experience, further exploration of the Mississippi was put off for well over a century.

In 1682, La Salle headed an expedition of 23 Frenchmen and 18 Native Americans that probed southward from French outposts on the Great Lakes. Upon reaching the Gulf of Mexico, he staged a ceremony to claim the Mississippi River and all its tributaries for France. This was no modest claim, for it included not only the entire river from Minnesota to the gulf, but a considerable part of North America extending from the Rockies to the Alleghenies. La Salle honored King Louis XIV in naming the area Louisiana. His maps inaccurately (and perhaps deliberately) showed the Mississippi River in the vicinity of Matagorda Bay (Texas), suspiciously close to New Spain's silver mines, which would have directly challenged Spain's claims there. In fact, upon his later return to the region, La Salle bypassed the Mississippi mouth – again, perhaps intentionally – and he was murdered in Texas in 1687.

The Mississippi Delta continued to elude sailors until 1699, when Canadian-born Pierre Le Moyne, Sieur d'Iberville, and his younger brother Jean-Baptiste Le Moyne, Sieur de Bienville, located the muddy outflow. They encamped 40mi downriver from present-day New Orleans on the eve of Mardi Gras and, knowing their countrymen would be celebrating the pre-Lenten holiday, christened the small spit of land Pointe de Mardi Gras – a name that would later have special cultural significance for New Orleans. With a Native-American guide, Iberville and Bienville sailed upstream, pausing to note the narrow portage to Lake Pontchartrain along Bayou St John in what would later become New Orleans.

French New Orleans

Iberville died of yellow fever in 1706, but Bienville remained in Louisiana to found

Nouvelle Orléans – so named in honor of the Duc d'Orleans – in 1718. Bienville chose his site on the Mississippi and the Bayou St John, which connected to Lake Pontchartrain and thereby offered more direct access to the Gulf of Mexico. The assignment of laying out New Orleans went to engineer Adrien de Pauger, whose plans from 1722 still outline the French Quarter today. Promotion of the endeavor fell into the hands of the shrewd Scotsman John Law, head of the Company of the West, an important branch of the Company of the Indies, which controlled trade between France and the rest of the world. Law's task was to populate Louisiana and to make a productive commercial port out of New Orleans. While Bienville's original group of 30 ex-convicts, six carpenters and four Canadians struggled against floods and yellow-fever epidemics, Law busily portrayed Louisiana as heaven on earth to unsuspecting French, Germans and Swiss, who soon began arriving in New Orleans by the shipload. To augment these numbers, additional convicts and prostitutes were freed from French jails if they agreed to relocate to Louisiana. This inauspicious start for the colony would have an indelible impact on the city's character for generations to come.

In just four years, the colony's population ballooned from 400 to 8000. This figure included African slaves, thousands of whom the French brought to New Orleans in its first decade. Whites born in New Orleans, mostly of French descent, came to be known as Creoles, and their French-derived culture quickly evolved into one that was unique to New Orleans. German immigrants gallicized their names, began to speak French and blended in. Black and white unions, although illegal, were not uncommon, and several new castes emerged based on the amount of African blood people had – quadroons were one-fourth black, octoroons one-eighth black. These people, too, spoke French and in time also became known as Creoles.

The number of free blacks – *les gens de couleur libre*, or 'the free people of color' – grew in New Orleans. Bienville, for one, owned 27 slaves in 1721, and freed two of them in 1733 after long years of service. Some slaves, after taking on additional work for wages, were permitted to buy their own freedom. Some free persons of color had slaves of their own. In 1724, French Louisianans adopted the Code Noir (Black Code), a document regulating the treatment and rights of slaves and free people of color. Freed slaves still had to carry passes to prove their status and they were prohibited from voting, holding public office or marrying someone of another race.

Colonial mercantilism was an economic failure, and the harsh realities of life in New Orleans discouraged civilian immigration – especially by women. As a result, the colonists created an exchange economy based on smuggling and local trade. To increase the female population, the Ursuline nuns brought young, marriageable women with them in 1728. They were known as 'cas-ket girls' because they packed their belongings in casket-shaped boxes. Looking about her, one recently arrived nun commented that 'the devil here has a very large empire.'

New Orleans under Spanish Rule

Realizing that Louisiana was a drain on the French treasury, French officials negotiated a secret pact – the 1762 Treaty of Fountainbleu – with King Charles III of Spain. In return for ceding to Spain the extensive Louisiana territory west of the Mississippi plus New Orleans, France gained an ally in its war against England. For Spain, Louisiana represented a buffer between its possessions in New Spain and the English colonies along the Atlantic coast. The 'Frenchness' of New Orleans was little affected throughout its administration by Spain.

Not until 1766 did Spain bother to assert its control, but by sending only a small

Yellow Fever

New Orleans' reputation as an unhealthy place was widespread and well deserved during the 18th and 19th centuries, when its residents were ravaged not so much by wild living but by the horrors of yellow fever. Symptoms of the disease showed themselves suddenly, and death soon followed. The epidemics frequently rose to biblical proportions. An 1853 epidemic resulted in almost 8000 deaths; about 10% of the residents who remained in the city after some 30,000 had fled.

Yellow fever's primary victims were male immigrants, children and laborers, many of whom lived and worked in squalid conditions. Yet no one was immune, and entire families were often lost. Numerous orphanages arose to care for children who survived their parents.

Many 'cures' were as harmful as the disease itself. 'Treatments' that hastened death included exorbitant bloodletting and large doses of calomel, a poisonous mercury compound, whose horrid effects mortified skin and bone, causing them to slough away. In 1836 one visiting physician commented, 'We have drawn enough blood to float a steamboat and given enough calomel to freight her'.

Morticians were overworked and underpaid during these epidemics. In the rush to entomb those who were suspected to be contagious, the undertaker lost the opportunity to embalm, preserve tissues on ice or even conduct services. Many cemeteries became putrid, fouled by the mass of bodies that could not be interred quickly enough.

Dr Carlos J Finlay, a Cuban, announced in 1881 that mosquitoes were responsible for spreading the disease, an explanation that was further proved by Walter Reed in 1905. This explained why the greatest risk was to those who spent a lot of time outdoors. Health authorities in Louisiana urged people to screen their homes and eliminate mosquito-breeding grounds, but apathy and disbelief led to one last epidemic in 1905.

HUGH D'ANDRADE

garrison and few financial resources with the politically inept Governor Don Antonio de Ulloa, Spain aggravated the locals' bitterness over becoming Spanish subjects. Ulloa only spoke Spanish, and after he attempted to forbid trade with French islands, a rebel force drove him from office in 1768. In response, Spain sent 2600 troops led by General Alejandro O'Reilly, an Irish native who had joined the Spanish military originally to fight England in the 'Seven Years War.' 'Bloody' O'Reilly, as he came to be known, squashed the rebellion by executing its leaders and arresting hundreds of others.

Participating in the rebellion were several hundred Acadians who had recently arrived in Louisiana. They had been deported by the British from Nova Scotia in 1755 after they refused to pledge allegiance to England, and left aboard unseaworthy ships. The largely illiterate, Catholic peasants were unwanted in the American colonies and elsewhere in the Americas. Their loyalty to France, however, appealed to French loyalists in New Orleans, who wanted increased popular support prior to the rebellion against Ulloa. Once the Spanish reasserted their control, the Acadians were no longer welcome in New Orleans, where the citified Creoles regarded them as country trash. Once again, the Acadians were banished, this time to the upland prairies of western Louisiana, where at last they were able to resume their lifestyle of raising livestock. For three decades, the wandering Acadians continued to arrive in Louisiana in the forced migration they called *le Grand Dérangement*.

Other former French subjects would soon arrive from Haiti. The slave revolt of 1791 in St Domingue abolished slavery in Haiti and established the country as the second independent nation in the Americas. Hundreds of slaveholders fled with their slaves to Louisiana, where they were free to maintain their way of life. Many former slaves also relocated to New Orleans as free people of color. They were joined in ideology by partisans of the French Revolution, which had abolished slavery in all French colonies. Wealthy New Orleans planters and merchants, however, rejected notions of equality

and denounced efforts to liberate slaves. Siding against France's revolutionary principles, Governor Carondelet deported activists and tried to quarantine the revolutionary contagion. But the seed was planted – in 1795 a failed slave uprising was widely supported by the lower-class whites of New Orleans.

Louisiana Purchase & Antebellum New Orleans

Like the French before them, Spanish officials became anxious to jettison the financial burden of Louisiana. In addition, they feared they would eventually have to fight the Americans to retain its control. Hence, Spain jumped at Napoleon Bonaparte's offer to retake control of Louisiana in 1800.

Meanwhile, US President Thomas Jefferson saw the need to seize the river capital of New Orleans, by force if necessary, to proceed on a path of western expansionism. Bonaparte knew that he risked losing New Orleans to the British and preferred that the territory be in American hands rather than under British control. Nevertheless, the US minister in Paris, Robert Livingston, was stunned by Bonaparte's offer to sell the entire Louisiana Territory – an act that would double the US's national domain – at a price of $15 million. On November 30, 1803, the Spanish flag on the Place d'Armes was quietly replaced by the French flag, which in turn was replaced by the American flag on December 20.

Little cheer arose from the Creole community, which envisaged Americans arriving in great numbers with their puritanical work ethic. Their Protestant beliefs and support for English common law jarred with the Catholic Creole way of life. In 1808 the territorial legislature sought to preserve Creole culture by adopting elements of Spanish and French law – especially the Napoleonic Code as it related to equity, succession and family. Elements of the code persist in Louisiana today.

Only one month after Louisiana's admission to the Union as the 18th state in 1812, President James Madison called for war against the British. His unpopular action barely registered with New Orleans residents until a British force assembled in Jamaica. Meanwhile, Louisiana governor William C Claiborne pursued ridding the state of smugglers such as Jean and Pierre Lafitte. Among other things, these Baratarian pirates conducted an illicit slave trade, years after the import and export of slaves had been outlawed in 1804. General Andrew Jackson arrived in Louisiana in November 1814, but locals were suspicious of his intentions when he imposed martial law. Their distrust of Jackson lessened when word spread that the British intended to free slaves willing to fight against the Americans. Meanwhile, Jackson convinced Jean Lafitte to side with the American forces in exchange for amnesty, thereby gaining the help of the pirate's band of sharpshooters and his considerable arsenal of weapons. Jackson also shocked many whites when he enlisted free black battalions and Choctaws. The Battle of New Orleans at Chalmette, just four miles from the French Quarter, was a one-sided victory for the Americans, with nearly 900 British losses versus only 13 US losses. Word soon arrived in New Orleans that the battle had actually begun after the US and Britain agreed to end the war.

New Orleans grew quickly as Americans moved to the increasingly busy port to make their fortunes, and soon the city's populace began spilling beyond the borders of the French Quarter. During the 1830s Samuel Jarvis Peters (1801–55), a wholesale merchant born in Quebec, purchased plantation land to build a new community upriver from the French Quarter. Peters helped create a distinctly American residential section, separated from the Creole Quarter by broad Canal St. He married into a Creole family and epitomized the American entrepreneur operating within the Creole host community.

Developers further transformed the 15 riverbank plantations into ostentatious American suburbs. By 1835 the New Orleans & Carrollton Railroad began providing a horse-drawn streetcar service along St Charles Ave, linking the growing communities of Lafayette, Jefferson and Carrollton. Today, these onetime suburbs are all part of Uptown New Orleans.

In spite of the Napoleonic Code's mandate for Jewish expulsion, and an anti-Semitic Southern Christian culture, trade practicalities led to tolerance of Jewish merchants. In particular, Alsatian immigrants augmented the small Jewish community in New Orleans and by 1828 they had established a synagogue. Judah Touro, whose estate was valued at $4 million upon his death in 1854, funded orphanages and hospitals that would serve Jews and Christians alike.

Americans took control of the municipal government in 1852, illustrating the erosion of Creole influence in New Orleans. American commerce had turned New Orleans into one of the world's wealthiest cities, but a political maelstrom had already appeared on the national horizon and would soon bring the city's prosperity to a crashing halt.

Civil War

During the first half of the 19th century, New Orleans' commercial ties to the North and to the rest of the world were much more developed than in any other city in the American South, and these connections had been instrumental in the city's rise to prominence. At the dawn of the Civil War, New Orleans was by far the most prosperous city south of the Mason-Dixon line. But Louisiana was a slave state, and New Orleans was a slave city, and it was over this very issue that the nation hurtled toward civil war. Politicians from the North increasingly spoke out against slavery, while Southerners began to clamor for secession from a Union that had grown hostile to their way of life. New Orleans wavered on the issue of secession. The city's merchants and bankers argued that New Orleans was economically tied to the North, but the tide shifted as the election of 1860 neared. Firebrand politicians warned that 'tame submission' to the North would lead to 'widespread ruin.' Abraham Lincoln, an Illinois Republican who was known for making statements such as 'I believe this government cannot endure permanently half slave and half free,' was elected president in November 1860, and incendiary newspaper editors responded by stating 'The Union is dead.' On January 26, 1861, Louisiana became the sixth state to secede from the Union, and on March 21 the state joined the Confederacy.

Fighting began in April at Fort Sumter, South Carolina, but the war didn't reach New Orleans until a year later. The Union readily achieved its objective to control the lower Mississippi River and New Orleans' port in April 1862. Captain David G Farragut led a US naval fleet up the Mississippi, bombarding Fort Jackson and Fort St Philip, which flanked the river south of New Orleans. The battle that took place there was brief but dramatic – likened to the 'breaking of the universe with the moon' by one particularly rhapsodic eyewitness – and Farragut's ships reached New Orleans a day later. It was the first Confederate city to be captured, and it would be occupied until the war's end in 1865.

New Orleanians, otherwise famous for their hospitality, didn't take too kindly to the occupation government or its leader, Major General Benjamin Butler. 'Beast' Butler, as the locals called him, was not intent on winning the hearts of the city's populace, and his presence unified the city in its hatred of him. Soon after the US flag went up in front of the US Mint, a New Orleanian named William Mumford cut it down, and Butler had the man hanged from the very same flagpole. The women of New Orleans, noting that the flag was not to be touched, began instead to insult Butler's troops by spitting on them and yelling insults. Butler's response to these recurring insults was to enact a measure specifying that women who partook in such 'unladylike' acts would be handled by law enforcement as women 'plying' their 'avocation.' Under Butler's rule, property was confiscated from citizens who refused to pledge loyalty to the Union.

On the other hand, Butler was also credited with giving the Quarter a much-needed cleanup, building orphanages, improving the school system and putting thousands of unemployed – both white and black – to work. But he didn't stay in New Orleans long enough to implement Lincoln's plans for 'reconstructing' the city. Those plans,

blueprints for the Reconstruction of the South that followed the war, went into effect in December 1863, a year after Butler returned to the North.

Reconstruction & Racial Fallout

The 'Free State of Louisiana,' which included only occupied parts of the state, was re-admitted to the Union a month later (the entire state wasn't re-admitted until after the war was over). The new state constitution abolished slavery and granted blacks the right to public education. The right to vote, which was extended to a few select blacks, soon followed. Two years later, a bloody riot erupted over attempts to extend suffrage to all black men, and the exceedingly violent police intervention in the melee led to the deaths of 34 blacks and two whites. It was a grim beginning for the Reconstruction period, foreshadowing an endless series of race-related struggles that would leave the people of New Orleans hardened, embittered and battered (see the boxed text 'Civil Rights in New Orleans').

In a move that caused no small amount of resentment among white Southerners, Louisiana's state constitution was redrawn to include full suffrage to blacks but not to former Confederate soldiers or rebel sympathizers. Blacks began challenging discrimination laws, such as those forbidding them from riding 'white' streetcars, and racial skirmishes regularly flared up around town.

White supremacist groups such as the Ku Klux Klan began to appear throughout the South. In New Orleans, organizations called the Knights of the White Camellia and the Crescent City Democratic Club initiated a reign of terror that targeted blacks and claimed several hundred lives during a particularly bloody few weeks. In the 1870s the White League was formed, with the twin purposes of ousting what it considered to be an 'Africanized' government (elected in part by newly enfranchised black voters) and ridding the state of 'carpetbaggers' and 'scalawags,' popular terms for Northerners and Reconstructionists who were then in government. By all appearances, the White League was arming itself for an all-out war

Open for business: Magazine St, Garden District   Paddlin' up the Mississippi

RICHARD CUMMINS

LEE FOSTER

RAY LASKOWITZ

All aboard the St Charles Ave streetcar – a New Orleans institution

New Orleans' fascination with voodoo, the occult and cemeteries endures. From simply adorned headstones to lavish tombs, these exotic boneyards prove that in death as in life, people never stop expressing themselves.

when police and the state militia attempted to block a shipment of guns in 1874. In an ensuing 'battle,' clearly won by the White League, 27 men were killed and scalawag Governor William Pitt Kellogg was ousted from office for five days until federal troops entered the city to restore order. Although Reconstruction ended in 1877, New Orleans remained at war with itself for many decades. Many of the civil liberties that blacks were supposed to have gained after the Civil War would be reversed by what became known as Jim Crow laws, which reinforced and in some ways ⬛ segregation and inequality.

As the 20th century approached, N⬛ leans attempted to get back to business the city staged the World's Industrial Cotton Centennial Exposition of 1884–5 herald its return to life. Although the exp⬛ was by most accounts a disappointing spec- tacle with lackluster exhibits (the awkward name was emblematic of muddled plan- ning), it did serve notice to the rest of the world that the city was once again turning its gaze outward. Manufacturing, shipping,

Civil Rights in New Orleans

Race relations in New Orleans have taken an up-and-down ride since whites and blacks began cohabiting the city nearly three centuries ago. Under French rule, Louisiana's Napoleonic Code included a *Code Noir* (Black Code), which carefully restricted the social position of blacks but also addressed some of the needs of slaves and accorded certain privileges to free persons of color. Under the Code Noir, abused slaves could legally sue their masters. Free blacks were permitted to own property and conduct business, in contrast to other parts of the Southern US where blacks had no such rights.

Many aspects of this code were dropped from state law after the US purchased Louisiana, but nevertheless blacks continued to enjoy liberties not seen elsewhere in the South. On Sunday, slaves in the city were permitted to sell their wares at markets such as Congo Square, where some were able to earn enough money to buy their freedom. At these markets, blacks were permitted to cele- brate African culture, and African music and spiritual practices continued to thrive here, more so than elsewhere in the generally intolerant USA.

But the Civil War and Reconstruction prompted a backlash throughout the South, with devastat- ing repercussions for African Americans. The slaves were free, but between the Civil War and 1954 institutionalized segregation and codified relations – known as Jim Crow laws – limited the move- ments and actions of all persons of color. For many in New Orleans' black Creole population – *les gens de couleur libre* (free people of color), who were accustomed to decent education and relatively comfortable standards of living – this meant that their social status took a dramatic turn for the worse.

With many blacks feeling the loss of their accustomed rights, New Orleans was a natural setting for the early Civil Rights movement. In 1896, a New Orleans man named Homer Plessy, whose one- eighth African lineage subjected him to Jim Crow restrictions, challenged Louisiana's segregation laws in the landmark *Plessy v. Ferguson* case. Although Plessy's case exposed the arbitrary nature of Jim Crow law, the US Supreme Court interpreted the Constitution as providing for political, not social, equality and ruled to uphold 'separate but equal' statutes. Separate buses, water fountains, bathrooms, eating places and courtroom Bibles became fixtures of the segregated landscape. Louisiana law made it illegal to serve alcohol to whites and blacks under the same roof, even if the bar had a partition for segregation.

Separate but equal remained the law of the land until the Plessy case was overturned by *Brown v. the Board of Education* in 1954. Congress passed the Civil Rights Act in 1964.

Today, New Orleans is governed by a multiracial council, and for much of the 1990s a popular black mayor, Marc Morial, presided over City Hall. Additionally, the city's police force has become increas- ingly mixed. Still, most of the city's elite is white, while the vast majority of the population is made up of blacks living at or near the poverty line. An uncodified brand of segregation is maintained by this disparity of wealth, and as elsewhere in the US, racial inequality is hardly a thing of the past.

...ville

...Orleans has always tried to keep its mind ...ousiness, but it has consistently shown a ...ndency to succumb to every vice known to ...umankind. As the song goes:

There is a house in New Orleans
They call the Rising Sun
It's been the ruin of many a poor gal
And me, I know I'm one...

As the 20th century began, many such houses were open for business all over town, catering to the natural and unnatural needs of men. Prostitution was such a flourishing business that it began to invade even the city's finer neighborhoods, and politicians, having little hope of ending the trade, sought at least to contain and control it. A district where prostitution would remain legal was created to the lakeside of the French Quarter, and it quickly gained renown as a modern Gomorrah – a domain of whores, pimps, madams, drug peddlers and a tragic number of wanton street urchins, a district whose very existence rested on its ability to foster and nurture any form of depravity.

This district, unofficially called Storyville, was proposed in 1897 by a city official named Sidney Story, and although Story reputedly lived a squeaky-clean life, his name will forever be synonymous with prostitution and vice. Storyville's residents simply called it 'the District.'

Some Storyville houses were sordid cribs enlivened by barrelhouse piano players like Jelly Roll Morton, a jazz pioneer who was also a journeyman card cheat and pimp, while others, such as one whorehouse capped with Moorish turrets, were genuinely posh.

WWI spelled the end for Storyville. In 1917, Secretary of the Navy Joseph Daniels ordered the district officially closed, expressing the navy's fears that legalized prostitution would cause the spread of social diseases among servicemen based at a New Orleans training camp. However, prostitution continued illegally along the same streets until the entire district was razed in the 1940s. A housing project now stands on the site and only a few of the original buildings survive.

trade and banking all resumed, and soon the city was again bustling with all the vigor of a major port.

Modern Adjustments

New Orleans snapped out of the Great Depression as WWII industries created jobs, and continued prosperity in the 1950s led to suburban growth around the city. Desegregation laws finally brought an end to Jim Crow, but traditions shaped by racism were not so easily reversed. As poor blacks moved into the city, many middle-class whites moved out. New Orleans' population quickly became predominantly black. The city's tax base declined, and many neighborhoods fell into neglect.

However, the French Quarter, which had become a dowdy working-class enclave after the Civil War, was treated to restoration efforts, and it emerged primed for mass tourism, which was becoming one of the city's most lucrative industries.

Even as the oil and chemical industries boomed in Louisiana, spurred on by low taxes and lenient environmental restrictions, New Orleans fastened its eyes on the tourist dollar. In the mid-1970s the Louisiana Superdome opened. The home of the city's NFL team, the Saints, it has also hosted Superbowls and presidential conventions and sparked a major revenue-earner for New Orleans: trade shows. All around the Superdome, new skyscrapers rose in the Central Business District, but by the end of the 1980s, the local oil boom went bust.

In 1978 the elections of New Orleans' first black mayor, Ernest 'Dutch' Morial, which marked a major shift in the city's political history. Morial, a Democrat, appointed blacks and women to many city posts during his two terms in office. Morial's tenure ended in 1986, and in 1994 his son, Marc Morial, was elected mayor and then reelected in 1998. In 2001 the younger Morial attempted to pass a referendum permitting him to run for a third term, but the city electorate turned him down. Ray Nagin became mayor in 2002.

Like most US cities at the end of the millennium, New Orleans benefited from trends toward urban revival, and crime has dropped in recent years. Still, New Orleans remains largely a poor city with a small tax base to support its public schools and social pro- grammes. Gentrification has mostly high- lighted a growing divide between the haves and have-nots. And, still, the divide is defined primarily by race.

GEOGRAPHY

At roughly the same latitude as Cairo and Shanghai, 30° north of the equator, New Orleans occupies the east sissippi River, about 90 m where the Mississippi emptie of Mexico.

If it wasn't for human interven of New Orleans would now be sw. The city's elevation averages 2ft be level. Elevated land, formed naturally b Mississippi's historic floods, exists near river levees, which generally serve as th city's crescent-shaped southern boundary.

Mississippi River Floods

For the better part of three centuries, people have gone to great lengths to prevent the Mississippi River, the largest river in North America, from spilling over its banks into the city of New Orleans. Upon settling the site in 1718, Jean-Baptiste Le Moyne, Sieur de Bienville, directed the construction of a mile-long, 3ft-high levee to protect the village from floods. With encouragement from Bien- ville, the French landed African slaves in Louisiana, in part to work on the levees. French prisoners whose sentences were commuted were also deported to work in Louisiana. By 1735 this labor force had extended the levees along both banks by about 30mi upstream and 12mi downstream. That year, high water breached or topped much of the system and filled the low areas to the north and northwest of the present French Quarter.

By 1812, continual building extended the levee system to Baton Rouge on the east bank and all the way to the confluence with the Red River on the west bank. However, the levees deteriorated under American control, particularly during the Civil War.

In the spring of 1927, a 100-year flood – so called because, according to local myth, floods of such size occur only once a century – devastated communities throughout the lower Mississippi Val- ley, inspiring a bevy of blues songs such as Blind Lemon Jefferson's 'Rising High Water Blues' and Bessie Smith's 'Muddy Water.' Congress' response to the disaster was less musical, but welcomed. In 1928, it passed the Flood Control Act, allotting funds to raise levees, dredge sediment from the river bottom and build floodways to divert high water into shorter paths to the Gulf of Mexico. The US Army Corps of Engineers, which had previously focused on channel improvements for naviga- tion, became responsible for flood control. So far, the efforts of the army corps have been success- ful. Recent floods have only inundated the same low-lying areas that experienced flooding during Bienville's time. During the early 1990s, the army corps completed an 8½mi above-ground flood- wall in New Orleans. The giant, steel floodgates at the foot of Canal St are normally open to allow traffic to reach the ferry. When closed, they represent a last-ditch defense against the rising water.

Of course, the point of so much defense would become moot if the river were to suddenly change its course – a prospect that appears inevitable if the river's history is any indication. Over many mil- lennia, the Mississippi has shifted its way across the wide flatlands from east Texas to the Florida Panhandle. As the naturalist writer John McPhee put it in his book *Control of Nature*, the river is 'like a pianist playing with one hand' – always seeking the shortest path to the gulf. Its current course, past New Orleans, is no longer the most direct, and the nearby Atchafalaya River, to the west, is clearly pointing a shorter way. If the Mississippi were to follow its natural inclinations and join with the Atchafalaya, New Orleans would bite the dust. The city would lose its freshwater source, its harbor and virtually all of its industry.

Upriver from New Orleans, the army corps wages an ongoing war against nature in an attempt to keep the Mississippi on course, but intervention in large-scale hydrologic processes is only a temporary fix in the geologic time frame. The will of the river never diminishes, and nature bides its time.

flows north toward the
... Lake Pontchartrain, which
... ...ern edge of New Orleans. By
...w-lying swamps along the lake,
...ave created neighborhoods that
...n massive pumps to carry storm
... the lake to avoid flooding.
...w Orleans is literally a fortress guarded
...130mi of surrounding river levees. We
...an assume that Fats Domino's hit song
'Walkin' to New Orleans' refers to travel
along the river levees, because no other land
connections exist. Motorists who are heading toward New Orleans on I-10 from either
the east or west travel over waterways on
elevated freeways.

CLIMATE

The Gulf of Mexico provides New Orleans
with plenty of moisture – the city receives

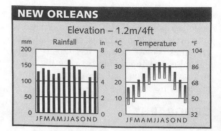

about 60 inches of rainfall annually. No
season is immune from rain.

In March, April and May the weather is
quite variable, with plenty of rain; but with
spring comes long stretches of sunny, mild
days that are perfect for the festivals.

Summer from June to August is hot and
steamy; your clothes stick to your skin and
you never feel dry. Brief afternoon showers,

Hurricane Season

As it passes through New Orleans, I-10 – the city's main freeway – is flanked by signs informing motorists that the interstate serves as a hurricane evacuation route. Local officials estimate that a full-scale evacuation of the low-lying, flood-prone city would take three days. Motorists caught in the typical rush-hour gridlock might imagine that such an evacuation could be impossible. Anyway, the only people likely to react to early warnings of approaching tropical storms would be visitors who would cancel their travel to New Orleans. Just remember that the average elevation here is 2ft below sea level and all evacuation routes cross open water.

Hurricanes in the Gulf of Mexico occur from June 1 to November 30, with the greatest frequency in late summer and early autumn.

A developing hurricane passes through several stages. A tropical depression is the formative stage, and a tropical storm is a strengthened tropical depression, with wind speeds between 39mph and 73mph. A Category-1 hurricane brings winds between 74mph and 95mph. This can produce a storm surge, or large waves, which can flood coastal roads. The most intense is a Category-5 hurricane, with sustained winds of 156mph or greater.

Fortunately, New Orleans has been spared a direct hurricane hit for more than 30 years. The last occurred when Hurricane Betsy crashed ashore in early September 1965, taking 74 lives throughout coastal Mississippi and Louisiana.

Following Betsy, the US Army Corps of Engineers began adding to the height of the 130mi of levees that protect all of Orleans Parish and some adjacent areas. The engineers' intention was to create a barrier capable of resisting the storm surges generated by winds of up to 130mph. Never-theless, if a storm such as Hurricane Andrew (1992), with 170mph winds, had veered directly toward New Orleans, a catastrophic disaster would have ensued.

Hurricanes are sighted well in advance. There are two distinct stages of alert: a Hurricane Watch, issued when a hurricane *may* strike in the area within the next 36 to 48 hours, and a Hurricane Warn-ing, issued when a hurricane is likely to strike the area. This is when you should consider canceling your visit or evacuating. Hotels generally follow evacuation orders and ask guests to leave. Ask at your hotel or hostel for more information as to the logistics of evacuation.

with thunder thrown in for dramatic effect, occur almost daily. On long summer days you can expect about eight or more hours of sunshine out of 14 possible hours. September and October are most likely to offer clear, temperate weather.

Winter temperatures average a comfortable 54°F, yet occasional drops in temperature, combined with the damp atmosphere, can chill you to the bone. Snow is rare in New Orleans. During December's short days, fog and rain conspire to allow only 4½ hours of sunshine a day.

Localized river fog often forms from December to May.

ECOLOGY & ENVIRONMENT

Ecologists are advising us to enjoy New Orleans while we still can. Many forces of nature threaten to either dramatically alter the city or wash it away entirely.

New Orleans is at the southern end of the broad Mississippi floodplain. The soil is loose and the water table is high, and while human engineering keeps the surging Mississippi contained most of the time, the geological record shows that the mighty river can't be kept down forever. Should global warming continue unabated, the resulting rise in sea level will place the city at increased risk of flooding. To facilitate that fate, the entire city is gradually sinking. The bigger threat, of course, is the prospect that a major flood will enable the Mississippi River to shift its course. (See the boxed text 'Mississippi River Floods' for more information.)

Meanwhile, wave erosion cuts away at almost 40 sq mi of coastal marsh each year,

Live Oaks & Their Be

The live oak (Quercus virginiana) emblematic tree in New Orleans. Be were harvested for shipbuilding, these nificent wide-spreading evergreens co the natural levees. Now they are relegated the parks and older neighborhood street where a Formosan termite infestation threatens their domain. A few great specimens in City Park are more than 500 years old; one tree, the John McDonald Oak, first sprouted in about 992 AD.

Beardlike Spanish moss (Tillandsia usneoides), which to some early New Orleanians resembled the bearded Spaniards who once explored the region, often drapes the broad oak branches. It is in fact not a moss (it's actually a relative of the pineapple), nor a parasite – it's an epiphyte, meaning it derives its nutrients from the air.

allowing brackish seawater to intrude inland. The gulf is advancing northward at a rate of a half mile per year.

Other hazards to the population and environment are the toxic emissions and river discharges from the many industrial and petrochemical plants that line the waterway between Baton Rouge and New Orleans. From the air at night, the string of plants resembles a foreboding film-noir scene. This section of the 'American Rhur' has also received the sobriquet 'Cancer Alley.' Louisiana leads the nation in toxic emissions, and a faint petroleum smell is often noted in parts of New Orleans.

You needn't worry, however, about the local drinking water. New Orleans' water is surprisingly good. By drawing its supply from below the river's surface north of the city, New Orleans avoids the floating pollutants and its own waste. Huge settling ponds effectively remove the suspended sediments, while chlorine and other treatments destroy bacteria and improve the taste.

Alligators

New Orleans boasts the largest gator population of any city in the USA, but the likelihood of actually running into one as you turn a corner is actually quite slim. Alligator nuisance control, operated by the Louisiana Department of Wildlife & Fisheries, reports the greatest amount of gator action following floods, usually in reclaimed marshland around the city's periphery.

GOVERNMENT & POLITICS

New Orleans is governed by an elected mayor and city council. (Parishes, as counties

...re called, originally were geo-
...nits outlined by the Catholic
...d they became political districts
...anish rule.)

...current mayor, Ray Nagin, took of-
...early 2002. At the time of his arrival
...ity Hall, many locals pointed to Nagin's
...ckground, which was in business rather
...nan in politics, as their main reason for voting him into office. It was widely felt that
what New Orleans needed was a straightforward business-driven policy to help the
city emerge from the economic doldrums
that had plagued it since the 1980s.

ECONOMY

New Orleans has revived its trade with Latin
America, resuming a relationship that thrived
in the 19th and early 20th centuries. The city
lost much of this trade to Miami in the 1960s,
but investments in coffee-bean silos and
cold-storage facilities for tropical fruits are
paying off. Even grain and steel exports from
inland plants are now reaching the Pacific
Rim after transshipment from barge to ocean
freighter at New Orleans' port.

Making up an increasing share of the
city's economy, tourism has seen steady
growth providing many low-paying service
jobs in hotels, restaurants and museums.

Wages in the State of Louisiana, as measured in income per person, lag behind the
wages in all other states except Mississippi
and Arkansas, where levels are destitute.
Even with its white-collar offices and well-
paying waterfront trades, New Orleans suf-
fers from declining earnings, and one
person in four lives below the poverty line.

During the 1970s New Orleans enjoyed a
booming economy propelled by the manu-
facture and financing of offshore oil rigs.
The economic turmoil of the 1981 oil price
crash reverberated throughout the state in
the following years, and the industry has
never fully recovered.

POPULATION & PEOPLE

Orleans Parish is home to approximately
500,000 people.

Diversity reigns in New Orleans. African
Americans constitute the majority, with

62% of the population, while whites comprise about 35%, and Hispanics around
3%. Many of the more recent arrivals have
ties to Central America, while Hispanics of
Cuban extraction are well established.

Despite its diversity, New Orleans shows
signs of geographic segregation, especially
for the most recent arrivals from Southeast
Asia. Strolling through the French Quarter,
one would never suspect that more than
12,000 Vietnamese and other Asians live
in New Orleans, mostly in the Versailles enclave at the far eastern edge of the city and
on the West Bank.

Gays and lesbians have long found ac-
ceptance in New Orleans, traditionally in
the lower French Quarter and Faubourg
Marigny, and increasingly in the Bywater.

ARTS

Music and architecture are New Orleans'
two greatest contributions to world culture,
but the Crescent City has been responsible
for its share of literary masterpieces, as well.
See the special section 'New Orleans' Musical Heritage' for more information on
New Orleans' music.

Architecture

Several New Orleans neighborhoods are
studies in distinct architectural styles and ad-
vanced preservationist techniques. While the
city has numerous landmarks, it is principally well-preserved areas such as the French
Quarter and the Garden District that make
New Orleans architecturally significant.

Historic preservation of the vernacular
architecture in the French Quarter has led to
what some critics regard as a 'Creole Disneyland.' It's an ironic comparison that really
ought to go the other way around, because
surely it's the small-scale charm of the Quarter that inspired Disney's Main St. In some
areas preservationists have gone overboard;
preservation is, after all, somewhat unnatural. The aim of restoration is not merely to
arrest a building's deterioration, but to restore
it to its original splendor – essentially turning
back the clock. Some longtime denizens miss
the rustic decay that marked the Vieux Carré
in days of old, but acknowledge that were it

not for preservationists the old Quarter would now be disappearing.

Efforts to preserve the quaint and distinctive elements of the French Quarter began when the federal government enlisted the efforts of the unemployed during the economic depression of the 1930s to restore the French Market and Pontalba Buildings. By the latter part of the 20th century, the preservationists' efforts began to leave a social impact on the French Quarter as working-class families were largely displaced due to high maintenance costs and rents.

Still, one cannot dismiss the accumulated impression that one gets from an overwhelming assortment of Creole houses and simple cottages. The familiar houses with overhanging balconies decorated by lacy, iron railings are among the most emblematic features of New Orleans. At the French Quarter's center, Jackson Square qualifies as one of the finest architectural spaces in the country.

For a closer examination of the architectural styles seen in the French Quarter, see the boxed text 'French Quarter Houses' in the Things to See & Do chapter.

The large mansions of the Garden District and Uptown are impressive both individually and collectively, and in some ways this part of town appears more naturally preserved than the French Quarter. The social makeup of these neighborhoods has pretty much remained the same over the years – they began as homes to the upper classes and remain so today. The prevalence of trees and dense gardens, and the absence of touristy shops and entertainment venues reinforces that these are neighborhoods where people actually live. One would be hard pressed to draw theme-park comparisons here.

Wealthy Americans settled the area and adopted Greek-revival architecture as a symbol of staunch classical tastes. The evolution of American design can be seen on tours that begin in the Lower Garden District and continue onto the Garden District proper (see the walking tours in the Things to See & Do chapter). Tours of the area around Audubon Park and the Tulane and Loyola campuses also offer much architectural splendor.

The most renowned local ar_ jamin Henry Latrobe. Latrobe _ Capitol in Washington, DC, anc_ worthy Baltimore Cathedral. After r_ in New Orleans in 1819, his early c_ sions included the St Louis Cathedral and the construction of the waterworks, their innovative pumping stations. Before succumbed to yellow fever, Latrobe de_ signed the Louisiana State Bank building, at 403 Royal St (see the Vieux Carré Walking Tour in the Things to See & Do chapter).

Another well-known architect is James Gallier Sr, whose son, James Gallier Jr, was also a distinguished architect. Gallier Sr is best known for the Greek revival–style Gallier Hall, at 545 St Charles Ave. He also took part in designing the Pontalba Buildings fronting Place d'Armes (which was renamed Jackson Square after the buildings went up).

Literature

Ever since Samuel Clemens acquired his Mark Twain pseudonym while piloting a steamboat on the Mississippi River, New Orleans has made an impression on American writers. You can pay homage to past greats at the March literary festival celebrating Tennessee Williams (see Public Holidays & Special Events in the Facts for the Visitor chapter).

George Washington Cable (1844–1925), described by Twain as 'the South's finest literary genius,' abhorred slavery and racism. He touched many Creole nerves with his fictional books *Old Creole Days* and, especially, *The Grandissimes*, both of which were set in New Orleans. His essays in *The Negro Question* (1885) are an indictment of the Code Noir and make compelling arguments for civil rights.

Author Kate Chopin (1851–1904) spent 14 years in New Orleans and southern Louisiana after marrying a cotton broker. She wrote her evocative accounts of the Creoles and Cajuns after returning to St Louis as a widow in 1882. Her second novel, *The Awakening*, was originally condemned for its portrayal of a young woman's adultery, but it was rediscovered in the 1970s as a masterpiece that evokes the region while

woman's discontent. Also look
...ction books *Bayou Folk* (1894)
...*t in Acadie* (1897).

...ulkner House, at 624 Pirate's Alley,
...e William Faulkner, at the onset of
...reer, briefly stayed with fellow author
...1am Spratling. An early novel, *The Mos-
itoes* (1926), is set in New Orleans, but it
s for the works *Light in August* (1932), *The
Sound and the Fury* (1929) and *As I Lay
Dying* (1932) that Faulkner was canonized as
one of America's greatest writers. For more
information on Faulkner, see the Things to
See & Do chapter.

Robert Penn Warren's fictional novel *All
the King's Men* (1946) captured a Pulitzer
for portraying Louisiana politics in the era
of Governor Huey Long. Warren then went
on to win more Pulitzer prizes for *Promises*
in 1958 and *Now and Then* in 1979.

Novelist Francis Parkinson Keyes, author
of the bestseller *Dinner at Antoine's* (1948),
lived at 1113 Chartres St.

While living at 632 St Peter St, playwright Tennessee Williams (1911–83) wrote
A Streetcar Named Desire (1947), which
portrayed Blanche Dubois' descent from an
elite family to life in the Quarter with her
sister and low-brow brother-in-law Stanley
Kowalski. As Williams descended down a
path of alcohol and drug abuse, his pathos
became increasingly evident in works such as
Suddenly Last Summer (1956), which was set
against a decadent New Orleans background.

**Tennesee Williams – the South's favorite
literary son**

Nelson Algren is rightfully claimed by
Chicagoans, but one of his most influential
novels, *A Walk on the Wild Side* (1956), is
set largely in New Orleans' decaying Storyville district. The saga of a Depression-era
scamp named Dove Linkhorn, it is perhaps
the definitive Crescent City novel.

Shirley Ann Grau writes fiction about the
American South with a sympathetic eye to-
ward African-American women. Among her
works set in New Orleans are *The Hard Blue
Sky* (1958) and *The House on Coliseum
Street* (1961).

Walker Percy's first novel, *The Moviegoer* (1961), is an existentialist portrayal of
a young New Orleans stockbroker, Binx
Bolling, whose despair and relationship
with his cousin Kate are revealed against a
muted Mardi Gras background.

John Kennedy Toole rose to posthumous
notoriety when his unforgettable portrayal of
hot-dog vendor Ignatius Reilly in *A Confederacy of Dunces* (1980) was published after
the author's suicide. No other book so readily prepares the visitor for the hapless and
semi-dysfunctional personalities that abound
in all spectrums of New Orleans society.

Romanian-born novelist and poet Andrei
Codrescu is best known for his travelogue
commentary on the vagaries of US culture,
Road Scholar (1993), which was turned
into a film. His offerings also include a
collection of essays, *The Muse is Always
Half-Dressed in New Orleans* (1993). Codrescu lives in New Orleans and teaches at
Louisiana State University.

New Orleans native Anne Rice established her credentials as a careful researcher
and gripping storyteller with *The Feast of
All Saints* (1979), which is a semifictional
account of *les gens de couleur libre* in antebellum New Orleans. Her best-selling vampire and witchcraft novels include *Interview
with the Vampire* (1976), followed by *The
Vampire Lestat* (1985), *The Queen of the
Damned* (1988) and *Lasher* (1993), among
others. If you yearn for more of her erotica
without the gore, look for her pseudonym
AN Roquelaure.

[Continued on page 33]

NEW ORLEANS' MUSICAL HERITAGE

As the hometown of an extraordinary nur early jazz stars, New Orleans holds a specia in the heart of all lovers of jazz music. N historians no longer get away with calling N Orleans the 'birthplace of jazz,' as any notion tha the music was born here – or in any one place – is now generally refuted. However, in its infancy jazz was certainly rocked and burped here. Jelly Roll Morton, King Oliver, Louis Armstrong, Sidney Bechet and many others strengthened their chops while suckling on the Crescent City's ample bosom.

New Orleans wouldn't be such an important place for music if music weren't so important to New Orleans. This is a celebratory city – surely more parades are staged here than anywhere else in the US – and in New Orleans no celebration is complete without music. Second-line parades, funerals, parties, brunches, festivals, fireworks, steamboat rides down the Mississippi – all are accompanied by music. As many a visitor to the city has observed, New Orleanians use music the same way they do a good pepper sauce – they pour it over everything.

New Orleans has always had a musical bent. The French and their descendants, the Creoles, were mad about ballroom dancing and opera. New Orleans boasted two opera companies before any other US city had even one. Meanwhile, slaves and free persons of color preserved African music and dance at public markets such as Congo Square. These European and African influences inevitably came together as French-speaking black Creoles, who prided themselves on their musicianship and training, began livening up traditional European dance tunes by adding African rhythms.

A proliferation of brass instruments after the Civil War led to a brass-band craze that spread throughout the South and the Midwest, and many musicians of the postwar generation learned how to play without learning how to read. These musicians 'faked' their way through a song, playing by ear and by memory, often deviating from the written melody. Thus, improvisation became another way to breathe extra life into musical arrangements. The stage was set for jazz.

Inset: Blowing brass in the French Quarter (Photo by Ray Laskowitz)

Bottom: Buddy Bolden changed the face of jazz

HAYDEN FOELL

Jazz Pioneers

Buddy Bolden One of the most problematic figures in jazz history is Charles 'Buddy' Bolden (1877–1931), New Orleans' first 'King of Jazz.' Very little is known about the cornetist's life or music, and no recordings survive. The details of his legend paint an attractive, larger-than-life picture, indicating that he made a huge

...sion on those who saw him play. Some said Bolden 'broke his
...' when he performed, while others mused that he would 'blow
...brains out' by playing so loud. One eyewitness account asserted
...at his cornet once exploded as he played it.

But the exaggeration veiling the actual truth about Bolden cannot
cheapen his stature. For roughly a decade, between 1895 and 1906,
he dominated a town already crowded with stellar musicians. People
were drawn in by Bolden's expressive and energetic playing, and audiences deserted the halls where rival dance bands were performing
when word spread that Bolden was playing somewhere else in town.
Naturally, all the young musicians of New Orleans wanted to be just
like him, and his influence was widely felt.

Sadly, Bolden went insane while still at the top of the New Orleans
music scene. He was institutionalized for 25 years, oblivious to the fact
that, after his abrupt departure from the scene, jazz had spread worldwide and had developed into many new styles. When Bolden died, he
was already long forgotten. Bolden is buried in an unmarked grave in
Holt Cemetery.

King Oliver After Bolden, New Orleans enjoyed a series of cornet-
playing kings, including Freddie Keppard, Bunk Johnson and Joe 'King'
Oliver. While Keppard's star passed over like a comet and Bunk lan-
guished in obscurity until he was rediscovered by 'trad' jazz enthusiasts in the 1940s, Oliver (1885–1938) made a break for Chicago,
where his Creole Jazz Band reached a much larger audience. Those
who followed Oliver's career say his sudden fame was deserved but
that he was past his prime when he reached Chicago. He was soon
overshadowed by his protégé, Louis Armstrong, whom Oliver sum-
moned from New Orleans in 1922. Together with Baby Dodds, Johnny
Dodds and Lil Hardin (Armstrong's wife), Oliver and Armstrong made
many seminal jazz recordings, including 'Dippermouth Blues.' By the
late '20s, Oliver had lost his chops – and his teeth – and his career
quickly went south. He hocked his horn and ended up supporting
himself as a fruit vendor in Savannah, Georgia, where he died in 1938.

Louis Armstrong Although he is sometimes referred to as 'King
Louie,' in the world of jazz Louis Armstrong (1901–71) is really beyond
royal sobriquets. The self-deprecating Armstrong is more widely
remembered as 'Satchmo.'

Armstrong made his greatest contributions to music during the
1920s, when he began to modify the New Orleans sound. New
Orleans jazz had always emphasized ensemble playing, but to better
utilize his own gifts for improvisation, Armstrong shaped his arrangements specifically to support his own driving improvised solos. With his
cornet riding above the ensemble, songs such as 'Muskrat Ramble' and
'Yes! I'm in the Barrel' had an intensity not heard before. If the music
sounds all too familiar today, it's because Armstrong's influence was
so far-reaching.

HAYDEN FOELL

As his popular Armstrong became summate showman, s jiving and mugging fo audience. His tours of Eur helped spread the popularit of jazz worldwide.

All of this, incredibly, was accomplished by the son of a prostitute. Armstrong grew up on the outskirts of New Orleans' notorious Storyville district, where he and his fellow street urchins would sing on the streets for pennies. While residing in the Waifs' Home for troubled youth, he began to learn the trumpet, and, obviously, he was a natural talent because he was soon playing professionally. Armstrong's big break came in 1922, when King Oliver hired him to play in his band in Chicago, and Satchmo never looked back. He only returned to New Orleans to play the occasional gig and, in 1949, to assume the role of Zulu on Mardi Gras.

Depth of the Talent Pool

The storyline from Bolden to Oliver to Armstrong neatly illustrates the evolution of jazz in New Orleans, but it leaves out many key players. At heart, New Orleans will always value the beauty of the ensemble; indeed, to consider all of the great musicians who played jazz early on is to regard a rare and wonderful collection of talent. Many musicians left New Orleans, but they carried the imprint of the city with them.

Their ranks included one who preferred to stand alone. Pianist **Jelly Roll Morton** was a controversial character – he falsely claimed to have 'invented' jazz while performing in a Storyville bordello in 1902 – but he had uncommon talents in composition and arrangement. **Kid Ory**, who hailed from nearby La Place, Louisiana, was also important in the development of jazz. His expressive 'tailgate' style on the trombone accompanied many of the first jazz stars, including Louis Armstrong, and when Ory moved his band to Los Angeles in 1919, he introduced jazz to the West Coast. **Sidney Bechet** was the first jazz musician to make his mark on the soprano saxophone, an instrument he played with vibrato and deep, often moody feeling. For 14 years clarinetist **Barney Bigard** was a key member of the Duke Ellington Orchestra.

The Barbarin family is legendary in New Orleans for producing some of the city's best-loved musicians, including drummer **Paul Barbarin** and his nephew, banjo and guitar player **Danny Barker**. Barker also wrote

Top: No one epitomizes New Orleans jazz like Satchmo

ular tunes for his wife, singer **Blue Lu Barker**. Members of the
family are still playing in New Orleans today.

is Prima also hailed from New Orleans, and although the Italian
pet maestro (composer of 'Sing Sing Sing' and 'Just a Gigolo')
ame linked to the snazzy Las Vegas entertainment scene, when his
me was up he came home and was laid to rest in Metairie Cemetery.

Blues

Despite its proximity to the Mississippi Delta, where the blues began,
New Orleans never became a blues capital the way Chicago did. The
blues have always been the domain of guitarists and harp players, and
New Orleans has always been primarily a brass and ivory city. But it
has never lacked great blues artists. Asked to name the king of New
Orleans blues, a local musician is likely to name trumpeter Louis Armstrong, whose blues-based solos of the 1920s and 1930s were equal
in expression and originality to those of any Delta guitarist of his day.

New Orleans has also been home to a few great blues guitarists,
beginning with Mississippi native Eddie Jones, who preferred to be known
as **Guitar Slim**. By the '50s, Guitar Slim was based in New Orleans, where
he packed patrons into nightclubs like the Dew Drop Inn. He wooed audiences with his anguished vocal style and agitated guitar licks. His biggest
hit – a gift from the devil, he said – was 'The Things I Used to Do,' which
sold a million copies. Other New Orleans blues guitarists include living
legends **Earl King**, whose 'Trick Bag' and 'Come on Baby' are essential
items on any New Orleans jukebox, and blind guitarist **Snooks Eaglin**.

R&B & Soul

Although New Orleans is still widely regarded as a jazz city, it is just as
much an R&B and soul city. Since the 1950s and 1960s, the city has
been churning out popular singers, drummers and piano players in
truly mind-boggling numbers.

New Orleans owes its solid reputation as a breeding ground for piano
players to a man named Henry Roeland Byrd – otherwise known as -
Professor Longhair. His rhythmic rhumba and boogie-woogie style of
playing propelled him to local success with tunes such as 'Tipitina' (for
which the legendary nightclub is named) and 'Go to the Mardi Gras.'
He did not tour, though, and his name soon faded away. His style of
playing, however, lived on in younger pianists like **Huey 'Piano' Smith**
who recorded 'Rockin' Pneumonia and the Boogie Woogie Flu' and the
eye-patched genius **James Booker**. In 1970, Professor Longhair was
barely making a living sweeping floors when promoter Quint Davis
tracked him down and booked him for that spring's Jazz Fest. That performance launched a decade of long-overdue recognition for one of
New Orleans' great performers. He died a peaceful death in 1980.

While Professor Longhair was still mired in obscurity, some very
unforgettable tunes came out of the Crescent City to rock the nation.
'Lawdy Miss Clawdy' was cut by **Lloyd Price**, with a backup band that
included **Dave Bartholomew** and **Fats Domino**, the duo credited with

shaping the 'New Orleans sound.' Bartholomew's trademark ar ments, built on soulful horns and a solid backbeat (laid dow drummer Earl Palmer), can be heard on many of the big hits of the ' including some of Little Richard's early recordings. In collaboration w Bartholomew, Domino would go on to become one of the city's mos successful musicians, recording a string of hit singles including 'Blueberry Hill,' 'My Blue Heaven' and 'Ain't that a Shame.'

The familiar expression 'see you later, alligator' naturally resulted in a catchy New Orleans pop song, recorded by **Bobby Charles** in 1955. The often-covered 'Ooh Poo Pah Doo' is also a local creation, and was first delivered by singer **Jessie Hill**. Other stars to emerge from the Crescent City during this period were the late, great **Johnny Adams**, who wooed the city with smooth, gut-wrenching ballads, and the dynamic pop duo **Shirley & Lee**, whose 'Let the Good Times Roll' became standard fare on radio playlists nationwide.

In the 1960s R&B in New Orleans and elsewhere fell under the spell of **Allen Toussaint**, a talented producer, songwriter and musician whose legion of hits is legendary. As the producer and talent developer at Minit Records, he exhibited a remarkable adaptability in molding songs to suit the talents of many of New Orleans' diverse young artists. The formula worked for **Ernie K-Doe**, who hit pay dirt with the disgruntled but catchy 'Mother In Law,' a chart-topper in 1961, and the coy 'A Certain Girl.' Toussaint also wrote and produced the **Lee Dorsey** hit 'Working in the Coal Mine,' which couldn't have been more different from the K-Doe songs.

Irma Thomas, the 'Soul Queen of New Orleans,' also frequentl collaborated with Toussaint. The former waitress was discovered in a talent show and was soon recording hits such as the sassy anthem 'Time Is on My Side' (later covered by the Rolling Stones) and the touching, autobi-

ographical 'Wish Someone Would Care.' A number of Toussaint-penned ballads, including 'It's Raining' and 'Ruler of My Heart,' lent definition to her body of work. These melancholic songs of resigned waiting and diminished expectations draw a compelling character portrait of the singer, who certainly experienced her share of ups and downs.

Toussaint's most enduring and successful partnership was with the Neville Brothers, who have reigned as the first family of New Orleans music for

Right: Professor Longhair pounds the keys

RINI KENGY

cades. **Aaron Neville**, whose soulful falsetto hallmarks one of the nstantly recognizable voices in pop music, began working with saint in 1960, when his first hit single, the menacing but pretty ver You,' was recorded. The association later yielded the gorgeous _et's Live.' But 'Tell It Like It Is' (1967), recorded without Toussaint, is the biggest national hit of Aaron's career.

Art Neville, a piano player from the Professor Longhair school, began performing with a group called the Hawkettes in the mid-'50s. In the late '60s, he formed the group Art Neville and the New Orleans Sound with guitarist Leo Nocentelli, bassist George Porter and drummer Zigaboo Modeliste, a group that would soon change its name to the **Meters** and define New Orleans funk music. The Meters later joined forces with George Landry, who as Big Chief Jolly was head of the Wild Tchoupitoulas Mardi Gras Indian gang (see the special section 'Mardi Gras' for more information); Landry also happened to be an uncle of the Nevilles. When **Wild Tchoupitoulas** began performing funk- and reggae-based Indian anthems (such as 'Meet de Boys on de Battlefront') in the mid-'70s, it marked the first time the four Neville brothers performed together – Charles and Cyrille rounded out the quartet.

The Meters and Allen Toussaint also contributed to the success of **Dr John**, who recorded his best-selling album *Right Place Wrong Time* with their support in 1973. Dr John began life as Mac Rebennack. He played guitar as a sideman for many New Orleans artists during the late '50s, but he switched to piano after his left index finger was shot off and sewn back on. He moved to Los Angeles and toured with Sonny and Cher in the mid-'60s before carving out his own unique blend of psychoactive soul and voodoo rock that have made him an enduring cult figure.

Rebirth of Brass

It could reasonably be argued that modern New Orleans music began with marching brass bands. Mobile brass outfits parading through the city's back streets for funerals and benevolent society 'second-line' parades during the late 19th century pretty much set the tone for things to come – Buddy Bolden, Freddie Keppard and even Louis Armstrong grew up idolizing the horn players who frequently played along the streets where these future jazz innovators lived. While early 20th-century ensembles such as the Excelsior, Onward and Olympia brass bands never became nationally recognized, their tradition did not die. Many brass bands today, including the current generation of the Onward, Olympia and the Tremé brass bands, still play very traditional New Orleans music, although surely they're jazzier than pre-20th-century bands were.

The brass band scene received a welcome infusion of new blood in the late 1970s with the emergence of the **Dirty Dozen Brass Band**. The Dirty Dozen were anything but traditional, fusing diverse styles of music from 'trad' jazz to funk to R&B to modern jazz. No longer a marching band, the Dirty Dozen continue to perform in clubs around town and tour frequently. They paved the way for the much funkier and streetwise **Rebirth Brass Band**, formed in 1983. Original members

of Rebirth, including trumpeter Kermit Ruffins, have mov
younger crew of musicians has kept the band alive, and it re
of the most popular groups in New Orleans, where Rebirth
regular club gigs. In recent years, brass music has continued to
in New Orleans, sometimes fusing with reggae music and eve
hop. Rappin' trombone player **Coolbone** is at the forefront of wha
terms the 'brasshop' movement.

Jazz Resurgence

When **Wynton Marsalis** released his first album in 1982, he was only 19 years old – and yet music critics proclaimed him a genius. Not since Louis Armstrong had a New Orleans musician been so well received on the national scene. It was the start of good things to come. Soon, Wynton's older brother **Branford Marsalis** was also making waves, and other young musicians who were studying with Winton and Branford's father, **Ellis Marsalis**, at the New Orleans Center for the Creative Arts, formed the nucleus of a New Orleans' jazz revival. These included pianist **Harry Connick Jr** and trumpeter **Roy Hargrove**. This wasn't another resuscitation of 'trad' jazz, though. The young turks of the '80s were clearly products of the post–Miles Davis and John Coltrane world. Since their beginnings in New Orleans, they have all relocated to other parts of the country, where media exposure and more money tend to be available.

The flow of talent from New Orleans hasn't ceased, and in recent years more rising stars have elected to stay at home, rather than seek the spotlight in New York or Los Angeles. The concentration of jazz artists in New Orleans is an obvious inspiration – this is an exciting time to be a musician or a fan of music in the Crescent City. **Henry Butler**, a blind pianist with extraordinarily quick hands, moved to California, but then returned to New Orleans, where he plays several nights a week in local clubs. He's been able to pursue several musical paths, from straight jazz to blues to funk and Latin. Trumpeter **Nicholas Payton** began his career recording classic New Orleans standards with a modern musical approach. He also joined forces with the ancient legend Buck Clayton in a Grammy-winning performance of 'Stardust.'

Trumpeter **Kermit Ruffins** may not have Payton's chops, but he's got more heart and is one of the most entertaining musicians in town. His shows often attract other musicians, who come for the chance to play with Kermit's band, the Barbecue Swingers – clearly a sign of a healthy music scene. Another trumpet player to watch is **Irvin Mayfield**, whose popular outfit, Los Hombres Calientes, includes yet another Marsalis brother, drummer **Jason Marsalis**, and the relative elder statesman, the legendary percussionist **Bill Sumners**. They've got a good thing going with their intense concoction of wildly expressive and percussive Latin jazz, and they put on a great live show.

Yet another trumpet player, **James Andrews**, has been gaining notice since the release of his album *Satchmo of the Ghetto*, on which Dr John (tinkling the ivories) and Allen Toussaint (producing) lend support. Andrews, who heads up an illustrious family of young musicians

...orty, a local celebrity since he was around eight years old,
...er brother), lays down some catchy, Toussaint-flavored licks
...um, but the album's title only perplexes (wasn't the original
...o also from the ghetto?). Additional musicians to check out
...e **Davell Crawford** (grandson of Sugarboy Crawford, of 'Jock-A-
fame), a funk-driven tour de force on piano and Hammond B-3,
...d **Donald Harrison Jr** (namesake son of the late Mardi Gras Indian
..hief), an inspired contemporary jazz innovator.

When in New Orleans, you're going to have to make some difficult
but enviable decisions, because on many nights several of these talented musicians will be performing at the same time in clubs around town.

Recommended Listening

To get up to speed on New Orleans music from the 1920s to the
present, here's a highly subjective list (in roughly chronological order)
of 10 great CDs, which are all widely available.

Louis Armstrong *Louis Armstrong 1925–26* (Chronological Classics) –
definitive early jazz recordings
Jelly Roll Morton *Jelly Roll Morton 1939–40* (Chronological Classics) –
the sound of Storyville
Sidney Bechet *Best of Sidney Bechet* (Blue Note, 1940s) – some sultry
playing by the soprano sax maestro
Professor Longhair *Collector's Choice* (Rounder, 1950s) – a good intro-
duction to one of New Orleans' most important R&B artists
Irma Thomas *Time Is On My Side* (Kent Soul, 1960s) – an essential
selection from the Soul Queen's songbook
The Meters *The Very Best of the Meters* (Rhino, 1970s) – steady, funky
instrumental grooves
Dr John *In the Right Place* (Atlantic, 1973) – psychoactive soul with an
Allan Toussaint groove
Wild Tchoupitoulas *Wild Tchoupitoulas* (Island, 1976) – a remarkable
collaboration, bringing together the Mardi Gras Indians, the Meters
and the Neville Brothers
Dirty Dozen Brass Band *Voodoo* (Columbia, 1989) – the second line
meets modern jazz
Wynton Marsalis *Standard Time, Volume 3* (Columbia, 1990) – jazz
standards by Wynton and his father, Ellis Marsalis
Nicholas Payton *Gumbo Nouveau* (Verve, 1996) – modern treatments
of New Orleans classics
Los Hombres Calientes *Los Hombres Calientes* (Basin Street, 1998) –
hip, modern, Latin sounds

Also, for a great overview of New Orleans R&B, blues and soul, check
out *Crescent City Soul: The Sound of New Orleans 1947–1974*, which
was issued as the 'official CD collection of the 1996 New Orleans Jazz
and Heritage Festival'. It includes everyone from Professor Longhair to
Dr John.

That was more than 10 selections, wasn't it? You didn't expect to go
away without a little *lagniappe*, did you?

Jazz Fest: a musical and cultural feast for the senses. For two weekends, New Orleans parties hard, eats and drinks her fill and grooves away to the sounds of the city's finest.

THOMAS DOWNS

RAY LASKOWITZ

JUDY BELLAH

The beat on the streets: a trumpeter goes solo (top left), while on Bourbon St the party rages all night long (top right). A bluegrass band does its twangin' thang in the French Quarter (bottom).

[Continued from page 24]

Georgia native Harry Crews made a brilliant detour to New Orleans with *The Knockout Artist* (1987), about a washed-up boxer who entertains at Uptown parties by knocking himself out.

Many mystery writers have tried to become New Orleans' version of Raymond Chandler. None has succeeded, but the mystery genre has nevertheless found a permanent home in New Orleans. You can't stop reading once you pick up one of James Lee Burke's novels about fictional New Orleans detective Dave Robicheaux (pronounced ro-bih-**cho**). Burke's books include *The Neon Rain* (1987), *Heaven's Prisoners* (1988, released as a film in 1996) and *Dixie City Jam* (1994), among others. In *Burning Angel* (1995), Burke broke away from the detective series to write a fictional account of organized crime and race relations. For yet another story about the mob in New Orleans check out John Grisham's *The Client* (1993).

Native son Elmore Leonard is another prolific detective and mystery novelist who occasionally pens a Western. His 1987 novel *Bandits* is set in New Orleans. In a shift from his regional nonfiction work, Tony Dunbar has also written the New Orleans detective novels *Crooked Man* (1994) and *City of Beads* (1995), featuring the Dubonnet Tubby character.

Cinema

New Orleans has no local film industry, but motion pictures set in the Big Easy have captured the city's cultural peculiarities in addition to its overstated politics, sex, violence and drinking. The musical genre, for which New Orleans once served as a staple location, has faded since 1958, when Elvis Presley starred in *King Creole*. Archives, however, are rich with footage of tap dancer Bill 'Bojangles' Robinson in *Dixiana* (1930) and jazz singer Billie Holiday's only screen appearance in *New Orleans* (1947). Louis Armstrong performed in *Hello Dolly!* (1969).

The highest-grossing film shot locally is director Oliver Stone's controversial *JFK* (1991), which includes numerous French Quarter scenes. Another hit, *De Walking* (1996) stars Susan Saranc Sean Penn in a true story about Sister. Prejean, a New Orleans resident whc votes time to death-row inmates and insp. discussion about the state's death penalty.

Andrei Codrescu's witty *Road Scholar* (1994) begins with his driving lessons in New Orleans before he hurtles across the US in a '59 Cadillac convertible.

Dennis Hopper and Peter Fonda play bikers in *Easy Rider*, the 1969 film classic. The scene of the two smoking pot in St Louis Cemetery No 1 upset the locals, since it introduced legions of youth to the New Orleans party scene.

Blaze Star, former governor Earl Long's main squeeze, told her story in an autobiography made into the 1989 movie *Blaze*, starring Paul Newman. Former governor Huey Long (Earl's brother, known as the 'Kingfish,' has been fictionalized in the Oscar-winning *All the King's Men* (1949), based on Robert Penn Warren's bestseller, and in *A Lion is in the Streets* (1953).

Hollywood has adapted many of Tennessee Williams' plays for film. His persistent portrayal of sexual repression and obsession often features New Orleans as a suitably decadent setting. In *Suddenly Last Summer* (1959), Katherine Hepburn as Violet Venable plots the forced lobotomy of her niece, played by Elizabeth Taylor, to preserve the reputation of her sexually irrepressible homosexual son. Vivian Leigh won an Oscar for best actress opposite a brutish Marlon Brando in *A Streetcar Named Desire* (1951), which also featured Oscar-winning supporting roles for Kim Hunter and Karl Malden. Filmed in and near the French Quarter, it deals with madness and rape. Don't bother looking for the famous streetcar that once ran on Desire St – it no longer exists. In a further disappointment, the name of the streetcar only sounds suggestive – it actually honors a woman named Desirée, rather than any particular form of yearning.

Louis Malle's *Pretty Baby* (1978), starring Brooke Shields as a pubescent streetwalker, was shot on location at the Columns Hotel. Julia Roberts plays a Tulane law student in

can Brief (1993), a film adaptation
. Grisham's bestseller. *Interview with*
.mpire (1994) features Tom Cruise and
. Pitt in the big-screen version of Anne
.e's novel.

Locals note that New Orleans police officers would never use French terms such as
'cher,' as did the fictional cops in *The Big*
Easy (1987). Its star, Dennis Quaid, was also
in *Undercover Blues* (1993) – one of the few
local films acknowledged in the local Planet
Hollywood restaurant's formulaic display.
Even devout fans of James Lee Burke's detective novels may flinch at the gratuitous
violence in the screen adaptation of *Heaven's*
Prisoners (1996), starring Alec Baldwin.

Michael Beaudreaux (pronounced **boo-**
dro) stars in *The Louisiana Story* (1945), a
semidocumentary about a young Cajun boy
who scouted the swamps for oil drillers.
The film's point of view – that Cajun culture and livelihoods can coexist with modern technology – is pure propaganda from
Standard Oil Company, which helped to
fund the production.

Writer-director Jim Jarmusch's black-
and-white film *Down by Law* (1986) stars
avant-garde jazzman John Lurie, grizzled
crooner Tom Waits and the crown prince of
Italian slapstick, Oscar winner Roberto
Benigni, as three down-and-outs at Orleans
Parish Prison. The repartee between the
three is the stuff of comic legend.

Other Hollywood films set in New Orleans, such as *Candyman II* and *Zombie vs*
Mardi Gras, had short runs at the box office. Nevertheless, *Zombie* has become
something of a cult classic.

SOCIETY & CONDUCT

Visitors to New Orleans are treated cor-
dially, even if they are never quite admitted
to the club; you need to have a few generations of New Orleans blood in order to be
fully accepted. However, conversation flows
easily between perfect strangers, whether
you're in a bar, at a restaurant or waiting in
line at the grocery store.

Cordial gestures abound. The use of 'no,
thank you,' 'yes, please,' 'ma'am,' 'sir' and
'How are you today?' might get you a better

room, a faster drink, a good table and at the
very least, a nod or a smile. Such politeness
generally crosses race and social lines in the
central parts of town. Out in some of the
dicier neighborhoods, people have tougher,
more inner-city manners.

New Orleans is not a fast-paced city. Service in restaurants and at shops can be slow.
Often someone serving you will be delayed
by a friendly conversation. The general attitude is that impatient people have their
priorities wrong. In New Orleans, life and
business are to be enjoyed, not rushed.

RELIGION

Roman Catholics predominate in New Orleans and the Cajun Country of southern
Louisiana, creating an anachronism amid the
Protestant 'Bible Belt' that shapes much of
the South. French and Spanish heritage, along
with a later influx of Irish, among others,
accounts for the Catholic preeminence.
Slaveholders were required by Bienville's
1724 Code Noir to baptize and instruct their
slaves in the Catholic faith – an edict not
rigidly followed. Nevertheless, Catholicism
is not uncommon among blacks today.

New Orleans' signature celebration –
Mardi Gras – is rooted in Catholic beliefs.
Carnival begins on 'Twelfth Night,' January
6 (the twelfth night following Christmas),
and continues to Mardi Gras, or 'Fat Tuesday,' which is the day before Ash Wednesday.
Catholics traditionally feast (hence in 'Carnival' the Latin root 'carne' or meat) before
Ash Wednesday, the beginning of Lent and
a period of penitence that continues until
Easter; see the special section 'Mardi Gras'
in the Facts for the Visitor chapter.

Slaves and immigrants from Haiti also
perpetuated their own belief systems brought
from West Africa. Voodoo rooted itself in
New Orleans as in other parts of the New
World – particularly in places like Brazil
and the Caribbean. Central African women
of the Fon and Yoruba tribes were especially
influential on the plantation estates and at
gatherings at Congo Square (now Louis
Armstrong Park). Much conjecture about
voodoo focuses on its mystery and on cere-
monies where worshipers enter a trance.

Small temples like the Voodoo Spiritual Temple at 828 N Rampart St, continue to serve worshipers.

Protestant Americans settled in the Uptown area and built the great churches that line St Charles Ave. After WWII, the influx of African Americans from the rural South augmented the Protestant presence in town.

LANGUAGE

Visitors expecting to hear French will be greatly disappointed. Nor should you expect to find a preponderance of the familiar Southern drawl. Instead, the dialect is most like that heard in the northeastern cities of Baltimore or Brooklyn. It reflects the same Irish, Italian and German roots, with some interesting Creole influences.

Many words have a unique meaning in New Orleans. When ordering a po'boy (equivalent to a hero or submarine sandwich in other parts of the US), you may be asked: 'You want it dressed?' An affirmative nod will get you lettuce, tomato and dressing (often mayonnaise). Check the Glossary for other locally employed terminology.

Local idioms abound. One may hear residents comment that they are going to 'make'

groceries, meaning they are go People also 'save' clothes, dish meaning they are going to put th away for later.

Sentence tags such as 'hear,' 'yeah 'him' or 'her' were once commonly hea the street. Cable's *The Grandissimes* tained the following example: 'I thi Louisiana is a paradize-me!' More recen examples appear in Toole's *Confederacy of Dunces*, such as when the underpaid character in The Night of Joy bar proclaims, 'I bet you give some color baby one-year-old a broom in he han', he star sweeping his ass off. Whoa!'

A possibly Southern trait found in the dialect at any level of society is the dropping of the final 'g' in words ending in 'ing'. For example: 'I was drivin' over to the Voo Carray to get a swimmin' suit.'

'Voo Carray' is an example of the local pronunciation of French. Its actual spelling is Vieux Carré. Many New Orleans streets have French names, and these are generally corrupted. Decatur is 'de-**cay**-ter,' Burgundy is 'bur-**gun**-dee,' Esplanade is 'es-plan-**aid**,' Chartres is '**char**-ters' and Carondelet is 'car-ahn-dah-**lette**.'

for the Visitor

TO GO

February through to April the climate w Orleans is most agreeable, coinciding the city's two most spectacular events – arnival and Jazz Fest. In May the heat begins intensifying, readying residents for summer. June marks the official beginning of the hurricane threat, which can last through to October and sometimes into November. The oppressive heat and humidity during the summer months causes many residents to flee to the Gulf Coast in Mississippi. August is simply stifling. If you're visiting in summer, prepare for the 'oven' effect of walking out of chilly 70°F air-conditioning into overwhelming tropical 95°F heat by wearing light clothes and bringing a sweater along for restaurants and theaters (not for most bars, however). Both September and October are months with agreeable humidity and temperatures for visitors. Christmas is an off-peak period with discounted accommodations and holiday food and decorations. Although winter temperatures during the large New Year's Eve celebration and the Sugar Bowl can be chilly, they are balmy in comparison with those in Midwestern US and Canada.

ORIENTATION

New Orleans is wedged between the meandering Mississippi River to the south and Lake Pontchartrain to the north. The original and most compact portion of the city parallels the river.

Within the city, the earliest settlements evolved on the relatively high ground along the river levee. Bienville's engineer, Adrien de Pauger, plotted a rectangular grid plan for Nouvelle Orléans around a central square, Place d'Armes, following the 'Laws of the Indies' precepts widely used by colonial powers in planning new cities. This became the Vieux Carré, or French Quarter. Colonial developers formed two additional municipalities bordering the Quarter, Faubourg Marigny and Faubourg Tremé (now more commonly referred to as the Tremé District).

Upriver from the town square, riverside plantations extended from the levee toward the lake in long, narrow rectangular plots. Their typical depth of 40 arpents (just under an acre) roughly coincides with Claiborne Ave, which paralleled the river, while St Charles Ave was intended to split the properties at the 20-arpent line. Anglo Americans subsequently subdivided and settled this area, generally referred to as Uptown.

One further feature had an impact on the city form. A subtle ridge of high ground near Bayou St John served as an early portage route between the river and the lake. Such so-called ridges were actually low natural levees. It attracted early plantation houses and other substantial homes, and became known as Esplanade Ridge, part of the City Park and Fair Grounds area, as is noted in this guide. Other bayou ridges include Metairie (**met**-ar-ee) and Gentilly.

Today, an important thing to note about getting around on New Orleans' streets is that 'avenues' are generally four-lane major thoroughfares and 'streets' are one or two lanes. Street numbering between the river and lake typically starts at the river. On routes that parallel the river, street numbers begin at Canal St. Because of the vagaries of the river, Uptown streets are labeled 'south' and downtown streets are 'north'.

The Mississippi River is the 'main street' and historical focal point for New Orleans. Directions, upriver or downriver, are relative to the water flow, which bends to all points of the compass; for example: 'The Convention Center is upriver from (or above) the French Quarter,' even though a compass would show that the Convention Center is south-southwest.

In addition, the river and Lake Pontchartrain serve as landmarks in 'river-side' or 'lake-side' directions: 'You'll find Louis Armstrong Park on the lakeside of the French Quarter – head toward the lake and you'll find it,' and 'Preservation Hall is on St Peter St toward the river from Bourbon St.'

The broad Canal St divides uptown from downtown. However, to add confusion, a large part of the city, from the Garden District to the Riverbend, is commonly referred to as Uptown.

People of different wealth, race and ethnicity create a checkerboard of neighborhoods in the compact city. It is often only a few steps from a ghetto to endowed estates. Note that the following overview is best accompanied by a look at a map.

Neighborhoods

The French Quarter (often shortened to 'the Quarter' and also known as the Vieux Carré) originally consisted of 44 blocks (it's now 80 blocks) centered on Place d'Armes (now known as Jackson Square) next to the river levee. The touristy upper Quarter is bounded by Canal St, where one finds most of the large convention-style hotels; Canal St separates the lower Quarter and the Central Business District (CBD). The lower Quarter, at the French Quarter's downriver boundary, meets Faubourg Marigny at Esplanade Ave, and both of these areas harbor the gay district. Below Faubourg Marigny is the transitional Bywater, fast becoming a burgeoning artists' neighborhood.

Beyond the Quarter's lake-side boundary at N Rampart St (named for the historic fortification that once surrounded the city) begins the African-American Tremé District. Away from the Quarter, lakefront City Park and the Fair Grounds (the site of Jazz Fest) are reached by Esplanade Ave.

On the river-side periphery of the CBD is the Warehouse District, a zone from Poydras St to Howard Ave, which is bounded by the river and St Charles Ave. The city encourages upscale galleries and developers to reuse the old warehouse spaces here. On the river-side boundary of the Warehouse District, you'll find the Ernest N Morial Convention Center and the Riverwalk Mall.

Downriver past the Canal St Ferry are the Aquarium of the Americas, Woldenberg Park and the Moonwalk. This general area is known as the Riverfront, and the Riverfront streetcar line traverses it before skirting the French Quarter.

St Charles Ave, the main Uptow and streetcar route from Canal S upriver past the Lower Garden Dist the Garden District to S Carrollton the Riverbend area.

MAPS

Good-quality maps of New Orleans are available from most bookstores, but free maps from a variety of sources are generally OK for most visitors. Car-rental agencies have heaps of maps, and so does the New Orleans Welcome Center on Jackson Square (see Tourist Offices, following). Most tourist offices also offer free copies of the *African American Heritage Map,* which shows points of historical interest in New Orleans along with contemporary enterprises.

Lonely Planet's handy laminated *New Orleans City Map* has all the key neighborhoods, a street index, and sights placed on the map. The map was designed to nicely complement this book.

American Automobile Association (AAA) members using AAA's *New Orleans & Vicinity Map* will appreciate the detailed 'metropolitan' coverage of the CBD and French Quarter, but the greatly simplified map of the city is disappointing.

TOURIST OFFICES
Local Tourist Offices

Right next to popular Jackson Square in the heart of the Quarter, the **New Orleans Welcome Center** *(Map 2, #86; ☎ 566-5031; 529 St Ann St; open 9am-5pm daily),* in the lower Pontalba Building, offers maps, up-to-date pocket guidebooks, listings of upcoming events, a variety of brochures and discount Regional Transit Authority (RTA) passes. The helpful staff can help you find accommodations in a pinch, answer questions and offer advice about New Orleans. However, relatively little information is available for the non-English speaker.

Information kiosks scattered through main tourist areas offer most of the same brochures as the Welcome Center, but their staff tend not to be as knowledgeable.

Jean Lafitte National Historic Park maintains a **National Park Service (NPS) Visitor**

...p 2, #134; ☎ 589-2636; 419 Deca-
...en 9am-5pm daily) in the French
. The park service's mission here is to
...et the history of the Mississippi Delta
New Orleans (the French Quarter and
Garden District are National Historic
...stricts), and it offers a variety of ranger-led
programmes, including talks and walks.

The **New Orleans Metropolitan Convention and Visitors Bureau** (☎ 566-5011; Ⓦ *www.neworleanscvb.com; 1520 Sugar Bowl Dr, New Orleans, LA 70112; open 8:30am-5pm Mon-Fri)* and the **Greater New Orleans Multicultural Tourism Network** (☎ 523-5652; Ⓦ *www.soulofneworleans.com; 1520 Sugar Bowl Dr, New Orleans, LA 70112; open 9am-5pm Mon-Fri)* share an address near the Superdome; neither has walk-in services, so you're best off calling, writing or checking the website. The Multicultural Tourism Network publishes a free visitor guide, *The Soul of New Orleans*, which is geared toward African Americans.

Information on Louisiana tourism can be obtained by mail from the **Louisiana Office of Tourism** *(☎ 342-8119, 800-414-8626; PO Box 94291, Baton Rouge, LA 70804)*.

Tourist Offices Abroad

The USA does not have a well-developed overseas tourist-office system. Contact your local US diplomatic mission (see Embassies & Consulates, later) concerning information from the United States Travel & Tourism Administration (USTTA). The best way to request that local information be sent by mail is by calling the **New Orleans Welcome Center** *(☎ 566-5031)* day or night. In the UK, contact the **New Orleans & Louisiana Tourist Office** *(☎ 020-8760-0377)*; there are no walk-in facilities. French visitors should contact Claude Teboul of **France Louisiane de la Nouvelle Orléans** *(☎ 01 45 77 09 68; 28 Boulevard de Strasbourg, 75010 Paris)*.

TRAVEL AGENCIES

The *Times-Picayune* Sunday travel section is a good place to search for discount travel deals. A few full-service travel agencies offer more than just cheap airline seats. Student and budget travelers can pick up Eurail

passes and other tickets from **STA Travel** *(Map 6, #22; ☎ 866-1767; 6363 St Charles Ave)* at the Loyola University Student Center. The **Four Corners Travel Agency** *(☎ 822-6244; 1000 N Broad Ave)* emerged in the 1960s to help minorities enjoy newfound equal access to public facilities.

AAA Travel Agency *(☎ 838-7500, 800-452-7198; 3445 N Causeway Blvd, Metairie)* offers complete travel planning for nonmembers and free maps and assistance for members.

DOCUMENTS

With the exception of Canadians, who only need proper proof of Canadian citizenship, all foreign visitors to the USA must have a valid passport, and most visitors must also have a US visa. It's a good idea to keep photocopies of these documents; in case of theft, they'll be a lot easier to replace.

Your passport should be valid for at least six months longer than your intended stay in the USA. Documents of financial stability and/or guarantees from a US resident are sometimes required, particularly for visitors from Third World countries.

Visas

A reciprocal visa-waiver programme applies to citizens of certain countries who may enter the USA for stays of 90 days or less without having to obtain a visa. Currently these countries are Andorra, Australia, Austria, Belgium, Brunei, Denmark, Finland, France, Germany, Iceland, Ireland, Italy, Japan, Liechtenstein, Luxembourg, Monaco, the Netherlands, New Zealand, Norway, Portugal, San Marino, Singapore, Slovenia, Spain, Sweden, Switzerland, the UK and Uruguay. Under this programme you must have a round-trip ticket on an airline that participates in the visa-waiver programme; you must have proof of financial solvency and sign a form waiving the right to a hearing of deportation; and you will not be allowed to extend your stay beyond 90 days. Consult with your travel agency or contact the airlines directly for more information.

Other travelers will need to obtain a visa from a US consulate or embassy. In most countries the process can be done by mail.

Visa applicants may need to 'demonstrate binding obligations' that will ensure their return home. Because of this requirement, those who are planning to travel through other countries before arriving in the US are generally better off applying for their US visa while they are still in their home country, rather than doing so while on the road.

The most common type of visa is a Non-Immigrant Visitors Visa (B1 for business purposes, B2 for tourism or visiting friends and relatives). A visitors visa is good for one or five years with multiple entries, and it specifically prohibits the visitor from taking up paid employment in the USA. The validity period for US visitor visas depends on what country you're from. The length of time you'll be allowed to stay in the USA is ultimately determined by US immigration authorities at the port of entry.

Tourist visitors are usually granted a six-month stay on first arrival. If you try to extend that time, the first assumption will be that you are working illegally, so come prepared with concrete evidence that you've been traveling extensively and will continue to be a model tourist. A wad of traveler's checks looks much better than a solid and unmoving bank account. Extensions are handled by the US Justice Department's **Immigration & Naturalization Service** (INS; Map 4; ☎ 800-375-5283; 701 Loyola Ave, room T8011; open 7:30am-2:15pm Mon-Fri), in the main post office.

Other Documents

Bring your driver's license if you intend to rent a car; visitors from some countries may find it wise to back up their national license with an International Driving Permit, available from their local automobile club. You'll also need a picture ID that shows your date of birth in order to buy alcohol (you must be 21 years old) or to enter bars and clubs. Make sure your driver's license has a photo on it, or bring some other form of ID.

A comprehensive travel or health insurance policy is very important for overseas visitors, and if you're coming from abroad, make sure that you carry a membership card or documentation.

EMBASSIES & CONSULATE
US Embassies & Consulates

US diplomatic offices abroad inclue following:

Australia (☎ 02-6214 5600) 21 Moonah Place Yarralumla ACT 2600
Canada (☎ 613-238 5335) 490 Sussex Dr, Ottawa, K1N 1G8 Ontario
Denmark (☎ 35 55 31 44) Dag Hammarskjölds Allé 24, 2100 Copenhagen
France (☎ 01 43 12 22 22) 2 ave Gabriel, 75008 Paris
Germany (☎ 030-238 5174) Neustädtische Kirschstrasse 4-5, 10117 Berlin
Ireland (☎ 1-668 8777) 42 Elgin Rd, Dublin 4
Japan (☎ 3-224 5000) 1-10-5 Akasaka Chome Minato-ku, 107 8420 Tokyo
Mexico (☎ 5-5080 2000) Paseo de la Reforma 305, Col Cuauhtémoc, 06500 Mexico City
Netherlands (☎ 70-310 92 09) Lange Voorhout 102, 2514 EJ, The Hague
New Zealand (☎ 644-462 6000) 29 Fitzherbert Terrace, Thorndon, Wellington
UK (☎ 020-7499 9000) 24 Grosvenor St, W1 1AE London

Consulates in New Orleans

Check the White Pages phone book (business listings) under 'Consulates' for diplomatic representation. Canada does not have a consulate in New Orleans; the nearest is in Miami. Other consulates include the following:

Denmark (Map 4, #23; ☎ 586-8300) 321 St Charles Ave
Dominican Republic (Map 4, #33; ☎ 522-1843) World Trade Center, 2 Canal St
France (Map 4, #41; ☎ 523-5772) 1340 Poydras St
India (Map 4, #16; ☎ 582-8000) 201 St Charles Ave
Japan (Map 4, #38; ☎ 529-2101) 639 Loyola Ave
Korea (Map 4, #23; ☎ 524-0757) 321 St Charles Ave
Mexico (Map 4, #33; ☎ 522-3596) World Trade Center, 2 Canal St
Spain (Map 4, #33; ☎ 525-4951) World Trade Center, 2 Canal St
Switzerland (Map 5, #34; ☎ 897-6510) 1620 8th St
Thailand (Map 4, #58; ☎ 522-3400) 335 Julia St
UK (Map 4, #23; ☎ 524-4180) 321 St Charles Ave

●wn Embassy

ourist, it's important to realize what country's embassy can and can't do. enerally speaking, it won't be much p in emergencies if the trouble you're in remotely your own fault. You are bound oy the laws of the country you are in and your embassy will not be sympathetic if you end up in jail after committing a crime locally, even if such actions are legal in your own country.

In genuine emergencies you might be able to get some assistance, but only if all other channels have been exhausted. For example, if you need to get home urgently, a free ticket home is exceedingly unlikely – the embassy would expect you to have insurance. If you have all your money and documents stolen, it might assist you in getting a new passport, but a loan for onward travel would be out of the question.

CUSTOMS

US Customs allows each person over the age of 21 to bring 1L of liquor and 200 cigarettes duty-free into the USA. Non-US citizens are allowed to enter the US with $100 worth of gifts from abroad. There are restrictions on bringing fresh fruit and flowers into the country and a strict quarantine on animals. If you are carrying more than $10,000 in US and foreign cash, traveler's checks, money orders or the like, you need to declare the excess amount. There is no legal restriction on the amount that may be imported, but undeclared sums in excess of $10,000 may be subject to confiscation.

MONEY

There are three straightforward ways to handle money in the US: cash, US-dollar traveler's checks and credit or bank cards, which can be used to withdraw cash from the many automatic teller machines (ATMs) across the country.

Currency

US dollars are the only accepted currency in New Orleans. The dollar is divided into 100 cents (¢) with coins of 1¢ (penny), 5¢ (nickel), 10¢ (dime), 25¢ (quarter) and the relatively rare 50¢ (half dollar). Quarters are the most commonly used coins in vending machines and parking meters, so it's handy to have a stash of them. Bills can be confusing to the foreign visitor, as they're all the same size and color. Bills come in denominations of $1, $2, $5, $10, $20, $50 and $100 – $2 bills are rare but perfectly legal. There are also two different $1 coins that the government has tried unsuccessfully to bring into mass circulation. You may receive the Susan B Anthony silver dollar occasionally as change from a machine; be aware that it looks similar to a quarter.

Exchange Rates

The travel section in the Sunday edition of the main New Orleans newspaper, the *Times-Picayune*, publishes current exchange rates as provided by AmEx. At press time exchange rates were as follows:

country	unit		dollars
Australia	A$1	=	US$0.66
Canada	C$1	=	US$0.68
euro zone	€1	=	US$1.04
Hong Kong	HK$10	=	US$1.28
Japan	¥100	=	US$0.84
New Zealand	NZ$1	=	US$0.53
UK	UK£1	=	US$1.57

Exchanging Money

Most major currencies and leading brands of traveler's checks are easily exchanged in New Orleans. You will also find various independent exchange bureaus. When you first arrive at the airport terminal, you can change money at **Travelex** (☎ 465-9647;

The Origin of $

New Orleans played a role in the origin of the US dollar sign during the Spanish colonial period of the late 1700s. Oliver Pollack, a wealthy Irish merchant engaged in the Mississippi River trade, made notations for 'peso' in his ledger that evolved from a separate 'P' and 'S' to an overlapping symbol by 1778. Further shorthand reduced the 'P' to a single slash.

open 8am-5pm) or at **Whitney National Bank** (☎ 838-6492; open 8:30am-3pm Mon-Thur, 8:30am-5pm Fri). Whitney charges a flat $5 foreign-exchange service fee. Travelex charges a sliding service fee ($2 for amounts up to $20, $4 for greater amounts). Since the exchange counters are only feet apart, get quotes from both, or wait till you can get downtown.

Better exchange rates are generally available at banks in the CBD. Typical opening hours are 10am to 5pm Monday to Thursday, 10am to 6pm Friday and 10am to 1pm Saturday. The **Hibernia National Bank** (Map 4, #13; ☎ 533-5712; 313 Carondelet St) and the main office of the **Whitney National Bank** (Map 4, #20; ☎ 586-7272; 228 St Charles Ave) both buy and sell foreign currency.

Cash US law permits you to bring in, or take out, as much as US$10,000 in American or foreign currency (including traveler's checks) without formality. Larger amounts must be declared to customs.

Traveler's Checks These are virtually as good as cash in the US; you don't have to go to a bank to cash a traveler's check, as most establishments accept checks just as they would cash. The major advantage of traveler's checks over cash is that they can be replaced if lost or stolen. Both AmEx and Thomas Cook, two well-known issuers of traveler's checks, have efficient replacement policies. Keeping a record of the check numbers is vital when it comes to replacing lost checks. Put this record in a safe place, separate from the checks themselves.

You'll save yourself trouble and expense if you buy traveler's checks in US dollars. Exchanging traveler's checks denominated in a foreign currency is much easier than it used to be, but is rarely convenient or economical. Purchase traveler's checks in large denominations such as US$100. Having to change US$10 or US$20 checks is inconvenient, especially as you may be charged service fees when cashing the checks at banks.

ATMs With a Visa or MasterCard and a PIN (personal identification number), you can easily obtain cash from ATMs ... greater New Orleans. The advantage o. ATMs is that you do not need to buy eler's checks in advance, you do not h. to pay the usual 1% commission on t. checks, and if you're from a foreign cour. try, you receive a better exchange rate. The disadvantage of credit cards is that you are charged interest on the withdrawal until you pay it back. In most cases you are also charged a fee for each withdrawal.

With the increasing interstate and international linking of bank cards, you can often withdraw money straight from your bank account at home. However, there is typically a terminal fee of $2 or more, and in some cases your bank back home will charge you an additional fee. Most ATMs in the area accept bank cards from the Plus and Cirrus systems, the two largest ATM networks in the USA.

Credit & Debit Cards Major credit cards are widely accepted by car-rental agencies and most hotels, restaurants, gas stations, shops and larger grocery stores. Many recreational and tourist activities can also be paid for by credit card. The most commonly accepted cards are Visa, MasterCard and AmEx. However, Discover and Diners Club cards are also accepted by a large number of businesses.

In fact, you'll find it hard to perform certain transactions without a credit card. Ticket-buying services, for example, won't let you reserve tickets over the phone unless you have a credit-card number, and it's virtually impossible to rent a car without a credit card. Even if you loathe credit cards and prefer to rely on traveler's checks and ATMs, it's a good idea to carry one for emergencies (Visa and MasterCard are your best bets).

If your bank debit card is affiliated with a major credit card company, businesses will accept it as they do a credit card. Unlike a credit card, a debit card deducts payment directly from your checking account. At some establishments (such as supermarkets, drugstores and gas stations), you can withdraw additional cash when you use your debit card.

...much money you need for visiting ...Orleans depends on your traveling ...e and the season when you visit. During ...e sweltering summer months, the same ...om that might cost $300 during Mardi ...Gras may go begging for under $50. Even restaurant menu prices fluctuate between the peak and off seasons – but not nearly so much as lodging prices. New Orleans' famed top-end restaurants will always test your credit-card limit. Alternatively, you can stay cheaply outside the French Quarter, live on po'boys and soul food and hit all the happy-hour drink specials.

Getting to New Orleans may take the biggest bite out of your budget. Car rental starts at about $40 a day. Parking a car in the French Quarter can be an expensive headache, particularly during busy tourist periods. If you're sticking close to the Quarter and along the St Charles Ave axis, you can save yourself that expense by hopping on a streetcar ($1.25 a ride) and walking. New Orleans also has a decent bus service. For excursions, organized tours may be available at less cost and hassle than renting a car. Nevertheless, if you plan to do a lot of traveling in southern Louisiana, a car may be essential.

Tipping

Tipping is a US institution that can be a little confusing for foreign visitors. Tipping is not really optional; the service has to be absolutely appalling before you should consider not tipping. In bars and restaurants, the waitstaff are paid minimal wages and rely upon tips for their livelihoods. Tip at least 15% of the bill or 20% if the service is great. You needn't tip at fast-food restaurants or self-serve cafeterias.

Taxi drivers expect a 15% tip. If you stay at a top-end hotel, tipping is so common you might get tennis elbow from reaching for your wallet constantly. Hotel porters who carry bags a long way expect $3 to $5, or $1 per bag; smaller services (holding the taxi door open for you) might justify only $1. Valet parking is worth about $2, and is given when your car is returned to you.

Bargaining

Almost everything at the **Flea Market** (Map 2, #48; French Market) is negotiable. Sometimes, you will automatically get a discount of about 10% if you're buying a quantity of books or recordings. When you shop also has a lot to do with the amount of bargaining that a seller will allow. Officially the Flea Market is open 24 hours; however, most vendors keep their own hours and most are open from 9am to 5pm. If the shop or service is open during the off-peak season and keeps regular hours, it is a sign of desperation. Most tour guides and shopkeepers prefer to spend the hot-wet-and-sticky months at a seaside cottage.

Taxes & Refunds

New Orleans' 9% sales tax is tacked onto virtually everything, including meals, groceries and car rentals. For accommodations, room and occupancy taxes, add an additional 12% to your bill plus $1 to $3 per person, depending on the size of the hotel.

International visitors to Louisiana can receive refunds on sales taxes (up to 10%) from more than 1000 Louisiana Tax Free Shopping (LTFS) stores. Look for the 'Tax Free' sign in store windows. Foreign visitors must show participating LTFS merchants a valid passport (Canadians may substitute a birth certificate or driver's license) to receive a tax-refund voucher. To get your refund at

The Dixie

The word 'Dixie,' synonymous with the South, traveled a peculiar road. Prior to the Civil War, the Citizen's Bank of New Orleans printed $10 banknotes. On the back of these bills appeared the French word dix (10). Southerners handling these bills began to refer to them as 'dixies.' A minstrel song, 'Dixie's Land,' by Daniel D Emmett, popularized the use of the word, and during the Civil War the Confederate States became affectionately known as Dixie. The phrase 'whistling Dixie' refers to the custom of Confederate soldiers to whistle the optimistic tune. No doubt the meaning of the expression was contrived by victorious Northerners.

the LTFS refund center at the New Orleans International Airport you must present the voucher(s) with the associated sales receipt(s), your passport and your round-trip international ticket indicating less than 90 days' stay. Refunds under $500 are made in cash; otherwise, a check will be mailed to your home address.

A complete listing of LTFS merchants is included in the *New Orleans Visitor Guide*, available free from the **New Orleans Tourist and Convention Bureau** (☎ 566-5005; W *www.neworleanscvb.com; 1520 Sugar Bowl Dr, New Orleans, LA 70112)*; tourists aren't really welcome to drop by, but you can call or check out the website. The guide includes instructions printed in French, German, Italian, Japanese, Portuguese and Spanish. Also included is a useful description of each store, including its address, opening hours and telephone number, which credit cards the store accepts and which languages are spoken by the store's staff.

POST & COMMUNICATIONS

New Orleans' **main post office** *(Map 4; ☎ 589-1135; 701 Loyola Ave)* is near City Hall. There are smaller branches throughout the city, including the **Airport Mail Center** (☎ 589-1296) in the passenger terminal; the World Trade Center *(Map 4, #34; ☎ 524-0033; 2 Canal St)*; the French Quarter *(Map 2, #112; ☎ 524-0072; 1022 Iberville St)*; and in the CBD at Lafayette Square *(Map 4, #45; ☎ 524-0491; 610 S Maestri Place)*. Post offices are generally open 8:30am to 4:30pm Monday to Friday and 8:30am to noon Saturday.

In the French Quarter, there are independent postal shops, including the **Royal Mail Service** *(Map 2, #64; ☎ 522-8523; 828 Royal St)* and the **French Quarter Postal Emporium** *(Map 2, #26; ☎ 525-6651; 1000 Bourbon St)*. These shops will send letters and packages at the same rates as the post office.

Postal Rates

Postal rates frequently increase, but at the time of writing the rates were 37¢ for 1st-class mail within the USA for letters up to 1oz (23¢ for each additional ounce) and 23¢ for postcards.

International airmail rates are 80¢ for a letter to any foreign country and 70¢ to for a postcard, depending on the destinatio It costs 60¢ to send a 1oz letter and 50¢ to send a postcard to Canada and Mexico. Aerogrammes are 70¢.

The **US Postal Service** (☎ 800-222-1811; W *www.usps.gov)* also offers a Priority Mail service, which delivers your letter or package anywhere in the USA in two days or less. The cost is $3.85 for 1lb. For heavier items, rates differ according to the distance mailed.

If you need to send something in a hurry, overnight Express Mail starts at $13.65. The Postal Service will even pick up your Express or Priority Mail packages for $12.50 per pickup.

Sending Mail

If you have the correct postage, you can drop your mail into any blue mailbox. However, to send a package that weighs 1lb or more, you must bring it to a post office. You can buy stamps and weigh your packages at all post office branches.

Receiving Mail

If you don't want to receive mail at your hotel, you can have mail sent to you at the main post office, marked c/o General Delivery, New Orleans, LA 70112. General Delivery is the US terminology for what is known as poste restante internationally. General Delivery mail is only held for 30 days. It's not advisable to try to have mail sent to other post offices in New Orleans.

Telephone

New Orleans telephones are run by Bell-South. The Yellow Pages has comprehensive business listings, organized alphabetically by subject. The New Orleans area code is ☎ 504, which includes Thibodaux and the surrounding area. Baton Rouge and its surrounding area, including St Francisville, uses the area code ☎ 225. Area code ☎ 318 applies to the northern part of the state.

When dialing another area code, you must dial ☎ 1 before the area code. For example, to call a Baton Rouge number from New Orleans, begin by dialing ☎ 1-225. At pay

nes, local calls start at 35¢, but long-
...ance charges apply to 'non-local' calls
...en within the same area code – to Thibo-
...aux, for example – and costs rapidly increase once you dial another area code. Hotel
telephones often have heavy surcharges.

Toll-free numbers start with ☎ 1-800 or
☎ 1-888 and allow you to call free within the
USA. These numbers are commonly offered
by car-rental operators, hotels and the like.
Dial ☎ 411 for local directory assistance; dial
☎ 1 + area code + 555-1212 for long-distance
directory information; dial ☎ 1-800-555-
1212 for toll-free number information. Dial
☎ 0 for the operator.

International Calls If you're calling from
abroad, the international country code for
the USA (and Canada) is ☎ 1.

To dial an international call direct from
New Orleans, dial ☎ 011 + country code +
area code (dropping the leading 0) + number. For calls to Canada, there's no need to
dial the international access code ☎ 011. For
international operator assistance, dial ☎ 00.

As a general rule, it's cheaper to make
international calls at night, but this varies depending on the country that you are calling.
The exact cost for making an overseas call
from a pay phone depends on the long-
distance phone company and the country in
question. For calls to Australia and Europe,
the cost is typically about $1.50 for the first
minute and $1 for each subsequent minute.
Calls to other continents usually cost about
twice as much.

To avoid having to keep feeding coins
into a pay phone while on a long-distance
call, you should use a credit card, subscribe
to a long-distance carrier or purchase a
phone debit card. Long-distance debit cards
allow purchasers to pay in advance and then
access their account through a toll-free 800
number.

Lonely Planet's ekno global communica-
tion service provides low-cost international
calls – for local calls, you're usually better
off with a local phonecard. The ekno service
also offers free messaging services, email,
travel information and an online travel
vault, where you can securely store all your

important documents. You can join online at
Ⓦ www.ekno.lonelyplanet.com, where you
will find the local-access numbers for the
24-hour customer-service center. Once you
have joined, check the ekno website for the
latest access numbers for each country and
for updates on new features.

Fax

Fax machines are easy to find in the USA –
at shipping outlets such as Mail Boxes and
Etc, photocopy outlets and hotel business-
service centers – but be prepared to pay
high prices (over $1 a page).

Aside from hotel fax machines, fax
services in the French Quarter include
French Quarter Postal Emporium (Map 2,
#26; ☎ 525-6651, fax 525-6652; 1000 Bour-
bon St), at St Philip St.

In the CBD there is a **Kinko's Copy Center** (Map 4, #49; ☎ 581-2541, fax 525-6272;
762 St Charles Ave; open 24hrs).

Email & Internet Access

New Orleans continues to lag behind other
cities in terms of online availability, but a few
services for traveling techies are available.
Your best bet is to have a widespread Internet Service Provider like AOL and use a local
New Orleans dial-up number. Carry your
own laptop to log on or send emails. When
making hotel reservations, be sure to ask if
your room is equipped with a modem line.

New Orleans Public Library (Map 4;
☎ 529-7323; Ⓦ http://nutrias.org; 219 Loyola
Ave), near City Hall, has terminals for free
Web access. Free access is also available at
the **Contemporary Arts Center** (Map 4, #64;
☎ 523-0990; 900 Camp St) in the CBD.
More central and more expensive are
Bastille Computer Café (Map 2, #108;
☎ 581-1150; Ⓔ e@netzero.net; 605 Toulouse
St; open 10am-11pm daily) and **Royal Access** (Map 2, #90; ☎ 525-0401; 621 Royal St);
both are in the French Quarter and charge
$5 for 30 minutes.

DIGITAL RESOURCES

The World Wide Web is a rich resource for
travelers. You can research your trip, hunt
down bargain airfares, book hotels, check

on weather conditions or chat with locals and other travelers about the best places to visit (or avoid!).

There's no better place to start your Web explorations than the Lonely Planet website at [W] www.lonelyplanet.com. Here you'll find succinct summaries on traveling to most places on earth, postcards from other travelers and the Thorn Tree bulletin board, where you can ask questions before you go or dispense advice when you get back. You can also find travel news and updates to many of our most popular guidebooks, and the subwwway section links you to the most useful travel resources elsewhere on the Web.

The *Times-Picayune* has a Destination New Orleans site on the Web at [W] www.neworleans.net or [W] www.nolalive.com, with listings of current events and other information for travelers.

Other useful websites, many of which serve as gateways to an infinite number of interesting links, include the following:

New Orleans Online ([W] www.neworleans online.com); great links to Mardi Gras sites

Offbeat Magazine ([W] www.offbeat.com)

WWOZ Radio ([W] www.wwoz.org); great links

Save Our Cemeteries ([W] www.saveour cemeteries.org)

Jazz Festival ([W] www.insideneworleans.com/ entertainment/nojazzfest)

Louisiana Music Factory ([W] www.louisiana musicfactory.com)

Neville Brothers ([W] www.nevilles.com); official site

Mardi Gras Indians ([W] www.mardigras indians.com)

BOOKS

If you're interested in finding out more about the city, many local bookstores are excellent resources for information (see the Shopping chapter for more information). In the French Quarter, Russell Desmond helps French and English speakers select new and used titles at his **Arcadian Books & Art Prints** (*Map 2, #71;* ☎ *523-4138; 714 Orleans Ave*).

Most books are published in different editions by different publishers in different countries. As a result, a book might be a hardcover rarity in one country while it's readily available in paperback in another. Fortunately, local bookstores and libraries can search by title or author, so these are the best places to find out about the availability of the following recommendations.

Lonely Planet

If you're exploring Louisiana, Mississippi, Alabama and the music capitals of Memphis and Nashville in Tennessee, pick up a copy of Lonely Planet's *Louisiana & the Deep South*. It's the perfect complement to this book. Also worth checking out is *New Orleans Condensed*. If you're traveling with children, it just so happens that LP publishes the book *Travel with Children*, by Cathy Lanigan and a slew of other intrepid parents who travel the globe with their children.

And if traveling is just an excuse to eat, check out *World Food New Orleans* for an introduction to the city's cuisines.

Guidebooks

Specialized guidebooks can really enhance your visit. Foodies will appreciate the pithy, no-nonsense review of more than 430 restaurants in Zagat's *New Orleans Restaurants*. New Orleans' rich diversity is naturally intriguing, but as with gumbo, it's difficult to identify the ingredients. For a real sense of place, read *Ethnic New Orleans* (1995), which uses maps and text to describe how the ethnic neighborhoods evolved. You can devise your own historical architecture tours using Leonard V Huber's *Landmarks of New Orleans* (Louisiana Landmarks Society, 1991). Special note should be taken of the architectural walking tours assembled more than 50 years ago by Stanley Clisby Arthur; numerous reprints of his *Old New Orleans* (1995) have received the careful attention of researchers at the Historic New Orleans Collection. You might have to ride to a couple of second-hand bookstores to find a copy of Louis Alvarez's excellent *The New Orleans Bicycle Book* (Little Nemo Press, 1984).

If you're planning on going afield, the Sierra Club's rough-hewn *Trail Guide to the Delta Country* (1992), edited by John P Sevenair, stands alone in offering hiking, bicycling and canoe outings geared to the outdoor crowd. The guide can be difficult to find, so you might need to phone or write the **Sierra Club** (☎ 482-9566; 5534 Canal Blvd, New Orleans, LA 70124). No visitor should venture into either the plains or wetland Cajun areas west of New Orleans without a copy of Macon Fry & Julie Posner's *Cajun Country Guide* (1993).

For out-of-town excursions, also pick up the free *Louisiana Traveling Kit* – it's hard to beat for short, uncritical descriptions of attractions, accommodations and restaurants throughout Louisiana. The kit is available from the **Louisiana Office of Tourism** (☎ 800-414-8626). Members of the American Automobile Association (AAA) can pick up a copy of the *Alabama, Louisiana, Mississippi Tourbook* for a list of mid-range to top-end restaurants and lodgings.

History

Pre-Columbian settlement is briefly treated in Robert W Neuman & Nancy W Hawkins' *Louisiana Prehistory* (1982). In *The Historic Indian Tribes of Louisiana* (1987), Fred B Kniffen and his fellow authors provide an excellent introductory review of history from 1542 to the present.

Gwendolyn Midlo Hall documents the development of an Afro-Creole culture during the 18th century in *Africans in Colonial Louisiana* (1992). Mary Gehman's slender monograph *The Free People of Color of New Orleans* (Margaret Media, 1994) offers a brief, nonacademic survey of Creole culture up to the present day. Her work is based on the unpublished work of Marcus Christian, who headed the 1930s New Orleans Black Writers Project of the Works Progress Administration (WPA).

Congo Square in New Orleans (1995), by Jerah Johnson, is a great little history (just 55 pages) about the important gathering place of slaves and free men of color during the 18th and 19th centuries. Published by the Louisiana Landmarks Society, it's available in most good bookstores in New Orleans.

The evolution of New Orleans' unique Franco- and Afro-Creole culture is further explored in *Creole New Orleans* (1992), a collection of six essays edited by Arnold R Hirsch & Joseph Logsdon. They make the point that it was no accident that the major challenge to discrimination came from a New Orleans resident, Homer Plessy, the man who took his case to the US Supreme Court in 1896 (see History in the Facts about New Orleans chapter for more information). For additional reading on the Civil Rights struggle in Louisiana, check out Adam Fairclough's *Race & Democracy* (1995). Stetson Kennedy's *Jim Crow Guide* (1959; reprint 1990) offers an eye-opening survey of the Jim Crow South.

Marshall Sprague re-creates the greatest land acquisition in US history – the 1803 Louisiana Purchase – in his book *So Vast So Beautiful a Land* (1974).

General histories dealing with New Orleans are not up to the standards of the above specialized works. Charles L DuFour wrote an archetypal chronology, *Ten Flags in the Wind: The Story of Louisiana* (1967). Cartoonist John Churchill Chase offers a witty lay history of New Orleans in *Frenchmen, Desire, Good Children & Other Streets of New Orleans* (1979).

Probably no other historical resource offers so much information on so many topics as the *Historical Atlas of Louisiana* (1995), by Charles Robert Goins & John Michael Caldwell. In addition to statewide maps that encompass Orleans Parish, it includes the routes of Native-American migration and colonial exploration, along with eight pages of maps and text specific to New Orleans.

Geography, Environment & Natural History

Southern Louisiana served as one of John James Audubon's prime areas for collecting and painting wildlife in the 1820s. Audubon's stature as one of the foremost artist-naturalists of his time came with the publication of his monumental *Birds of America* (1827–38). Most of his written chronicles about New Orleans are captured in the widely available second volume of *Audubon and His Journals*, edited by Maria R Audubon (1897; reprint 1986).

The Mississippi River has attracted the attention of many authors. *The Lower Mississippi* (1942), Hodding Carter's contribution to the Rivers of America series, remains a classic.

Wildlife lovers should also take a look at *Louisiana Birds* (1955) and *The Mammals of Louisiana* (1974), both written by George H Lowery Jr and published by Louisiana State University Press.

Mardi Gras

You can learn so much about the city of New Orleans by researching the topic of Mardi Gras – and you can start with any of a great number of books. Henri Schindler's *Mardi Gras New Orleans* (1997) is a fond remembrance of the days when the old-line *krewes* (crews) Comus, Momus and Proteus ruled the day. These are the krewes that stopped parading when antidiscrimination measures aimed to add color to their all-white membership, so in that respect outsiders might not sympathize with Schindler's sentiment. He is, however, one of the preeminent historians on the subject, and this is a thoroughly researched and beautifully illustrated book. (Expensive, too, at $50 a pop.)

An alternative and more critical view is expressed in James Gill's fiery *Lords of Misrule: Mardi Gras and the Politics of Race in New Orleans* (1997). This is also the much cheaper way to go.

Carol Flake captures the physical and cultural decay of the city in her chronicle of the Carnival season, *New Orleans: Behind the Masks of America's Most Exotic City* (1994). Unfortunately, Flake's return to New Orleans coincided with the vicious controversy over the integration of Mardi Gras krewes. She paints a bleak picture of social collapse rather than a rosy scene of healthy evolution.

Anything about the Mardi Gras Indians is bound to be a fascinating read, and Michael P Smith's *Mardi Gras Indians* (1994) reflects the author-photographer's remarkable access to a fairly closed society.

Music

In Search of Buddy Bolden (1978), by Donald Marquis, is essential reading if you are interested in the origins of jazz. *Remembering Song* (1982), by Frederick Turner, is another good book portraying the lives of a selection of New Orleans' key jazz originals.

You could read half-a-dozen books about the life of Louis Armstrong. His autobiography, *Satchmo* (1954), is a classic – an engaging and fascinating depiction of old New Orleans. Later, academic historians actually refuted some of Armstrong's history – but the great jazzman can certainly be forgiven if he improvised a little.

General

Folk tales of Louisiana told by Louisianans were recorded in the late 1930s by the Federal Writers Program of the WPA and compiled by Lyle Saxon, Edward Dreyer & Robert Tallant in *Gumbo Ya Ya* (1945; reprint 1991). Within this volume, Robert McKinney's story 'Kings, Baby Dolls, Zulus & Queens' is almost worth the book price alone for its description of black Mardi Gras celebrations during an era of segregation. Other stories by Creole writers refer to the ostracism that resulted from any trace of 'café au lait' among white Creoles. The unique aspects of New Orleans cemeteries also get special attention.

New Orleans probably has more books about its cemeteries than any other city in the world. The best one is Robert Florence's *New Orleans Cemeteries: Life in the Cities of the Dead* (1997). A self-proclaimed cemetery hound Florence has dug up some of the more intriguing stories about the USA's most fascinating resting places. The book is beautifully illustrated, with photographs by Mason Florence.

In 1991 the ultimate political race from hell featured Edwin Edwards (the crook), David Duke (the Klan) and Governor Buddy Roemer (tainted incumbent). John Maginnis follows the antics of the three unpopular candidates in *Cross to Bear* (Darkhorse Press, 1992).

If you must have access to all the facts, try lugging the enormous *Encyclopedia of Southern Culture* (1989) up a flight of stairs. Edited by Charles Reagan Wilson & William Ferris, it offers comprehensive coverage of everything from agriculture (page 1) to women's life (page 1515).

NEWSPAPERS & MAGAZINES

Locals will sometimes complain about New Orleans' only daily newspaper, the *Times-Picayune*. Nevertheless, with approximately a quarter of a million readers, it has the largest circulation of any newspaper in Louisiana. For 50¢ daily or $1.50 on Sunday – a few 'bits' more than when a *picayune* represented a fair exchange – it offers visitors a daily entertainment calendar and a glimpse of local society in the living section. Don't miss the Friday *Lagniappe* entertainment guide. The *Times-Picayune* is perhaps the only US newspaper that includes occasional editorials on French issues. The paper's editors traditionally lean toward the Democratic Party. Don't be surprised to see plenty of front-page murder stories in New Orleans, which has a higher-than-average crime rate.

The *Louisiana Weekly*, which has been published in New Orleans since 1925, offers an African-American perspective on local and regional politics and events. Billing itself as 'the people's paper,' the *New Orleans Data News Weekly* focuses on local news. The monthly newspaper *La Prensa* features bilingual articles for Hispanic readers.

For alternative news and entertainment listings, pick up a copy of the free weekly newspaper *Gambit*. Its sporadic distribution makes it somewhat difficult to find; it's surprisingly scarce in coffee shops. The monthly *Offbeat* magazine provides a complete music and entertainment calendar with good reviews of local performances. It's available free at record stores and coffee shops.

The monthly *New Orleans Magazine* is a glossy, tourist-oriented advertisement that offers better-quality writing about the city than you might expect from most city magazines. *Where New Orleans* is a monthly publication that offers maps of attractions; it's strictly for visitors.

A few magazines about the South deserve a mention. Foremost is *Southern Exposure*, a bimonthly journal that carries on the muckraking tradition of Stetson Kennedy's 1946 book by the same name. Many of its articles on social issues, politics, the economy and regional culture are cited by other researchers. The bimonthly *Oxford American*, published in William Faulkner's hometown of Oxford, Mississippi, preserves the literary tradition of the South.

See Gay & Lesbian Travelers, later, for more information on alternative media.

RADIO

Community radio station WWOZ FM 90.7 offers the most jazz, with a mix of blues, R&B and Cajun and an odd assortment of ethnic music. Its mission is to promote the music of southern Louisiana, and the more you listen to the station, the more you realize just what an incredibly musical place this is. You're really keeping an ear to the ground when you tune in – the deejays keep you posted on all the comings and goings of the city's home-grown talent.

Station WWNO FM 89.9 broadcasts a predominantly classical format but plays jazz from 10:30pm to 1am. It's the city's only National Public Radio affiliate, offering morning and evening news programmes.

News and literary programming is broadcast by WRBH FM 88.3. Newscasters read the entire local paper on air for the blind and print-handicapped (a boring exercise for some, but useful for those who have blurred vision after a night on Bourbon St).

A zydeco music show is hosted by Kateri Yager every Saturday from 10am to 1pm on WSLA AM 1560.

PHOTOGRAPHY & VIDEO

New Orleans is a city where details tell the story, so if you're photographing any significant others, make sure that they're not entirely obscuring the ornate cast iron that inspired you to shoot the picture. ('Uh, honey, scoot on over jest a little.')

For professional photo processing and services near the downtown area, there's **Primary Color** (☎ 581-3444; *1116 Magnolia St*) at Calliope St. It's in a sketchy neighborhood near the Superdome and is only worth going to if you can drive there.

[Continued on page 49]

Mardi Gras

Carnival is New Orleans' leviathan holiday, a beautiful, undulating, snakelike festival that first rears its head on January 6 (the Feast of the Epiphany) and, weeks later, unfolds in all its startling, fire-breathing glory – to terrify and delight the millions who worship it.

In New Orleans, Mardi Gras operates on the subconscious. It's the flame that burns in the city's soul, the elaborate overture that tells us what the city is all about. It's a baroque fantasy, a vibrant flower, a circus, a nightmare, a temptation from the devil.

One telling little fact, offering a glimpse of how deeply ingrained Mardi Gras is in New Orleans' culture, is that in 1699 on **Lundi Gras** (Mardi Gras Eve), Pierre Le Moyne, Sieur d'Iberville took possession of the Louisiana territory and named his first encampment Pointe de Mardi Gras. He was just a little way downriver from the future site of New Orleans. It may be a stretch to say that New Orleans was founded on Mardi Gras – in fact, it was founded 19 years after d'Iberville claimed the territory – but locals can truthfully claim their Mardi Gras tradition dates back three centuries. Over that time, Mardi Gras has evolved into one of the greatest spectacles in the world.

Each year, on the day before Mardi Gras, the mayor of New Orleans steps down so that Rex, the King of Carnival, may rule the city for 24 hours. It's only a symbolic gesture, but it's quite a statement nevertheless.

During Mardi Gras, entire sections of New Orleans – the French Quarter and major thoroughfares such as Canal St and St Charles Ave – are tied up in knots. Public transportation comes to a halt, schools are closed and the postal service stops delivering the mail.

Mardi Gras permeates all levels of New Orleans society. Families of all classes and colors come out before each parade. All over the city imaginative people create theatrical costumes for seasonal masquerade parties. These events, when characterized by the peculiar local brand of perfectionism, become fantastic flights from time and place. Meanwhile,

RAY LASKOWITZ

Title Page: Rex may be king, but nobody outdoes the queen, as this beautiful headdress shows (Photo by Richard Cummins)

Inset: What are you looking at? A mask stares out from a float. (Photo by Richard Cummins)

Bottom: Snap up a colorful doll as a Mardi Gras souvenir

some of the city's most impoverished inhabitants are among its most passionate celebrants on Mardi Gras. For the Mardi Gras Indians, who hail from some of the poorest, most crime-ridden neighborhoods in the country, the day goes way beyond celebration – it marks a reaffirmation of their unique cultural identity.

Above all, Mardi Gras is a hell of a party, and New Orleans, in its characteristic generosity, welcomes travelers from around the world to join in the revelry.

HISTORY

To understand and appreciate Mardi Gras it is helpful to first become familiar with the history, for many of the traditions that shape the holiday today actually acquired their significance centuries ago. New Orleans is the rare American city where people take care to preserve the spirit of ancient rites like Carnival.

Pagan Rites

Carnival's pagan origins are not lost on anyone in New Orleans. They can be traced all the way back to the ancient Greeks, who held pre-spring festivals in which people sought purification through flogging. These rites were passed down to the Romans, whose Lupercalia (as they called the festival) was celebrated in an atmosphere of characteristic debauchery. During Lupercalia, all social order broke down as citizens and slaves, men and women cavorted in masks and costumes and behaved in a totally lawless and licentious manner. Sadism, masochism and prostitution were the order of the day, followed by a period of recovery and introspection. An ox was sacrificed, and its blood was believed to wash away the sins of the people. Similar pagan rites were practiced by Druid priests in France, culminating in the sacrifice of a bull.

The early Catholic Church failed to appreciate this tradition, but after trying unsuccessfully to suppress it, the church eventually co-opted the spring rite and fit it into the Christian calendar. In Rome, it came to be

Top Left: Highly coveted Carnival booty adorns a bike

Top Right: 'Hey! We're over here!' – a destination totem to help you find your way known as *carnevale* ('farewell to the flesh'), referring to the fasting that began on Ash Wednesday. For many centuries the celebration, lasting several days, continued to be characterized by chaos and public lewdness, with the pervading sense of violence in the air.

By the 17th century in Venice, a sophisticated theatrical sensibility turned Carnival into a baroque masquerade in which citizens transformed themselves into characters of the commedia dell'arte and ran rampant on the city's streets. The festival continued to thumb its nose at social conventions, and a preponderance of satyr costumes indicates the holiday's pagan origins had not been forgotten. This theatrical form of Carnival became the custom in France, and variations of it spread to French outposts in the New World.

Creole Carnival

Early generations of Creoles loved to dance, and they celebrated the Carnival season with balls and a full calendar of music and theater. The Creoles also had a penchant for masking, and on Mardi Gras the people of the city would emerge from their homes wearing grotesque, sometimes diabolical, disguises and masks.

From the beginning, the spirit of Carnival appears to have crossed race lines and permeated every level of society. Early on, Creoles of color held Carnival balls to which slaves were sometimes invited. The popularity of masking among blacks was made evident by an ordinance, passed during Spanish rule, which prohibited blacks from masking. The fear was that blacks, effectively disguising their color, might easily invade elite white balls. Several times, masking was altogether outlawed by authorities who distrusted the way in which masks undermined the established social order. This didn't stop people from masking, though, and on Mardi Gras, the citizenry tended to blend into an unruly, desegregated mob.

Carnival remained primarily a Creole celebration for several decades after the Louisiana Purchase made New Orleans a US city, and Creoles

TOM DOWNS

Bottom: There's a whole lotta love in the room as Twelfth Night party revelers ring in the Carnival season continued to elaborate on the festivities. By the 1830s, parades replete with ornamented carriages, musicians and masked equestrians had become an important part of the Mardi Gras celebration. But the public splendor was short-lived, and by the mid-19th century, Creole Carnival revelers had begun withdrawing into their ballrooms. Many Creoles lamented that New Orleans had become too American, too practical-minded, to sustain such a fanciful holiday as Mardi Gras.

Carnival's 'Golden Age'

Ironically, Mardi Gras was saved not by Creoles, but by a secretive group of wealthy Americans who resided in the Garden District. Calling themselves the **Mistick Krewe of Comus**, these men made their first public appearance after dark, their floats illuminated by flambeaux (torches), on Mardi Gras in 1857. On that night, the stage was set for Carnival as we know it today.

New clubs modeled themselves on Comus, calling themselves 'krewes' (which was supposed to be an ersatz Old English spelling of 'crews'). **Rex** first appeared in 1872, **Momus** a year later and **Proteus** in 1882. Pompous parades, presided over by a king, coursed through the streets at night, delighting audiences with elaborately decorated, torch-lit floats fashioned from horse-drawn carriages. Mythological and some-times satirical themes defined the parades, making these processions coherent theatrical works on wheels. The parades would end at a theater or the opera house, where exclusive balls would close out the evening.

Rex naturally anointed himself 'King of Carnival' and his krewe also contributed several lasting traditions. He contributed the official colors of Carnival – purple, green and gold, which New Orleanians continue to work into their Mardi Gras attire – and the anthem of Carnival, a corny tune called 'If I Ever Cease to Love.' Additionally, the Rex parade featured floats that depicted biting political satire, which would become a recurring motif shared by other krewes.

Also in the late 19th century, another krewe, the **Twelfth Night Revelers**, introduced several practices that would outlive the krewe's parading days. The first Carnival 'throws,' which are trinkets tossed from a float to spectators, were proffered in a Revelers' parade as early as 1871. Throws would not become standard parade practice until much later (see the 'Throws' boxed text, later).

Carnival rose to new heights during the years that followed the Civil War, and as New Orleans coped with the hardship and insult of 'carpet-bag' rule, the importance of Mardi Gras as the cultural focal point of the year was cemented. At times, the seriousness with which Carnival was regarded in New Orleans was exhibited in rather extreme ways. In 1890, two parades, those of Comus and Proteus, reached the edge of the French Quarter at the same time. In a heated dispute over which krewe would enter the Quarter first, several krewe members appeared ready to draw swords, but the confrontation was resolved without violence.

Black Carnival

Very little has been written to document early black Carnival, but it seems unlikely that blacks ever ignored the most festive holiday in New Orleans. Parades and musical processions surely took place in the area around Congo Square, and black Creole balls were held even before the Louisiana Purchase.

In 1885 one of the most significant and enduring traditions of black Carnival was born when a Mardi Gras Indian gang, calling itself the Creole Wild West, made its first appearance. Eventually, an untold number of black Indian gangs – the Wild Tchoupitoulas, Yellow Pocahontas and Golden Eagles, among many others – would enter the city's

Mardi Gras Indians

New Orleans' black Indian gangs, who are otherwise known as the Mardi Gras Indians, are a dazzling example of authentic, unsanctioned inner-city artistry.

Indian gangs began appearing in Mardi Gras parades in the 1880s, when a group calling itself the Creole Wild West came masked in the feathered finery of Plains Indians. Since then, many gangs have come and gone, including the Wild Tchoupitoulas, Yellow Pocahontas and Wild Magnolias, which were led by now-legendary 'big chiefs' such as Big Chief Jolly, Tootie Montana and Bo Dollis.

Over the years, black Indian suits seem to have grown more extravagant. Although the Indians generally hail from the poorest, most crime-ridden parts of town, they devote extraordinary amounts of time and money toward the creation of their suits. Sewing, a point of pride among Indians, is done by hand, and it is an interesting sight to see tough, streetwise young men perusing the aisles in stores dealing in sewing supplies, sequins and brightly colored feathers. Layers of meaningful mosaics are designed and created in patterns of neatly stitched sequins. Multilayered feathered headdresses – particularly those of the big chiefs – are more elaborate and flamboyant than the headgear worn by Las Vegas show performers. The making of a new suit can take the better part of a year, and in the course of this arduous work, trickles of blood frequently seep into the suit's fabric as needles prick the sewer's nimble fingers.

On Mardi Gras, many suits are still unfinished, but Indian gangs still roam the backstreets looking for a showdown with another gang, or hoping to find an appreciative audience. (Claiborne Ave, to the lakeside of the Tremé District, is where spectators frequently wait for the Indians to appear.) Indian suits are closer to completion by the time Indian gangs march the city's backstreets again weeks later on St Joseph's night (roughly midway through the Lenten season), and have usually reached their full splendor by Super Sunday (which usually takes place sometime in April), when the gangs reappear to show off to crowds of admirers. On these occasions, visitors are not advised to go looking for Indians unless they are comfortable with venturing into the backstreets of this often violent city. For most people, the easiest way to check out the Indians is to see them perform at Jazz Fest or at nightclubs.

backstreets on Mardi Gras, dressed in elaborately beaded and feathered suits and headdresses. A canon of black Indian songs was passed down from generation to generation, with lyrics often fusing English, Creole French, Choctaw and African words until their meaning was obscure.

From the beginning, 'masking Indian' was a serious proposition. Tribes became organized fighting units headed by a **Big Chief**, with **Spy Boys, Flag Boys** and **Wild Men** carrying out carefully defined roles. Tremendous pride was evident in the costly and expertly sewn suits, and when two gangs crossed paths, an intense confrontation would ensue as members of each tribe sized each other up. Often violence would break out. And as is the case with many of Mardi Gras' strongest traditions, this was no mere amusement.

Other black traditions emerged around the turn of the 20th century. The **skull-and-bones gangs** (influenced, some think, by Mexican Day of the Dead artwork) were men dressed up like skeletons who would chase frightened little kids around black neighborhoods on Mardi Gras morning. Their purported 'purpose' was to put a little fear in the youngsters in order to make the kids behave. A band of prostitutes calling themselves the **Baby Dolls** also began masking on Mardi Gras. Dressed in bloomers and bonnets, they danced from bar to bar, turning tricks along the way.

The black krewe of **Zulu** first appeared in 1909, with members initially calling themselves the Tramps and parading on foot. By 1916, when the Zulu Social Aid & Pleasure Club was incorporated, the krewe had floats, and its antics deliberately spoofed the pomposity of elite white krewes. Zulu members paraded in black face, and their dress was a wickedly absurd interpretation of African tribal culture, as if to say, 'Is this really how you see us?' Krewe hierarchy included a witch doctor, a mayor, the absurdly uppity Mr Big Shot and a phalanx of tribal warriors bearing shields and wearing grass skirts. In time, Zulu's members would **Bottom:** Flamboyant include some of the city's more prominent black citizens. Jazz star Louis Mardi Gras Indians Armstrong reigned as King Zulu in 1949, and although his float broke

TOM DOWNS

into pieces during the parade (fortunately, in front of a bar), he had no complaints. As he summed up the experience, 'I always been a Zulu, but King, man, this is the stuff.'

Modern Carnival

The 20th century has seen the coming and going of dozens of different krewes, each adding to the diversity and interest of Carnival. Iris, a women's krewe, was formed in 1917 and began parading in 1959. Gay krewes began forming in the late '50s, with **Petronius**, the oldest gay krewe still in existence, staging its first ball in 1962. (Petronius is not a parading krewe.)

Today's 'superkrewes' began forming in the 1960s. **Endymion** debuted as a modest neighborhood parade in 1967; now its parades and floats are the largest, with nearly 2000 riders and one of its immense floats measuring 240ft in length. Endymion is so big, its ball is held in the Louisiana Superdome. While Endymion was still fledgling, **Bacchus**, which began in 1969, shaped the trend for bigger things to come. From its start, Bacchus deliberately set out to break Carnival tradition, wowing its audiences by anointing celebrity monarchs (including Bob Hope, Jackie Gleason, Kirk Douglas and William Shatner) and opening its ball to the paid public. **Orpheus**, a superkrewe founded by musician Harry Connick Jr, first appeared in the mid-1990s.

Tradition was dealt another blow when the old-line krewes Comus, Proteus and Momus stopped parading in the early 1990s. City council member Dorothy Mae Taylor challenged these all-white krewes to integrate, and their response was to retreat from the streets, continuing their elite Carnival traditions in private.

Despite many changes, and although rambunctious tourists generally outnumber rowdy locals during Mardi Gras, the holiday continues to mark the zenith of New Orleans' festive annual calendar. And despite the grayish ooze of trash, spilled beer, piss and vomit that's ground into the city's gutters by thoughtless mobs, a hearty spirit manages to shine

RAY LASKOWITZ

Bottom: A detail from one of the extragavant Mardi Gras floats through, somehow linking today's Carnival to those of 18th-century France and even to the Lupercalia of ancient Rome. The masking tradition, carried out primarily in the French Quarter and Faubourg Marigny, upholds an ancient and enchanting Mardi Gras aesthetic. Night parades continue to haunt St Charles Ave and Canal St with surreal and terrifying floats, Mephistophelian masked riders and infernal *flambeaux*. The skull-and-bones gangs and black Indians continue to carry out their spontaneous rituals. When it comes right down to it, the good, the bad and the ugly are all parts of Mardi Gras tradition.

EXPERIENCING CARNIVAL

Carnival begins slowly, with related events, parties and parades becoming more frequent as Mardi Gras nears. (Mardi Gras, translating as 'Fat Tuesday,' is used here specifically to refer to the actual day, rather than to the entire season; Carnival refers to the season from January 6 to Fat Tuesday.) During the final, culminating weekend, particularly on Lundi Gras and Mardi Gras, many things are scheduled to occur simultaneously, and you will have to make some decisions. Preplanning and prioritizing are definitely in order, as getting around town grows more difficult with each passing day (a bicycle will grant you the greatest mobility). Be prepared also to improvise a little.

Twelfth Night

The beginning of Carnival is signaled early in the evening of January 6, as a rowdy band calling itself the **Phunny Phorty Phellows** parades down St Charles Ave aboard a streetcar. If you happen to be in town on this night, you might catch some of the season's first throws (see the 'Throws' boxed text, later). Later in the evening, Twelfth Night masquerade parties are held around town. While many of these are private affairs, some clubs have revelries to ring in the season. You may want to ask around at various clubs in town to see if anything's doing. (Mid-City Rock & Bowl has been known to hold Twelfth Night parties open to the public; see the Entertainment chapter.)

Mardi Gras R&B

Hundreds of songs have been recorded to get people into the spirit of Mardi Gras in New Orleans. Some R&B Mardi Gras tunes are flat-out great songs that get ample play on local radio – especially on WWOZ-FM 90.7 – during Carnival season.

Classic R&B favorites include Professor Longhair's 'Mardi Gras in New Orleans,' with Fess' infectious, exuberant whistling; Art Neville's catchy 'Mardi Gras Mambo,' which he recorded way back in 1955, long before the Meters or the Neville Brothers reached national stardom; James 'Sugar Boy' Crawford's cryptic 'Jock-A-Mo,' a song built on Mardi Gras Indian chants; and Al Johnson's 'Carnival Time,' which serves as a litmus test of sorts, because if this tune doesn't draw the Carnival spirit out of you, then you just don't have it.

Parades

The parade season is a 12-day period beginning two Fridays before Fat Tuesday. Most of the early parades are charming, almost neighborly processions that whet your appetite for the later parades, which increase in size and grandeur each day, until the awesome spectacles of the superkrewes emerge during the final weekend.

A popular preseason night procession, usually held three Saturdays before Fat Tuesday, is that of the **Krewe du Vieux**. By parading before the official parade season and forgoing motorized floats (nearly all krewe members are on foot), Krewe du Vieux is permitted to pass through the Quarter. It's a throwback to the old days, before floats and crowds grew too large, when parading krewes typically traversed the Quarter while onlookers packed the sidewalks and balconies. The themes of this notoriously bawdy and satirical krewe clearly aim to offend puritanical types.

A lovely night parade presented by the predominantly black krewe of **Oshun** (named for a West African goddess) has been rolling very early in the season on the Uptown route (detailed in the following section). Other krewes that traditionally parade during the first weekend are **Pontchartrain**, with a Mid-City promenade known for its marching-band contests; **Sparta**, with an Uptown night parade that features traditional touches like *flambeaux* carriers and a mule-drawn float; and **Carrollton**, a 75-year-old krewe that rolls down St Charles Ave on Sunday afternoon.

In some years, parades are held every night of the subsequent week, getting larger as the weekend gets near. Toward the end of the week, the highly secretive **Knights of Babylon** present their attractive traditional parade, replete with *flambeaux* and riding lieutenants (eerily reminiscent of hooded Klansmen); it follows the Uptown route but continues toward the lake on Canal St and down Basin St for a few blocks. On Friday night before Mardi Gras, Uptown is the domain of **Hermes**, with its beautiful nighttime spectacle maintaining the aloof mystery of 19th-century Carnival processions. Hermes is followed directly by **Le Krewe d'Etat**, whose name is a clever, satirical pun: d'Etat is ruled by a dictator, rather than a King. However menacing this modern krewe may be, d'Etat's floats and costumes nevertheless reflect fairly traditional standards of beauty, and in recent years its glowing skull-and-crossbones krewe necklaces have been among the best throws of Carnival.

Mardi Gras weekend is lit up by the entrance of the superkrewes, with their monstrous floats and endless processions of celebrities, marching bands, Shriner buggies, military units and police officers. Unlike the traditional krewes, the superkrewes, following a 'more is better' mentality, are as flashy as a Vegas revue. The crowds of spectators also grow larger by the day, and that comfortable corner you'd staked out for yourself earlier in the week is now likely to be overrun by tourists. All of these considerations aside, if you've been in town all week, you'll be ready for something bigger by this time. (A few nonsuperkrewes parade on the weekend as well.)

On Saturday afternoon, the all-women's krewe, **Iris**, parades down St Charles Ave with more than 30 floats and 750 krewe members. Iris is followed by **Tucks**, an irreverent krewe with the inspired alliterative motto of 'Booze, Beer, Bourbon, Broads' and a giant toilet-seat float, which spectators are encouraged to throw unwanted beads into.

Throws

Parading Carnival krewes don't just aim to entertain – they also give things to people. They toss trinkets, called 'throws', from their Carnival floats as they cruise by crowds of people. Regardless of how cheap or garish the throws are, people want 'em. You have to work to get them, and the more you get, the more you'll want. The traditional plea 'Throw me something, mister!' is a holdover from the days when all krewe members were men. People say that, but in some instances a simple 'Throw me something!' will suffice.

The standard item tossed from Carnival floats is a string of plastic **beads**. By the end of Mardi Gras, aggressive throw-catchers can proudly drape several pounds of beads around their necks.

Quantity isn't the only issue. Creative throws, like Zulu's famous hand-painted coconuts, are among Carnival's highest prizes. 'Medallion beads' (or 'krewe beads') bearing an emblem representing the krewe get bigger with each Carnival season, as krewes strive to satisfy their fans' increasing hunger for bigger, better and badder booty. **Doubloons**, minted aluminum coins bearing krewe insignia and themes, are also popular collector's items. Other things you may acquire along a parade route range from plastic cups to Beanie Babies and bags of potato chips.

The smaller, common plastic beads coveted by spectators a generation ago have come to be called **tree beads**, for their ignominious fate is to be tossed into the branches of the live oaks along St Charles Ave, where some actually hang on long enough to see the following year's Carnival. They can also be strung together to make elegant Christmas tree ornaments.

A word of caution: When a throw lands on the street, claim it by stepping on it, then pick it up. If you try to pick it up without first stepping on it, someone else will surely step on your fingers – and then insist that the object is by rights theirs!

RAY LASKOWITZ

Right: 'Throw me something, mister!'

On Saturday night, the megakrewe **Endymion** stages its spectacular parade and Extravaganza, as it calls its ball in the Superdome. With 1900 riders on nearly 30 enormous, luminescent floats rolling down Canal St from Mid-City, the Endymion parade is one of the season's most electrifying events. The krewe's massive, 240ft steamboat float is the biggest in New Orleans.

On Sunday night the **Bacchus** krewe wows an enraptured crowd along St Charles Ave with its celebrity monarch and a gorgeous fleet of crowd-pleasing floats.

Monday night is parade night for **Proteus**, which returned to action in 2000. Proteus' parade is an old-style affair, replete with riding lieutenants, *flambeaux* and lovely hand-painted floats. The main event of the evening is staged by **Orpheus**, a spirited and stylish superkrewe founded by singer-pianist Harry Connick Jr (who hails from New Orleans). Connick rides annually and he always enlists a handful of movie stars and musicians to join his 1000-member krewe. Orpheus is such a huge parade, you may have to wait several hours before seeing the famous, 140ft Leviathan float. It's a spectacular float, and most people are glad they waited.

On Mardi Gras morning, **Zulu** rolls its loosely themed and slightly run-down floats along Jackson Ave, where the atmosphere is very different from the standard parade routes. Folks set up their barbecues on the sidewalk and krewe members distribute their prized hand-painted coconuts to a lucky few in the crowd. When Zulu reaches St Charles Ave, it follows the Uptown route toward Gallier Hall for a spell before ending up on Orleans St and the Tremé District.

Zulu typically runs blithely behind schedule while the King of Carnival, **Rex**, waits farther Uptown for clearance on St Charles Ave. Rex's parade is, naturally, a much more restrained and haughty affair, with the monarch himself looking like he's been plucked from a deck of cards, as he smiles benignly upon his subjects. Rex's floats are beautifully

JOHN NEUBAUER

Left: A samba dancer sashays her way through the French Quarter constructed and hand-painted, but in terms of throws, some loot-hungry spectators frequently note Rex's shocking stinginess.

On Mardi Gras afternoon you can continue to watch parades. The populist spirit of the **truck parades**, haphazardly decorated semis loaded up with people line-dancing and throwing beads, is sociologically interesting but minimally entertaining. If you've been in town all weekend, you'll be paraded-out by this time and there's plenty going on elsewhere around town.

Routes There are two primary Carnival parade routes in Orleans Parish. The **Uptown parade route** typically follows St Charles Ave from Napoleon St to Canal St (where these parades actually begin and end can vary, but this stretch is fairly constant). The Zulu parade departs from this course by rolling down Jackson Ave until it reaches St Charles Ave, at which point it follows the standard route toward Canal St. The **Mid-City parade route** begins near City Park and follows Orleans Ave to Carrollton Ave and then onto Canal St, down toward the French Quarter, hooking into the Central Business District (CBD) in order to pass the grandstands at Gallier Hall.

These lengthy routes, which can take several hours for some of the larger krewes to traverse, obviously afford many vantage points from which to see the parades. But your choice is fairly straightforward: Either head away from the crowded Quarter to get a more 'neighborhood' feel, or stick close to the corner of Canal St and St Charles Ave, where the crowds are thickest and a raucous, sometimes bawdy party atmosphere prevails. Grandstands (with paid admission) are set up along St Charles Ave in the area between Lee Circle and Gallier Hall, and parading krewe members tend to go into a bead-tossing frenzy through this corridor.

If catching throws is of highest priority, here's a tip: Near the end of parade routes, krewe members often discover they've been too conservative early on, and they tend to let loose. However, by this time the excitement level of the parade may already have passed its crescendo.

Walking Parades On Mardi Gras there are many 'unofficial' walking parades that are worth seeking out and, in some cases, even joining.

The **Jefferson City Buzzards**, a walking club that has been moseying from bar to bar on Mardi Gras morn since 1890, starts out at 6:45am at Laurel St near Audubon Park. If you're into drinking early, you are likely to run into them at drinking establishments between there and the Quarter. Since 1961, jazzman Pete Fountain's **Half-Fast Walking Club** has been making similar bar-hopping rounds, starting out from Commander's Palace at around 8am.

Downtown has its own morning activities, the biggest event being the parade of the **Society of St Anne**. This is a gloriously creative costume pageant – krewe members, clad in elaborate hats, capes, makeup and masks or, in some cases, in very little at all, march through the Bywater, Faubourg Marigny and the French Quarter to the jazzy rhythms of the Storyville Stompers. The parade starts around 10am in

King Cakes

Of all Mardi Gras traditions, none is more kitschy than the king cake. Every year, on Twelfth Night (January 6), the first king cakes emerge from bakeries all over New Orleans and soon appear in offices – including the mayor's – and at Twelfth Night parties throughout the city.

The king cake is an oval, spongy Danish pastry with gooey icing and purple, green and gold sugar on top. More importantly, it always contains an inedible, peanut-size plastic baby somewhere inside. The baby is the key – it's what perpetuates the king cake tradition. The rule is, whoever is served the piece of cake with the baby inside (careful – don't swallow that baby!) has to buy the next cake. Some office workers eat king cake five days a week between Twelfth Night and Mardi Gras.

The king cake originated in 1870, when the Twelfth Night Revelers used it to select a queen for the 'Lord of Misrule' and a Carnival tradition was born. Early king cakes contained an uncooked golden bean instead of a baby, and the recipient of the bean was crowned king or queen of a Carnival krewe. That ritual is still maintained by some krewes, but such important matters are no longer left to chance. The bean, or baby, is always planted in the piece of cake served to a preselected king or queen. It seems the king cake has lost some of its clout.

Nevertheless, king cakes are big business. One local bakery chain claims to sell 30,000 king cakes a day. According to local statisticians, 750,000 king cakes are consumed annually in the New Orleans metropolitan area.

the Bywater, and the colorful procession, which strives to re-create scenes from 19th-century oil paintings of French Mardi Gras, flows down Royal St all the way to Canal St, where it sometimes arrives in time to run into the Rex parade.

Another costume-oriented downtown walking parade is that of the **Krewe of Cosmic Debris**, which convenes at around noon in Faubourg Marigny. The krewe's wandering musical voyage through the French Quarter is largely determined by which bars it elects to patronize along the way.

RAY LASKOWITZ

Left: Cool cats – even children have a role to play in the celebrations

Costume Contest

Mardi Gras is meant to be a citywide costume party, and many New Orleanians take a dim view of visitors who crash their party without a costume. Needless to say, people take their costumes very seriously. On Fat Tuesday, exquisitely attired maskers, human beasts and exhibitionists mingle and a spirit unique to Mardi Gras animates the streets; this is all-ages material, folks.

This unbound creativity is distilled into two costume contests – a high-proof one for adults and a watered-down one for the entire family. The notorious **Bourbon St Awards**, attracting a large number of gay contestants, is staged not on

RAY LASKOWITZ

The Law of Mardi Gras

New Orleans has fostered a reputation as a permissive city, and Mardi Gras is obviously a time of unbridled debauchery. But don't come expecting utter lawlessness. Overall, the New Orleans Police Department does a commendable job maintaining order, despite immense, spirited crowds consuming unbelievable quantities of liquor. Along parade routes and in the French Quarter, cops are everywhere. If their ranks appear to have swelled, it's because the entire force is working long shifts, with little time for rest in between. Rule No 1 is don't push your luck with tired cops!

Surprisingly, the presence of so many overworked cops does not interfere with the general merriment of Carnival. The attitude of the police during Carnival is to let people have their fun, but officers draw the line at potentially dangerous behavior. If a cop tells you to watch what you're doing, don't try to argue. If you start with the 'Aw, but ossiffer...' routine, you're likely to end up in the slammer – and you probably won't be released until Mardi Gras is over.

Many special laws go into effect during Carnival. Here are a few that visitors ought to bear in mind:

- Do not park your car along a parade route within two hours of the start of a parade – it's guaranteed that your car will be towed.
- Do not cross police barriers unless permitted to do so by an officer.
- During parades, do not cross the street if it means stepping between members of marching bands or in front of moving floats.
- It is against the law to throw anything at the floats (except for Tucks' toilet float).
- Police tend to look the other way (figuratively, anyway) while women expose their breasts in the French Quarter. But don't expect the same tolerance elsewhere.
- It isn't true that it's okay to have sex in public.

Top: Beads aplenty

RAY LASKOWITZ

Bourbon St (as it once was) but in front of the Rawhide Bar at Burgundy and St Ann Sts; it begins at noon. The cleaner **Mardi Gras Maskathon** is held in front of the Meridien Hotel on Canal St, after the Rex parade concludes.

Balls

You can't expect to roll into town on Friday night and on Fat Tuesday gain admittance to one of the invitation-only society functions that typify the Carnival ball season. You can, however, buy your way into a party put on by one of the more modern krewes, including **Orpheus** (☎ 822-7211), **Tucks** (☎ 288-2481), **Bacchus** (W *www.kreweofbacchus.org*) and **Endymion** (☎ 736-0160; W *www.endymion.org*). Gay krewes include **Petronius** (☎ 525-4498) and the **Lords of Leather** (☎ 347-0659).

Information

A glossy magazine, *Arthur Hardy's Mardi Gras Guide*, is an indispensable source of information and a worthwhile souvenir. Published by an obsessive Carnival aficionado, the annual publication appears in book-stores each year before Twelfth Night. In addition to loads of Mardi Gras trivia, it includes parade schedules and route maps. Similar information is offered by the *Gambit Weekly's* monthly publication, the 'Natives' Guide to New Orleans,' which publishes a Carnival edition during February or March, depending on the date of Mardi Gras. *OffBeat*, a music magazine, offers invaluable information on Mardi Gras–related events.

Future Mardi Gras Dates

Mardi Gras can occur on any Tuesday between February 3 and March 9, depending on the date of Easter. Dates for the next several years are:

2003	March 4
2004	February 24
2005	February 8
2006	February 28
2007	February 20
2008	February 5
2009	February 24

RICHARD CUMMINS

Top: Badge of honor: a detail from an Endymion costume

Left: Gold, purple and green, the colors of Mardi Gras

[Continued from page 48]

More convenient is **Liberty Camera Center** *(Map 4, #24; ☎ 523-6252; 337 Carondelet St)*. **Downtown Fast Foto** *(Map 4, #27; ☎ 525-2598; 327 St Charles Ave)* offers quick color print and E-6 slide processing.

In the Riverbend area you'll find the **Camera Shop** *(Map 6, #17; ☎ 861-0277; 7505 Maple St)*. Opposite Delgado Community College, **Moldaner's Camera** *(Map 7, #6; ☎ 486-5811; 622 City Park Ave)* provides reliable photo-finishing services.

Overseas visitors thinking of purchasing videos should remember that the USA uses the National Television System Committee (NTSC) color TV standard, which is not compatible with other standards like Phas Alternative Line (PAL). Unless you find worthwhile PAL-format videos (available in some Canal St shops), it's best to avoid those seemingly cheap movie purchases.

TIME

New Orleans is on Central Standard Time, one hour behind the East Coast's Eastern Standard Time and six hours behind Greenwich Mean Time (GMT). In early April, all US clocks move ahead one hour for Daylight Saving Time (which roughly corresponds to British Summer Time); clocks move back one hour in October. When it's noon in New Orleans, the time elsewhere is as follows:

Auckland	9am next day
Chicago	noon
London	6pm
New York	1pm
Sydney	7am next day
Tokyo	6am next day

ELECTRICITY

Electric current in the USA is 110-115V, 60Hz AC. Outlets may be suited for flat two-prong or three-prong grounded plugs. If your appliance is made for another electrical system, you will need a transformer or adapter; if you didn't bring one along, buy one at Radio Shack (which has several locations around town) or another consumer electronics store.

WEIGHTS & MEASURES

New Orleans residents resist the metric system. Draft beer is commonly offered by the pint. Dry weights are in ounces (oz), pounds (lb) and tons, but liquid measures differ from dry measures. One pint equals 16 fluid oz; 2 pints equal 1 quart, a common measure for liquids such as milk, which is also sold in half gallons (2 quarts) and gallons (4 quarts). Gasoline is measured in the US gallon, which is about 20% smaller than the imperial gallon and equivalent to 3.79L. Distances are in feet (ft), yards (yd) and miles (mi). Three feet equals 1yd (0.914m); 1760yd, or 5280ft, equal 1mi. Temperatures are in degrees Fahrenheit, whereby 32°F is freezing. There is a conversion chart on the inside back cover of this book.

LAUNDRY

Drinkers and pool players will appreciate the many New Orleans bars that offer self-service laundry facilities. Most of these are operated by the Igor's chain – with locations Uptown along St Charles and Magazine St and downtown on Esplanade Ave (see the Entertainment chapter for more information). Laundries are easily found all over New Orleans, or you could try **Hula Mae's Laundry** *(Map 2, #17; ☎ 522-1336; 840 N Rampart St)*.

TOILETS

A recording by Benny Grunch, 'Ain't No Place to Pee on Mardi Gras Day,' summarizes the situation in the French Quarter. While tour guides delight in describing the unsanitary waste-disposal practices of a bygone era, the stench arising from back alleys is actually far more recent in origin.

You'd think New Orleans would commemorate 300 years of French influence (as the city did in 1999) by adopting the French *pissoir* (urinal) – or in any case do *something* for the hordes of visitors guzzling 29oz Hurricanes in French Quarter streets. But the only public restrooms open in the evening are in the **Jackson Brewery mall** *(Map 2, #117; 620 Decatur St)*. Another public restroom is available in the **French Market** *(Map 2, #59)*.

HEALTH

New Orleans is a typical First-World destination when it comes to health. For most foreign visitors no immunizations are required for entry, although cholera and yellow-fever vaccinations may be required of travelers from areas with a history of those diseases. There are no unexpected health dangers, excellent medical attention is readily available, and the only real health concern is that a collision with the medical system can cause severe injuries to your financial state.

If you do require emergency treatment while in Orleans Parish, you can request an **ambulance** (☎ *911*). Or have someone take you to the emergency room (ER) at a major hospital with a well-staffed trauma center. The **Medical Center of Louisiana** (Map 4, #4; ☎ 903-2311; 1532 Tulane Ave), formerly known as Charity Hospital, offers free services to those who qualify and assesses fees on a sliding scale for others.

Nonprescription medications and contraceptives can be purchased in the pharmacy section of drugstores like **Walgreens**, which has two locations (☎ 822-8073; 3311 Canal St at Jefferson Davis Pkwy • ☎ 943-9788; 1100 Elysian Fields Ave, near St Claude St) within a short drive of the French Quarter. There's also another **Walgreens** (Map 4, #9; ☎ 568-9544; 900 Canal St), which is open until midnight. Many outlying **Rite Aid** stores are open 24 hours; there's one close to the French Quarter (Map 6, #40; ☎ 896-4575; 3401 St Charles Ave) at Louisiana Ave.

There's also a **NO/AIDS task force hotline** (☎ 945-4000).

WOMEN TRAVELERS

Intoxicated bands of young men in the Quarter and along parade routes are a particular nuisance for women. Otherwise respectable students and businessmen are transformed by New Orleans – they expect to drink and carouse in a manner that is not acceptable in their home towns. Women in almost any attire are liable to receive lewd comments. More provocative outfits will lead to a continuous barrage of requests to 'show your tits.' This occurs on any Friday or Saturday night, not just during Mardi Gras. Many men assume that any woman wearing impressive strands of beads has acquired them by displaying herself on the street.

Conducting yourself in a common-sense manner will help you to avoid most problems. For example, you're more vulnerable if you've been drinking or using drugs than if you are sober; you're more vulnerable alone than if you're with company; and you're more vulnerable in a high-crime urban area than in a 'better' district. Of course, any serious problems you encounter (including assault or rape) should be reported to the **police** (☎ 911). The YWCA offers a **Rape Crisis Hotline** (☎ 483-8888), as well as a **Battered Women's Hotline** (☎ 486-0377).

There's a New Orleans branch of **Planned Parenthood** (Map 6, #55; ☎ 897-9200; 4018 Magazine St), which provides health-care services for women, including pregnancy testing and birth-control counseling.

GAY & LESBIAN TRAVELERS

The gay community in New Orleans revolves around the lower French Quarter, below St Ann St, and the adjacent Faubourg Marigny neighborhood. While many businesses in the area are gay owned and gay oriented, and most residents are gay, many of the clubs cater to a mixed crowd.

The **Lesbian & Gay Community Center** (Map 3, #34; ☎ 945-1103; 2114 Decatur St) is a great resource center where you can pick up all of the numerous free rags available in New Orleans. The people working there often have time to tell you what they personally think of just about any bar, club, restaurant or cabaret performer in the city.

The **Faubourg Marigny Book Store** (Map 3, #21; ☎ 943-9875; 600 Frenchmen St) is the South's oldest gay bookstore and is a good place to learn about the local gay scene. While you're there, pick up a copy of The Weekly Guide, a free pamphlet that's chock-full of information about gay and lesbian businesses, entertainment venues, hotels and guesthouses. It features a pull-out bar guide section.

For nightlife ideas, gay and lesbian readers should out the free biweekly tabloids Southern Voice and Ambush Magazine.

Both magazines are published in New Orleans and offer adult entertainment suggestions throughout the Gulf South, although *Ambush* tends to do a better job of covering the gay scene beyond New Orleans.

DISABLED TRAVELERS

Thanks to the federal Americans with Disabilities Act, more and more lodgings and transit agencies are meeting the needs of disabled people. Even older hotels are obligated to provide wheelchair access, although accessible bathroom accommodations are primarily found only at newer properties. Wheelchair ramps and/or elevators are available at the ferry crossings. A few of the RTA buses offer a lift service. For information about paratransit service (alternate transportation for those who can't ride regular buses), call the **RTA** (☎ 827-7433). The Riverfront streetcar line features Braille kiosks, platform ramps and wide doors that allow anyone to board easily. Unfortunately, the St Charles Ave streetcar line has not been modified for wheelchair passengers.

The French Quarter is especially difficult for disabled travelers. Beware that rough masonry sidewalks hinder wheelchair travel and can be equally challenging for near-sighted individuals. Few of the picturesque galleries projecting over the Quarter's streets are accessible to wheelchairs.

Of course, most federal facilities and parks – including Lafitte National Historic Park – offer access for the disabled. Another popular destination is the platform trail over the swamp at the Louisiana Nature Center. See the Things to See & Do chapter for more information on attractions.

SENIOR TRAVELERS

The age at which senior benefits begin varies, although travelers aged 50 years and older (although more commonly it's 65 and up) can expect to receive discount rates at such places as hotels, museums and restaurants. Some national advocacy groups that can help seniors in planning their travels are the **American Association of Retired Persons** (AARP; ☎ 202-434-2277; 601 E St NW, Washington, DC 20049), representing Americans

50 years or older, and **Elderhostel** (☎ 877-426-8056; 11 Avenue De Lafayette, Boston, MA 02111), for people 55 and older.

NEW ORLEANS FOR CHILDREN

With the exceptions of the Audubon Zoo and the Aquarium of the Americas, most activities for children are set apart from the city's major attractions for adults. For specially scheduled children's activities, check out the brief 'kid stuff' listing that appears in the *Times-Picayune*'s living section each Monday. For more detailed listings on the following places, see the Things to See & Do chapter.

In eastern New Orleans, the **Audubon Louisiana Nature Center** (Off Map 1; ☎ 246-5672; 5601 Read Blvd), in Joe W Brown Memorial Park, enthralls kids with exhibits of reptiles, amphibians and birds.

The **Louisiana Children's Museum** (Map 4, #56; ☎ 523-1357; 420 Julia St), in the Warehouse District, caters to kids from ages one to 12.

The Maple Street Bookstore – renowned for its 'Eracism' bumper stickers – operates the **Children's Book Shop** (Map 6, #16; ☎ 866-4916; 7529 Maple St). Cozy readings take place here.

Accent on Children's Arrangements (Map 4, #52; ☎ 524-1227; 701 S Peters St) is a service that takes the kids off your hands and engages them in organized activities. Some of the bigger, more expensive hotels also provide childcare services.

USEFUL ORGANIZATIONS

With more than 5500 Louisiana members, the nonprofit **Nature Conservancy** (☎ 338-1040; PO Box 4125, Baton Rouge, LA 70821) is an influential force in preserving plants, animals and natural communities by protecting the lands and waters they need to survive. Call or write to find out about scheduled hikes, canoe trips and other field trips.

The Sierra Club advocates for environmental protection throughout the USA. The **New Orleans Group of the Delta Chapter** (☎ 482-9566; 5534 Canal Blvd, New Orleans, LA 70124) is active in promoting low-impact visits to natural sites in southern Louisiana.

The headquarters for the local **American Automobile Association** *(AAA; ☎ 838-7500; 3445 N Causeway Blvd, Metairie)* provides its members with maps, suggestions for accommodations, as well as travel-planning services. AAA also offers **emergency road and towing services** *(☎ 800-222-4357)* for its members.

Hostelling International (HI), the name of the International Youth Hostel Federation and American Youth Hostels, has its local office at the **Marquette House Hostel** *(Map 5, #13; ☎ 523-3014; 2249 Carondelet St)*. Membership costs $25 and entitles you to some of the lowest bed rates in the US for an entire year.

LIBRARIES
If you're interested in finding out more about the city, the **Louisiana Room** *(☎ 596-2610)*, on the 3rd floor of the **New Orleans Public Library** *(Map 4; ☎ 529-7323; w http://nutrias.org; 219 Loyola Ave)*, is an excellent resource for books, newspapers and maps. The library's website includes a link to a complete catalog.

UNIVERSITIES
New Orleans' foremost private universities are Tulane and Loyola, which are nestled next to each other in Uptown on St Charles Ave, opposite Audubon Park. Both buildings are architecturally impressive.

In response to the cholera and yellow-fever epidemics, seven physicians founded **Tulane University** *(Map 6; ☎ 865-5000; 6823 St Charles Ave)* in 1834. It now boasts 22,000 students in 11 colleges and schools, including a law school and school of medicine. Among Tulane's most noted graduates are the president of France, Jacques Chirac, who wrote a thesis on the port of New Orleans, and former speaker of the US House of Representatives Newt Gingrich, who opposed university censorship of the student newspaper in 1968. The **Amistad Research Center** *(Map 6, #26; ☎ 865-5535)*, the world's largest African-American archive, and the **Hogan Jazz Archives** *(Map 6, #21)* are two of Tulane's attractions; both are discussed in the Things to See & Do chapter.

Operated by Jesuits since 1917, **Loyola University** *(Map 6; ☎ 865-2011; 6363 St Charles Ave)* is best known for its College of Music, School of Business and Department of Communications.

The historically black, private campuses of Dillard and Xavier universities are well known for excellence. Founded in 1869, **Dillard University** *(Map 1; ☎ 283-8822; 2601 Gentilly Blvd)* was an important meeting site for civil rights leaders. The oldest building on the present campus is the 1934 library building, but the stately Avenue of the Oaks is Dillard's most attractive feature. Established in 1915, **Xavier University** *(Map 1; ☎ 486-7411; 1 Drexel Dr)* is the only historically black Roman Catholic university in the USA. Xavier boasts a fine College of Pharmacy.

The public **Southern University at New Orleans** *(SUNO; Map 1; ☎ 286-5000; 6400 Press Dr)* is a relative newcomer, founded in 1959. Its Center for African and African American Studies and Fine Arts boasts a large collection of African art. SUNO was the first major college in the US to be headed by a black woman, Chancellor Dr Dolores Spikes.

The largest public campus in New Orleans is the **University of New Orleans** *(UNO; Map 1; ☎ 280-6000)*, on the lakefront, where 16,000 students study on a site that formerly housed a coast guard station. The history department is gaining a reputation for its cutting-edge approach to Louisiana history. The Keifer Lakefront Arena attracts thousands for large concert events.

CULTURAL CENTERS
Visitors from France are often surprised to discover that French is rarely spoken in New Orleans. The odd truth is that from 1916 until 1968, the Louisiana Board of Education actually forbade classroom instruction in the French language. Pride in Louisiana's French-speaking heritage re-emerged in 1968 when Representative James Domengeaux founded Codofil (le Conseil pour le Développement du Français en Louisiane). The University of New Orleans offers assistance through the **Council for International Visitors** *(☎ 539-9432)*. **Alliance Française**

(Map 5, #24; ☎ 568-0770; 1519 Jackson Ave), near Prytania St, offers a French-language curriculum.

The **Amistad Research Center** *(Map 6, #26; ☎ 865-5535)*, on the Tulane campus, specializes in African-American history. See Tulane University in the Things to See & Do chapter for more information.

The NPS operates the **Isleño Center** *(☎ 682-0862)* within St Bernard Parish.

DANGERS & ANNOYANCES

Many areas in New Orleans suffer from high-crime rates. For the tourist, the possibility of getting mugged is always something to consider, even in areas you'd think are safe (eg, the Garden District). Naturally, solo pedestrians are targeted more often than people walking in groups, and daytime is a better time to be out on foot than night. If you are traveling alone, avoid entering secluded areas such as the cemeteries and Louis Armstrong Park. Instead, plenty of group tours go to St Louis Cemetery No 1, and even if you don't care to join the tours, it might be a good idea to wait for them and thereby avoid walking alone on the grounds. Avoid wandering into the Quarter's unfrequented residential areas late at night or straying across N Rampart St toward the lake.

Large crowds typically make the French Quarter a secure around-the-clock realm for the visitor. However, if your hotel or vehicle is on the margins of the Quarter, you might want to take a taxi back at night. The CBD has plenty of activity during weekdays, but it's relatively deserted at night and on weekends. At night stay out of dimly lit parks. The clubs near S Carrollton Ave in the Riverbend are generally problem free.

Until you are familiar with the terrain, you should confine your Uptown wanderings to the corridor between St Charles Ave and Magazine St that includes the Garden District. But even this area is not entirely safe. With a few exceptions, the Irish Channel area riverside from Magazine St is not recommended for the visitor.

In the Quarter, street hustlers frequently approach tourists. You can simply walk away – no hard feelings. Also be aware that just about anywhere, especially in bars, cashiers might have a tendency to 'assume' a tip by short-changing tourist customers. Keep tabs on prices and the amount of the bills you hand over, then count your change.

Pedestrians crossing the street do not have the right of way and motorists (unless they are from out of state) will not yield. Whether on foot or in a car, be wary before entering an intersection, as New Orleans drivers are notorious for running yellow and even red lights.

LEGAL MATTERS

Although it may seem that anything goes, even New Orleans has its limits. Anyone under the age of 18 on the streets after 11pm is violating the city's curfew. During Mardi Gras in 1996, more than 2500 people found themselves behind bars. Women who flash their breasts may get the attention of the police (and many others) but are not typically arrested unless they expose themselves repeatedly. For the most part, the police are interested in crowd control; it's only when things begin to get out of hand that they intervene.

The police are less lenient about a few other matters: dropping your pants, grabbing or groping another person and urinating in public can all land you in jail. Don't join those who come on vacation and leave on probation.

If you are arrested, you're allowed to remain silent. There is no legal reason to speak to a police officer if you don't wish, but never walk away from an officer until given permission. All persons who are arrested are legally allowed to make one phone call. If you don't have a lawyer or family member to help you, call your embassy. The police will give you the number upon request.

The headquarters for the **New Orleans Police Department** *(Map 7, #40; emergencies ☎ 911, nonemergencies ☎ 821-2222)* is at 715 S Broad St.

Alcohol

The legal drinking age for the city is 21, despite efforts to push it back to 18. You can be arrested for carrying open glass or metal containers on the street – grab a plastic 'go cup' when leaving a bar.

Drinking and driving can get you in big trouble. Driving while intoxicated (DWI) is a serious crime; you are considered legally drunk when your blood alcohol level reaches 0.10 – about two drinks, although this depends on the person. In addition, motorists are prohibited from carrying open containers of alcohol in vehicles.

Gambling

The legal age for gambling is also 21, and businesses with gaming devices (usually video poker machines) out in the open are closed to minors. Even cafés with gaming devices are off-limits to minors, unless the games are contained within private rooms or booths.

BUSINESS HOURS

While New Orleans is a true 24-hour center of activity, businesses tend to be incredibly lax about operating hours. It's the Big Easy! Some businesses never remove signs stating, 'Come in! We're open.' The proprietors of small shops are notorious for getting up late, closing early, stepping out for extended periods, ignoring a ringing phone or locking the doors to hide from creditors.

In any case, stated business hours are usually 9am to 5pm. Note that some stores lock their doors during slow periods for safety reasons; look for a bell to ring for entry. Liquor stores are open until 9pm, and there's always the corner drugstore, usually open until midnight (if not 24 hours), which sells everything from snacks to nail polish to cough medicine.

PUBLIC HOLIDAYS & SPECIAL EVENTS

Any excuse to celebrate – those are words that New Orleanians live by, and the locals are so good at celebrating they hardly need national holidays. In fact, what's known as 'the holidays' throughout the rest of the USA – meaning the season from Thanksgiving through to New Year's – seems more like a warm-up in New Orleans, for on the heels of 'the holidays' comes Mardi Gras,

the king of all celebrations in New Orleans. The Christmas lights and house decorations go down, and the Mardi Gras fringe and masks go up. Mardi Gras season lasts about six to eight weeks.

The city's other great festival, Jazz Fest, is a concentrated dose of good music – but good music, in lesser concentrations, is a commodity that New Orleans enjoys year-round.

The city also celebrates New Year's Eve, St Patrick's Day and Halloween with its characteristically whole-hearted and flamboyant style.

Note that when national holidays fall on a weekend, they are often celebrated on the nearest Friday or Monday so that everyone enjoys a three-day weekend.

January
New Year's Day January 1 is a national holiday.

Sugar Bowl This NCAA football game between two of the nation's top-ranking college teams takes place on or around New Year's Day. It originated in 1935 and fills the Superdome (Map 4) to capacity; call ☎ 525-8573 for information.

Twelfth Night The Carnival season kicks in on January 6 (12 nights after Christmas) as the Phunny Phorty Phellows dust off their costumes and assemble at the Willow St car barn prior to an evening ride on the St Charles Ave streetcars.

Battle of New Orleans Celebration On the weekend closest to January 8, volunteers stage a re-creation of the decisive victory over the British in the war of 1812 at the original battleground in Chalmette National Historical Park (Off Map 1); call ☎ 281-0510 for details. A noontime commemoration on Sunday in Jackson Square features a military color guard in period dress.

Martin Luther King Jr Day On the third Monday in January, a charming midday parade, replete with brass bands, makes its way from the Bywater to the Tremé District down St Claude Ave.

Mardi Gras Parades Early Carnival parades in January or February tend to be the most outlandish, such as the annual Krewe du Vieux parade that passes right through the French Quarter. Early in the Carnival season each year, the *Times-Picayune* runs a 'Carnival Central' section with maps of all the parades.

February
Mardi Gras Parades The greatest free show on earth really heats up during the three weeks before Mardi Gras, culminating with multiple

parades each day. Routes vary, but the largest krewes stage massive parades with elaborate floats and marching bands that run along portions of St Charles Ave and Canal St. None enter the French Quarter.

Mardi Gras Day In February or early March, the outrageous activity reaches a crescendo as the French Quarter nearly bursts with costumed celebrants. It all ends at midnight with the beginning of Lenten penitence.

Presidents' Day The third Monday in February is a national holiday.

March

Black Heritage Festival On the second weekend in March, the city celebrates African-American contributions to food, music and the arts at the Audubon Zoo (Map 6; ☎ 861-2537).

St Patrick's Day Just when you thought the city would calm down, the festivities pick up again on March 17. On the actual day, a major Irish pub crawl through the French Quarter follows a parade through the Irish Channel, starting at Race and Annunciation Sts. The prior weekend (if the 17th falls on a weekday) also features a motley

New Orleans Jazz & Heritage Festival

'Jazz Fest', as New Orleans' second-biggest festival is more commonly known, started as a celebration of the city's 250th anniversary in 1968, attracting jazz musicians such as Louis Armstrong, Dave Brubeck, Duke Ellington, Woody Herman, Ramsey Lewis and Pete Fountain. After struggling with poor attendance, 'Jazz Fest' moved to the Fair Grounds in 1972 and expanded to two weekends in late April and early May. The organizers also began to showcase a variety of musical forms besides jazz and experienced success.

Jazz Fest offers something for just about everyone's musical tastes. You can hear headliners, cult favorites and relative unknowns on more than 10 stages. At one stage you can listen to zydeco, while others might offer R&B, rock, gospel, bluegrass, reggae, Latin and, of course, jazz.

The 'heritage' part of the festival refers to Louisiana and local arts, crafts and food. This continues downtown at Armstrong Park's Congo Square, where African food and crafts are emphasized.

It's highly recommended to arrive at the Fair Grounds hungry – the plethora of eating options is staggering, and prices are reasonable. But you'll have to decide what exactly you're hungry for: a plate of boiled crawfish (it's peak season!), shrimp étouffée, catfish or oyster po'boys, a heaping helping of jambalaya or red beans and rice, soft-shell crab (also in season), the tastiest crawfish pie, zesty gumbo, crawfish Monica, barbecued anything, crab-stuffed mushrooms, even cherry 'sno balls' and strawberry shortcake, plus cuisine from other cultures (gyros, Cuban sandwiches, fried plantains), and the list goes on and on. With over 60 vendors to choose from, this is an excellent place to get your culinary bearings. And for some reason everything at Jazz Fest tastes more delicious than it might elsewhere!

In addition, plan for heat and sun at the Fair Grounds – bring sunscreen and a brimmed hat and wear light-colored clothing. Keep yourself well hydrated – and although it may be the perfect thirst-quencher, not with beer! Only a few tents at Jazz Fest are ventilated (hardly air-conditioned, but at least shaded). Most stages are open-air, and you'll end up standing for long periods of time. It's a good idea to bring a blanket or ground cover for resting between concerts, and a rain poncho just in case.

You can check the schedules in January (they're not available earlier) and you should make reservations as soon as possible to save money and ensure that you get your favored weekend dates. Daily passes cost $18 in advance or $25 at the gate. The Fair Grounds are open daily from 11am to 7pm, and there are many nightly performances at other sites throughout New Orleans. For information, call or write the **New Orleans Jazz & Heritage Festival** (☎ 522-4786; ⓦ www.nojazzfest.com; 1205 N Rampart St, New Orleans, LA 70116). Tickets are available through **Ticketmaster** (☎ 522-5555).

Ditch your car, as you cannot count on getting one of the few $20 parking spaces near the Fair Grounds. The **RTA** (☎ 827-7433) operates its regularly scheduled No 82 Esplanade bus from the French Quarter. Special shuttles are available from the New Orleans Jazz & Heritage Festival at an additional cost. Air-conditioned shuttle buses run back and forth from major hotels on Canal St and cost around $10 for a round trip. If you can find a taxi, the special-event price from the Quarter is $3 per person.

parade, beginning at Molly's at the Market (Map 2, #44; ☎ 525-5169), where a boisterous group tosses cabbages and carrots to the crowd.

Tennessee Williams Literary Festival The end of March features five days dedicated to the great American playwright, with plays (by Williams and others), lectures (on subjects such as humor and the art of storytelling), literary- and gay-heritage walking tours, nostalgic panels starring Williams' surviving chums and – natch! – a cocktail party. The festival runs through the last weekend of the month, with events held at Le Petit Théâtre du Vieux Carré (Map 2, #109) as well as elsewhere in the French Quarter. Call ☎ 581-1144 for information.

Easter Although that big bunny makes his rounds, Easter isn't nearly as much fun as Mardi Gras. The Christian holiday falls on the first Sunday after a full moon in March or April.

Isleños Arts & Crafts The Canary Islanders who settled in St Bernard Parish celebrate their folk life (a culture based on the use of natural resources) during the last week of March. They stage demonstrations and host a crawfish-eating contest at the Isleño Center (☎ 682-0862), 7mi south of Chalmette and 1½mi east of Poydras on Hwy 46.

April

Spring Fiesta Since 1935, locals have donned antebellum outfits to host visitors in historic homes normally closed to the public. Tours are given over a five-day period in April or May beginning on the first Friday after Easter. Fees vary, but you can find out the details by contacting the Spring Fiesta Association (☎ 581-1367).

Crescent City Classic Runners from all over the globe compete in a 10K race from the Jackson Brewery to Audubon Park on the first Saturday of the month. Contact the *Times-Picayune* (☎ 861-8686) for details.

French Quarter Festival Twelve stages throughout the French Quarter showcase New Orleans music, plus local lifestyles, during the second weekend of April.

Jazz Fest The Fair Grounds Race Track (Map 7) – and, at night, the whole town – reverberates with good sounds, plus food and crafts, through two weekends in the latter part of April and early May. See the boxed text 'New Orleans Jazz & Heritage Festival,' earlier, for details.

May

Tomato Festival In Chalmette, Our Lady of Prompt Succor Church (☎ 271-3441; 2320 Paris Rd),

features a pre-Miss Louisiana beauty pageant along with musical performances on the first weekend of the month.

Memorial Day A national holiday takes place on the last Monday in May.

Greek Festival On Memorial Day weekend, the Greek community offers food and the entertaining Hellenic Dancers. The festival is held on the grounds of the Greek Orthodox Cathedral of the Holy Trinity Church (☎ 282-0259; 1200 Robert E Lee Blvd), near Bayou St John.

June

French Market Tomato Festival During the first weekend of the month, you'll find food and entertainment in the French Market (Map 2, #59; ☎ 522-2621).

Grand Prix du New Orleans If you thought crossing the street in New Orleans was dangerous before, check out what happens when it really becomes a racetrack on the second weekend of June.

Carnival Latino On the last weekend in June, the Riverfront comes alive with the sounds and flavors of Latin America.

July

Independence Day Since the Civil War, folks in these parts have regarded July 4, with evident disdain, as a 'Yank' holiday. Nevertheless, New Orleanians are not known to pass up a good time. Food stalls and entertainment stages are set up on the Riverfront and fireworks light up the night sky.

Essence Music Festival On Independence Day weekend, *Essence* magazine sponsors a star-studded line-up of musical performances at the Superdome (Map 4). Started in 1995, the event has featured Stevie Wonder and other renowned black recording artists.

Wine & Food Experience Find out which wine to drink with your catfish during a four-day foodie event in July; for information call ☎ 529-9463. Sometimes, the event occurs in late June or May.

August

Blessing of the Shrimp Fleet It's an Isleño tradition to parade decorated boats, then party. Festivities annually alternate between the fishing villages at Delacroix Island or Yscloskey in St Bernard Parish. Contact the Isleño Center (☎ 682-0862) for information.

September

Labor Day The first Monday in September is a national holiday.

October

Swamp Festival For four days in early October, the Audubon Institute (☎ 801 2537; ⓦ www.audu boninstitute.org/swampfest/ releases swamp critters into the hands of visitors at both the Audubon Zoo and Woldenberg Park. Both events feature Cajun food, music and crafts.

Columbus Day The second Monday in October is a national holiday.

Halloween Celebrated on October 31, Halloween is a holiday not taken lightly in New Orleans. Most of the fun is the giant costume party throughout the French Quarter. In addition, the New Orleans Metropolitan Convention and Visitors Bureau (☎ 566-5011) coordinates a parade plus a monster bash and Anne Rice Vampire Lestat Extravaganza at the Convention Center.

November

All Saints Day On November 1, many residents honor the dead by sprucing up the local cemeteries.

Veterans Day November 11 is a national holiday.

Celebration in the Oaks If unnatural holiday decorations turn you on, you might check out the colorful constellations of light at City Park. It's a unique New Orleans take on the spirit of Christmas in America – a little bit Vegas, a little bit Disneyland, right in the middle of the oak trees (of course!). As a clincher, you can view it in its entirety from your car only (turn off those headlamps). A separate walking tour visits the botanical garden and carousel area. The huge power cord (imagine God reaching for it beneath the Christmas tree) is plugged into the socket every night after dark, from the last week of November through to the first week in January. Admission is $10 per motor vehicle and $5 per person for the walking tour.

Thanksgiving A national holiday observed on the fourth Thursday in November, this is the day that Americans stuff themselves with turkey dinners. (Picture Grandma chomping on that turkey leg.)

December

Christmas – New Orleans Style During the month of December, St Charles Ave is a festival of light, as many of New Orleans' poshest homes are lavishly decorated and illuminated for the holidays. This is also a great time to tour historic homes. The lobby of the Fairmont Hotel (Map 4, #8) in the CBD is transformed into a gaudy but charming Christmas grotto, its walls and ceiling concealed by shredded cotton. And of course, the Celebration in the Oaks continues all through the month (see November, previous). On Christmas Eve, St Louis Cathedral (Map 2, #96) attracts a tremendous crowd for its midnight choral mass. Many restaurants offer réveillon dinners on Christmas Eve. Contact French Quarter Festivals (☎ 522-5730, 100 Conti St, New Orleans, LA 70130) for a complete schedule of events, open homes and réveillon menus.

Feux de Joie Fires of joy light the way along the Mississippi River levees above Orleans Parish and below Baton Rouge on Christmas Eve. To reach the giant bonfires, you must either endure incredible traffic along the narrow River Rd or spend a fortune to see the fires from a riverboat; call ☎ 524-0814 for information. Another option is to take I-10 to La Place (27mi) or even Burnside (50mi) to see the spectacle.

New Year's Eve Revelers – mostly drunk tourists – pack the French Quarter, especially around Jackson Brewery (Map 2, #117), where the Baby New Year is dropped from the roof at midnight. Adding to the frenzy are thousands of college football fans, in town for the annual Sugar Bowl, which takes place on New Year's Day (see January, earlier).

WORK

It perhaps goes without saying that New Orleans is not a magnet for migrating professionals. Tourism puts butter on most people's bread in this town, and passers-through who have a way with people can usually find work in related businesses. Many of the city's bars and restaurants hire seasonal labor, and some get downright desperate for reliable help during Carnival and Jazz Fest.

If you're really hard up for cash, or just want to gain greater insight into the character of Ignatius Reilly (of John Kennedy Toole's novel *A Confederacy of Dunces*), you might enlist with the folks at **Lucky Dog** (☎ 523-9260; 517 Gravier St).

Getting There & Away

AIR

The area is served by one main airport, New Orleans International Airport (MSY). About 98% of the flights that pass through here are domestic – the only 'international' flights are with other North and Central American countries. New Orleans is a medium-size air traffic hub, overshadowed by major hubs at Dallas–Fort Worth, Houston and Atlanta.

Airline phone numbers are listed under Airline Offices, later in this chapter. For options on getting from the airport to your lodging, see the Getting Around chapter.

Departure Tax

A standard airport departure tax of $24 is charged to passengers traveling between the USA and foreign cities. If you purchased your ticket to New Orleans in the USA, the tax will normally be included in the ticket price. Tickets purchased abroad may not include this tax. In addition to the airport departure tax, visitors arriving from a foreign country will be charged a $6.50 North American Free Trade Agreement (Nafta) tax, which may also be included in the price of your ticket, depending on where the ticket was purchased. To pay for additional airport security since the events of September 11, the US government has imposed a $2.50 (maximum of $5) tax per flight.

Other Parts of the USA

New Orleans International Airport's proximity to major hubs at Dallas–Fort Worth, Houston and Atlanta make it easy to find a convenient flight or connection to and from just about anywhere in North America. A good place to begin your search for the cheapest and/or most convenient flight is the Sunday travel section of the *Times-Picayune* newspaper, as well as similar sections in the *New York Times*, *Chicago Tribune* and *Los Angeles Times*, in which you'll find any number of travel agency ads. The Friday travel page of the *Wall Street Journal* offers many useful tips for business travelers.

Regional airlines (those serving fewer destinations than the intercontinental biggies) may also be a good bet on short or heavily traveled routes, as they require neither a round-trip purchase nor a Saturday night's stay to get an economical fare. Southwest Airlines covers the western USA fairly completely, with frequently scheduled flights from its hub in Houston. Southwest also offers services to Florida, so you can expect airfares there to remain reasonable. Southwest often offers rates undercutting major airlines and runs specials, such as 'companion fares' that allow two people to travel for the price of one. Delta Air Lines sometimes offers discount flights to compete with Southwest.

Most large domestic airlines dominate a major hub airport, with radiating 'spokes' connecting to other cities. If you book a flight through a carrier's hub, your ticket will typically be cheaper, and you can select from more frequent flights than if you demand nonstop service. Also, by doing a little research on such airline systems, you can figure out why your favorite airline in one travel corridor may be a costly and inconvenient choice in another.

Fares change often, but nearly all of the best fares require an advance purchase of seven to 21 days. Low round-trip fares to either Dallas–Fort Worth, Atlanta or Memphis typically cost from $150 to $170, while those to Houston are about $130. Fares to the East Coast fluctuate the most, with New York round trips ranging from $180 to $350 during a recent 30-day period. Round-trip fares to the West Coast typically cost around $300, while a round-trip fare to Chicago hovers around $200. A comparable round-trip fare will get you to Orlando, Florida, where you can lunch with Disney characters.

Latin America

New Orleans has long-standing business ties with Caribbean sugar and Central American fruit and coffee plantations, so there are decent services to and from Latin America. Cancún's beaches are less than two hours away aboard daily Aeroméxico or Grupo TACA flights; economy round-trip tickets average $550. Aeroméxico continues to Mexico City via Cancún. Flights to San Juan in Puerto Rico typically cost $600 on American Airlines. Grupo TACA provides daily flights to Belize and El Salvador, as well as Costa Rica, Honduras and Panama. Many other flights to/from Central and South America go via Miami, Houston, Dallas–Fort Worth or Los Angeles. Most countries' major airlines, as well as US airlines such as United and American, serve these destinations. Continental has flights between New Orleans and about 20 cities in Mexico, Central America and the Caribbean via Houston.

Canada

Despite the tremendous influx of Canadian visitors during the winter months, the only direct flights from Canada to New Orleans originate out of Toronto. Travelers must typically make connections at US gateways, although US-Canadian airline partnership agreements do offer 'through ticketing.'

Northwest Airlines offers extensive Canadian service, but you may find lower fares on other airlines.

The availability and cost of through-ticketed flights varies depending upon the time of year, the distance traveled and the whim of the industry. Typical economy round-trip fares include Toronto (C$900) Montreal and Quebec (C$650), Winnipeg (C$1000), Edmonton (C$1200) and Vancouver (C$900). To save money, catch a ride to a US gateway to take advantage of competitive domestic US fares. Call a travel agency or check the newspapers for specific details.

The UK & Continental Europe

British Airways arrives in the USA at many gateways, with connecting service on US Airways or American Airlines domestic flights. Cheaper flights to New Orleans from London may involve landing in New York City. You should also consider traveling to either Atlanta, Orlando, Houston or Dallas–Fort Worth, depending on international fares, and taking a low-fare domestic connecting flight. Westbound passengers usually depart London mid-morning and, after making a domestic connection, arrive in New Orleans about 12 hours later during the evening. Eastbound flights go overnight with a travel time of 11 hours.

A straightforward economy round-trip ticket is around £1000, and a business-class round-trip ticket costs about £4500. Cheaper fares vary with the season; summer (June through to August) and Christmas are the peak periods, and weekends may also be more expensive. Economy or APEX tickets, which usually must be purchased 21 days in advance and involve cancellation penalties if you change your plans, cost from £300 to £1000 for a round trip. Bargain fares from around £200 can be found using one of the less popular international airlines from London to New York and continuing on with a US domestic flight. Charter flights typically cost around £400 for a round trip. The business of discounting tickets is so well developed in Britain that you can get heavily discounted 1st-class and business-class tickets as well as cheaper economy tickets.

The weekly London magazine *Time Out*, the *Evening Standard* and the various give-away travel papers are all good sources of ads for finding cheaper fares. Good agencies for low-priced tickets in London include the following:

STA (☎ 020-7937 9962, W www.statravel.co.uk) 40 Bernard St, London WC1N 1LS
Trailfinders (☎ 020-7628 7628, W www.trail finder.com) 1 Threadneedle St, EC2R 8JX
Travel Cuts (☎ 020-7255 1944) 295A Regent St, London W1R 7YA

London generally offers the best value for crossing the Atlantic; however, indirect flights from Paris cost about €872. From Amsterdam, KLM–Royal Dutch Airlines offers direct service with Continental Airlines for about €1200 for a round trip. Lufthansa makes connections with United Airlines between Frankfurt and New Orleans for approximately €600. Continental offers direct flights to Newark and Houston from most European cities. Ditto for American Airlines to Dallas–Fort Worth, Delta to Atlanta and Northwest to Detroit and Memphis.

Asia
None of the many Asian carriers currently offer direct flights to New Orleans – most serve the Los Angeles or San Francisco gateways. Continental flies nonstop from Tokyo to Newark (economy round-trip fares cost ¥89,000). Eastbound flights from Tokyo to Newark leave in the early evening and arrive in the early evening after traveling for 11½ hours. Add another 1½ hours to the westbound travel time. American, United and Northwest Airlines also fly using Asian routes and offer connecting flights from West Coast gateways. Ticket consolidators purchase blocks of tickets and typically offer them at a discount from the airlines' prices – don't be shy about asking your travel agent about ticket-consolidator deals.

Australia & New Zealand
Neither Qantas nor Air New Zealand currently fly directly to New Orleans. Both airlines fly to Los Angeles and offer service to New Orleans on a connecting domestic flight, sometimes on a code-sharing flight designed to make you think it's all the same airline. United Airlines does have convenient connecting flights to New Orleans from both Sydney and Auckland. With the advent of long-range 747-400 aircraft, most services now fly over Hawaii, so at least the Pacific is covered in one mighty leap. From Auckland to Los Angeles, it takes 12 to 13 hours and from Sydney to Los Angeles, 13½ to 14½ hours. Typical economy round-trip fares from the Australian east coast are around A$2700; fares from New Zealand cost NZ$2300.

Weekend travel sections in major city newspapers in Australia and New Zealand have ads for travel agencies specializing in cheap fares. In Australia, Flight Centre and STA have competitively priced tickets. STA also operates in New Zealand.

Airline Offices
A few airlines have offices in the Central Business District (CBD). **American Airlines** *(Map 4, #8)* is quartered in the Fairmont Hotel, 123 Baronne St. Airlines with ticket counters at the New Orleans International Airport include the following:

Aeroméxico (☎ 800-237-6639)
Air Canada (☎ 888-247-2262)
AirTran (☎ 800-825-8538)
American Airlines (☎ 800-433-7300)
America West (☎ 800-327-7810)
British Airways (☎ 800-247-9297)
Continental Airlines (☎ 523-9739, domestic ☎ 800-732-6887, international ☎ 800-231-0856)
Delta Air Lines (domestic ☎ 800-221-1212, international ☎ 800-241-4141)
Frontier Air Lines (☎ 800-265-5505)
Grupo TACA (☎ 800-535-8780)
Jet Blue (☎ 800-538-3583)
KLM–Royal Dutch Airlines (☎ 800-374-7747)
Lufthansa (☎ 800-645-3880)
Midwest Express (☎ 800-452-2022)
Northwest Airlines (domestic ☎ 800-225-2525, international ☎ 800-447-4747)
Southwest Airlines (☎ 464-9240, 800-435-9792)
TWA (☎ 800-433-7300)
United Airlines (domestic ☎ 800-241-6522, international ☎ 800-538-2929)
US Airways (☎ 800-428-4322)
Vanguard (☎ 800-826-4827)

BUS

As is typical throughout the South, you can rely on good bus services to New Orleans. **Greyhound** (☎ 800-231-2222, in Spanish ☎ 800-531-5332) is the only regular long-distance bus company serving the city. All trains and Greyhound buses share the **New Orleans Union Passenger Terminal** (Map 4; 1001 Loyola Ave), which is also known as Union station, seven blocks upriver from Canal St. The terminal includes a **Travelers' Aid counter** (☎ 525-8726, for airport counter ☎ 528-9026) and an inexpensive cafeteria, which offers red beans and rice for under $3. Note the murals by Conrad Albrizio, created for the terminal dedication in 1954, depicting New Orleans' history from early exploration to the modern age.

From New Orleans, there are three morning, three afternoon and three evening Greyhound buses to Baton Rouge. Travel time is under two hours, and the round-trip fare is $26. Other frequent departures and round-trip fares include the following:

Chicago	$172
Houston	$92
Jackson	$58
Lafayette	$33
Memphis	$85
Mobile	$50

Bicycles for bus travel must be boxed (boxes are not available from Greyhound) and cost an additional $15 each way.

TRAIN

Three **Amtrak** (☎ 800-872-7245) trains serve New Orleans at **Union Passenger Terminal** (Map 4; ☎ 528-1610; 1001 Loyola Ave).

The *City of New Orleans* train runs to Memphis, Jackson and Chicago, departing New Orleans at 2:10pm Thursday to Monday and arriving in Chicago the following morning.

Another train originating in New Orleans is the *Crescent Route*, serving Birmingham, Atlanta, Washington, DC, and New York City. It departs at 7:20am on Monday, Thursday and Saturday and arrives in Atlanta in time for dinner. There's a one-night layover; trains travel daily between Atlanta and New York.

New Orleans is on the *Sunset Limited* route between Los Angeles and Miami. Westbound trains are scheduled to depart on Tuesday, Thursday and Sunday at 1:45pm, but they are notorious for being late. Eastbound trains depart on Wednesday, Friday and Sunday at 10:30pm. Again, because of poor performance, don't count on the guaranteed 2½-hour layover.

All three trains offer coach seating as well as different levels of sleeping-car accommodations. Amtrak Thruway Bus Connections offers coordinated service with guaranteed train connections between New Orleans and Baton Rouge on one through-ticket. Bicycles are accepted on all trains when packed in the large, roomy boxes provided at the station; the boxes cost $5 and the transport charge for the bike is $7 – you will only need to remove the pedals, loosen the post to drop the seat and loosen the neck to turn the handlebars sideways.

CAR & MOTORCYCLE

Call **Auto Driveaway Co** (☎ 737-0266; 7809 Airline Dr, Metairie) if your travel plans are flexible and you are willing to follow a time constraint that does not allow for sightseeing side trips. If you agree to drive one of these cars, you'll usually have time just to take the most direct route from point A to point B. But it's free, so people do it – and it's cheaper than the bus or train, which also preclude side trips. Your chances of getting a drive-away car are better if you offer to travel to regions rather than specific destinations. Drive-away companies typically request a substantial deposit, valid driver's license and proof of liability insurance coverage.

As if to emphasize that New Orleans is an isolated piece of high ground, all freeway approaches to the city travel over lakes and bayous and are designated as hurricane-evacuation routes away from the city. Interstate 10 (I-10) is the nation's major east–west route along the southern boundary, linking Jacksonville with Los Angeles via Mobile and Houston. Baton Rouge and Lafayette are also on I-10 west of New Orleans. If you're heading for a destination beyond New Orleans, you can skirt downtown congestion by exiting I-10 and taking the I-610 shortcut. Alternatively, you can completely avoid the metro area by following the north shore of Lake Pontchartrain on the I-12 between Slidell and Baton Rouge.

The north–south routes I-55 (to Chicago) and I-59 (to Chattanooga) meet I-10 to the west and east of New Orleans on either side of Lake Pontchartrain.

On the east bank of the Mississippi River, Hwy 61, the infamous Airline Hwy of ill repute, offers an alternate route from New Orleans to Baton Rouge. Another older route, Hwy 90, crosses the Huey P Long Bridge as it follows a southerly course between Mobile and the Cajun bayous south of Lafayette. Both Hwy 90 and the short I-310 connect New Orleans with the West Bank plantations upriver along the so-called 'River Rd' (Hwy 61).

BICYCLE
Bicycling is a great way to explore the state. Louisiana gives bicyclists the same rights and responsibilities as motorists; however, the interstate freeways and highway bridges near New Orleans are closed to bicyclists; use Hwy 90 or Hwy 61 instead. All of New Orleans' free state-operated ferries crossing the Mississippi River offer bicycle transport. Outside of the city, the crossings cost $1.

For information and maps of cross-country touring routes, contact **Adventure Cycling** (☎ 406-721-1776; PO Box 8308QO, Missoula, MT 59807). The company's suggested east-west trek across Louisiana crosses the Mississippi River about 100mi north of New Orleans at St Francisville.

HITCHHIKING
Travelers hoping to thumb their way around Louisiana may be in for an unpleasant surprise. On the whole, hitching is much less common in the US than elsewhere in the world, and for good reason. With true horror stories and urban myths to deter people from sharing their rides, thumb-mode travel is now almost nonexistent. As hitching is never entirely safe, travelers who decide to

do it should understand that they are taking a potentially serious risk.

That said, for people who do choose to hitch, the advice that follows should help to make the journey as fast and safe as possible. Officially, hitchhiking is legal in Louisiana, but it *is* frowned upon by police and the highway patrol and you can expect hassles. Local laws may be more stringent. As signs at the on-ramps will tell you, pedestrians are not allowed on major highways. Try to travel in pairs and always let someone know where you are planning to go.

RIVERBOAT
Visitors to New Orleans during Mark Twain's time arrived by boat via the Mississippi River. This once common mode of travel continues to be offered by a few paddle-wheel riverboats and ocean-going cruise ships. Costs are high compared to other travel modes – the era of steerage passage is over. River travel is now typically offered as a package tour or excursion that includes top-end food and lodging.

With headquarters in New Orleans, the **Delta Queen Steamboat Company** (Map 5; ☎ 800-543-1949; 30 Robin St Wharf) offers occasional paddle-wheel riverboat travel to and from ports on the Mississippi River, including St Paul (14 nights), St Louis (seven nights) and Memphis (five nights). It also connects New Orleans with riverboat ports on Mississippi River tributaries such as Pittsburgh (12 nights), Nashville (nine nights) and Chattanooga (10 nights); all times are for downriver travel – add at least one day for each five days to head upriver. In addition, voyages on the *Delta Queen* occasionally ply the Intracoastal Waterway between New Orleans and Galveston (six nights).

Riverboat fares typically start at $375 per person for three nights in a simple double-occupancy berth and include all meals and entertainment, but they do not include the $90 to $100 port and departure tax. The company operates two paddle-wheel riverboats, the *Mississippi Queen* and the handsomely restored *Delta Queen*, which was originally launched in 1927 and still follows the steam-powered tradition.

Getting Around

The compact and level nature of the French Quarter and downtown riverfront areas make walking and bicycling the preferred ways to get around for most visitors. As in cities throughout the USA, public transit in New Orleans has deteriorated as transportation funds have been diverted to subsidize motorists. Nevertheless, visitors will find that the buses, streetcars and ferries generally serve the most popular attractions (with the glaring exception of Union Passenger Terminal). In fact, riding the streetcars or ferries is an exciting attraction in itself.

THE AIRPORT
New Orleans International Airport (*MSY; Map 1; ☎ 464-0831*) ranks 40th in the USA in passenger volume on account of it being a destination rather than a transfer airport. A single terminal is connected to four concourses. Luggage lockers are available in each concourse, immediately past the security area. There is no need for gigantic tramways or moving walkways here – even passengers fresh from Bourbon St are not likely to get lost. Baggage and ground transportation are on the lower level. Don't light up inside the terminal. However, some gates have designated smoking areas.

Information
There is a main **information booth** (*open 8am-9pm daily*) at Concourse A and B. Nearby there's a **Travelers' Aid information booth** (*☎ 464-3522; open 9am-9pm*) in the eastern baggage claim. New Orleans airport has a post office near Concourse C next to Whitney National Bank.

Money
A branch of the **Whitney National Bank** (*☎ 838-6492; open 8:30am-3pm Mon-Thur*) and ATM are in the terminal, near Concourse C. Exchange rates at **Travelex** (*☎ 465-9647; open 8am-5pm daily*), operated by Mutual of Omaha, are posted. You may be inclined to comparison shop, but it's best to

wait until you can get downtown on a weekday for better currency-exchange rates.

Telephones
White courtesy phones and a free phone connection to various airport services are scattered throughout the terminal. Pay phones that accept credit cards are widely available.

TO/FROM THE AIRPORT
New Orleans International Airport is in Kenner, 11mi west of the city center.

Shuttle
Most visitors take the **Airport Shuttle** (*☎ 522-3500*) to and from the airport. It's a frequent service between the airport and downtown hotels for $10 per passenger each way. It's a cheap and courteous introduction to the city, although it can be time-consuming, especially if you are the last to be dropped off. At the airport, buy tickets from agencies in the baggage area below the arrival gates. You can purchase a round-trip ticket at your hotel or just pay the driver. Be sure to call a day ahead to arrange for a departure pickup, which is typically two hours prior to your flight.

Bus
If your baggage is not too unwieldy, the **Louisiana Transit Company** (*☎ 818-1077*) offers the cheapest ride downtown aboard its Jefferson Transit Airport Express, route E2, for $1.50. Passengers can exit at stops along Airline Hwy (Hwy 61) and along Tulane Ave, but must flag the bus to board in most locations. The bus makes two regular stops: opposite ticket door No 7 on the upper level of the airport's main terminal, and downtown on Tulane Ave and Loyola St, opposite the public library.

During the day, buses run the full route every 23 minutes. From 6:45pm to 6am, buses only operate between the airport and Carrollton Ave, where for $1.25 you can continue to downtown on the Regional Transit Authority's (RTA) No 39 Tulane bus.

Car

The quickest way to drive between the airport and downtown is to take I-10. If you're coming from downtown on I-10, take exit 223 for the airport; going to downtown, take exit 234, as the Superdome looms before you. An alternative route is Airline Hwy (Hwy 61), a surface street with an endless series of stoplights.

Taxi

A taxi ride from the airport costs a flat rate of $28 for one to two passengers. Each additional passenger costs another $12. More than four passengers are not allowed. Taxi stands are on the lower level, immediately outside the baggage claim area.

TO/FROM UNION PASSENGER TERMINAL

New Orleans provides few options for passengers arriving by bus and train. Although it's tempting to walk the short distance to the French Quarter, you should be wary of going solo through the deserted Central Business District (CBD) at night. Cab fare to the corner of Bourbon and Canal Sts costs about $5.

As incredible as it may seem, local buses do not directly serve the New Orleans Union Passenger Terminal (Map 4; 1001 Loyola Ave), which is also known as Union station. In front of the station, arriving passengers must search for the sheltered stop across broad Loyola Ave at Howard Ave. The No 17 S Claiborne Ave bus goes to the edge of the French Quarter at Canal and Rampart Sts. The fare is $1.25, plus 25¢ for a transfer. During the weeks preceding Mardi Gras, a sign directs passengers to board one block down Loyola Ave at Julia St.

Although Union Passenger Terminal provides neither bicycle lockers nor secure racks, **Amtrak** (☎ 800-872-7245) is obligated to offer a baggage-check service to passengers. You can check a bike as stored baggage by paying $1.50 per day.

BUS

The Regional Transit Authority (RTA) offers a decent bus and streetcar service (see

Streetcar, following). Call the **RTA Rideline** (☎ 248-3900) for bus-route information. The only sure way to get bus schedules is to visit the **RTA office** (101 Dauphine St, 4th floor).

Fares cost $1.25 and transfers are 25¢ extra, except on express buses, which charge a $1.50 fare. All buses require exact change. Consider purchasing an RTA Visitor Pass, which is good for unlimited travel on buses and streetcars. A one-day pass costs $4; a three-day pass is $8. Visitor Passes are available from most hotels (ask the concierge) and at the RTA office.

From the French Quarter, most destinations are served by buses that stop at the intersection of Basin and Canal Sts. All stops have signs noting the route name and number – you may have to explore all four corners of an intersection to find the stop you want. The free *New Orleans Street Map*, available from information booths at the airport and downtown, shows most route numbers and lists the route names you can expect to see displayed on the front of the bus.

The **Louisiana Transit Company** (☎ 818-1077) operates Jefferson Transit buses, which serve the airport and Metairie, in Jefferson Parish. The Causeway Blvd route E5 connects Jefferson Hwy near the river with W Esplanade Ave near the lake. The fare is $1. This bus carries bikes, but you'll need a bike permit (see Bicycles, later in this chapter).

You can cross the Greater New Orleans Bridge aboard **Westside Transit** (☎ 367-7433) buses. Board the Lapalco Blvd bus in New Orleans at the corner of Loyola and Tulane Aves to cross to the Gretna terminal on the West Bank. Up to two bikes can be carried. The fare is $1.50.

STREETCAR

Streetcars are making a comeback in New Orleans. The two existing lines, described here, will soon be linked by a Canal St line, which is slotted to begin operation in early 2004. And rumor has it that the famous streetcar named *Desire*, which once provided Blanche Dubois with a ride and Tennessee Williams with a title, may return to action sometime in the foreseeable future.

St Charles Ave Streetcar Line

When the St Charles Ave streetcar route opened as the New Orleans & Carrollton Railroad in 1835, it was the nation's second horse-drawn streetcar line. The line was also among the first systems to be electrified when New Orleans adopted electric traction in 1893. Now it is one of the few streetcars to have survived the automobile era – it continues to serve local passengers and introduce visitors to the preferred commuter mode of the early 20th century, when fares cost a nickel. There is no need to worry about breakdowns when you hear the intermittent thunka-thunka sound – it's just the air compressor. The streetcars' brakes, doors and even the fare box operate on compressed air.

Check out the streetcar-era suburbs, with their Georgian architecture and ornate churches that evolved along the tracks extending from Canal St uptown to S Carrollton Ave (see the St Charles Ave Streetcar Tour special section in the Things to See & Do chapter). Of course, you can get off the streetcar and explore along the way, as the line serves many of the attractions and walking tours listed in this book.

The fare is $1.25 each way (exact change is required), and a transfer to RTA buses costs 25¢. Both the one- and three-day Visitor Passes (see Bus, earlier) are valid on the streetcar. The 13mi round trip from the corner of Canal and Carondelet Sts takes 1½ hours. Although the St Charles Ave streetcar operates 24 hours, with frequent peak-hour service, it only runs hourly from midnight to 4am. Unfortunately, the streetcars are not wheelchair accessible.

Riverfront Streetcar Line

In 1988 the wheelchair-accessible Riverfront streetcar line began operating vintage red cars on the old dockside rail corridor wedged between the levee and flood wall. The 2mi route runs between the Old US Mint, in the lower end of the French Quarter near Faubourg Marigny, and the upriver Convention Center, crossing Canal St on the way. The fare costs $1.50 (an additional quarter is required if you use an RTA transfer). It operates from 6am to midnight.

CAR & MOTORCYCLE

Bringing a car to downtown New Orleans is a costly proposition that may actually hinder your visit and create headaches when dealing with the traffic and parking congestion. The narrow one-way streets and crowds in the Quarter are not conducive to driving, and hotels often charge extra for parking. The CBD is also crowded – many small parking lots use lifts to make room for more cars. Of course, a vehicle is essential if you are not staying in the downtown area or if you wish to take excursions not accessible by transit.

See Orientation in the Facts for the Visitor chapter for information on getting around the streets of New Orleans.

Parking

Downtown on-street parking is typically for short-term use. Parking meters offer 12 minutes for a quarter, with a two-hour limit, from 8am to 6pm Monday to Friday. Exceptions are numerous, so be sure to read all posted restrictions to avoid citations or towing. Enforcement is particularly efficient in areas where motorists are deemed capable of paying – for example, the Warehouse District's premier restaurant and gallery area along Julia St supports two or three parking patrols.

Although free parking on the street is often available in the lower end of the French Quarter (try along Esplanade Ave), it's generally a better idea to pay to park. The **U-Park Garage** *(Map 2, #147; ☎ 522-5975; 716 Iberville St)*, near the upper end of Bourbon St, charges $5 for the first hour or $19 for 24 hours. Other garages concentrated in the upper area of the Quarter charge similar rates.

The sound of car alarms from illegally parked vehicles being towed is frequently heard in the Quarter. If you park your car in a driveway, within 20ft of a corner or crosswalk, within 15ft of a fire hydrant or on a street-sweeping day, you will need about $75 (cash or credit card) plus cab fare (do not walk) to retrieve your car from the **Auto Pound** *(☎ 565-7450; 400 N Claiborne Ave)*.

Rental

All the big car-rental companies are found in New Orleans, particularly at the airport,

GETTING AROUND

along with a host of smaller or local operators. If you are staying downtown and only visiting the French Quarter – where hotel parking charges, parking fines and congested traffic make cars an encumbrance – you do not need a car. An option for visitors planning on taking an excursion is to pick up a rental car downtown when checking out of your hotel, then drop it off at the airport when you leave. Companies such as Agency, Avis and Hertz have offices downtown, in addition to airport locations. In any case, airport rates are generally better than city ones.

Rates go up and availability lessens during special events or large conventions. It's always worth phoning around to see what's available. Booking ahead usually ensures the best rate. A compact car typically costs $30 to $40 a day or $150 to $200 a week. On top of that, there is a 13.75% tax and an optional $9 to $15 a day loss/damage-waiver or LDW (insurance). Some credit cards pick up the insurance tab, but check with your credit-card company to make sure. Also, your own automobile insurance policy may automatically cover your rental vehicle. If so, it's wise to carry a copy of your insurance policy. Basic liability insurance, which will cover any damage you may cause to another vehicle, is required by law and is included in the price of renting a car. This is sometimes called third-party coverage. Most rates include unlimited mileage; if a rate looks like a real bargain, it may be because you're going to get hit for a mileage charge.

Most companies require that you be at least 25 years of age and have a major credit card, as well as a valid driver's license. A few agencies will accept a hefty cash deposit in lieu of a credit card. Some will also rent to those younger than 25, although younger drivers may have to pay extra.

Some of the larger agencies in or near the downtown area include the following:

Avis (☎ 523-4317, 800-3311-1212) 2024 Canal St
Budget Rent-a-Car (Map 2, #110; ☎ 565-5600, 800-527-0700) 1317 Canal St
Enterprise (☎ 522-7900, 800-325-8007) 1939 Canal St
Hertz (Map 4, #73; ☎ 568-1645, 800-654-3131) 901 Convention Center Blvd

The lowest rates are available by renting older cars for local travel from **Econo-Cars** (☎ 827-0187; 4417 Earhart Blvd). The agency offers three-day minimum rentals at $90 or a week for $180, including insurance.

TAXI

Hailing a cab is easy in downtown New Orleans, except when parades are blocking streets and when peak events are taking place. Taxi stands are located in front of most hotels, and cabs queue like predators to intercept late-night revelers on the streets adjacent to Bourbon St.

One downside to staying Uptown or visiting the nightclubs is the difficulty in hailing a cab. You will usually need to call. Also, it's best to give an address *and* cross streets, rather than just cross streets.

As some stranded travelers have found out, it can sometimes be pointless to call ahead for a taxi pickup – especially during Mardi Gras or Jazz Fest. Drivers are choosy and may actually decline to pick up a passenger if the destination is a bit out of the way. During Carnival parades, when travel is especially difficult, many drivers refuse to travel beyond the downtown area after being hailed on the street.

Another problem is the restricted service area of the cab companies. One passenger reported calling ahead to United Cabs to schedule an early-morning ride from a rental-car return lot in Kenner to the airport terminal. No cab was waiting at the prescribed time. After the passenger had made two additional calls and missed the flight, the dispatcher explained that United Cabs do not serve Kenner – except for pickups at the airport.

If you telephone through for a taxi your request is typically quickly met, yet none of the taxi services can be recommended as being completely reliable. **White Fleet Cabs** (☎ 948-6605) and **United Cabs** (☎ 522-9771) will pick up passengers at the airport or anywhere within New Orleans. **Metairie Cab** (☎ 835-4242) specifically serves the outlying suburbs. Rules are made to be broken, but don't plan on taking a taxi with a crowd of more than four people. Telephone calls for a pickup are usually answered promptly, but pre-scheduled pickups are usually subject to error.

Fares from the French Quarter to the Bywater are around $8, to the Garden District $10 or more and to Mid-City it's about $10; add an additional $1 for more than one passenger and a 15% tip. During Jazz Fest, the cabs charge a $3 special events fare from the French Quarter to the Fair Grounds, but availability is limited.

MISSISSIPPI RIVER FERRIES

The cheapest way to cruise the Mississippi River is aboard one of the state-run ferries. Ferries operate daily between Canal St and the West Bank community of Algiers, and between Jackson Ave and Gretna, another West Bank suburb. Another ferry travels between Chalmette, where the battlefield is, and lower Algiers. All begin service at either 5:45am or 6am and continue to 9pm or 9:15pm, except the Canal St Ferry, which operates until 11:45pm or midnight. In the vicinity of New Orleans, the ferries are free; further afield (see the Excursions chapter), there's a toll of $1 for cars. Boats leave the terminals at the following times:

Algiers On the quarter hour and three-quarters hour
Canal St On the hour and half-hour
Chalmette Every quarter hour
Gretna On the quarter hour and three-quarters hour
Jackson St On the hour and half-hour

BICYCLE

On the positive side of the ledger for riders, New Orleans is flat and relatively compact. On the negative side are the heavy traffic and potholes, which make fat tires a near necessity. Oppressive summer heat and humidity also discourage some bicyclists.

Routes

Residents typically follow either Burgundy or Dauphine Sts to traverse the French Quarter between the CBD and Faubourg Marigny, where the bicycle is the travel mode of choice. Esplanade Ave is somewhat busy, but the cars can go around you as you pedal from the French Quarter to the Fair Grounds or City Park. At City Park you should avoid Weisner Blvd where it crosses I-610 and instead travel through the western side of the park to Lakeshore Dr. Roads and paths along the lake are typically bicycle friendly. Racers favor workouts in City Park on the Roosevelt Mall oval and along Lakeshore Dr.

Many visitors travel from the French Quarter through the Warehouse District on Magazine St. Prytania St is a good choice for crossing through the Lower Garden District. The rest of Uptown is readily traversed, from Jackson Ave to Audubon Park, on quiet residential streets such as Camp and Chestnut Sts. A complete circuit of town can be completed from Uptown by following either Napoleon Ave to Octavia St, or State St to the neutral ground (median) bike path on Jeff Davis Parkway leading to Bayou St John. Return to the French Quarter on Esplanade Ave. It's a good idea to have a bike light if you plan to return in the evening (especially during the short winter daylight hours).

From S Carrollton Ave, the river levee offers a continuous off-road bicycle route upriver to near the airport.

Bicycling on the West Bank is a breeze. You can take the Canal St Ferry to Algiers, follow the levee downriver on Patterson Rd and detour around the US Navy Hospital before returning to Patterson Rd via Odean St. Continue to the Chalmette Ferry, but beware that returning on the St Bernard Hwy is not for beginners – you might want to go back in the same direction.

Rental

Bicycles can be rented for around $15 to $20 a day. Rental bikes are available from **French Quarter Bicycles** (Map 2, #76; ☎ 529-3136; 522 Dumaine St) and nearby in the Faubourg Marigny from **Bicycle Michael's** (Map 3, #17; ☎ 945-9505; 622 Frenchmen St).

See Organized Tours, later, for information on tours offered to cyclists.

Public Transportation

You can readily transcend the river barrier by incorporating the ferry service into your rides. All state-operated ferries offer free transportation for bikes. Bicyclists board ahead of cars by walking down the left lane of the ramp to the swinging gate. You must wait for the cars to exit before leaving.

Unfortunately, the RTA does not allow bikes on buses and streetcars. In Jefferson Parish, three bus routes offer fold-down racks, which carry up to two bikes on the front of the bus: **Louisiana Transit's** (☎ 818-1077) Airport Express route E2 and Causeway Blvd route E5, and **Westside Transit's** (☎ 367-7433) Lapalco Blvd route between Gretna and New Orleans. For these buses, you will need a bike permit; apply in person (with a photo ID) between 10am and 2pm, Monday to Friday, or by appointment at one of two locations: (☎ 364-3450) 118 David Dr, Metairie or (☎ 364-3450) 21 Westbank Expressway, Gretna.

WALKING & JOGGING

The compact French Quarter and adjacent downtown hotels are ideally suited to the pedestrian. In fact, there is no better way to participate in the action along Bourbon St or to appreciate the local architecture than on foot. Aside from the French Quarter, some of the other areas that are best toured on foot include the Warehouse District galleries around Julia St; anywhere along the river levee; and Faubourg Marigny, wedged between Esplanade and Elysian Fields Aves below the French Quarter. Should a sudden thundershower catch you without an umbrella, many shops offer plastic ponchos for less than $1.

To walk through the Garden District or Audubon Park, ride the St Charles Ave streetcar from downtown. To leave the frenzy and noise behind, consider taking the Canal St Ferry to Algiers for a stroll through quiet neighborhoods or along the West Bank levee, which offers vistas of New Orleans and river shipping.

The best uninterrupted jogging paths are along either the levee above Audubon Park or the West Bank levee. Joggers have also worn pathways between the St Charles Ave streetcar tracks. Be sure to run facing the approaching streetcar so you will be aware of its approach and be able to step aside while it passes. Many joggers also circle

the Superdome on the plaza level – each lap is slightly more than a quarter mile.

Beware that pedestrians do not have the right-of-way and will find their lives in danger should they attempt to challenge motorists. Local motorists consider it a courtesy to honk at pedestrians in the street before speeding by – only out-of-state drivers are inclined to slow down or stop.

See Dangers & Annoyances in the Facts for the Visitor chapter for more information on pedestrian safety.

ORGANIZED TOURS

Few cities offer the variety of worthwhile organized tours available to New Orleans visitors. Although independent travelers sometimes scoff at being herded about, group tours can be an entertaining crash course on local history and architecture and can serve to orient new visitors to potentially unsafe areas.

If you do decide to take a tour, choosing one after perusing the tour companies' ubiquitous handbills may call for the 'eenie-meenie-mynie-moe' method. Some people habitually let a hotel concierge make a decision for them, but before you do that, be warned that concierges don't generally spend their free time taking walking tours, and some of them may actually receive kickbacks for recommending a particular company's tours. This can not only add to the price for you, but it also unfairly limits your choices. In some of the larger hotels, tour companies such as Grayline actually set up 'information' desks where you can be certain you won't receive honest advice about competing companies.

For swamp and plantation tours, see the Excursions chapter.

Walking Tours

At times it seems everyone and their mother is conducting walking tours in New Orleans, so it's worth taking the time to choose a tour carefully. Don't just stroll into one of the phony 'information' centers that have infested the French Quarter. All a tour operator needs to do to be recommended by one of these outfits is to put a little cash in the man's hand. It makes no difference if the tours are good or bad. (And some of the best tours refuse to pay.)

Many tours today are more about showmanship than insight into the fascinating city of New Orleans. A good tour guide will ballast an entertaining story with a deep understanding of the history behind it. New Orleans has no shortage of tall tales, but as usual truth is stranger than fiction. Your guide should be able to discern the difference.

Friends of the Cabildo (☎ 523-3939) is a nonprofit organization that offers daily two-hour French Quarter walks. Knowledgeable guides emphasize history, architecture and folklore. As a bonus, the price includes admission to two of the four Louisiana State Museums: the Cabildo, the Presbytère, the Old US Mint or the 1850 House. Tours start at the **1850 House Museum Store** (Map 2, #87; 523 St Ann St) at 10am and 1:30pm Tuesday to Sunday and at 1:30pm Monday. Tickets per adult/child are $10/8.

Gay Heritage Tour (☎ 945-6789), Robert Batson's well-regarded company, gets high marks for its humor and historical insight. The 2½-hour walk through the Quarter is chock-full with colorful anecdotes about local characters, including Tennessee Williams, Ellen DeGeneres and Clay Shaw. Everyone is welcome to come along, regardless of their sexual orientation. Tours cost $20 per adult and depart (with a minimum of four people) from the **Alternatives Shop** (Map 2, #23; 909 Bourbon St) on Wednesday and Saturday at 1pm.

Jean Lafitte National Historic Park (Map 2, #134; ☎ 589-2636; 419 Decatur St) offers free walks of the French Quarter led by park rangers. The free tours are limited to 30 people and are very popular. To get tickets, you must arrive at the park office at 9am, and one person cannot get tickets for the entire family – each person must show up for their own ticket.

Historic New Orleans Walking Tours (☎ 947-2120; ☒ tourneworleans.com), led by author Robert Florence, reinvests a percentage of its earnings in the restoration of old tombs. Florence has a savvy sense for what people want to hear, and he backs that up with a scholar's knowledge. His two-hour voodoo

and cemetery tour (adult/senior & student $15/13), which includes a visit to St Louis Cemetery No 1 and the Voodoo Spiritual Temple, is highly recommended. The company also offers a Garden District tour (adult/senior & student $14/12), including Lafayette Cemetery No 1, and a French Quarter Mystique tour (adult/senior & student $12/10) that delves into the facts and myths of the Vieux Carré. For details on where the tours depart from check the website.

Le Monde Creole (Map 2, #106; ☎ 568-1801; 624 Royal St) has tours that lead visitors past the closed doors of the Quarter and into some of the city's secluded courtyards. Guides specialize in the history of the Locoul family, a 19th-century Creole clan, and by investigating their story the tours offer a slice of every day Creole life. Tours are offered twice daily Tuesday to Sunday and cost $18 per adult.

Carriage Rides

Tour guides offering carriage rides through the French Quarter are certified by the city – which means that they at least have a modest understanding of the Quarter's history. However, you should be aware that Mark Twain's admonition, 'Get your facts first, then you can distort them all you please,' certainly applies to the carriage-guide business. Historical embellishment is commonplace.

Carriages depart day and night, until midnight, from Jackson Square. You will not be disappointed if you consider the tours to be fun orientation rides. Half-hour tours for up to four people cost $50.

African American Heritage Tours

This company (☎ 504-288-3478) offers three-hour city-wide van tours that explore the African-American heritage of New Orleans, the USA's most African city. The company also gives all-day tours of a French-speaking Cajun village, with an emphasis on zydeco music, as well as plantation tours. The van will swing by to pick you up at your hotel. Tickets cost $45 for the city tour, $75 for the Cajun tour and $85 for the plantation tour; a minimum of 10 people are needed for the last two tours.

GETTING AROUND

Things to See & Do

THINGS TO SEE & DO

The Best of the Big Easy

- Atmospheric architecture
- Audubon Zoo, among the USA's best
- Riverboat calliope music – if you're not too close to it
- Jackson Square buskers
- St Charles Ave streetcar
- Oak trees and mansions along St Charles and Esplanade Aves
- Quiet Bayou St John
- Royal St balconies and courtyards
- Cemeteries, especially St Louis Cemetery No 1
- The Mardi Gras exhibit at the Presbytère

Sightseeing in New Orleans is not difficult, as most sights are in the French Quarter or along a few narrow corridors sprocketing from it. Sights not within walking distance of the central area are easily reached by public transit. Within these narrow parameters, however, New Orleans packs in enough historic buildings, museums, restaurants, clubs, curiosities and amusements to draw many travelers back time and time again.

FRENCH QUARTER (MAP 2)

Locals call it the Vieux Carré, or 'Old Quarter,' but the French Quarter is much more than a historic district. It's the cultural and geographic focal point of New Orleans, the antiquated centerpiece that time left alone, but never forgot.

At its heart is Jackson Square, a public garden defined by the striking architectural symmetry and daily cultural chaos that surrounds it. It's possible to spend the better part of a day here acquainting yourself with New Orleans' history at the four Louisiana State Museums, and catching the ever-changing street scene from a sidewalk bench.

The Quarter is easily navigated on foot. It's just six blocks by 13 in a grid pattern, and it's densely packed with shops, bars, restaurants and things of interest. A visitor

can walk these blocks time and time again, on each occasion noticing something new that had never caught his or her eye before.

The upper Quarter, nearest Canal St, is most touristy. Architectural restrictions are relatively lenient here, particularly between Canal and Iberville Sts, permitting high-rise hotels and chain shops. Within the upper Quarter are the signature attractions that the whole world equates with New Orleans. The boisterous crowds and noisy bars along Bourbon St contrast wildly with the more sober antique shops and galleries that line Royal St. Both streets offer some of the oldest Creole restaurants in the city.

Below Orleans Ave (which divides the quarter in half) things quiet down, and most of the buildings are private residences with the odd corner shop or guesthouse thrown in. This lower quarter is occupied by many gay people and young, hip migrants with nary a string to tie them down. These people are drawn by New Orleans' creative, party-town atmosphere. Many wealthy New Orleanians own town houses in the Quarter, which they use for entertaining. The French Market, in the lower Quarter near the river, is a historic structure that now houses the Farmer's Market and Flea Market, which offer cheap trinkets from Louisiana and around the world (see the Shopping chapter for more information).

Since 1937, when the Vieux Carré gained its historic-district status, the population in the Quarter has plummeted from more than 12,000 to about 5000 today. There has been an even greater decline in the proportion of blacks and children in the population mix as the area has grown more affluent and less family oriented.

Vieux Carré Walking Tour

A walk through the French Quarter's narrow streets and passageways is primarily an appreciation of the elegant architectural vestiges of the 18th-century Spanish colony. The French Quarter also has its mysterious

French Quarter Houses

No city in the US offers such an extensive district of historic architecture as New Orleans' French Quarter, but apart from the ring of landmarks around Jackson Square and a few churches and modern hotels, the French Quarter's building stock consists mostly of rather modest residential structures. It's the collective effect of so many aged houses, distinguished primarily by minute details, that makes the French Quarter truly beautiful.

There are not many surviving structures from the French and Spanish colonial periods, but architects from those times (before the Louisiana Purchase in 1803) introduced many characteristics that influenced later New Orleans designers. The French adapted to New Orleans' torrid, wet climate by constructing West Indies–style galleries; these kept houses shaded and allowed families to keep their windows open when the rains came. The Spanish introduced secluded courtyards connected to the street by long, draft-drawing carriageways, and also began New Orleans' continuing love affair with wrought-iron ornamentation.

During the Spanish period, the French Quarter was decimated by two major fires, and subsequent architects took the precaution of building with brick, set between hand-hewn wooden posts, instead of with wood. Through the 19th century, when most of the surviving French Quarter was built, construction of this type predominated in the French Quarter.

Various building types pop up throughout the Quarter, but the three most prevalent types are cottages, town houses and shotgun houses.

The typical Creole cottage, of a type originally seen during the Spanish period, is topped by a gabled roof, sometimes with dormer windows that illuminate a finished attic. Shuttered doors and tall windows face the street. The interior is quartered into equal chambers, each with side windows or doors, and no hallway.

Spanish influences can also be observed in the town houses that line Royal and Chartres Sts. From the street, these wide row houses appear crammed against one another. They are usually two or three stories tall. Balconies and galleries extend from the facade, while interior courtyards reached by carriageways afford open-air privacy. The ground level is often occupied by a business, and in some examples a squat mezzanine, or *entresol*, serves as a storage space.

American town houses, with interior hallways instead of carriageways, are also common in the French Quarter. These generally date from 1840 and after, a period also marked by the emergence of cast iron. Cast iron is molded rather than tinkered into shape, and can be mass produced. The design possibilities were also much greater. Many town houses in the French Quarter and elsewhere in New Orleans are festooned with elaborate cast-iron filigrees, often with leafy motifs, grape clusters and ears of corn.

The shotgun house was a low-rent, mass-produced type of residence popular in the late 19th century, and many blocks leading toward Rampart St are lined with uniform examples. A shotgun, thus-named supposedly because a single bullet could be fired from front to back through the doorways of all of the rooms, is one room wide, with each room leading to the next in succession. Rooms have side windows, allowing in some cases for cross-ventilation. 'Double-shotguns' are duplexes, with mirror-image halves occupied separately. Some, called 'camel-back shotguns,' have a 2nd floor above the back of the house. Over time shotguns have come to be prized for their high-ceilinged, spacious rooms and Victorian styling. Shotgun houses are common throughout New Orleans.

charms. Intriguing stories can be sensed, if not always seen, and this certainly enhances the Quarter's allure.

This tour should take about two hours (more if you're touring some of the historic houses, buying art, drinking in the bars, etc).

Some sights given just a cursory description here are examined in greater detail later in this chapter.

Begin your walk at the **Presbytère** on Jackson Square and head down Chartres St. At the corner of Dumaine St, go left. Halfway up the block at No 632 stands **Madame John's Legacy**, run by the Louisiana State Museum. This French colonial house was built in 1788 and acquired its name when George Washington Cable used it as the setting in his story 'Tite Poullette.' Its raised basement of briquette *entre poteaux* construction offered protection from floods. An iron gate set in the brick wall across the street is graced by devil's pitchforks, a common motif in the Quarter that continues to keep trespassers and evil spirits at bay.

Return to Chartres St. At the corner of Ursulines Ave, the **Ursuline Convent** is partly obstructed from view by a wall surrounding its grounds. Built in 1745–50, it is the oldest structure in the Quarter and the only French-colonial building still standing in New Orleans (see Ursuline Convent, later).

Directly across Chartres St, at No 1113, the **Beauregard-Keyes House** dates back to 1826 and combines Creole- and American-style design. Civil War General PGT Beauregard rented rooms here after his wife died, and author Francis Parkinson Keyes lived here from 1942 to 1970.

Walk along Ursulines Ave to Royal St and turn right. Halfway up the block, at No

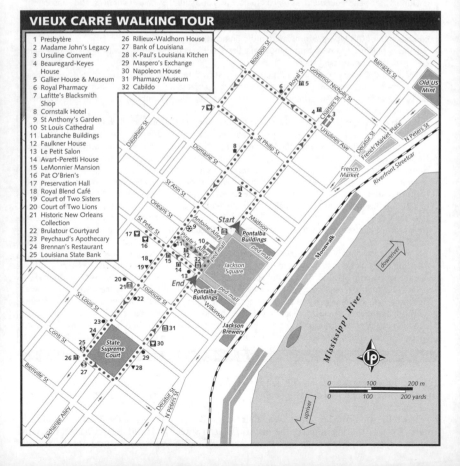

VIEUX CARRÉ WALKING TOUR

1 Presbytère
2 Madame John's Legacy
3 Ursuline Convent
4 Beauregard-Keyes House
5 Gallier House & Museum
6 Royal Pharmacy
7 Lafitte's Blacksmith Shop
8 Cornstalk Hotel
9 St Anthony's Garden
10 St Louis Cathedral
11 Labranche Buildings
12 Faulkner House
13 Le Petit Salon
14 Avart-Peretti House
15 LeMonnier Mansion
16 Pat O'Brien's
17 Preservation Hall
18 Royal Blend Café
19 Court of Two Sisters
20 Court of Two Lions
21 Historic New Orleans Collection
22 Brulatour Courtyard
23 Peychaud's Apothecary
24 Brennan's Restaurant
25 Louisiana State Bank
26 Rillieux-Waldhorn House
27 Bank of Louisiana
28 K-Paul's Louisiana Kitchen
29 Maspero's Exchange
30 Napoleon House
31 Pharmacy Museum
32 Cabildo

1118, the **Gallier House** is a Greek-revival town house, built in 1857 by architect James Gallier Jr for his family. The house is now a museum.

Cross Royal St and backtrack to the corner of Ursulines to take a peek at the **Royal Pharmacy**. The soda fountain, a perfectly preserved relic from the USA's malt-shop days, is no longer in use, but the owners of the pharmacy feel it's too classic to pull out.

Continue heading up Ursulines Ave and then left onto Bourbon St. The ramshackle one-story structure on the corner of St Philip St is a great little tavern called **Lafitte's Blacksmith Shop**. This is a National Historic Landmark, and although stories connecting it with the pirate Jean Lafitte are probably not true (legend has it he ran a blacksmith shop here with his brother), the little cottage stands out for its exposed brick-between-post construction. Most of the houses in the Quarter are built in this style, but the brick and framework is almost always concealed in stucco or wood. It is believed that the building dates to the end of the 18th century. Have a drink and then walk down St Philip St and back to Royal St.

When it comes to classic New Orleans postcard images, **Royal St** takes the prize. Many of the structures along the following stretch are graced by cast-iron galleries and potted plants hanging from the balconies. Take it slow and appreciate the details.

At No 915 the **Cornstalk Hotel** stands behind one of the most frequently photographed fences anywhere. The cast-iron fence with its cornstalk motif was manufactured in 1859 and has seen many coats of paint over the years. (See the Places to Stay chapter for details on staying here.)

Continue on to Orleans Ave, where stately magnolia trees and lush tropical plants fill **St Anthony's Garden**, behind **St Louis Cathedral**. At night, a lamp illuminates a statue of St Anthony, which casts dramatic shadows against the back of the cathedral. Vistas of the cathedral's steeple are available from anywhere along Orleans Ave, which divides the French Quarter in half.

Alongside the garden, **Pirate's Alley** is an inviting walkway that calls for a little detour.

The name is purely a romantic one, as the alleyway never harbored pirate activity. Jean Lafitte and his gang were long gone when the passageway was first opened in 1831.

The first buildings to the right, Nos 622–624 Pirate's Alley, are just two of the **Labranche Buildings**, which wrap around Royal St to St Peter St. Note the original wrought-iron balconies, some of the finest in town, which date to the 1840s. The houses were built by the pirate Jean Baptiste Labranche, a sugar planter. Continue along Pirate's Alley, and later you'll catch another look at the Labranche Buildings around the block.

At 624 Pirate's Alley the small but charming **Faulkner House Bookstore** opened in 1990 and very quickly became a focal point for New Orleans literary circles. It is so named because in 1925 author William Faulkner briefly lived in the house (the street was then called Orleans Alley). Poet Andrei Codrescu and novelist Richard Ford frequently drop in to visit owner Joe DeSalvo.

Turn right down Cabildo Alley to St Peter St. Note the unusual house at 620 St Peter St, with curved stairs leading up to its main entrance on the 2nd floor. It's known as **Le Petit Salon**, because in the 1920s civic-minded women gathered here to discuss ways to preserve local culture. The house's bow-and-arrow balcony motif is a visual play on words: The arrows are worthy of an archer's quiver, but the bows are of the sort that dainty girls wear in their hair.

Turn right up St Peter St, toward Royal St. At No 632 St Peter, the **Avart-Peretti House** is where Tennessee Williams lived in 1946–7, when he was writing his most famous play, *A Streetcar Named Desire*.

When you reach the corner of Royal, take a look at **LeMonnier Mansion**, at No 640, which is commonly known to be New Orleans' first 'skyscraper.' Begun in 1795, the structure grew to three stories tall by 1811 (a fourth floor was added in 1876). Until that time, building in New Orleans was generally limited to two floors, for fear that the 'swampy' soil couldn't support taller buildings. The building's 1811 owner, Dr Yves LeMonnier, left his initials in the wrought-iron balcony that overlooks the street corn

Continue to the next site, which is on the same side of St Peter St. Halfway up the block you'll reach **Pat O'Brien's**, a bar famous for its syrupy signature beverage, the 'Hurricane.' Without bothering to taste the overpriced drinks you can breeze through Pat's large scenic courtyard, take in the raucous scene, and re-emerge on Bourbon St. (The bar doesn't open till 10am, so if it's too early, continue to the next sight, on the same side of the street.) When you leave Pat O'Brien's courtyard, return to St Peter St, and head in the direction of Royal St.

On your way, at No 726, you'll pass the rustic facade of **Preservation Hall**, where old-time jazz musicians perform nightly to a packed house. (If it's nighttime, you'll hear the trumpets and trombones blaring through the open windows.) When you reach Royal St, turn right.

The **Court of Two Sisters**, at 613 Royal St, where sisters Emma and Bertha Camors operated a variety store from 1886 to 1906, is now a famous Creole restaurant with a shaded courtyard that draws continuous raves and expensive food that is consistently disappointing.

Continue on Royal St. From the solid line of facades built to the sidewalk, or banquette, large interior courtyards are hidden behind most of the carriage gates. The Creole custom was to orient a home toward the rear, with more personal style accorded to interiors where families spent most of their time; by contrast, facades were relatively unostentatious and deliberately unrevealing. Some courtyards are now occupied by art retailers, but you can go in without buying anything. You can also enjoy a pleasant coffee or a meal in an alfresco courtyard setting at the **Royal Blend café** (see the Places to Eat chapter).

At the corner of Royal and Toulouse Sts stand a pair of houses built by Jean François Merieult in the 1790s. The corner house, called the **Court of Two Lions**, at 541 Royal St, has a well-known gate on the Toulouse St side, flanked by marble lions atop the entry posts. The house next door is home to the **Historic New Orleans Collection**, at 27–533 Royal St. Built in 1792, it is a rare survivor of the 1794 fire. Organized tours of the house and adjacent structures are available; see the Getting Around chapter.

Across the street, at No 520, a carriageway leads to the picturesque **Brulatour Courtyard**, which has been made famous by the countless artists who have drawn and painted it. It's now occupied by the Sutton Collection art dealers and is open during business hours.

On the next block, the massive **State Supreme Court Building** was the setting for many scenes from the movie *JFK*. Opened in 1909, the white marble and terracotta facade stands in attractive contrast with the rest of the Quarter.

Across the street, an antique gun shop at No 437 (now James H Cohen & Sons) occupies the former premises of **Peychaud's Apothecary**. Legend has it that the cocktail was invented here.

A few doors down, at No 417, the famed **Brennan's Restaurant** has been serving Creole cuisine since 1955. Vincent Rillieux, the great-grandfather of artist Edgar Degas, owned the property and may have commissioned the building's 1802 construction. The building housed the Banque de la Louisiane, the first bank established after the Louisiana Purchase, and in 1841 it became the home of boy-wonder chess-champ Paul Morphy.

Louisiana State Bank, at No 403, was designed by nationally acclaimed architect Benjamin Henry Latrobe in 1820, shortly before his death from yellow fever.

The **Rillieux-Waldhorn House**, at No 343, is another former bank built by Rillieux shortly after the great fire of 1794. Its wrought-iron balconies and knee braces are notable examples of Spanish colonial design. The Waldorn antique shop has been on the premises since 1881.

Across the street, pause to admire the interior of the Greek revival-style **Bank of Louisiana**, at No 334, which was built in 1826. The building has served in many capacities since the bank was liquidated in 1867, including a stint as the State Capitol. The building now houses a police station and a visitor center.

Head down Conti St to Chartres St and turn left. From here it's a straight shot back to Jackson Square, with several interesting sights along the way. Facing the back of the State Supreme Court is **K-Paul's Louisiana Kitchen**, at 416 Chartres St, where super-chef Paul Prudhomme introduced modern Cajun cuisine to the world.

Maspero's Exchange, at No 440, is a restaurant formerly known as La Bourse de Maspero, the slave-trading house and coffee shop of Pierre Masperos.

On the opposite corner of the street at No 500, **Napoleon House** is a treasured ancient bar with stucco walls. At the beginning of the 19th century, the building's owner, former Mayor Nicholas Girod, hatched a plot to rescue Napoleon Bonaparte from his prison on St Helena and to keep the deposed emperor in an apartment above the bar. Unfortunately the emperor died before the elaborate plan was carried out.

The La Pharmacie Francaise sign, above No 514, calls attention to the **Pharmacy Museum**. In 1823 the shop was run by the USA's first licensed pharmacist.

As Jackson Square comes into view, you'll reach the Presbytère's near-identical twin, the **Cabildo**. The benches in front are a good spot to stop for a while. Musicians and other street entertainers are almost always performing here.

Jackson Square (Map 2)

Jackson Square is one of the most attractive public spaces in the USA. The park itself is well groomed and pleasant enough, but the surrounding architecture is what makes Jackson Square visually spectacular. A striking symmetry is created by the two Pontalba Buildings flanking the square and the nearly identical Cabildo and Presbytère structures on either side of St Louis Cathedral, which is the square's structural centerpiece. All around the square a host of street musicians, painters, tarot-card readers and mimes compete for the attention of tourists milling about the banquette.

The square was part of Adrien de Pauger's original city plans, laid out in 1722, and it began its life as a military parade ground called Place d'Armes. Madame Micaëla Pontalba transformed the muddy grounds

Madame Pontalba

The woman behind the Pontalba Buildings on Jackson Square, Madame Michaela Pontalba, is one of New Orleans' more remarkable historic characters. She is often referred to as a baroness, although in truth she had divorced her husband before he inherited the title of baron from his father. She attained her powerful status by fusing the wealth of the two richest families in Louisiana (Almonaster and Pontalba) through her own shrewd dealings after an ill-fated attempt on her life by her father-in-law.

Micaëla was born in 1795, when her father, Don Andrés Almonaster y Roxas, was 71 years old. Almonaster had arrived in Louisiana a penniless Spanish notary in 1769 and amassed a fortune through land transfers and rental income. In fact, Almonaster's contribution to the beautification of Jackson Square far exceeded his daughter's later additions, for it was Almonaster who commissioned the Cabildo, St Louis Cathedral and the Presbytère. But Micaëla led the more interesting life.

At 16, Micaëla married her cousin, Joseph Xavier Célestin Delfau de Pontalba and moved to Paris to live with his family. It was an arranged marriage, and although the couple had three children, they seemed to have developed no affection for one another. Before their first son was born, Célestin asked Micaëla to sign over her fortune to him – apparently he was afraid she might die in childbirth – and she refused. In 1834, they separated.

Micaëla, however, was unwilling to give up her share of the Pontalba riches. Angered by her demands, her husband's father, Baron Joseph Xavier de Pontalba, shot her while she was visiting in France. Thinking that she was dead, the baron turned the gun on himself and committed suicide. Although seriously injured, Micaëla survived and left Paris with two of her three sons for her native New Orleans in 1848, sans title but with her wealth intact. After commissioning – some say even designing – the upper and lower Pontalba Buildings and converting the dowdy Place d'Armes into the elegant Jackson Square, Madame Pontalba returned to Paris, where she died in 1874.

into beautiful groomed gardens and re-named the square to honor Andrew Jackson, who led the American forces in the Battle of New Orleans before serving two terms as the seventh president of the USA (1829–37); see the boxed text 'Madame Pontalba' for more information.

In the middle of the park stands **Jackson monument** *(Map 2, #97)* – Clark Mills' bronze equestrian statue of Jackson, which was unveiled in 1856. The inscription, 'The Union Must and Shall be Preserved,' was an added – and locally unwelcome – sentiment from General Benjamin Butler, the Yankee commander of occupying forces in 1862.

St Louis Cathedral (Map 2, #96)

During the Christmas Eve midnight mass, the Cathedral of St Louis, King of France *(☎ 525-9585; donations accepted; open 9am-5pm Mon-Sat, 1pm-5pm Sun)*, draws a large standing-room only crowd of worshipers. The cathedral is the focal point for New Orleans' sizeable Catholic community. Marie Laveau, the voodoo queen who practiced a hybrid voodoo-Catholicism, worshiped here during the height of her influence in the mid-19th century.

In 1722, a hurricane destroyed the first of three churches built here by the St Louis Parish, established in 1720. Architect Don Gilberto Guillemard dedicated the present cathedral on Christmas Eve in 1794, only weeks after it was saved from a devastating fire by a combination of shifting winds and a firebreak provided by the empty lot where the original Cabildo had burned down six years earlier. Extensive remodeling from 1849 to 1851 was designed by French-trained architect JNB DePouilly. In 1850, the cathedral was designated as the metro-politan church of the Archdiocese of New Orleans. Pope Paul VI awarded it the rank of minor basilica in 1964.

Buried in the cathedral is its Spanish bene-factor, Don Andrés Almonaster y Roxas, who also financed the Cabildo and the initial construction of the Presbytère – not bad for a minor official who arrived in New Or-leans as a poor Spanish notary. He gained his wealth from rents after he acquired real estate facing the Place d'Armes. His daughter, Madame Pontalba, later built the Pontalba Buildings to complete Jackson Square (see the boxed text 'Madame Pontalba').

Cabildo (Map 2, #95)

The first Cabildo was a single-story struc-ture destroyed by the Good Friday fire of 1788. Reconstruction was delayed by the city's more pressing needs for a prison, cathedral, and police and fire stations. It turned out to be fortuitous that architect Gilberto Guillemard, who was busy with the St Louis Cathedral, did not hurry the reconstruction. The December 1794 fire would have likely destroyed a new Cabildo and the almost completed cathedral as well. Tenants in the rebuilt Cabildo *(☎ 568-6968; 701 Chartres St; adult/senior & student $5/4, child under 12 free; open 9am-5pm Tues-Sun)*, dedicated in 1799, have included the Spanish Council (for which the building is named), the City Hall government from 1803 to 1853, the Louisiana Supreme Court from 1853 to 1910 and the Louisiana State Museum from 1911 to the present.

Three floors of exhibits emphasize the significance of New Orleans in a regional, national and even international context. It is a challenge to see it all in part of a day. You might try to quickly survey the lower floor, paying attention to the pre-Columbian In-dian artefacts and the colonial exhibits that most interest you. You can overlook Jack-son Square from the Sala Capitular (Span-ish Council room) on the 2nd floor. This is where the Louisiana Purchase documents were signed, transferring the extensive territory from Napoleonic France to the US. Other displays depict the Battle of New Orleans, including the role of free blacks and members of the Choctaw tribe in Major General Andrew Jackson's force, which decisively defeated General Packenham's British troops in 1814. The 3rd-floor ex-hibits of racial and ethnic groups from the American period are among the most inter-esting, with artefacts and shocking depic-tions of African slaves next to Civil War military displays that show free people of color in support of the Confederacy.

Presbytère (Map 2, #84)

Although architect Gilberto Guillemard originally designed the Presbytère (☎ 568-6968; 751 Chartres St; adult/senior & student $5/4, child under 12 free; open 9am-5pm Tues-Sun) to be a rectory for the St Louis Cathedral in 1791, the building was never directly used by the church after it was completed in 1813. Instead, the cathedral administrators rented the building to the city for use as a courthouse before selling it to them in 1853. Ownership was transferred to the Louisiana State Museum in 1911.

The Presbytère has a permanent exhibit, called 'Mardi Gras: It's Carnival Time in New Orleans,' that's essential viewing for visitors wanting to learn about Louisianan culture. The exhibit delves into all of the major topics, with vibrant displays of masks and costumes, parade floats, Mardi Gras Indian suits and historic photos. Documentary videos and detailed signage help convey the meaning behind many of carnival's complicated traditions.

1850 House (Map 2, #87)

The 1850 House (☎ 568-6968; 523 St Ann St; adult/senior & student $5/4, child under 12 free; open 9am-5pm Tues-Sun) is one of the apartments in the lower Pontalba Building. Madame Micaëla Pontalba, daughter of Don Andrés Almonaster y Roxas, continued her father's improvements around Jackson Square by building the long rows of red-brick apartments flanking the upper and lower portions of the square. She was also responsible for renaming the once barren parade grounds, the Place d'Armes, after her friend Andrew Jackson. Initial plans for the apartments were drawn by the noted architect James Gallier Sr. In 1927, the lower Pontalba Building was bequeathed by William Ratcliffe Irby to the Louisiana State Museum, and three years later the city acquired the upper Pontalba Building, where Micaëla once lived.

Now, knowledgeable volunteers from the Friends of the Cabildo give tours of the apartment, which includes the central court and servants' quarters with period furnishings throughout. Innovations include the use of bricks imported from the East Coast, extended porches to create covered walkways, and the upstairs galleries, which have cast-iron railings in place of wrought iron. Repeated along the railings are the initials AP, signifying the union of the Almonaster and Pontalba wealth.

The guides are available Tuesday to Friday from 11am to noon and 1pm to 2pm, and Saturday from 11am to noon. At all other times tours are self-guided.

French Market (Map 2, #59)

For more than 200 years, New Orleans trade has focused on the high ground beside the river levee. Native Americans conducted the earliest commerce by offering hides to Europeans, and French colonials followed with an open-air market. The Spanish built the first structure in 1791 to house butchers, as well as regulate the often abused sale of food, but it was destroyed by hurricane and fire. In 1813, city surveyor Jacques Tanesse designed a replacement market, the Halle des Boucheries (Butcher's Market).

In the 1930s the WPA (Works Progress – later, Works Project – Administration) extensively renovated the city-managed French Market (French Market Place; open 24 hrs) from St Ann to Barracks Sts. See the Shopping chapter for information on the vendors currently operating at the market.

Cafés have occupied the Butcher's Market building since 1860. Café du Monde (Map 2, #98; ☎ 581-2914; 800 Decatur St; open 24 hrs), the market's oldest tenant, sells loads of its packaged chicory-blend coffee and boxed beignet mix to visitors (see the Places to Eat chapter for more information).

New Orleans Jazz National Historic Park (Map 2, #46)

The headquarters for the Jazz National Historic Park (☎ 877-520-0677; 916 N Peters St; admission free; open 9am-5pm) does not have much to offer yet – there's no historic exhibit pulling all the stops. Such a thing is sorely missing in the 'Cradle of Jazz.' However, the center does have educational musical programmes on most days of the week. Many of the park rangers are musicians and knowledgeable lecturers, and their programmes discuss musical developments, cultural changes, regional styles, myths, legends, and musical techniques in relation to the broad subject of jazz. By 2005, the center should be ready to relocate to its permanent headquarters in Louis Armstrong Park.

Ursuline Convent (Map 2, #40)

After a five-month voyage from Rouen in France, 12 Ursuline nuns arrived in New Orleans to care for the French garrison's miserable little hospital and to educate the young girls of the colony. They were the first nuns in the New World. The French Colonial Army planned and built the existing convent and girls' school between 1745 and 1752, making it the oldest structure in the French Quarter and the Mississippi Valley. It is also one of the few surviving examples of French-colonial architecture in New Orleans. The nuns moved Uptown in 1824.

Guided tours of the fully restored convent *(☎ 529-3040; 1112 Chartres St; adult/senior/child $5/4/2, child under 8 free)* include a visit to the Chapel of Archbishops, built in 1845. The chapel's stained-glass windows pay tribute to the Battle of New Orleans (Andrew Jackson credited his victory to the Ursulines' prayers for divine intervention) and to the Sisters of the Holy Family, the black Creole nuns established in 1842 by Archbishop Antoine Blanc. Tours of the Ursuline Convent are offered Tuesday to Friday at 10am, 11am, 1pm, 2pm and 3pm; and Saturday and Sunday at 11:15am, 1pm and 2pm.

Old US Mint (Map 2, #15)

This unremarkable Greek-revival building appears out of place among the Creole buildings of the lower Quarter. From 1838 to 1861 and again from 1879 to 1910, the New Orleans Mint struck US coinage bearing the 'O' mint mark. The Confederate States of America briefly produced coins after seizing the mint in 1861. The current meager exhibits about the Old US Mint are likely to disappoint all but the most starved coin enthusiasts looking for a quick fix.

After serving as a US Mint, a federal prison and a US Coast Guard office, the building was transferred to the Louisiana State Museum, which opened its doors to the public in the 1980s.

The Old US Mint *(☎ 504-568-6968; 400 Esplanade Ave; adult/senior $5/4; open 9am-5pm Tues-Sun)* has two gift shops which offer a good selection of jazz recordings and an array of coins and Confederate currency minted in New Orleans. The price of entry also entitles you to a look at the New Orleans Jazz Exhibit and the Houma Indian Arts Museum.

New Orleans Jazz Exhibit (Map 2, #15)

If you wouldn't give a nickel to see where coins were once minted, the Old US Mint's exhibit on New Orleans jazz might lure you in. The exhibit is an intriguing assemblage of memorabilia and photographs, as well as the dented horns, busted snare drums, and homemade gut-stringed bass fiddles played by some of the Crescent City's most cherished artists. All artefacts are organized chronologically with historical notes, and as you peruse the exhibit, the museum's piped-in music comes alive. As history, though, the exhibit has more holes than a clarinet.

Houma Indian Arts Museum (Map 2, #15) You might not think jazz and Houma art go together, but in Louisiana it does. The Old US Mint's exhibit of contemporary folk art by Houma Indians is an impressive and often humorous collection of colorful wood carvings depicting men and animals – many of them life-sized. The room dedicated to model fishing boats and pirogues, the dugout canoes traditionally used by Native Americans and Cajuns to navigate Louisiana swamps, is also worth lingering in.

Historic New Orleans Collection (Map 2, #104)

The Historic New Orleans Collection *(☎ 504-523-4662; W www.hnoc.org; 533 Royal St)* is housed in a complex of historic buildings, anchored by Merieult House. Beginning in 1970, it has displayed private collections of art and historical documents that attract visitors, local researchers and foreign scholars. The exhibits may be a bit dry and academic for some tastes. A gift shop offers historical postcards, new and used books and other collectibles.

Williams Gallery These rotating exhibits *(admission free; open 10am-4:30pm Tues-Sat)* provide visitors with an opportunity to gain an understanding of different aspects of local history. For example, one past exhibit featured historical photographs, videos and oral histories to document the changes that mechanization brought to southern Louisiana's rural sugarcane-growing areas.

Merieult History Tour (Map 2, #108) Unlike the undocumented anecdotes fed to tourists by the French Quarter's ubiquitous carriage guides, the Historic New Orleans Collection's version of Louisiana's past is meticulously researched. The handsome gallery displays are housed in the landmark Merieult House, built in 1792. Showcased are the original transfer documents of the 1803 Louisiana Purchase. If the guide leaves something out, you can pick up a handy listing of each room's contents to find out more on your own. It's a bit fast paced, especially if you want to inspect the many early maps showing the city's evolution, or such disturbing items as an 1849 broadside advertising '24 Head of Slaves' (individual children for sale for $500 or entire families for $2400). Nevertheless, no better, short introduction to the history of the city is available.

Merieult House, a rare survivor of the 1794 fire, is an almost overlooked part of the tour. It was extensively remodeled in 1832, reflecting the American influence of the period. In one room, sections of plaster are removed to expose the traditional brick-and-post construction, and another room is sheathed with barge boards from river barges dismantled at the end of a downriver trip.

Tours are given Tuesday to Saturday at 10am, 11am, 2pm and 3pm. The cost is $4.

Williams Research Center (Map 2, #130) In 1996, the Historic New Orleans Collection moved its research facilities *(☎ 504-523-4662; 410 Chartres St; open 10am-4:30pm Tues-Sat)* to a beautifully refurbished police station. It really isn't of interest to the casual visitor, but if you have specific queries about almost any building in New Orleans the staff at this research center can help. The archives contain more than 300,000 images and a comprehensive block-by-block survey of the French Quarter. Ink pens are not permitted inside.

St Louis Cemetery No 1 (Map 2)

New Orleans' oldest cemetery (it dates to 1789), St Louis Cemetery No 1 *(admission free; open 8am-3pm)* has a rare beauty, enhanced by natural decay wrought by time. If you visit just one cemetery, this one near the French Quarter is certainly a good choice. Time and a willingness to explore the grounds are essential. Wandering at your own leisure, you can appreciate the statuary and ornate ironwork and stumble (literally) upon many historic tombs.

Voodoo queen **Marie Laveau** purportedly rests here. Fittingly, mystery surrounds her crypt. A family tomb not far from the entrance has the names Glapion, Laveau and Paris (all branches of Marie Laveau's family) etched in its marble front, and a commemorative plaque identifies it as Laveau's 'reputed' resting site. Debates concerning *which* Marie Laveau – mother or daughter, if either – was actually buried here will never be resolved, but popular consensus has designated this as Laveau's memorial. People come here to scratch an 'x' in the tomb's plaster, presumably to pay their 'respects' to the voodoo queen. However, living members of the Glapion family consider this practise vandalism – there is no spiritual significance to these chicken scratches, and visitors are strongly discouraged from desecrating this or any other tomb.

In the adjacent family tomb rests **Ernest 'Dutch' Morial**, New Orleans' first black mayor. Morial was mayor from 1978 to 1986, and he died in 1989.

Civil Rights figure **Homer Plessy** also rests in the cemetery, as do real-estate speculator **Bernard de Marigny**, architect **Henry Latrobe** and countless others.

The **Italian Mutual Benevolent Society Tomb** is responsible for the tallest monument in the cemetery. Like a lot of immigrant groups in New Orleans, the Italians formed a benevolent association to pool funds and assist in covering burial costs. The tomb is large enough to hold the remains of thousands. In 1969, to the obvious shock of the families who own tombs here, a demented rape scene in the movie *Easy Rider* was filmed in St Louis Cemetery No 1. Note the headless statue called 'Charity' on the Italian society tomb – urban myth maintains that actor Dennis Hopper was responsible for tearing the head off.

The cemetery gates are open and you are free to wander around on your own. It can be hard to find all of the noteworthy sights, and a good walking tour will help you see all of them (see Organized Tours in the Getting Around chapter). Even if you are not interested in a tour, it's a good idea to coincide your visit with one in order to ensure that you are not alone within the cemetery walls. Vandalism and statuary theft are the most common crimes here, but solitary visitors within the secluded grounds might be risking their personal safety.

Voodoo

Voodoo has in no small way contributed to New Orleans' reputation as the 'least American city in America.' It is perceived as both a colorful spectacle and a frightening glimpse of the supernatural, and this has proved to be an irresistible combination. Scores of shops selling voodoo dolls, gris-gris (amulets) and other exotic items attest to the fact that visitors to New Orleans can't help but buy into the mystique of voodoo.

All the hype aside, voodoo has remained a vital form of spiritual expression for thousands of practitioners. It came to the New World via Haiti, aboard slave ships from West Africa. A hybrid American form of voodoo developed as people from many different tribal communities contributed various spiritual practices – including animism, snake worship, ancestor worship and making sacrifices to deities, called *loas*.

In Haiti, voodoo played an integral role in the slave rebellions that led to Haitian independence at the end of the 18th century. (Haiti is, in fact, the second-oldest nation in the Americas, having gained its independence just 28 years after the USA.) Haitian *vodoun* cults became military units as vodoun priests urged their followers to fight for freedom, and the bravery of the rebels was probably abetted by vodoun charms carried for protection. Haitian landowners fled the island, many settling with their slaves in New Orleans, and this influx hastened the spread of voodoo. Liberated black Haitians also migrated to New Orleans, and this influx hastened the spread of voodoo.

In New Orleans, voodoo fused with Catholic beliefs as saints and deities became interchangeable for followers of both religions. And it grew extremely popular as more people turned to voodoo conjurers for advice, fortune telling, herbal medicine, love charms and revenge against their enemies. These conjurers became increasingly influential in the community, and some of the more successful were wealthy and often controversial.

Little is known about the famous 19th-century diviners with spectacular names like Doctor John, Doctor Yah Yah and Sanité Dédé. Even the known facts about the life of Marie Laveau, the most famous voodoo queen, continue to baffle historians. Half a century or more after their deaths, their biographies were committed to writing by historians who relied solely on hearsay and scant newspaper clippings. But no matter how true or false, their stories are fascinating.

Doctor John

By all accounts, Doctor John was an impressive sight to behold. Born in Africa and raised as a slave in Cuba, he had scars on his face, was immense in stature and could conjure up terrifying facial expressions. Legend has it he intimidated his master into granting him his freedom. After traveling the world as a sailor, Doctor John settled in New Orleans, where he established himself as the most influential voodoo king of his day.

Mortuary Chapel (Map 2, #77)

An unfounded fear of yellow-fever contagion led the city to forbid funerals for fever victims at the St Louis Cathedral. Built in 1826 near St Louis Cemetery No 1, the Mortuary Chapel (☎ 525-1551; 411 N Rampart St; donations accepted; open 7am-6pm daily) offered hasty services to victims, as its bell tolled constantly during epidemics. In 1931, it was renamed Our Lady of Guadeloupe Church. Inside the chapel, you'll see a statue of St Jude, patron saint of impossible cases, and a curious statue of St Expedite, a saint who probably never existed (on the plaque there are quotation marks around his name).

Voodoo Spiritual Temple (Map 2, #19)

A visit to Priestess Miriam Williams' Voodoo Spiritual Temple (☎ 504-522-9627; 828 N Rampart St; donations accepted; usually open 10:30am-5pm Mon-Fri, sometimes Sat) will convince you that voodoo is alive and well. The sageness and integrity of Priestess Miriam suggests that voodoo, with its reputation for trickery, has gotten a bum rap.

Voodoo

The evidence suggests he was a flim-flam artist. Doctor John had an army of spies working for him – household servants in the employ of prominent families – and he used information gleaned from these sources to bribe people and determine the course of events. At the time of his greatest influence, in the 1840s, Doctor John had clients in every stratum of society on both sides of the color line.

Despite Doctor John's nefarious dealings, he had a profound effect on New Orleans voodoo. Doctor John popularized the religion, introduced whites to its periphery and is sometimes credited with developing the voodoo-Catholic hybrid.

Marie Laveau

In many peoples' minds, voodoo means just one person: Marie Laveau. She is remembered as a beautiful and charismatic woman who had become one of the most powerful people in New Orleans by the mid-19th century. Her fame grew as she presided over spectacular rituals at Congo Square, where people of all colors paid to watch her do her thing. Marie Laveau popularized voodoo like never before or since.

Confusingly, there were actually two people known as Marie Laveau, a mother and daughter, and it is unclear where the influence of one gave over to the other. Certainly the illusion of eternal youth added to the Marie Laveau mystique.

Throughout her life, the elder Marie Laveau (also called the Widow Paris) remained a Catholic, and she insisted that her voodoo followers, too, observed the Catholic faith. Her healing methods often involved prayer in St Louis Cathedral.

Like Doctor John, Laveau had many tricks up her sleeve. She started out as a hairdresser. Entering the homes of upper-class white women as a coiffeuse gave her an inside view of the ruling class, and she used her knowledge to her advantage. By the time she was a voodoo queen, she had spies in upper-class homes throughout New Orleans.

Reports on Laveau's activities suggest that there was much more to her practice than nonpractitioners were permitted to witness. Only devoted followers were admitted to the rituals she presided over at her house on St Ann St and in the bayous around New Orleans. According to sensational accounts, related after her death, Laveau's followers danced naked around bonfires, drinking blood and slithering on the ground like snakes before engaging in all-out orgies.

The younger Marie Laveau was unable to maintain the success of her mother, and ultimately resorted to running a quadroon whorehouse for the pleasure of wealthy white men.

One of these two women is believed to be buried in St Louis Cemetery No 1, but no one can say for certain which Marie Laveau it is.

Miriam founded the Voodoo Spiritual Temple, in a converted storefront two doors down from Hula Mae's laundry, in 1990. The site she chose is just a few blocks from Congo Square, where Marie Laveau is said to have performed her theatrical public rituals in the mid-19th century. In Miriam's dimly lit temple, altars to many deities are endowed with such worldly offerings as cigarettes, liquor, money, candles, toys, photographs and statuettes, and the walls are covered with colorfully patterned cloths. In a back room, a snake relaxes in its vivarium, and on occasion, with a transfixed countenance, Priestess Miriam will take it out and lift it up, the snake appearing to move its body according to her will. In an adjacent shop Miriam does a modest trade in books, postcards, votive candles and other voodoo artefacts.

To neophyte eyes (all are welcome to visit the Voodoo Spiritual Temple), the temple is exotic and thrilling. Miriam, herself, is an impressive presence with her face beaming proudly and her hair radiating upward. But Miriam is unconcerned that her shop or the dramatic handling of the snake might conform to prevailing misconceptions about voodoo. She often seems dismissive of literal perceptions.

'It's OK that people should have a false opinion of voodoo, because all conceptions are initially false. Ideas progress toward the truth. Every thought is a misconception until something in it touches the thinker in some way. That's what voodoo is like. It is silent. It is an energy that vibrates into our minds.'

Historic Voodoo Museum (Map 2, #63)

This fascinating museum (☎ 523-7685; 724 Dumaine St; open 10am-8pm daily; adult/ senior/child $7/5.50/3.50) has an intricately arrayed collection of voodoo artefacts and is worth visiting. Tours of the museum are self-guided, and some of the items raise questions for which there is seemingly no answer. Carefully read the handout as you pass through the rooms; otherwise, there is little to explain the exhibited arcana.

Beauregard-Keyes House (Map 2, #39)

Greek-revival structures such as this house, built in 1826, with slave quarters and a rear courtyard, are uncommon in the Quarter. After the war, it was the home of Confederate General Beauregard for one year (1866). Beauregard made his mark on US history when he gave the order to Confederate forces to fire upon Fort Sumter in Charleston, South Carolina, thus beginning the Civil War.

The house's other illustrious resident was the author Francis Parkinson Keyes, who lived here from 1942 until her death in 1970. Beginning in 1926, she became well known for her serialized travel correspondence in *Good Housekeeping* – much of her success came from her incredible ability with foreign languages. She published 51 novels, including many that were set locally, such as *Crescent Carnival* (1942), the bestseller *Dinner at Antoine's* (1948) and *Steamboat Gothic* (1952). Her novel *Madame Castel's Lodger* (1962) is set in this house, which at the time belonged to General Beauregard.

Tours of the Beauregard-Keyes House (☎ 523-7257; 1113 Chartres St; adult/senior/ child $5/4/2) operate on the hour from 10am to 3pm Monday to Saturday and are

Historic House Tours

New Orleans offers a nice array of fine old houses that are open for tours. The following list (in order of construction) includes a few of the more significant homes. The two earliest homes on the list represent French-colonial city and plantation houses.

Merieult House (French Quarter) 1792; rebuilt 1832
Pitot House (Bayou St John) 1799
Beauregard-Keyes House (French Quarter) 1826
Hermann-Grima House (French Quarter) 1831
1850 House – lower Pontalba Buildings (French Quarter) 1850
Gallier House (French Quarter) 1857
Longue Vue House (Metairie) 1942

not as interesting as the individuals who lived there. A gift shop offers most of Francis Parkinson Keyes' books.

Gallier House Museum (Map 2, #29)

New Orleans owes much of its architectural heritage to James Gallier Sr and James Gallier Jr. They are both renowned for their Greek-revival designs. In 1857 Gallier Jr began work on this impressive French Quarter town house (☎ 525-5661; 1118 Royal St; adult/senior $6/5, child under 8 free; open 10am-3:30pm Mon-Fri), incorporating numerous innovations – such as interior plumbing, skylights and ceiling vents – into the design. A cistern provided fresh water to the kitchen, which in turn provided hot water to the upstairs bath. It is carefully furnished with period pieces. Access to the cast-iron gallery overlooking Royal St and other handsome homes is an added highlight of the worthwhile tour.

Hermann-Grima House (Map 2, #101)

Samuel Hermann, a Jewish merchant who married a Catholic, introduced the American-style Federal design to the Quarter in 1831. Hermann sold the house in 1844 to Judge Grima, a slaveholder, after he reportedly lost $2 million during the national financial panic of 1837. Cooking demonstrations in the authentic open-hearth kitchen are a special treat on Thursday from October to May.

Tours of the Hermann-Grima House (☎ 525-5661; 820 St Louis St; adult/senior $6/5) are offered from 10am to 3:30pm Monday to Friday.

Faulkner House (Map 2, #94)

Considered one of the greatest American novelists, William Faulkner (1897–1962) briefly rented an apartment in a town house on Pirate's Alley at the onset of his career. (At the time, the narrow passageway was called Orleans Alley.) In 1925, he moved to New Orleans from Mississippi, worked as a journalist at the Times-Picayune and met Sherwood Anderson, who helped him publish his first novel, Soldier's Pay (1926). He also contributed to the Double Dealer, a literary magazine published in New Orleans. The site of Faulkner's New Orleans stay is now home to Joe DeSalvo, who runs a bookstore (☎ 524-2940; 624 Pirate's Alley; open 10am-6pm daily) in the front rooms.

US Custom House (Map 2, #162)

The fortresslike US Custom House (423 Canal St) covers a square block. Construction on it began in 1849 and was supervised by Lieutenant PGT Beauregard, who later commanded Confederate forces. During the Reconstruction period after the Civil War, it served as the headquarters for African Americans in Abraham Lincoln's Republican party. Blacks held a majority in the Louisiana legislature, and two African Americans filled the office of lieutenant governor: Oscar J Dunn and Pickney Benton Stewart Pinchback. Meetings took place in the enormous 'Marble Hall' on the 2nd floor.

The construction of the building is also interesting. A cofferdam surrounded the excavation while the foundation was under construction; cotton bales used to seal the dam gave rise to stories that the building was founded on bales of cotton. Despite a mat of cypress timbers, the foundation has settled about 3ft under the weight of the brick and granite structure. All four sides of the building are identical.

Maspero's Exchange (Map 2, #123)

Pierre Maspero operated La Bourse de Maspero, a coffeehouse and one of many slave-trading houses in New Orleans. He was a tenant in the building that now houses the restaurant Maspero's Exchange (☎ 524-8990; 440 Chartres St) – not to be confused with Café Maspero on Decatur St. Regular markets for the abhorrent trade in human chattel occurred on Exchange Alley (now Exchange Place), between Conti and Canal Sts, and at the market beyond the Quarter's wall, now Louis Armstrong Park across Rampart St. Following the Good Friday fire of 1788, Don Juan Paillet built this structure, later to become the scene of slave trading, with an entresol (a mezzanine floor with a low ceiling that was visible from the exterior through the arched windows). This cramped room, then only reached by a ceiling door from the bottom floor, is where the African slaves are said to have been imprisoned while awaiting their sale. It is now a dining room – a rather discomfiting and tasteless use of the space.

One other historical note about Maspero's is worth mentioning: With British troops approaching in 1814, this building served as the headquarters for the local Committee of Public Safety, charged with marshaling citizens to fight under General Andrew Jackson.

J&M Music Shop

Cossimo Matassa's J&M Music shop, where New Orleans musicians recorded some of the biggest R&B hits in the 1950s, closed down years ago, but the site, now home to **Hula Mae's Laundry** *(Map 2, #17; ☎ 522-1336; 840 N Rampart St; open 10am-9pm daily)*, is still standing and contains a few items of interest to New Orleans music historians. The old J&M sign is still embedded on the sidewalk by the entrance. Inside, by the dryers and folding tables, one wall is dedicated to a photo and history exhibit that tells some of the story behind this historic spot. It was here that Fats Domino and Dave Bartholomew established the 'New Orleans Sound,' and countless oldies but goodies were recorded right there where those people are folding their clothes, including Lloyd Price's 'Lawdy Miss Clawdy.'

Musée Conti Historical Wax Museum (Map 2, #99)

Every city in America with a tourism industry of any size must have a wax museum, right? New Orleans' version, the Musée Conti *(☎ 525-2605; 917 Conti St; adult/senior/child $6.75/6.25/5.75; open 10am-5:30pm daily)*, waxes philosophical about local historical figures, including Andrew Jackson, Huey Long, Louis Armstrong and Napoleon Bonaparte (caught in the bathtub for some reason); the lifelike exhibits then detour suddenly toward more sensational personalities like Frankenstein's monster (chained down, for your protection) and the

Swamp Thing (unchained!). Some of your favorite celebrities, past and present, are sure to be on hand.

TREMÉ DISTRICT (MAP 2)

Immediately to the lake-side of the French Quarter's early walls (now N Rampart St) grew New Orleans' first suburb, the Tremé District, an area traditionally populated by black Creoles. The neighborhood's population is for the most part poor and many of the shotgun houses, which closely resemble their French Quarter counterparts in style and construction, are run-down and, in some cases, derelict. In recent years, some Tremé denizens have begun to make an effort to restore their homes, possibly a sign that gentrification is beginning. There aren't many reasons to wander into the Tremé beyond curiosity or an abiding interest in African-American culture. Shops and businesses are few and far between. At night, walking the streets of the neighborhood can be risky.

St Augustine's Church (Map 2, #6)

The celebrated architect who virtually rebuilt the St Louis Cathedral in 1849–51, JNB DePouilly, designed St Augustine's Church *(☎ 525-5934; 1210 Governor Nicholls St)*. It opened in 1842 and it is the second-oldest African-American Catholic church in the country. One of its stained-glass panels depicts the Sisters of the Holy Family, the order of black Creole nuns founded in 1842 by Henriette Delille and Archbishop Antoine Blanc. Today, the small congregation works to provide food for the needy and to maintain the Tomb of the Unknown Slave. Many jazz funerals can be seen leaving the church before parading the streets of the Tremé District.

Louis Armstrong Park (Map 2)

The park, which commemorates legendary jazz cornetist Louis Armstrong, is usually very quiet and some consider it unsafe to wander into alone, especially at night. The park is surrounded by fences that project an unwelcoming atmosphere. That's too bad, because a public space with a jazzy name on this particular spot makes sense and, one would think, really ought to be a cultural focal point for New Orleans.

In the mid-19th century, the area was just outside the city's walls (Rampart St, as the name suggests, was the town limit), and slaves and free persons of color met in a market here called **Congo Square**. African music and dances were permitted here, while in the rest of the US people of African descent were forced to repress their traditional culture. In the early 20th century, **Storyville**, a hotbed of early jazz music among other things (see the boxed text 'Storyville' in the Facts about New Orleans chapter), occupied the adjacent neighborhood, to the lakeside of Basin St. Ironically, most of this area's historic architecture was razed in the 1950s to clear space for the park and for housing projects.

Seeing the **Louis Armstrong statue** is the most popular reason to go inside the park, and while you're here, also check out the **bust of Sidney Bechet**, a tribute to the jazz clarinetist. Other structures here include the **Mahalia Jackson Theater** and the **Municipal Auditorium**, where music and other cultural events take place. The radio station WWOZ airs out of Armstrong park.

The park's **arched entrance**, at the corner of Rampart and St Ann Sts, is picturesque in a dated sort of way and really creates a festive carnival atmosphere when the bare bulbs that spell 'Louis Armstrong Park' are lit up. (Unfortunately, when the bulbs burn out, funds are not always available to replace them.) Congo Square, located on roughly the same spot as the 19th-century market, is a quiet corner of the park where musicians sometimes play. During Jazz Fest, cultural events are held here.

In the near future, the **New Orleans Jazz National Historic Park** (Map 2, #46; ☎ 504 589-4806) will be based at **Perseverance Hall** (Map 2) in the park. Tune in to WWOZ and other cultural media to learn about concerts and parades sponsored by the National Park Service.

Backstreet Museum (Map 2, #7)

The term 'backstreet' refers to African-American traditions that have flourished independently from mainstream white culture since the city's early days. Despite prevailing poverty and the lack of official sanction and funding, many of the city's most distinctive traditions, such as jazz funerals, second-line parades and the Mardi Gras Indians, emerged in African-American neighborhoods such as the Tremé District, the 9th ward and even in housing projects. The backstreets were routes that parades traditionally followed without permission of the police. No official permits were required to block traffic along thoroughfares in these neighborhoods.

Things have certainly changed over the years. Today, most large parades must have a police escort and follow predetermined routes. Also, for many traditionalists, jazz funerals have lost some of their cachet as drug dealers and gangsters have also been honored with a jazz band accompanied by pistol-packing youths firing bullets into the sky. At the same time, funding has become less of a problem as some of these traditions have benefited from foundations created by Jazz Fest and the new Jazz National Historic Park.

The former Blandin's Funeral Home has been converted into this charming little 'powerhouse of knowledge,' run by documentarian Sylvester Francis. The front parlors house exhibits of New Orleans' vital backstreet culture with Indian suits, social aid and pleasure-club banners, and some extraordinary raw video footage. Francis, a photographer and filmmaker who has documented parades and backstreet events since 1980, is just the man to head up such a project. He's about as knowledgeable as anybody on these subjects. His guided tours sometimes gloss over the fascinating details and history – there's really too much to say about any of these interesting subjects on a short tour – but be sure to ask him lots of questions as he guides you from room to room. Occasionally, special events are held with stellar entertainment.

The Backstreet Museum (☎ 504-525-1733; 1116 St Claude Ave; donations accepted; open 10am-5pm Tues-Sat) is open odd hours (call ahead to arrange a visit).

THINGS TO SEE & DO

New Orleans African American Museum (Map 2, #5)

For some visitors, the main draw to the Tremé might be this museum *(Noaam; ☎ 565-7497; 1418 Governor Nicholls St; adult/senior/child $5/3/2; open 10am-5pm Mon-Fri, 10am-2pm Sat)*. Established to preserve, interpret and promote African-American art, culture and history, Noaam is in a historic plantation home and it can be a very quiet spot indeed. This is obviously an institution with potential that has yet to attract much interest. The exhibits can be uneven, and business is slow (on a recent visit, they turned the lights on especially for us).

FAUBOURG MARIGNY & BYWATER (MAP 3)

If you're heading downriver out of the French Quarter, by crossing Esplanade Ave you enter the Faubourg Marigny, which was developed by the colorful plantation owner Bernard Xavier Philippe de Marigny de Mandeville in the mid-19th century. Originally a Creole suburb, the Marigny today is one of New Orleans' gay hubs, and the neighborhood supports a vibrant bohemian scene as well. Some of the city's hottest music clubs line Frenchmen St (see the Entertainment chapter for listings).

The Marigny really comes into its own as the sun goes down and the sidewalks simmer in light cast from doorways just beginning to open for dinner. The concentration of restaurants, bars and live-music clubs makes Frenchmen St the street to watch.

The neighborhood is also worthy of an afternoon stroll to observe the rustic elegance of its buildings, most of which are private residences. **Washington Square Park**, at the heart of the neighborhood, is a peaceful and well-shaded park where you can escape the touristy French Quarter and rest your boots in peace.

As rents in the Marigny rise, greater numbers of poor, creative types have been moving further downriver to the careworn but up-and-coming Bywater area. There are few sights of interest to tourists, but the Bywater is a decent and inexpensive part of town to stay, eat and drink in. See the Places

Faubourg Craps

Faubourg Marigny, just across Esplanade Ave from the French Quarter, gets its name from the Creole plantation owner Bernard Xavier Philippe de Marigny de Mandeville, whose colorful sense of humor and love of a good time left an unforgettable impression on downtown New Orleans.

In 1800, young Marigny was sent to London, where he studied the English language and learned a game of dice the English called 'hazard,' which hadn't yet been introduced to America. When he returned to New Orleans, he brought with him a pair of dice and commenced teaching the Creoles of New Orleans the new game, which came to be known in local parlance as 'craps.'

Unfortunately, Bernard Marigny was unsuccessful at his own game and he forfeited much of his wealth losing at dice. An urgent need for cash forced him to subdivide his vast estate, and the resulting development was named the Faubourg Marigny. In naming the streets of his new development, Marigny continued to exhibit the romantic and fanciful sensibility that had no doubt contributed to his inability to manage his own finances. Among the names he applied to the streets of Faubourg Marigny were Poets, Music, Love, Good Children and, of course, Craps.

Ironically, Rue de Craps became the site of no fewer than three churches, which is why the street's name was eventually changed to Burgundy. The game of craps, meanwhile, went on to become a national pastime.

Bernard Marigny lived to the ripe old age of 83, but an endless series of unsavvy business deals cost him the remainder of his fortune and he died penniless in 1868.

to Stay, Places to Eat and Entertainment chapters for more information.

St Roch Cemetery (Map 3)

Just a few blocks from the Faubourg Marigny (driving is recommended), St Roch cemetery *(Cnr St Roch Ave & N Roman St; open 9am-4pm daily)* is as one of New Orleans' most intriguing resting places. And that's no small feat! It is named after an obscure saint, a French native, whose prayers are said to have protected Rome from the Black Plague. During New Orleans' bouts with yellow fever, Catholics who prayed to St Roch (pronounced 'St Rock') are believed to have been spared, and the small chapel within the cemetery grounds was raised in his honor.

Entering this walled necropolis, you pass through an elegant wrought-iron fence; the grounds' paved paths are lined with family and society tombs, some magnificent, some decrepit. The real fascination here is within the chapel itself.

The main reason to schlep out here is to cast your peepers on the curiosities displayed behind a small gated chamber, to your right as you enter the chapel. The strange collection of ceramic body parts (healed ankles, heads, breasts), prosthetics, leg braces, crutches and false teeth that hang from the walls and cover the floor are *ex-votos*, or testaments to the healing power of St Roch. Marble floor tiles are inscribed with the words 'thanks' and '*merci*.' Each of these items represents a prayer answered by the prolific, strangely named saint, who, the decaying evidence suggests, is currently enjoying a semiretirement.

CBD & WAREHOUSE DISTRICT (MAP 4)

On the other side of Canal St from the French Quarter, the Central Business District (CBD) and the Warehouse District comprise the American commercial sector that was established after the Louisiana Purchase in 1803. Soon after the Stars and Stripes were raised over the Cabildo, merchants, brokers and manufacturers from New England flooded into New Orleans and industriously transformed it into a bustling port. The American sector, then called the Faubourg St Mary, developed into a nexus of offices, banks, warehouses and government buildings, with Lafayette Square at its core.

Canal St was the division between the French and American parts of town, and it still represents the boundary between Uptown and Downtown. That's no false distinction,

as some citizens of New Orleans, set in their Uptown or Downtown ways, never seem to find any reason to cross Canal St. The wide median down the middle of Canal St was considered part of neither the French nor American sector and for that reason came to be called the 'neutral ground' – in time, all medians in New Orleans would be referred to by that idiosyncratic term. Lee Circle marks the area's downtown boundary.

Toward the lake, extending to Claiborne Ave, is the modern City Hall, the Louisiana Superdome and new office buildings and convention hotels. Most of this modern area was formerly an African-American neighborhood called Back o' Town, with Perdido St running through Black Storyville, an extension of the seamy red-light district. Louis Armstrong's birthplace, like every other house in the area, was bulldozed to make room for the characterless structures that now stand here.

The Warehouse District faded in its importance as the port shrank in size, but the 1984 Louisiana World Exposition focused attention on the area, as former warehouses were converted into lofts and exhibit spaces for artists. A number of shops, restaurants and music clubs now make it an exciting part of town. The district is defined by Poydras St, Magazine St, Howard Ave and the river. The change in emphasis from water and rail transportation to highways has led to an industrial decline along the riverfront, and the area was redeveloped with a Convention Center and a shopping mall.

Most of the sights and museums in the CBD and Warehouse District are a good walk from the French Quarter, and with the exceptions of both streetcar lines and the No 11 Magazine bus, public transportation here isn't the best. Wear good walking shoes if you plan to explore thoroughly.

Aquarium of the Americas (Map 4)

At the Aquarium of the Americas (☎ 504-581-4629; Canal St; adult/senior/child 2-12 yrs $13.50/10/6.50; open 9:30am-5pm), which is operated by the Audubon Institute, you can go eye-to-eye with giant tropical creatures such as the Amazon's arapaima *(Arapaima gigas)*, get a look at spotted moray eels *(Gymnothorax moringa)* and hawksbill turtles *(Etetmochelys imbricata)* in a walk-through Caribbean reef tube, or watch incredible specimens of gulf species through 14ft-high windows. Mr Bill, the 40-year-old sawfish, shares the giant gulf tank with an oil platform that doesn't leak. Of course, the Mississippi River and Delta wetland environments are also displayed.

The air-conditioned aquarium is at the foot of Canal St, adjacent to Woldenberg Park and next to the Canal St Ferry. Use the Riverfront streetcar if you don't want to walk from the French Quarter. Be sure to pick up a programme listing times for special presentations such as the penguin feed and diver shows. The gift shop is a good place to pick up books on Louisiana's natural history.

Discounts on admission are offered in tourist magazines such as *Where*. You can

Mississippi Riverboats

New Orleans' current fleet of steamboats are theme-park copies of the old glories that plied the Mississippi River in Mark Twain's day. Gone are the hoop-skirted ladies, wax-mustachioed gents, round-the-clock crap games and bawdy tinkling on off-tune upright pianos. In their place are pudgy tourists, clad in white shorts, Bourbon St T-shirts and tennis shoes, who are content to rest their plump bottoms on plastic stadium seats. The evenings are given over to urbane jazz cruises. The calliope organ survives, but even this unique musical instrument loses some of its panache when applied to modern schmaltz like 'Tie a Yellow Ribbon on the Old Oak Tree.' Alas, romance is forever relegated to the past.

Still, few visitors to New Orleans can resist the opportunity to get out on the Mississippi and watch the old paddle wheel propel them upriver and back down for a spell. It's a relaxing pastime that the entire family can enjoy.

Some steamboat trips have actual destinations. The battlefields of Chalmette are just a little way downriver from New Orleans, and the Audubon Zoo is a short ride upriver from the Aquarium of the Americas.

John James Audubon Riverboat *(Map 4; ☎ 586-8777; W www.auduboninstitute.org; one way/round trip $12/15)* runs daily short trips between the Aquarium of the Americas and Audubon Park and Zoo. The boat moves slowly and the journey takes one hour. Combination tickets for the two attractions and the boat ride are available.

New Orleans Paddlewheels *(Map 4; ☎ 524-0814, 800-445-4109; W www.neworleanspaddlewheels.com; trips $16-$22, jazz cruise $45)* has two boats, the *Creole Queen* and the *Cajun Queen*, that run six two-hour cruises every day. Battlefield cruises depart at 10:30am and 2pm. The two-hour dinner and jazz cruise, featuring a live Dixieland jazz combo, boards nightly at 7pm and departs at 8pm. For all cruises, passengers board at the Canal St Wharf.

Steamboat Natchez *(Map 4; ☎ 586-8777, 800-233-2628; W www.steamboatnatchez.com; trips $16-22, jazz cruise $26-46)* doesn't go to Chalmette or the zoo, but it's the closest thing to an authentic steamboat running out of New Orleans today. The *Natchez* is steam-powered and has a bonafide calliope on board (an organist performs your favorite pop classics on the 11:30am and 2:30pm cruises). The evening dinner and jazz cruise takes off at 7pm nightly. The *Natchez* boards behind the Jackson Brewery.

RINI KEAGY

get a variety of combination tickets that include the zoo, the aquarium and the Zoo Cruise aboard the *John James Audubon* riverboat, which docks here (see Audubon Zoological Gardens under Garden District & Uptown, later in this chapter, for more information on the Zoo Cruise). For the best prices, double-check coupon offers against such combinations. Other combination tickets good for the aquarium and adjacent IMAX theater offer a saving of about 15%.

National D-Day Museum (Map 4, #68)

The monumental D-Day Museum (☎ 504-527-6012; Ⓦ *www.ddaymuseum.org; 923 Magazine St; adult/senior/child $10/6/5; open 9am-5pm daily*) opened its doors in June 2000 to extraordinary fanfare. The museum's founder, bestselling WWII historian Stephen Ambrose, was on hand, as were filmmaker Stephen Spielberg, actor Tom Hanks and a gaggle of network news anchors. The museum, touted as the only one of its kind, is a 70,500-sq-ft structure presenting WWII with boats, planes, weapons and uniforms used in the Allied effort. A special feature with a local angle is a pair of Higgins boats, the landing craft that enabled the Allies to invade Normandy by sea. The boats were designed and produced by New Orleans entrepreneur Andrew Higgins. According to Ambrose, General Dwight D Eisenhower once said that Higgins 'won the war for us.'

The upstairs exhibits are really a narrative documentary. Authentic and replicated artefacts encased in glass serve to heighten the drama created in multimedia accounts of what happened on the ground at Normandy, Iwo Jima and elsewhere during WWII. Oral-history stations with recorded first-hand accounts, and the Academy Award–winning film *D-Day Remembered* (which screens daily) add context to the exhibits and help to make this a worthwhile stop.

Historic Buildings (Map 4)

Many of the CBD's historic buildings can be seen through the windows of a slow-moving St Charles Ave streetcar, and are covered in the St Charles Ave Streetcar Tour special section in this chapter. To see others requires zigzagging a few side streets on foot.

The lighted colonnade of the **Hibernia National Bank** (*Map 4, #13; 812 Gravier St*), built in 1920, once rose above all of New Orleans. Its neighbor, the **New Orleans Cotton Exchange** (*Map 4, #14; 231 Carondelet St*) and the cornucopia of tropical produce gracing the entrance to the **United Fruit Company** (*Map 4, #26; 321 St Charles Ave*) building hint at the industries upon which New Orleans was built. **Factors Row** (*Map 4, #25; 806 Perdido St*) was the site where Degas painted *The Cotton Market in New Orleans* while visiting his uncle's office in 1873. The 13 identical red-brick houses lining **Julia Row** (*Map 4*), between Camp and St Charles Sts, were built in 1832. The fan transoms above the doorways are indicative of the row's aristocratic appeal – also note the servant's wings that project from the rear. The **lighthouse** (*Map 4, #50; 743 Camp St*) was built in 1922 to house a center called the Lighthouse for the Blind, and is now home to a glass store. Across the street, **St Patrick's Church** (*Map 4, #51; 724 Camp St*) was built between 1838 and 1840 by Irish immigrants making a break from the French-speaking Catholic parishes of New Orleans.

Canal St Ferry (Map 4)

A short ferry ride from the foot of Canal St to Algiers is the best way to get out on the water and admire New Orleans from the traditional river approach. Ride on the lower deck next to the water, and you're likely to see the state bird, the brown pelican. The state-run ferry is free and runs between 6am and midnight, leaving Canal St on the hour and half-hour, and returning from Algiers on the quarter-hour.

Harrah's Casino (Map 4)

The national casino chain arrived in New Orleans in 1999, and while one would think all manner of vice would be welcome in the Big Easy, Harrah's (☎ 533-600, 800-427-7247; 4 Canal St; open 24 hrs), near the foot of Canal St, has had a hard go of it thus far. Within a year of opening, the casino was already reporting disappointing attendance and complaining about its enormous state-tax burden. In spite of its best efforts to fit in, with a stately new brick home and a perfunctory Mardi Gras parade every night, Harrah's still manages to make its guests feel like they're in Sparks, Nevada – not exactly what tourists usually have in mind when they come to New Orleans. Nevertheless, people do trickle in for the casino gambling, buffet dining, free parking and hotel discounts. (Harrah's has no hotel of its own, but has agreements with some local hotels.)

World Trade Center (Map 4, #34)

New Orleans' pint-sized World Trade Center (2 Canal St), formerly known as the Trade Mart, was briefly the tallest building in town when its 33rd floor was completed in 1968. Special pumping and foundation technology had to be developed to keep such high-rises from sinking into the mud. The unattractive building's only remaining draw is its revolving observation deck, the **Top of the Mart Lounge** (☎ 522-9795; open 10am-11pm Mon-Thur, 10am-midnight Fri, 11am-1am Sat, 2pm-11pm Sun). This slowly revolving bar offers spectacular views of the French Quarter and the Mississippi River for the price of a mixed drink. Also check out the stained-glass murals that depict the history of the city.

Contemporary Arts Center (Map 4, #64)

This tremendous exhibition and performance space (☎ 528-3805; 900 Camp St; adult/child $5/3, admission free Thur; open 11am-5pm Tues-Sun) occupies a renovated warehouse. The steel ceiling above the impressive central stairway honors prominent figures in local arts. Among the many acknowledged artists are painter and sculptor Fritz Bultman, visual artist and sculptor Enrique Alferez, architect Charles Rousseve and his wife, Noma, who was the first director of Xavier's Fine Arts Department, and Ellsworth Woodward, the first director of Newcomb's Fine Arts Department.

Dozens of multimedia exhibits appear each year in the gallery spaces. Also featured on the two stages are performances of plays, performance art, dance programmes, musical concerts and video screenings.

Louisiana Children's Museum (Map 4, #56)

This educational museum (☎ 523-1357; 420 Julia St; admission $6; open 9.30am-4:30pm Tues-Sat, noon-4.30pm Sun) is like a high-tech kindergarten. Generous corporate sponsors have helped create hands-on exhibits such as a supermarket, complete with stocked shelves and check-out registers, and a TV news studio, where young anchors can see themselves on monitors as they forecast a July snowstorm in New Orleans. In the rush to build newer, bigger and better exhibits, the museum has failed to maintain some of the existing displays – 'Mayday!' calls on the tugboat radio go unheard and most kids abandon ship. Overall, however, the nonprofit museum and volunteers have done a good job in providing attractions for everyone from toddlers to 12-year-olds.

The museum is also open on Monday during the summer months. Children under 16 must be accompanied by an adult. The admission price is for anyone over a year old.

Lee Circle (Map 4)

Called Place du Tivoli until it was renamed to honor Confederate General Robert E Lee after the Civil War, Lee Circle has lost some of its earlier cachet. Just a few dozen paces away, an elevated freeway structure disturbs some of the traffic circle's symmetry, and gas stations occupy two of its corners. Nevertheless, the **Robert E Lee monument** (Map 4, #65) at its center, dedicated in 1884, still refuses to turn its back on the North – for that's the direction the statue faces.

Also on Lee Circle, **K&B Plaza** (Map 4, #70; 1055 St Charles Ave; open 8:30am-4:30pm Mon-Fri) is a modish office tower dating to 1963 with an indoor/outdoor sculpture gallery. The outdoor sculptures, featuring Isamu Noguchi's The Mississippi, can be viewed anytime.

Civil War Museum (Map 4, #67)

Dedicated to presenting Louisiana life during the Civil War, this museum (☎ 523-4522; 929

Camp St; adult/senior & child $5/2; open 10am-4pm Mon-Sat) is housed in sturdy old Confederate Memorial Hall, designed by Thomas Sully. Opened to the public in 1891, it's the oldest operating museum in the state. Entering the hall, with its exposed cypress ceiling beams and exhibition cases, is worth the price of admission alone, and the exhibit itself is likely to exceed expectations.

The museum makes little effort to reinterpret history, or lament past sins. The closest thing to a point of view are a few harsh words (mostly quoting federal officials in Washington, DC) about General Benjamin 'Beast' Butler, the locally reviled head of the Union forces that occupied New Orleans during the war. The agenda seems to be to humanize those who fought on the losing side of a grizzly war, and to that end the exhibits really falter by neglecting unpleasant topics such as slavery.

Of course, there are rifles and pistols from the war, along with other strangely beautiful artefacts of the industrial age, but what really makes this museum worth a visit is the endless collection of personal effects that belonged to officers and soldiers and their families back home. Knapsacks, playing cards, tobacco pouches and undergarments are fastidiously arranged within the display cabinets. Display cases densely packed with curious items, such as Jefferson Davis' slippers and an impressive array of oddly styled hats, conjure up the past in a surprisingly touching way.

The Civil War Museum is a block from Lee Circle.

Ogden Museum of Southern Art (Map 4, #66)

This regional museum (☎ 539-9600; 925 Camp St; open 10am-5pm Mon-Sat) has emerged from the stellar Southern art collection of New Orleans entrepreneur Roger Houston Ogden. In addition to the still-growing permanent collection, the museum exhibits other private collections, and it is affiliated with the Smithsonian Institute in Washington, DC, giving it access to that bottomless collection.

LOWER GARDEN DISTRICT (MAP 5)

While it might be said that this is the Garden District's bedraggled older sibling, at one time the Lower Garden District was one of the country's poshest and most elegant suburbs. On its many tree-lined thoroughfares stand countless Greek-revival houses that once were part of a cohesive, classic-style faubourg. The neighborhood's long decline is slowly being reversed, and strolling through the area around Coliseum Square often requires sidestepping contractors and building supplies as homes are being restored.

In the early 19th century, French-born surveyor Barthélémy Lafon drew plans for a community that would be the envy of other classically obsessed planners of his day. Street names honored Greek gods, nymphs and muses, and attractive tree-lined canals along their median strips provided drainage to the river. By the 1830s, the city's elite had built their mansions here, also paying homage to the Greeks with columned galleries looking out over cultivated gardens burgeoning with pecan trees, banana trees and fish ponds. Gazebos and horse stables further announced that life was good in the area. New Orleans' craze for cast-iron struck the mid-century denizens of the Lower Garden District, who adorned and fenced in their homes with ornate metallic designs, which today lend the area a rustic grace.

The neighborhood's glory was short-lived. The wealthy soon moved further uptown to the newer, more fashionable Garden District, and many of the larger residences of the Lower Garden District were divided into rental units to accommodate immigrants from Germany and Ireland, many of whom were employed on the docks. With the introduction of housing projects and the construction of an entrance to the Mississippi River bridge, the neighborhood deteriorated. The bridge ramp has since been demolished, reducing the traffic that once marred the neighborhood, and as rents in the French Quarter have risen, many boutique shops have moved to Magazine St. Similarly, an influx of professionals, artists and hipsters seeking fixer-uppers and cheap rents has breathed new life into the area.

THINGS TO SEE & DO

Lower Garden District Walking Tour

The best way to take in the Lower Garden District is to do a brief walking tour and perhaps some shopping along Magazine St. Strolling the neighborhood's well-shaded streets is only recommended during the daytime.

If you're arriving by streetcar, disembark at Terpsichore St (named after the Greek muse of dance) and walk one block toward the river. At Prytania and Terpsichore Sts, a small neutral ground creates an open feeling, as was intended in Lafon's original street plan. Turn right on Prytania, then left onto Euterpe St, so named for the Greek muse of lyrical poetry. Toward the far end of the block on the right, at 1420 Euterpe St, is **John Thornhill House** which was built in 1847 and purchased in 1854 by Thornhill, a wealthy cotton factor. Union troops confiscated the house from 1863 to 1866 for use as the headquarters of the Freedmen's Bureau, responsible for establishing the first black school in New Orleans.

Continue to **Coliseum Square**, the focal point of the fashionable Faubourg Annonciation, as this part of the district was known

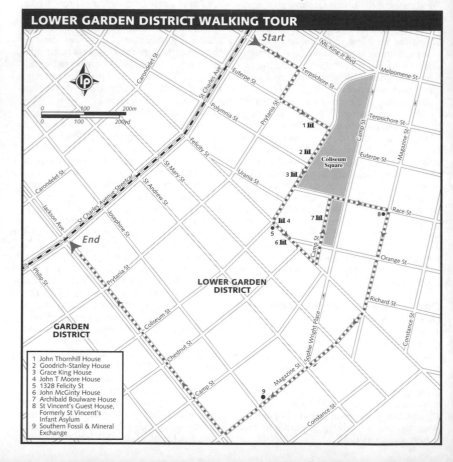

LOWER GARDEN DISTRICT WALKING TOUR

1 John Thornhill House
2 Goodrich-Stanley House
3 Grace King House
4 John T Moore House
5 1328 Felicity St
6 John McGinty House
7 Archibald Boulware House
8 St Vincent's Guest House, Formerly St Vincent's Infant Asylum
9 Southern Fossil & Mineral Exchange

during its heyday. Coliseum Square is a pleasant-enough public space, with old oaks offering ample shade, but it doesn't exactly bustle with activity. Rather than linger in the park, bear right on Coliseum St. At 1729 Coliseum St, the **Goodrich-Stanley House** was built in 1837 by jeweler William M Goodrich. Goodrich later sold the house to the British-born cotton factor Henry Hope Stanley, whose adopted son, Henry Morton Stanley, went on to become famous for finding the missing Scottish missionary, Dr David Livingston. It was Stanley who first uttered the famous question, 'Dr Livingston, I presume?' He was subsequently knighted and founded the Congo Free States. The house originally stood a few blocks away, at 904 Orange St, and was moved to its current spot in 1981.

Behind a handsome wrought-iron fence, at 1749 Coliseum St, is the papaya-hued **Grace King House**, named for the Louisiana historian and author who lived here from 1905 to 1932. It was built in 1847 by banker Frederick Rodewald and features both Greek Ionic columns on the lower floor and Corinthian columns above.

At Race St, cross Coliseum St, but continue along the brick pathway to Felicity St, whose well-preserved cobbled sidewalk lends it a more distinctive antiquated feel. Until 1852, the uppermost part of New Orleans ended at Felicity St. Turning the corner affords a view of the tastefully preserved **John T Moore House**, at 1309 Felicity St. The house combines Victorian and Italianate styles and features sweeping balconies with elaborate cast-iron railings. It was built in 1880 by architect James Freret for his family. Moore, whose name the house bears, was Freret's father-in-law and he originally owned the property. Opposite the house, at **1328 Felicity St**, is a gorgeous entry door of beveled glass that's worth inspecting (bearing in mind that staring too long and hard might make the residents uneasy).

Proceed on Felicity St toward the river. Just a few paces away, at No 1322, stands the attractive 1870 **John McGinty House**, a fine example of Italianate masonry architecture. As you approach Camp St, note the

Leafy Prytania St traverses the
Lower Garden and Garden Districts

scars left in the cobblestones, evidence of uprooted streetcar tracks that once delivered wealthy residents to their front doors.

Turn left on Camp St. A row of fine homes includes the **Archibald Boulware House**, at 1531 Camp St, built in 1854. Turn right on Race St and continue along the brick wall that fences **St Vincent's Guest House**, formerly St Vincent's Infant Asylum, at 1507 Magazine St. Turn the corner onto Magazine St for a better view of the buildings. A sign from the orphanage days still hangs from the finely styled cast-iron gallery in front. The orphanage was built in 1864 with assistance from federal troops occupying the city. It helped relieve the overcrowded orphanages filled with youngsters of all races who lost their parents to epidemics. A former orphan, Margaret Haughery became widely known as 'the orphans' friend' for donating money and food from her successful bakery, and there is a **statue** on the corner of Prytania and Clio Sts honoring her. The orphanage is now a guesthouse, St Vincent's, which offers afternoon teas (see the Places to Stay chapter).

Continue down Magazine for a look at shops and galleries that reflect the current tastes of denizens of the Lower Garden District (see the Shopping chapter). An intriguing break in the line of Magazine St antique stores is the **Southern Fossil & Mineral**

Exchange, at 2045 Magazine St. This little shop-museum seems to want to scare people away with its entire skeleton of an alligator suspended from the ceiling and an enormous cave bear raising its paw, along with some 'fossil jewelry.' With items like Tyrannosaurus rex eggs, the shop's owners make an unassailable claim of having 'the oldest stuff on the block.' Everything is for sale.

At Jackson St, turn right toward St Charles Ave. You can either commence exploration of the Garden District (see Garden District Walking Tour, following) or hop back on the streetcar.

GARDEN DISTRICT (MAP 5) & UPTOWN (MAP 6)

With the Garden District as its centerpiece, and St Charles Ave as its primary spine, Uptown New Orleans is a living and splendid architectural museum that contrasts dramatically with the more crowded, old-world French Quarter. Block upon block of glorious mansions stand as symbols of the bustling trade and enterprise that made New Orleans one of the world's wealthiest cities in the mid-19th century.

Americans began settling further beyond Canal St as development followed the streetcar tracks through the towns of Lafayette, Jefferson and Carrollton, virtually leaving Barthélémy Lafon's Lower Garden District tract in the dust. These upriver towns, laid out on expansive plantations, were populated almost exclusively by Americans, and the area reflects their wealth and taste for Greek-revival architecture. Commodious street plans allowed for larger, more ostentatious houses and lush gardens. Gradually, all of these towns became part of the city of New Orleans: Lafayette was annexed in 1852, Jefferson in 1870 and Carrollton in 1874.

Garden District Walking Tour

Like the French Quarter, the Garden District is a National Historic District, where architectural preservation ordinances attempt to maintain the character of the area. Its boundaries are roughly those of the former city of Lafayette: St Charles Ave to Magazine St, between Jackson and Louisiana Aves. The

area of greatest architectural interest is the lower half, below Washington Ave. Ironically, this premier enclave is not particularly safe to walk in at night. Plan to explore the neighborhood during daylight hours.

Begin your walk at Jackson Ave and St Charles Ave, and follow Jackson Ave toward the river. On the corner of Coliseum St is **Buckner House**, at 1410 Jackson St, built in 1856 for cotton merchant Henry S Buckner. The architect was Lewis E Reynolds. With wide galleries on four sides, it is the largest home in the Garden District. If it isn't feeding time, you'll notice that a finely conditioned Dalmatian watchdog complements the stateliness of this mansion. Continue to the corner of Chestnut St and turn right.

At the corner of Philip and Chestnut Sts, the house at **1238 Philip St** was built in 1853 for merchant John Rodenberg. Semioctagonal bay windows rise above a brick wall covered with tropical mandevilla vine on the Chestnut St side of the house, contributing an interesting effect to the Greek-revival structure. This side wing with the bays was added in 1869.

Halfway down the same block of Chestnut St, a rustic garage benefits from an elegant decay rarely seen in the Garden District, as crumbling plaster is permitted to expose the underlying brick. The garage is your first view of the estate at **1315 First St**, a glorious Italianate-style house laced with cast-iron ornamentation. The house was designed by architect Samuel Jamison for cotton factor Joseph Carroll.

Before you stray from the corner of Chestnut and First Sts, backtrack a bit to **Anne Rice's house**, called 'Rosegate,' at 1239 First St. Regrettably, this attractive home, named for the rose motif on the cast-iron fence, doesn't appear in any outward way to be haunted, or occupied by an eccentric author of occult novels. (In the past, the Rice's invited their fans to tour the home, but when the neighbors complained about long lines on the sidewalk the tours were discontinued.)

Head up First St toward Prytania St, where many of the district's finest old homes stand. The **Louise S McGehee School**, at No 2343, occupies one of the Garden District's most impressive mansions. Built in 1872 – later than other grand mansions in the district – the house combines decorative French second empire and classic styles. The architect is unknown, but stylistic clues suggest it may have been James Freret. The building has been home to the all-girls academy since 1929.

Continue on Prytania St, heading toward Washington St. Past Second St, the **Chapel of Our Lady of Perpetual Help**, at No 2521, was designed in 1856 by Henry Howard. It was built for Henry Lonsdale, a merchant who made his fortunes in gunnysacks and coffee. A block further down, the lovely **Charles Briggs House**, at No 2605, certainly stands out. Designed by James Gallier in 1849, the house's Gothic-style pointed-arch windows and Elizabethan chimneys are unique in the neighborhood.

Colonel Short's Villa, at No 1448 Fourth St, was home to a Confederate officer. The house was seized by federal authorities during the Civil War, but was returned at the war's end to Short, who lived there until his death in 1890. It is an impressive home, designed by architect Henry Howard, and it is distinguished by a cornstalk cast-iron fence

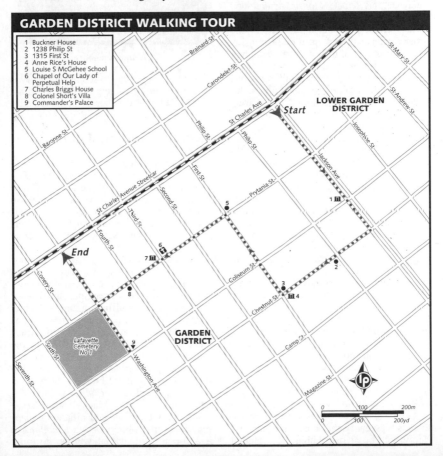

GARDEN DISTRICT WALKING TOUR

1 Buckner House
2 1238 Philip St
3 1315 First St
4 Anne Rice's House
5 Louise S McGehee School
6 Chapel of Our Lady of
   Perpetual Help
7 Charles Briggs House
8 Colonel Short's Villa
9 Commander's Palace

LOWER GARDEN DISTRICT

Start

End

GARDEN DISTRICT

Lafayette Cemetery No 1

0   100   200m
0   100   200yd

that outclasses the more famous cornstalk fence in the French Quarter because of its fewer layers of paint.

From Colonel Short's Villa, continue to Washington St, where you have several choices: You can explore **Lafayette Cemetery No 1** (see following), walk a block onto Washington St toward a rewarding lunch at **Commander's Palace** (see the Places to Eat chapter) or turn right toward St Charles Ave and the streetcar.

Lafayette Cemetery No 1 (Map 5)

Established in 1833 by the former City of Lafayette, this cemetery *(open 9am-2:30pm)* is divided by two intersecting footpaths that form a cross. Fraternal organizations and groups, such as the Jefferson Fire Company No 22, took care of their members and their families in large shared crypts. Some of the wealthier family tombs were built of marble, with elaborate detail rivaling the finest architecture in the district. But most tombs were constructed simply of inexpensive plastered brick. You'll notice many German and Irish names on the aboveground graves, testifying that immigrants were devastated by 19th-century yellow-fever epidemics. Not far from the entrance is a tomb containing the remains of an entire family that died of yellow fever.

The cemetery was filled within decades of it opening, and before the surrounding neighborhood reached its greatest affluence. By 1872, the prestigious Metairie Cemetery had already opened and its opulent grounds appealed to those with truly extravagant and flamboyant tastes.

An unusual event occurred at Lafayette Cemetery in July 1995, when author Anne Rice, who lives just a few blocks away, staged her own funeral here. She hired a horse-drawn hearse and a brass band to play dirges, and she wore an antique wedding dress as she laid down in a coffin – because, she said, she wanted to experience her funeral *before* she was dead. (The newsworthy stunt coincided with the release of one of Rice's novels, so it wasn't pure frivolity.)

As with all the cemeteries in New Orleans, there is no security and sometimes lone visitors might be at risk within the secluded

Author Anne Rice

grounds. A good way to see the cemetery is to join a tour, or coincide your visit with a tour so that you're not alone on the grounds. The gates close early – don't get locked in!

Audubon Zoological Gardens (Map 6)

The Audubon Zoo *(☎ 861-2537; adult/senior/ child $9/5.75/4.75; open 9am-5pm daily)* is among the USA's best zoos. It is the heart of the Audubon Institute, which also maintains the Aquarium of the Americas (see CBD & Warehouse District, earlier) and the Louisiana Nature Center (later in this chapter).

The zoo is divided into distinct sections. **Louisiana Swamp** displays flora and fauna amid a Cajun cultural setting, which shows how the Cajuns harvested Spanish moss for use as furniture stuffing, among other details. The authentic fishing camp comes complete with shrimp trawls, crawfish traps and an oyster dredge. Alligators laze on the muddy bank of the bayou when they're not hibernating during the winter. Year-round in the exhibit, you'll see bobcats *(Lynx rufus floridamus)*, red foxes *(Vulpes vulpes)*, endangered Louisiana black bears *(Urses americanus luteolus)* and alligators snapping at a turtle *(Macroclemys temminicki)*, a 200-pound giant that wiggles its pink tongue as bait. Human intrusions into the swamp environment are poignantly represented with a *traânasee* cutter, used by fish and game trappers to create access across shallow swamps, and an 'Xmas Tree' oil-well cap, reminding us of the much larger corporate threat to the swamp environment.

The **Audubon Flight Exhibit** is best on quiet days, when you can enter the giant cage to sit and observe the bird species portrayed by ornithologist-artist John James Audubon in *Birds of America*. Of course, there are ducks galore, but you will be mesmerized by the brilliant plumage of species such as the scarlet ibis *(Eudocimus ruber)* and glossy ibis *(Plegadis falcmellus)*, among others.

Most visitors are awed by the 'magnificent seven' in the **Reptile Encounter**, which displays representatives of the largest snakes in the world – from the king cobra that grows to over 18ft in length to the green anaconda that reaches 38ft. Many local species of nonpoisonous and poisonous snakes are also on display.

At **Butterflies in Flight** you enter a humid greenhouse that is home to thousands of fluttering exotic butterflies, including tropical swallowtails *(Papilioniddae)* and iridescent morphos *(Morphidae)*. Tropical birds and plants are also on display. The enclosure is worth the additional admission cost, but shed any unnecessary clothes before entering.

The Audubon Zoo, on the riverside of Magazine St and Audubon Park, is accessible from the French Quarter via the Zoo Cruise (see following) and the No 11 Magazine bus, or you can take the St Charles Ave streetcar and walk 1½mi through shady Audubon Park. Look for discount coupons in tourist magazines such as *Where*.

Zoo Cruise The Audubon Zoo Cruise offers a unique way to see the zoo and the Aquarium of the Americas in a day. Combined discount tickets for the riverboat cruise, zoo and aquarium are available.

The boat departs the aquarium at 10am, noon, 2pm and 4pm. It leaves the zoo at 11am, 1pm, 3pm and 5pm, departing from the Audubon Landing near the Australian Outback exhibit.

Tulane University (Map 6)
The Tulane University (☎ 865-4000) was founded in 1834 as the Medical College of Louisiana in an attempt to control the repeated cholera and yellow-fever epidemics. In 1847, the University of Louisiana merged with the school. Paul Tulane's $1 million donation in 1883 initiated significant expansion – plus it immortalized his name. The highly regarded medical school has since moved downtown to Tulane Ave. Tulane's law programme is also well respected.

The **University Center** *(Map 6, #22)* features a bookstore, ATM and a **box office** (☎ 861-9283) that sells tickets for sporting and special events. Downstairs there's a bulletin board for information on apartment rentals, sublets and ride shares. The *Hullabaloo*, the campus newspaper published during the school year, is a good source for campus happenings, such as free Friday open-air concerts and work opportunities.

Amistad Research Center (Map 6, #26)
In Tilton Memorial Hall, the Amistad Research Center (☎ 865-5535; 6823 St Charles Ave; open 9am-4:30pm Mon-Sat) is one of the nation's largest repositories specializing in African-American history. Even if you didn't come to New Orleans to study, the rotating exhibits offer insight on ethnic heritage that you're not likely to get from any other source. A video of the Amistad adventure is shown for free. The displayed works of art from the Aaron Douglas Collection are another reason to drop by – a few of the works are copied for sale.

Hogan Jazz Archive (Map 6, #21)
This specialized research library (☎ 865-5688; 3rd floor, Joseph Merrick Jones Hall, 304 Freret St; open 8:30am-5pm Mon-Fri, 9:30am-1pm Sat) is worth visiting if you're writing a book about jazz, or are just seriously into jazz history. Most of its great wealth of material is not on exhibit; the librarian will retrieve items from the stacks for you. The collection includes stacks of 78rpm recordings, including early sides recorded by the Original

[Continued on page 101]

ST CHARLES AVE STREETCAR TOUR

Crooking more than 5mi through the heart of uptown New Orleans, St Charles Ave offers a relentless panorama of 19th-century mansions, stately churches, age-old oak trees, alluring parks and slow-moving joggers. Linking the Central Business District (CBD) with the Lower Garden District, the Garden District, Uptown and Riverbend, the walk along St Charles Ave is longer than most visitors would care to take. But by hopping aboard the St Charles Ave streetcar – an essential activity while you're in New Orleans – you can see many of the city's greatest houses and churches while chugging the entire length of the street at a leisurely 10mph. The streetcar costs just $1.25 each way, and riding it out and back takes about 90 minutes. It's usually jam-packed during the heavy morning and afternoon commute, making those periods less suitable for sightseeing.

Audubon Park statue
(Photo by Richard Cummins)

Catch the streetcar heading toward Uptown at the corner of St Charles Ave and Common St. If you want air-conditioning, just pull down the window.

The first landmark you'll see on this tour is the streetcar itself. Its entire path – the neutral ground that splits St Charles Ave – is on the National Register of Historic Places. New Orleans claims that this is the world's oldest continuously operating streetcar line, dating back to September 1835, when the New Orleans & Carrollton Railroad company began running horse-drawn streetcars on St Charles Ave. After the tracks were laid, people began to move into the rural hinterlands upriver from the French Quarter and the American sector surrounding Lafayette Square, and in two decades of furious building, the area was transformed from rural countryside to a continuous series of posh suburbs. The streetcars were electrified in 1893, and the classic olive-green cars in use today were built in 1922–4.

Trundling along, you reach the monumental Greek-revival **Gallier Hall** on the right at No 545. Gallier Hall served as City Hall from its completion in 1853 until 1957. To the left, across from Gallier Hall, is **Lafayette Square**, the focal point of the old American sector.

Map labels:
S Claiborne Ave
Palmer Park
CARROLLTON
S Carrollton Ave
Carrollton Station Streetcar Barn
End
Camellia Grill
Levee Park
St Charles Ave
Broadway St
RIVERBEND
Greenville Hall
Tulane University
Holy Name of Jesus Church
Loyola University
Audubon Park
Exposition Blvd
Wedding Cake House
Palmer House ('Tara')
Jefferson Ave
UPTOWN
Milton H Latter Memorial Library

Line up for pecan
waffles at the end of
your tour
(Photo by
Rick Gerharter)

The streetcar clicks and clacks past several wino hotels that are completely incongruous with St Charles Ave's upscale reputation before reaching **Lee Circle** and skirting the **Robert E Lee monument**. The circle was called Place du Tivoli when the area was laid out in 1807, but it was renamed in 1884 (a time when anti-Reconstructionist sentiments ran extremely high) to honor the Confederate general.

Chugging beneath the freeway overpass, the streetcar enters the Lower Garden District, famous for its streets named after ancient Greek muses. On the right-hand side of the block, between Calliope and Clio (muses of heroic poetry and history, respectively) Sts, note the sturdy **Jerusalem Temple**, at No 1137, which was built in 1916 and serves as the headquarters for a local chapter of the Shriners (whose reputation rests on their penchant for fezzes and tiny cars – an attitude perfectly adaptable to New Orleans).

The first bend in the track occurs at Felicity St, which marked the northern limit of the city of New Orleans until 1852. Nearby, at the corner of St Mary St (on your left), the comely **Zion Lutheran Church** (1871) is a Gothic-revival structure built entirely of wood.

At Jackson Ave, the streetcar begins to pass along the edge of the Garden District. To see what really distinguishes this lovely neighborhood, you have to get off the streetcar and traverse the shady sidewalks between St Charles Ave and Magazine St.

At Sixth St, on your right, rises the tall Gothic bell tower of the prestigious **Christ Church Cathedral**, an Episcopal church built in 1886. Entombed in the choir aisle is Reverend Leonidas Polk, the first bishop of Louisiana and a general of the Confederate States of America. You leave the Garden District after passing Louisiana Ave, but St Charles Ave itself is just getting warmed up.

Between Peniston and General Taylor Sts, on the right, the grand white columns of the **Columns Hotel** rise above a porch patio where drinks are served into the wee hours. Louis Malle's *Pretty Baby* was filmed in the hotel. Catty-corner from the Columns Hotel is the red-brick **Rayne Memorial Methodist Church**, a landmark built in 1887. Peer through the oaks for a glimpse of the church's shingled steeple. In a few blocks, after you cross Milan St, the distinctive **Touro Synagogue** appears on the left. The synagogue, noted for its Moorish design and inlaid ornamentation, was dedicated in 1909.

Napoleon Ave, roughly the midway point on the streetcar line, reflects New Orleans' early-19th-century admiration for the French emperor. Nearby street names – Austerlitz, Constantinople, Marengo, Milan and Jena – commemorate Napoleonic victories.

At Jena St, on the right, stands **Sacred Heart Academy**, a Catholic school for girls established in 1887. The building dates to 1900, and its colonial-revival style is enhanced by distinctly New Orleanian touches such as louvered shutters.

At Soniat St, look to the left for the tile-roof of the neo-Italianate mansion that occupies an entire block. It's the **Milton H Latter Memorial Library**, a branch of the New Orleans Public Library system, which was built in 1906 as a private residence. It's worth a stop on the way back. At Arabella St, on your right, stands the **Palmer House**, curiously modeled on Tara, the house in the film *Gone with the Wind*. It was built in 1941, just two years after the blockbuster movie was released.

Past Nashville Ave, to the right, the residences on the Rosa Park cul-de-sac are among the most admired in New Orleans. Just off the corner of Rosa Park, at 5809 St Charles, is the oft-admired **Wedding Cake House**, a delectable Victorian colonial-revival home.

Crossing Calhoun St, you see Audubon Park on the left and the campuses of two of the city's universities on the right. The impressive group of red-brick Tudor Gothic buildings are part of the Jesuit **Loyola University**, established in 1904. It's the largest Catholic university in the South. Between the two campuses, the spire that belongs to the red-brick, Gothic-revival **Holy Name of Jesus Church** is plainly visible in a gap between St Charles Ave's oak trees. **Tulane University** was founded in 1834. Facing St Charles Ave are Tulane's gray-stone Gibson Hall, built in 1894, and Tilton Hall, built in 1902.

Both campuses face **Audubon Park**, named for the famed naturalist John James Audubon. The park extends about 1½mi to Magazine St; from Magazine St to the river is the Audubon Zoo and Levee Park, which surrounds the zoo.

Between Broadway and Pine Sts, on the left, **Greenville Hall** (1882) is part of Loyola University. Built in an architectural style dubbed 'steamboat Gothic,' it features twin galleries with carved posts. The crowning cupola contains a statue of St Mary left over from when the building housed St Mary's Dominican College for women.

St Charles Ave ends in an area called the Riverbend, formerly the town of Carrollton. As the streetcar turns onto Carrollton Ave, you can look to the left and see the gentle grassy slope of the Mississippi River levee. Also to the left, you'll soon see the **Camellia Grill**. This is a good place to end your streetcar tour, grab a bit to eat and board a returning car. If you're really into trains, you can stay aboard until Willow St and walk two blocks to have a look at the **Carrollton Station Streetcar Barn**, where the cars rest overnight.

[Continued from page 97]

Dixieland Jazz Band in 1917, and you can ask to listen to rare tracks if you like. There's also a wealth of oral histories, photos and early concert posters. Curator Bruce Raeburn is a great man to talk to if you come with questions about jazz. For the more casual visitor, the Storyville Room, with its emphasis on Jelly Roll Morton (who played piano in the district's bordellos during the early 20th century) may be of interest.

Newcomb Art Gallery (Map 6, #18) In 1886, Josephine Louise Newcomb founded **H Sophie Newcomb College** (☎ 865-5328) in memory of her daughter. It was the first degree-granting women's college in the US to be established as a coordinate division of a men's university. It has its own campus of red-brick buildings facing Broadway, adjacent to the main Tulane campus.

The Newcomb Art Gallery *(Woldenberg Art Center; admission free; open 10am-5pm Mon-Fri, noon-5pm Sat & Sun)* features a permanent exhibit of the college's collection, including Newcomb Pottery, rotating exhibits from the university's art collection, nationally recognized traveling exhibits and contemporary student and faculty exhibits. Flanking the gallery entrance are two important Tiffany stained-glass triptychs depicting figurative scenes, 'The Resurrection' and 'The Supper at Emmaus.'

ESPLANADE RIDGE (MAP 7)

Esplanade Ave, like St Charles Ave Uptown, is an exquisite residential concourse with a neutral ground running down the middle and a continuous oak canopy shading its lovely manses. All it lacks is a streetcar line. Esplanade Ridge is graced by a placid bayou and a racetrack, and it abuts New Orleans' largest park. The houses are less ostentatious than their Uptown counterparts, and they are classier for it.

Esplanade Ridge is a strip of subtly higher ground extending from Bayou St John to the French Quarter, and early settlers quickly recognized the advantages of building their homes here as a precaution

against the seasonal floods that washed away the surrounding flatlands. The area around Bayou St John is one of the oldest in New Orleans.

There isn't much to entertain the sightseer, beyond an easy walk admiring the old homes. Upscale restaurants are clustered around the corner of Esplanade Ave and Ponce de Leon St. A visit to City Park can easily segue into lunch or dinner around this culinary nexus.

In addition to a regular horse-racing season, the **Fair Grounds Race Track** *(Map 7)* is also the site of the huge springtime New Orleans Jazz & Heritage Festival (see Public Holidays & Special Events in the Facts for the Visitor chapter).

Bayou St John Walking Tour

Graced with a variety of residential architectural styles, the placid Bayou St John is a pleasant place to stroll. It's actually the oldest part of New Orleans. French Canadians began settling the area before the founding of New Orleans. Long before that, Native Americans used the waterway to reach a ridge along what is now Esplanade Ave (or Esplanade Ridge), and this portage was the shortest link between Lake Pontchartrain and the Mississippi River. When the explorers Iberville and Bienville learned of this path, they decided it was the ideal place to settle. A canal built by Governor Carondelet later extended the bayou to the edge of the French Quarter, nearly connecting the lake and the river. Navigation ended with the filling of the canal in 1927.

This tour is largely an appreciation of the beautiful houses that line the Bayou St John. None of the following houses are open to the public aside from the Pitot House. It's a good idea to plan your exploration of this neighborhood during the opening hours of the house in order to go inside this grand old structure. Start this walk at Esplanade Ave and Moss St, which follows the curve of Bayou St John.

The first stop is the **Pitot House** *(☎ 482-0312; 1440 Moss St; adult/senior/child $5/3/2; open 10am-3pm Wed-Sat)*, a French colonial plantation-style house built in 1799. James

Pitot, who was the first mayor of the incorporated city of New Orleans, acquired it in 1810. Built without corridors, the en suite (adjoining) interior rooms allow air to circulate through the louvered shutters on the windows and upstairs back porch. The house features a double-pitched roof and stucco-covered briquette *entre poteaux* construction.

Follow Moss St along the levee toward the **Magnolia Bridge**, a restored iron span built around the turn of the 20th century. It is now a pedestrian and bicycle crossing. Keep your eyes peeled for turtles along the water's edge. During the early morning,

you can often see at least one old-timer working his crab trap in the bayou. Do not cross the bridge (unless you already want to bag this tour).

Our Lady of the Rosary Rectory, at No 1342, was built as the home of Evariste Blanc, probably in 1834. It exhibits a combination of styles characteristic of the region. The high-hipped roof and wraparound gallery, reminiscent of West Indies houses, were actually the preferred styles of the early French Canadians who settled Bayou St John. Classic details suggest this building is of a later period.

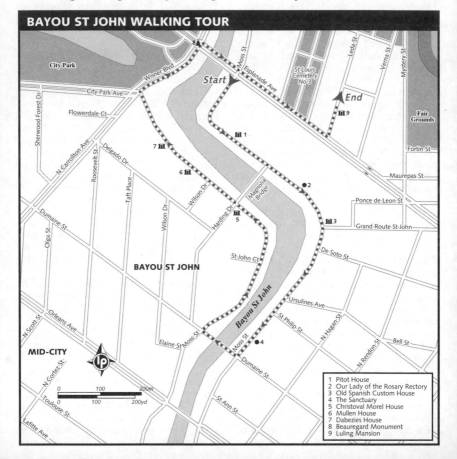

BAYOU ST JOHN WALKING TOUR

1 Pitot House
2 Our Lady of the Rosary Rectory
3 Old Spanish Custom House
4 The Sanctuary
5 Christoval Morel House
6 Mullen House
7 Dabezies House
8 Beauregard Monument
9 Luling Mansion

The **French colonial-style house** at No 1300 was built for Captain Elie Beauregard around 1807 by Robert Alexander, who also built the first US Custom House.

A bit further along, at No 924, is **The Sanctuary**, built in 1816–22 by Blanc on land originally granted in 1720–1 to French Canadians. The once swampy property was later transferred to Don Andrés Almonaster y Roxas, the real-estate speculator who commissioned St Louis Cathedral on Jackson Square in the French Quarter.

At Dumaine St, cross the bridge to the other side of Bayou St John (and likewise, to the other side of Moss St), and continue back along the levee toward the Pitot House. A decidedly American influence can be seen in the 1½-story Greek-revival design of the **Christoval Morel House**, at No 1347, built in the late 1840s.

The whimsical arch supports of the **Mullen House**, at No 1415, are attributed to the ship carpenters employed by Thomas Mullen, who was a partner in the Mullen & Kennedy Shipyard near the Esplanade Bridge in the 1850s.

Among the airy California bungalows built in the Arts and Crafts style is the notable **Dabezies House**, at No 1455. Its cobblestones came from Decatur St when that street's bricks were pulled out. Continue along the levee back to Esplanade Ave.

At the Esplanade Bridge, you can see the entrance to City Park, on the left, and the **Beauregard Monument**, dedicated to the French Creole Confederate general. Turn right and cross to **St Louis Cemetery No 3**, just a block away. The cemetery was established in 1854 at the site of the old Bayou Cemetery and is worth strolling through for at least a few minutes (longer if you're a cemetery enthusiast). James Gallier Jr designed the striking monument for his mother and father, who were lost at sea.

Continue one more block along Esplanade Ave to the largest house in the neighborhood, the **Luling Mansion**, at 1438 Leda St. James Gallier Jr and Richard Esterbrook created the Italianate-villa design in 1865 for Florence Luling, an Alsatian-born cotton factor. (Luling actually made his fortune

selling turpentine to the Yanks during the Civil War.) The villa was sold in 1871 to the Louisiana Jockey Club. Its landscaped gardens once extended from the Fair Grounds Race Track to Esplanade Ave.

CITY PARK (MAP 7)

At 1500 acres, City Park (☎ 504-482-4888) is the nation's fifth-largest urban park. The city acquired the property in 1850 and began improvements in 1896. It is well known for its live oaks draped with Spanish moss and its bayou lagoons, especially along the narrow strip fronting City Park Ave. Unfortunately, I-610 slices through the park, ruining the solitude and habitat of the central area. The larger, lake-side portion has been reduced to four golf courses, plus a riding stable.

Most visitors just explore the remaining one-third nearest Esplanade Ridge where there are kiddie rides, cafeterias and tennis courts, as well as the New Orleans Museum of Art. For more information about outdoor activities in City Park, see the entries later in this chapter.

From the French Quarter, City Park is easily reached aboard the No 48 Esplanade bus. Esplanade Ave ends at the park entrance. The park is closed to bicyclists in the evening, but the issue is moot as cyclists will not find that City Park offers a convenient route to the lakeshore.

New Orleans Museum of Art (Map 7, #5)

Founded in 1910, the New Orleans Museum of Art (☎ *504-488-2631; 1 Collins Diboll Circle; adult/senior/child $6/5/3; open 10am-5pm Tues-Sun*), originally a gift from philanthropist Isaac Delgado, continues to grow as the collection of fine art is now valued at more than $200 million and covers three large floors. On the 1st floor are major traveling exhibits, which typically attract crowds and feature associated lectures, films and workshops. A sampler of recent exhibitions included Fabergé in America, Sacred Arts of Haitian Voodoo and Andrew Wyeth: the Helga Pictures.

If you're not here for a special exhibit, you might consider starting with the 3rd-floor permanent exhibits, where pre-Columbian, Native-American and African art set the stage for European influences, shown on the 2nd floor.

The museum is reached from the French Quarter by the No 48 Esplanade bus. You can also get there from the Riverbend area aboard the No 90 Carrollton bus. The **Courtyard Café** *(Map 7, #5)* offers lunch and snacks from 10:30am to 4:30pm.

Botanical Gardens (Map 7)

This 12-acre garden *(☎ 504-482-4888; adult/child $3/1; open 10am-4:30pm Tues-Sun)* was built by the WPA and features a showpiece Art Deco pool and fountain, as well as a bevy of old statues. Native and exotic plant specimens from tropical and semitropical environments excite the senses.

Carousel Gardens & Storyland (Map 7, #1)

For children, the main attractions to City Park are these charmingly dated theme parks on Victory Ave.

The centerpiece of Carousel Gardens *(admission $1, child under 2 free)* is a restored antique carousel, housed in a 1906 structure with a stained-glass cupola. In the 1980s, residents raised $1.2 million to restore the broken animals, fix the squeaky merry-go-round and replace the Wurlitzer organ. The results are naturally spectacular. Other rides on the grounds include a small roller coaster, a tilt-a-whirl and bumper cars. The City Park Rail Road is also boarded here. Rides at Carousel Gardens cost an additional $1 each, and an $8 pass will allow you unlimited rides for the day.

Storyland *(☎ 504-483-9382; admission $2, during Christmas season $3; usually open 11am-2:30pm Wed-Sun)* has no rides, but the park's fairytale statuary is plenty of fuel for young imaginations. Children can play among – and climb upon – such larger-than-life figures as the Jabberwocky from *Alice in Wonderland*, or enter the mouth of the whale from *Pinocchio*. If these characters seem strangely similar to Mardi Gras floats, it's because they were created by master float-builder Blaine Kern. Storyland is open later

on Saturday and Sunday. During the Christmas season, it's lit up like a Christmas tree.

Dueling Oaks (Map 7, #4)

During the 19th century, hot-headed Creoles responded to challenges to their honor by arranging pistol duels behind St Louis Cathedral or here, in a shaded oak grove on the former Allard Plantation. A famous duel on this spot between a Baton Rouge newspaper editor and one Alcée La Branche refutes the notion that the pen is mightier than the sword. After three attempts in which the combatants missed each other from 40yd away, the fourth duel felled the editor. Only one of the historic trees still stands near the Museum of Art, but it is joined by younger oaks too young to recall the violence of yesteryear.

LAKESHORE PARK (MAP 1)

Locals cool off, bike, skate or just check each other out for nearly 10mi along a narrow shoreline strip fronting Lake Pontchartrain. The park extends from the Southern Yacht Club, marked by the lighthouse, to the Inner Harbor Navigation Canal. It's still a long way from Santa Monica, and you shouldn't enter the polluted water, but it beats driving across the mind-numbing Pontchartrain Causeway to see the lake. Near the yacht club are numerous restaurants suitable for lunch, but don't make a special trip out here for dinner.

METAIRIE CEMETERY (MAP 1)

Having visited other New Orleans cemeteries doesn't quite prepare you for the stunning architectural splendor and over-the-top extravagance of Metairie Cemetery *(☎ 486-6331; 5100 Pontchartrain Blvd; admission free)*. Established in 1872 on a former race track (the grounds, you'll notice, still follow the oval layout), Metairie Cemetery is the most American of New Orleans' cities of the dead, and, like the houses of the Garden District, its tombs appear to be attempts at one-upmanship.

This is the final resting place for many of New Orleans' most prominent citizens, and some of the cemetery's inhabitants are fairly famous. William Charles Cole Claiborne,

Tales of the Crypts

The best way to become intimate with the Crescent City's past is to visit one of its splendid boneyards.

The city's necropolises exhibit all the diversity and style of the surrounding city. In death, as in life, the wealthy mingle with the poor, with just enough elbow room for all to express some – or, in many cases, ample – personal style. Ornate marble tombs rise to the sky like Gothic churches amid rows of inner-city apartments for the dearly departed (it is even possible to rent). Some neglected sections – postmortem ghettoes, if you will – have attracted the attention of preservationists, such as local historian Robert Florence, who hope to restore these important emblems of a unique culture.

The vast majority of the graves in New Orleans are aboveground, and while no small amount of grandiosity inspired the more extravagant high-rise tombs, this practice of building up rather than down originated out of necessity. As early New Orleanians discovered, the region's high-water table makes for wet digging; getting a buoyant wood coffin 6ft underground meant first scuttling it to ensure that it would sink. Even then, a heavy rain could easily draw it back up to the surface again, and the dreadful sight of cadavers washing down flooded streets in the young city was not uncommon. So aboveground tombs constructed of brick and surfaced with plaster became the norm – and grandpa stayed put.

There are several distinct styles of tombs. The wall vaults that surround many cemeteries are often called 'ovens' because in the summer months they are known to get hot enough to slowly incinerate the bodies within. Once a body is decomposed – after a year and a day, according to a rule of thumb – these vaults can be reopened for the interment of a newly deceased person. Family tombs are the most common type of tomb. The cemetery equivalent of two-story, single-family homes, they are privately owned and typically house the remains of several generations. Stepped tombs, marked by steps on all sides, lack stable foundations and have a tendency to sink below ground. The stepped tomb is the only one of these five styles that is designed to contain just one body – all the others are intended for multiple burials. You are most likely to see these in St Louis Cemetery No 1, as they were no longer in use when later cemeteries were established. The grandest tombs are the society tombs, so called because they were funded by benevolent associations to ensure proper burial for members of a certain community. Many of these majestic monuments are dedicated to particular 19th-century immigrant groups, who pooled funds to take care of their dead. Professions, religious denominations and branches of the military are also commonly represented in the cemetery. The larger society tombs have more than 20 vaults, and as these are reused over time, the population within these monuments can reach staggering numbers.

What really makes New Orleans' cemeteries visually enthralling is the incredible array of expressive, creative and often strange statuary and ornamentation that adorn many of the crypts. Angels praying with slumped wings and shoulders, grieving mothers tenderly cradling lethargic (perhaps dead) babies, wrought-iron crosses and gates, and stained-glass mosaics all play on light and shadow to create glorious surroundings for the dead. Some cemeteries are rapidly decaying, with broken tablets and loose plaster falling about the tombs, making them decidedly eerie.

Sadly, over the years many statues have been vandalized and even stolen. Some of the more elaborate pieces can fetch thousands of dollars on an underground market. New Orleans police recently exposed a ring of grave robbers, implicating Royal St antique dealers. Through this kind of thoughtless profiteering, the city is being drained of an attribute that should be preserved, treasured and above all protected.

There are more than 40 cemeteries in New Orleans. This book highlights just a few of them: St Louis Cemetery No 1, just outside the French Quarter; Lafayette Cemetery No 1, in the Garden District; Metairie Cemetery, just west of City Park; and St Roch Cemetery, a few blocks toward the lake from Faubourg Marigny. See the appropriate neighborhood sections for more information on each of these cemeteries. Also see Organized Tours in the Getting Around chapter to find out about informative cemetery tours.

Louisiana's first American governor, is here, as is Confederate General PGT Beauregard. Jefferson Davis was laid to rest here, only to be moved to Richmond, Virginia, two years later. Trumpet player Louis Prima occupies a family tomb inscribed with the refrain from his signature song, 'Just a Gigolo' – 'When the end comes they'll know/I was just a gigolo/Life goes on without me.'

But the real highlight here is architecture. Many of the family tombs and monuments gracing Metairie Cemetery's concentric ovals are stunning, bringing together stone, bronze and stained glass. The statuary here is often elegant, touchingly sad and even sensual. Highlights include the **Brunswig mausoleum**, a pyramid guarded by a sphinx statue; the **Moriarty monument**, the reputed 'tallest privately owned monument' in the entire country; and the **Estelle Theleman Hyams monument**, with its stained glass casting a somber blue light over a slumped, despondent angel statue, .

Visitors can drop by the funeral home on the grounds and select either the 'Soldier, Statesmen, Patriots, Rebels' or 'Great Families and Captains of Commerce' self-guided tours. You will be given a map and loaned a recorded cassette and tape player (no charge).

Seeing everything on the 150-acre grounds is most easily accomplished by car. Tape tours take about an hour, but stretching this out by getting out of your car for a closer look at the tombs is highly recommended.

LONGUE VUE HOUSE & GARDENS (MAP 1)

Longue Vue (☎ 488-5488; 7 Bamboo Rd; open 10am-4:30pm Mon-Sat, 1pm-5pm Sun) is an ornate home built in the early 1940s by the late Edith and Edgar Stern – heirs to the Sears & Roebuck fortune and among the leading philanthropists of the 20th century. The gardens include the formal Spanish Court, with trademark fountains modeled after Spain's Alhambra garden by Ellen Biddle Shipman, and a contrasting Wild Garden with a natural-forest walk. Visitors can also tour the fine-arts gallery, featuring rotating exhibits with such themes as textiles, clocks and Staffordshire pottery.

To get to Longue Vue House, take Canal St bus Nos 40, 41, 43 or 44 and get off at City Park Ave, which becomes Metairie Rd past the freeway. Either walk about 1mi along Metairie Rd beside the Metairie Cemetery or wait for a Jefferson Transit Metairie Rd bus. Bamboo Rd is on the left (south) immediately past the bridge over the drainage canal. Motorists can drive toward the lake from the French Quarter on I-10 and take Metairie Rd exit 231. Guided tours last about one hour and cost $7/3 per adult/child ($10/3 around Christmas time).

AUDUBON LOUISIANA NATURE CENTER (OFF MAP 1)

In eastern New Orleans near the Lake Forest Mall, more than 80 acres of swampy habitat and a small **museum** (☎ 246-5672; Joe Brown Memorial Park, Nature Center Dr; adult/senior/child $4.75/3.75/2.50; open 9am-5pm Tues-Fri, 10am-5pm Sat, noon-5pm Sun) introduce the visitor to the local ecology and wildlife. The museum includes both hands-on exhibits for the kids and hands-off displays such as live venomous snakes. A large picture window and microphone allow you to see and hear the birds outside. Many of the caged animals were either orphaned or injured and are being tended by the center's staff. One guest, the barred owl (Strix varia), frequents the swamps and has a distinctive cry that sounds like 'who cooks for you.'

Immediately outside the museum is a pond inhabited by nutria. Also nearby is an example of a Tchefuncte home and a garbage heap of the sort that archaeologists get excited about. The Tchefuncte people inhabited the bayous about 2000 to 2500 years ago. It is known that these hunter-gatherers ate deer, rabbits, geese, alligators and fish; curiously, however, the rubbish pile contains neither crawfish nor crab remains.

Over a mile of raised platform walkway allows visitors to enter the cypress swamp and reach other trails. Plenty of spur trails and convenient benches allow wildlife observation away from crowds. A duckweed-covered pond awaits at the outermost part of the trail. Occasional traffic sounds remind the visitor of the developments threat to these wetlands.

A laser **planetarium** offers light shows that cost $5, which are presented Friday and Saturday at 9pm, 10:30pm and midnight, plus 3:30pm on Saturday and Sunday.

To get to the nature center from downtown, board the No 64 Lake Forest express bus at the intersection of Canal and Basin Sts (on the lakeside next to the movie theater). Motorists can follow the bus's course west on I-10 to Read Blvd (exit 244) – head toward the river to the park entrance at Nature Center Dr and continue past the tennis courts to the center. The gift shop offers a good selection of nature guides.

COOKING CLASSES

You are not likely to learn how to make complex French sauces in a short, introductory cooking demonstration. However, you can learn how to make a few of the one-dish Cajun and Creole meals that are relatively easy to prepare when you're in a hurry. The two courses listed here offer entertaining lectures followed by a lunch made up of the dishes you have watched the chefs prepare. If you're in town for a couple of days, you might take both courses; they're not much more expensive than an equivalent lunch. The **Hermann-Grima House** *(Map 2, #101; ☎ 525-5661; 820 St Louis St)* also has cooking demonstrations (see the French Quarter, earlier in this chapter).

New Orleans School of Cooking (Map 2, #133)

The three-hour demonstration offered by this school *(☎ 525-2665, 800-237-4841; [W] www.neworleansschoolofcooking.com; 525 St Louis St)* features everyday Creole cooking. An introduction to the area's geography and history is woven into the course, explaining how Creole cuisine evolved. The menu consists of gumbo, jambalaya, bread pudding and pralines served with a Dixie beer. Classes at the New Orleans School of Cooking are available in time for lunch daily from 10am to 1pm and cost $25; a shorter class, which is conducted with a video presentation, is available daily from 2pm to 4pm for $20. Call ahead to make a reservation.

Cookin' Cajun (Map 4, #43)

This two-hour demonstration at Cookin' Cajun *(☎ 586-8832; Riverwalk Mall)* is a bit more rushed than the School of Cooking course (it leaves out the geography and history lesson), and the menu typically features jambalaya, oysters Rockefeller or shrimp Creole. Cookin' Cajun is in the Creole Delicacies Gourmet Shop. Call for class times and reservations; classes cost $20.

BICYCLING

New Orleans is a great city to bicycle in – it's flat and compact. Just watch out for those mammoth potholes, which can swallow skinny tires. Better yet, hop on a fat-tire mountain bike, and you've got the perfect urban swamp cruiser. For casual bicycling, pedal through City Park (during daylight hours only as the park is closed at night) and around the lakefront and in a loop around Audubon Park and the riverside Levee Park. See the Getting Around chapter for bicycle-rental information and for information about touring either on your own or with a group.

FISHING

Louisiana isn't called the 'Sportsman's Paradise' on the strength of top-secret Olympic training facilities hidden back in the bayous. Fishing (along with hunting) has always been a way of life in the waterlogged lower half of the state. For every pick-up truck you spot on Louisiana's highways and byways, rest assured there's a small fishing boat stored in a garage or behind a shotgun shack somewhere.

To get a nonresident recreational fishing license, call the **Louisiana Department of Wildlife & Fisheries** *(☎ 568-5616, 888-765-2602)*, or check the Yellow Pages for sporting goods shops that issue licenses; the sheriff's office also sells licenses. Fees for licenses vary depending on the length of the fishing trip and whether you add a saltwater stamp; a basic three-day freshwater license costs $13.

In the Gulf of Mexico, Louisiana's commercial live catch leads the nation – an auspicious indication of the sport fishing potential below the Intracoastal Waterway. Freshwater fishing also affords ample action, with catfish, sacalait (white perch), redfish and bass.

Casual anglers can try the stocked lagoons in **City Park** *(Map 7; ☎ 483-9376)*. The fishing season begins in March. There's no equipment rental, but inexpensive cane poles are sold at the boat rental near the **Casino Building** *(Map 7, #3)* in City Park.

GOLF
Only a streetcar ride from downtown, the 18-hole **Audubon Park golf course** *(Map 6)* is open to the public.

City Park is home to the **Bayou Oaks Golf Course** *(Map 7; ☎ 483-9396; Zachary Taylor Dr)*, with greens fees ranging from $10 to $18. All courses are open from dawn until dusk. There's also a **driving range** *(☎ 483-9394; open 9am-10pm Mon-Fri, 8am-10pm Sat & Sun)*, across from the main Bayou Oaks Clubhouse. A large bucket of balls costs $6.

GYMS
The **YMCA** *(Map 4, #63; ☎ 568-9622; 920 St Charles Ave; open 5am-9pm Mon-Fri, 9am-5pm Sat, 12:30pm-5pm Sun)*, at Lee Circle, has complete facilities, which include a swimming pool, indoor track and weight machines. The cost is $8 per day.

One Canal Place Fitness Center *(Map 2; ☎ 525-2956; Canal Place, 1 Canal St; day use $12; open 6am-10pm Mon-Fri, 9am-6pm Sat-Sun)* has weight machines, treadmills and aerobics classes.

If you want to rub elbows with real professionals, head for the **Mackie Shilstone Spa** *(Map 5, #16; ☎ 566-1212; 2111 St Charles Ave)* in the Avenue Plaza Hotel. When you get off the elevator on the 2nd floor, you are greeted by a life-size autographed photo of New Orleans' native and professional baseball star Will Clark. Shilstone is a personal trainer for many professional athletes. To use the spa it costs $5 for guests and $9 for visitors.

HORSEBACK RIDING
Cascade Stables *(Map 6, #60; ☎ 891-2246; 6500 Magazine St)* offers a 45-minute horse ride ($20) and lessons ($25 per hour) in Audubon Park.

City Park Riding Stables *(Map 1; ☎ 483-9398; 1001 Filmore Ave; open 9am-7pm Mon-Fri, 9am-5pm Sat & Sun)* offers lessons for groups ($25 per hour); private lessons are also available, but these cost more. Riders must be over six years old and have hard-soled boots.

TENNIS
Audubon Park Tennis Courts *(Map 6; ☎ 895-1042; 6320 Tchoupitoulas St; open 8am-7pm Mon-Fri, 8am-6pm Sat)* has well-maintained courts.

The **City Park Tennis Center** *(Map 7, #2; ☎ 483-9382; open 7am-10pm Mon-Thur, 7am-7pm Fri-Sun)* offers 36 lighted courts. Both hard and soft courts are available along with locker rooms, racquet rental, a pro shop and lessons from USPTA pros.

Places to Stay

Most visitors to New Orleans stay within easy reach of the French Quarter or inside the Quarter itself. In the upper Quarter and along Canal St, there is a concentration of large hotels with all the conveniences you'd expect from top-end tourist accommodations. The Central Business District (CBD) and the Warehouse District are where you'll find most of the convention-oriented hotels.

For traditional Creole charm, consider staying in the lower Quarter or even in the Faubourg Marigny, where numerous small hotels and guesthouses have been fashioned from old Creole cottages and houses. Many of these have secluded courtyards, where you can escape the heat and the tourist rush.

Elsewhere around town myriad options are worth exploring. In particular, the Garden District and Uptown offer grand old guesthouses within a block or two of the historic St Charles streetcar line, which links visitors to the French Quarter and most Uptown sights. Esplanade Ridge is home to a few old mansions that have been converted into magnificent B&Bs; these are particularly convenient for Jazz Festers.

New Orleans has three youth hostels. Two are near the Garden District, and the other is in Mid-City.

Room rates vary depending on the time of year, with peaks during Mardi Gras and Jazz Fest and to a lesser degree around New Year's Eve, and according to New Orleans' very busy convention calendar. Advance reservations are recommended well ahead of time during these periods, whether you plan to bunk down at a hostel or stretch out in a classy hotel, and you can expect the rates to be double the norm. Off-season discounts kick in when occupancy rates drop. During the hot, wet and sticky summer months, desperate innkeepers drastically reduce rates at the most costly properties, so you should consider the comfort value of a modern air-conditioned room during these times.

You can often find discounts from the so-called 'rack rate' quoted to guests who arrive without a reservation. Discounts of 10% or more are commonly granted to members of the American Automobile Association (AAA), as well as senior citizens, students, military personnel, government employees and those with some corporate affiliations. Even someone walking in off the street without a reservation can often negotiate a discount if armed with the knowledge that occupancy is down; ask your shuttle or taxi driver how business is. Conversely, don't expect a discount at a hotel that is booked for a convention. (The ☎ 800 numbers of the hotel chains are not your best bet for getting a good deal or checking on room availability. These national hotlines also can't guarantee a particular room – say, one with a balcony or a view. Lower rates are often quoted if you use the local numbers.)

In addition to the room rates quoted over the phone and the Internet, all hotels in New

Ten Unique Hotels

New Orleans has more than its share of unique and wonderful places to stay. The following stand out just a notch above the rest. All are listed in greater detail in this chapter.

Gentry House (French Quarter) Creole bargain
Soniat House (French Quarter) Creole luxury
Melrose Mansion (Faubourg Marigny) For bottomless pockets
Lamothe House (Faubourg Marigny) For Marigny bar hoppers
India House Hostel (Mid-City) Funky hostel
Sully Mansion (Garden District) Garden District gem
Fairmont Hotel (CBD) Swanky 20th-century digs
House on Bayou Road (Esplanade Ridge) Jazz-Fest find
Josephine Guest House (Lower Garden District) Mardi Gras guesthouse
Benachi House (Esplanade Ridge) Southern splendor

Orleans charge a 12% room tax, plus a $1 occupancy tax per person. You can also add about $15 to $20 a day if you choose to park a car at most of the lodgings in the French Quarter or CBD. Charges for telephone calls can also inflate your bill.

Unless you are just passing through, don't scrimp by booking a discounted room near the airport or along one of the highways. Your savings will be lost when you must either pay a taxi fare or exorbitant parking fees to join in the fun in the Quarter.

CAMPING

For the best tent camping, head out to one of four state park camping grounds within a half-hour drive of New Orleans. All have toilets, hot and cold running water, showers, electrical hookups and shaded sites. These are St Bernard Parish State Park, Bayou Segnette State Park, Fontainebleau State Park, and Fairview-Riverside State Park. You'll need a car or a good bicycle if you're planning to spend your nights out in these parks and your days in New Orleans. Fontainebleau and Fairview-Riverside are covered in the Excursions chapter.

St Bernard Parish State Park (Off Map 1; ☎ 682-2101; camp sites $12), the most convenient camping ground, is about 13mi southeast of New Orleans. It's near the Mississippi River and features wooded lagoons, short nature trails and a swimming pool. The Jean Lafitte National Historic Park (see the Excursions chapter for details) is nearby. Take Hwy 46 along the east bank of the Mississippi to Bayou Rd and turn right on Hwy 39. The park entrance is within a mile on your left. Camp sites are on a first-come, first-served basis and include water and electricity.

Bayou Segnette State Park (Map 1; ☎ 736-7140; camp sites $12, cabins $65), on the west bank of the river, is another place that campers can stay at. It offers 100 reservable camp sites with water and electricity. Cabins, which can accommodate up to eight people, are available and include linens and cookware. The park was built at the confluence of several canals that have partially drained the former swamp, creating a bottomland hard-

wood environment with good boat access to swamps and bayous all the way to the Gulf Coast. The popular boat launch is open 24 hours. To get there from New Orleans, cross the Greater New Orleans Bridge and follow Business Hwy 90 (Westbank Expressway) upriver about 10mi to the bayou entrance at Drake Ave, which is on your left.

New Orleans West KOA (Map 1; ☎ 467-1792; 11129 Jefferson Hwy; camp/RV sites $22/31) is upriver from town, almost all the way to the New Orleans International Airport. From New Orleans, take I-10 exit 223A; it's 3mi down Williams Blvd to Jefferson Hwy, where you take a left. KOA offers a shuttle service to and from the French Quarter.

The closest privately operated RV parks and camping grounds are along the Chef Menteur Hwy (Hwy 90) in eastern New Orleans (east of the Inner Harbor Navigation Canal).

Mardi Gras Campground (Off Map 1; ☎ 243-0433, 800-290-0085; 6050 Chef Menteur Hwy; camp sites $23) isn't outdoorsy, or even attractive, but it might be worth calling if you're hard up for an inexpensive place to pitch your tent. It's behind a gas station, near I-10 exit 240A. Prices are higher during Jazz Fest.

HOSTELS

Two hostels can be reached from the French Quarter on public transit: One is a block

In a Pinch...

If you're going to arrive in New Orleans with no hotel reservation, you may be in luck. During ordinary times (ie, *not* during Carnival or Jazz Fest) many hotels around town are underbooked. In hopes of filling up as many rooms as possible at the last minute, these hotels often turn some of their last-day bookings, at reduced rates, over to the **New Orleans Welcome Center** (Map 2, #86; ☎ 566-5031; 529 St Ann St; open 9am-5pm daily). Travelers can stop by the center, right on Jackson Square, to find out what's available. The helpful clerks will even assist in securing reservations.

Save Up & Reserve Early for Festivals

Although you are encouraged to join in the fun and frivolity of Mardi Gras or Jazz Fest as much as possible, you will first need to make some very businesslike telephone calls.

Get your accommodations sorted well in advance – at least two or three months ahead of time; otherwise, you may be left out in the cold (and it can be cold during Mardi Gras). After staying at the perfect place while attending a festival, many folks make their reservations for the next year as they're checking out; some plan even further in advance.

During Mardi Gras, room rates are typically double or even *triple* the published rack rates. During Jazz Fest, room rates rise nearly as much. Most of the prices listed in this book are rack rates, so a little math will be required to figure out what a given hotel might charge during Mardi Gras.

Other holidays that are big in New Orleans, making preplanning and a bigger budget necessary, are New Year's (when the Sugar Bowl adds to an already festive atmosphere) and Halloween.

away from the St Charles Ave streetcar, and one is in Mid-City near Canal St. They're predominantly used by foreign visitors; local lodgers are discouraged, as are overly extended stays. They all offer a kitchen, baggage storage, heat or air-conditioning depending on the season, and communal areas, where it's easy to make friends. All are also well known to the airport shuttle drivers. The no-curfew policies will no doubt be appreciated by guests intent on making the most of New Orleans' round-the-clock action. Hostel bulletin boards offer a wealth of local information and travel tips.

HI Marquette House Hostel (Map 5, #13; ☎ 523-3014; e hineworlc@aol.com; w www .hiayh.org; 2253 Carondelet St; dorm beds members/nonmembers $19/22, private rooms $50/53) is a Hostelling International (HI) property on the margins of the Garden District. The 176-bed facility consists of four buildings that are kept impressively clean. Dorm rooms and private rooms sleep up to four people. Picnic tables in the backyard are an ideal place to meet fellow travelers. Internet access is available in the lobby, and there are two laundries nearby (one is in a bar). Sheet rental is an additional $2.25, and the cost for the coin-operated rental lockers will add up if you need to repeatedly get to your things. To get there from Union Passenger Terminal, walk five blocks toward the river on Howard Ave to St Charles Ave and take the Uptown streetcar to Jackson Ave and walk northwest one block to Carondelet St; the hostel is half a block to the left. You don't

need to be a member of HI to stay here. Membership to the hosteling organization ($25 a year in the USA) can be purchased at the desk and primarily entitles you to access or discounts at a network of hostels across the USA.

India House Hostel (Map 7, #36; ☎ 821-1904; w www.indiahousehostel.com; 124 S Lopez St; dorm beds $14, private rooms $35), half a block off Canal St in Mid-City, has a free-spirited party atmosphere. A large aboveground swimming pool and cabana-like patio decor add ambience to the three well-used old houses that serve as dorms. Bunk beds include linen and tax. For a unique experience, ask about the private Cajun shacks out back, which come with pet alligators. Guests can use the washer and dryer, and log onto the Internet. Children are not permitted to stay at this hostel. To get there from the Union Passenger Terminal, cross Loyola Ave in front of the depot and take any Claiborne Ave bus ($1.50 fare with transfer) to Canal St, where you transfer to any Canal St bus heading toward the lake. Cross Canal St after you get off at Lopez St.

HOTELS
French Quarter (Map 2)
It's possible to be too close to the noisy activity in the French Quarter. Guests staying near Bourbon St should not turn in until they are ready to pass out, and even then the early morning trash pickup and street sweeping can wake the dead. Ask about courtyard-facing rooms, which are significantly quieter.

You can generally find somewhere quieter in the predominantly residential areas of the lower Quarter.

Those really wanting cheap digs in the Quarter will end up curling up on a bench in Jackson Square, where they're likely to get the shove from the cops. (See Lower Garden & Garden Districts, and Faubourg Marigny & Bywater for inexpensive options.)

Mid-Range Half a block from the Rampart St music clubs, **Gentry House** *(Map 2, #21; ☎ 525-4433; W www.gentryhouse.com; 1031 St Ann St; rooms $85-125)* is a converted double shotgun owned by kind Sadie Gentry, who personally dashes out for fresh croissants each morning for her guests. Most rooms open up onto a lush garden patio inhabited by a cat, a friendly dog and several dozen geckoes. Furnishings are well worn and darn comfortable (mattresses are in good shape), and each room comes with a fridge and coffee maker. Some rooms are large enough for families. Credit cards are not accepted and the rates given here include taxes.

Le Richelieu *(Map 2, #12; ☎ 529-2492, 800-535-9653; W www.lerichelieuhotel.com; 1234 Chartres St; rooms $85-180, suites from $200)* is a very convivial spot, on the quiet side of the Quarter. Le Richelieu's red-brick walls once housed a macaroni factory, but extensive reconstruction in the early 1960s converted it into a conservative-looking hotel. Its rooms are handsomely decorated in quasi-baroque stylings (Liberace on a subdued day) and the price includes parking. At night, guests can admire the phosphorescent swimming pool while having a drink on the patio.

Chateau Hotel *(Map 2, #54; ☎ 524-9636; W www.chateauhotel.com; 1001 Chartres St; rooms $79-139, suites $129-209)* used to be called the 'Chateau Motor Hotel,' but recently its owners decided 'Chateau Hotel' sounded more upscale. In other words, this ain't really no chateau, but at least parking is free and the rooms are spotless. The price includes a continental breakfast.

Cornstalk Hotel *(Map 2, #52; ☎ 523-1515; W www.travelguides.com/bb/cornstalk; 915 Royal St; rooms $75-185)* is famous for its cast-iron fence, which is possibly the most photographed fence in the USA. The colorful cornstalks were cast in 1859 and today they attract a steady stream of admirers. The rooms inside are also attractive, with high ceilings, antique furnishings and private baths. This is a regular stop for the horse-and-buggy tours that roam the French Quarter, so if there's a drawback to staying here, it would be the stench of horse manure that pervades the sidewalk in front.

Andrew Jackson Hotel *(Map 2, #53; ☎ 561-5881, 800-654-0224; W www.historic innsneworleans.com; 919 Royal St; rooms $119-149, suites from $179)* is next to the Cornstalk Hotel, but the horses just trot right by it. Its rooms are spacious and comfortable and overlook a scenic courtyard.

Hotel St Pierre *(Map 2, #18; ☎ 524-4401, 800-225-4040; W www.historicinnsneworleans.com; 911 Burgundy St; rooms $79-139, suites $159-185)* is a cluster of historic Creole cottages with interior courtyards and modern furnishings. It's relatively quiet but still near the center of the action.

Lafitte Guest House *(Map 2, #25; ☎ 581-2678, 800-331-7971; W www.lafitteguesthouse.com; 1003 Bourbon St; rooms $159-199)* is an elegant three-story French manor house (c. 1849) with 14 guestrooms. The riotous Bourbon St hubbub does not typically extend down to this corner, although Lafitte's Blacksmith Shop tavern is on the opposite corner.

Hotel Provincial *(Map 2, #55; ☎ 581-4995, 800-535-7922; W www.hotelprovin cial.com; 1024 Chartres St; rooms from $129, suites from $259)* does its best to make you feel as if you are in Europe. Its 100 rooms, in finely restored buildings, have high ceilings, are cluttered with antique furnishings and open onto interior courtyards. Parking costs $13 a day.

Hotel Villa Convento *(Map 2, #38; ☎ 522-1793, 800-887-2817; W www.villaconvento.com; 616 Ursulines Ave; rooms $89-155)*, half a block from the Ursuline Convent, has comfortable rooms on a quiet block. It has one 'family' room, with loft bedding, but only kids 10 years and up are welcome. According to a growing number of unreliable storytellers, this was the legendary 'House of the Rising Sun.'

Ursuline Guest House *(Map 2, #27; ☎ 525-8509, 800-654-2351; 708 Ursulines Ave; rooms $95-125)* is an old Creole cottage that's rustic in a good way. The shuttered front rooms are just a short step up from the sidewalk, perhaps too close to the neighborhood's stream of yammering late-night pedestrians, but the back rooms are sheltered from the street. Same-sex couples will feel welcome here.

Place d'Armes Hotel *(Map 2, #72; ☎ 524-4531, 800-877-4623; Ⓦ www.turbotrip.com/usa/la/neworleans/placedarmes; 625 St Ann St; rooms $85-$200, suites from $169)* is a romantic red-brick building that dates to the late 18th century. Its picturesque courtyard is graced by a trickling fountain and a swimming pool. The hotel is only a block from Jackson Square.

The Creole House Hotel *(Map 2, #22; ☎ 524-8076, 800-535-7858; Ⓦ www.big-easy.org; 1013 St Ann St; rooms $50-200)* has three historic houses on the lakeside of the Quarter. Rooms are ordinarily furnished but comfortable and quiet. One of the houses stands on the presumed site of voodoo queen Marie Laveau's 19th-century residence. Rampart St jazz clubs are just a block away.

Top End One of the city's venerable old hotels (it opened in 1907), **Hotel Monteleone** *(Map 2, #149; ☎ 523-3341, 800-535-9595; ⓌЕ www.hotelmonteleone.com; 214 Royal St; rooms $200-230)* is also the French Quarter's largest. The narrow streets hardly allow one to stand back to admire its handsome, white, terracotta exterior. (Preservationists eventually put a stop to building on this scale below Iberville St.) The rooms were brought up to date a decade ago, and rates drop significantly during the summer.

Soniat House *(Map 2, #30; ☎ 522-0570, 800-544-8808; ⓌЕ www.soniathouse.com; 1133 Chartres St; rooms $175-295, suites $325-600)* is a meticulously restored 1830 town house with lacy ironwork, beautiful antique furnishings and a courtyard cooled by a lily pond. It is the pinnacle of Creole style, and because it has that elusive blend of warmth and elegance this may well be New Orleans' premier lodging. Children under 12 are not welcome.

Omni Royal Orleans *(Map 2, #115; ☎ 529-5333, 800-843-6664; ⓌЕ www.omniroyalorleans.com; 621 St Louis St; rooms $200-279, suites from $450)* offers arguably the best furnishings and in-room amenities of any large hotel in the Quarter. Rates depend on the room size and the season. Services include a beauty salon and babysitting, and the Omni Royal's rooftop observation deck affords a stunning view.

Royal Sonesta *(Map 2, #119; ☎ 586-0300, 800-766-3782; ⓌЕ www.royalsonestano.com; 300 Bourbon St; rooms from $289, suites from $500)* offers a choice between rooms with balconies overlooking noisy Bourbon St or quiet courtyard-facing rooms. (The quiet rooms cost less.) It was built to look old, but with 500 rooms it is oversized for this section of the Quarter and obviously not kin to its smaller, antiquated neighbors. Just the same, all the stops are pulled and this is a comfort zone.

Bourbon Orleans Hotel *(Map 2, #70; ☎ 523-2222, 877-999-3223; ⓌЕ www.wyndham.com/hotels/msybo/main.wnt; 717 Orleans Ave; rooms $99-119, suites from $229)* is, hic, a big place with rooms (217 of 'em) graced by Queen Anne furnishings and marble bath tubs. Before Mardi Gras they have to grease the sidewalk pillars to keep revelers from climbing up onto the balconies.

Tremé District (Map 2)

On Esplanade Ave, along the edge of the Tremé District, are several reasonably priced places worth considering for their historic trimmings and proximity to the Quarter.

Maison Esplanade *(Map 2, #1; ☎ 523-8080, 800-490-8542; 1244 Esplanade Ave; rooms $50)* is a historic home with an exterior stairway (the story behind this has something to do with 19th-century taxes on interior stairs) and nine modest, antique-furnished rooms with private bath. Pets are permitted and parking is free.

Rathbone Inn *(Map 2, #3; ☎ 947-2100, 800-947-2101; ⓌЕ www.rathboneinn.com; 1227 Esplanade Ave; rooms $50-250)* is a well-preserved 1850s mansion with inexpensive rooms. Some rooms sleep up to eight people and there is free parking.

Hotel Storyville (Map 2, #2; ☎ 948-4800, 866-786-7984; W www.hotelstoryville.com; 1261 Esplanade Ave; suites $80-250) is another nice old property with a variety of suites that sleep two to four people. All units have a small kitchen and parking is free.

Faubourg Marigny & Bywater (Map 3)

Immediately below Esplanade St, the Faubourg Marigny is an attractive alternative to the Quarter. Its grid-defying street pattern is speckled with colorful old cottages, many of which have been converted into homey B&Bs. Savvy, straight night owls feel the pull of the lively Frenchmen St scene (and the seamier, lower Decatur St bars, nearby), and same-sex couples are drawn to the neighborhood by accommodations that make a special effort to cater to them. Beyond the Marigny, the low-rent Bywater has become another creative neighborhood to watch. From either neighborhood, it is possible to walk to the Quarter, but it's more than a mile from the Bywater to the lower Quarter so cabs are recommended after dark.

Lamothe House (Map 3, #27; ☎ 947-1161, 800-367-5858; W www.new-orleans.org; 621 Esplanade Ave; rooms $59-134), separated from the Quarter only by Esplanade St's oak-shaded neutral ground, is a grand old place with 11 guest rooms. It's tastefully furnished with antiques of the sort you won't feel guilty sitting or sleeping on. This is a suitable place to rest your head after you've had enough of the action on nearby Frenchmen St. If the main house is booked, they might be able to get you a room just around the block, at their smaller, but equally inviting **Marigny Guest House** (Map 3, #27; rooms $59-$175), which has the same phone and address as Lamothe House.

Lion's Inn B&B (Map 3, #23; ☎ 945-2339; W www.lionsinn.com; 2517 Chartres St; rooms $50-110, quads $120) welcomes all sexual persuasions with four nice rooms in a renovated house. It's just a few blocks down from Frenchmen St.

The Frenchmen (Map 3, #35; ☎ 948-2166, 800-831-1781; W www.french-quarter.org; 417 Frenchmen St; rooms $119-169, suites from $189) consists of three, thoroughly refurbished 1850s houses that share a courtyard swimming pool. Rooms (some with balcony) have high ceilings and stylish furnishings. It offers a 24-hour concierge and a spa. Guests here are perfectly pivoted for scoping the nightlife of the Marigny and the lower Quarter.

A Quarter Esplanade (Map 3, #13; ☎ 948-9328, 800-546-0076; W www.quarteresplanade.com; 719 Esplanade Ave; suites $90-175) is a comely Italianate mansion with a leafy back courtyard and swimming pool. Its smartly furnished rooms have small kitchens and private baths.

Girod House (Map 3, #12; ☎ 944-7993; 835 Esplanade Ave; rooms $90-175) is run by the same people that operate A Quarter Esplanade. It is an all-suite guesthouse fashioned out of the 1833 Creole home built by New Orleans' first mayor, Nicholas Girod. The rooms are completely modern and have kitchens.

Hotel de la Monnaie (Map 3, #37; ☎ 947-0009; 405 Esplanade Ave; suites $100-190) is the largest hotel in this part of town, with five floors of stately suites. Built in the 1980s to look much older than it really is (and to smell like money), it features interior courts and river views from the top floors. The suites have minikitchens and can sleep four to six people. If you're traveling with a group or family, the price tag starts to look reasonable.

Melrose Mansion (Map 3, #7; ☎ 944-2255, 800-650-3323; W www.melrosemansion.com; 937 Esplanade Ave; suites $225-450) is one of New Orleans' premier crash pads. It is an exquisite 1884 Victorian mansion with fastidiously polished antique furnishings. This is a retreat for well-heeled honeymooners and slick Hollywood swells, not for families with children. The hotel's superior service begins with a stretch limousine sent to fetch guests at the airport.

Mazant Guest House (Map 3, #25; ☎ 944-2662; 906 Mazant St; singles with shared/private bath $29/39, doubles with shared/private bath $40/44), in the lower Bywater, is an attractive, two-story former plantation house with kitchen facilities and 11 varied guest rooms (ask about your choices when making your reservation). It's a bit removed from the action, but the Mazant's selling points are its warm, homey charm and extremely reasonable rates. Furnishings are faded antiques. The Mazant attracts European guests who often make use of the kitchen and parlor, making this a fairly social place to stay. Ask about rooms that afford more privacy. Free off-street parking is available, and there are bicycles available for guests' use. Vaughan's bar, with live music on Thursday night, is just a few blocks away. Credit cards are not accepted.

Bywater Bed & Breakfast (Map 3, #4; ☎ 944-8438; W www.bywaterbnb.com; 1026 Clouet St; rooms $65-75), also in the Bywater, is a popular lesbian artist hang-out that houses a folk-art collection. There are three rooms with shared bath.

CBD & Warehouse District (Map 4)

The CBD is not the place to stay if you're looking for that distinctive New Orleans atmosphere. The hotels here tend to be modern, utilitarian chains or posh high-rises catering to business people on expense accounts. The nearby Warehouse District, despite its promising arts-district leanings, does not offer bright alternatives. Its proximity to the Convention Center has attracted more hotel chains to accommodate undiscriminating conventioneers. Reasons to stay in these parts of town include: proximity to the French Quarter; finding a sweet deal; Mardi Gras parades passing through this part of town; wanting a view of the Superdome; your employers are paying the bill and this is where they chose to put you.

That said, there are a handful of truly outstanding exceptions. During slower periods, prices for nicer mid-range places come down to 'budget' levels, so try these before resorting to the rinky-dink chains.

Budget There is very little to recommend about the **Days Inn** (Map 4, #1; ☎ 586-0110, 800-325-2525; W www.daysinn.com; 1630

B&B Madness

New Orleans has hundreds of B&Bs, many of them in charming old homes with not so much as a sign out front to indicate that their rooms are available to travelers. Their obvious selling points are intimate surroundings, historic architecture, generally convivial hosts, early morning victuals and, in many cases, a traditional Creole courtyard in which to escape the maddening crowds. Some of these hidden B&Bs are right in the French Quarter. Other neighborhoods in which to consider seeking out your home away from home are the Faubourg Marigny, Esplanade Ridge and the Garden District.

Bed & Breakfast, Inc (☎ 488-4640, 800-729-4640; W www.historiclodging.com; 1021 Moss St, PO Box 52257, New Orleans, LA 70152-2257) represents a number of good B&Bs as well as other short- and long-term rentals in New Orleans. The website is an excellent start to your search; they'll also send a free brochure to you.

Bed and Breakfast & Beyond (☎ 896-9977, 800-886-3709; W www.nolabandb.com; 3115 Napoleon Ave) represents a handful of B&Bs on Esplanade Ave and in the Uptown area. Staff are very helpful in finding the right accommodations for you.

Louisiana B&B Association (☎ 225-346-1857, 800-395-4970; W www.louisianabandb.com; PO Box 4003, Baton Rouge, LA 70821-4003), a wing of the Louisiana Office of Tourism, can help you reserve B&B accommodations anywhere in the state of Louisiana, and offers several select choices in New Orleans. Check out the website, or call for a free, illustrated brochure.

Canal St; rooms $79-99). It stands beside the elevated freeway, is a long walk down a dicey couple of blocks to the Quarter, and its rooms are bland. But it's worth trying if you're making late arrangements during a busy time of year.

Ramada Inn & Suites Downtown Superdome (Map 4, #5; ☎ 586-0100, 800-535-9141; W www.ramada.com; 1315 Gravier St; rooms $75-85), near City Hall, is a high-rise with nearly 200 basic rooms and a swimming pool. It's a little removed from the Quarter, but a free shuttle service is available.

Comfort Suites Downtown *(Map 4, #22; ☎ 524-1140, 800-524-1140;* W *www.com fortinn.com; 346 Baronne St; rooms $129)* has modern rooms with cheap, corporate decor. It's just a block outside the Quarter.

Hampton Inn *(Map 4, #15; ☎ 529-9990, 800-292-0653;* W *www.neworleanshampton inns.com; 226 Carondelet St; rooms $89-199)* is less sterile than the average chain hotel. It's two blocks from the Quarter, and the streetcar begins its Uptown run just around the corner.

Mid-Range One of our top choices for the neighborhood is **Le Pavillon** *(Map 4, #35; ☎ 581-3111, 800-535-9095;* W *www.lepavil lon.com; 833 Poydras St; rooms $50-145, suites from $400)*. It's an elegant place (operating since 1907) with plenty of marble in the lobby and plush, modern rooms. During slow periods this hotel offers some astounding deals for same-day reservations.

Holiday Inn Downtown Superdome *(Map 4, #10; ☎ 581-1600, 800-535-7830;* W *www .holidayinnneworleansla.com; 330 Loyola Ave; rooms from $90-230)* is easily recognized by the 18-story-high clarinet painted on the side of the tall, 300-room building. Rooms are equipped with coffeemakers and dataports. It's near the Superdome and City Hall.

Holiday Inn Select *(Map 4, #69; ☎ 524-1881, 888-524-1881;* W *www.hiselect.com; 881 Convention Center Blvd; rooms $59-229)* was built in the 1990s to resemble a 1930s Art Deco hotel. Room rates depend on events scheduled at the Convention Center across the street. It has a pool.

Radisson Hotel *(Map 4, #2; ☎ 522-4500, 800-333-3333;* W *www.radisson.com/new orleansla; 1500 Canal St; rooms $79-139)* is a large chain hotel a few blocks up Canal St from the French Quarter. It's neat and fairly convenient, and efficiently run.

Top End A small and luxuriant hotel, **Lafayette Hotel** *(Map 4, #44; ☎ 524-4441; 800-525-4800;* W *www.lafayettehotel.com; 600 St Charles Ave; rooms from $165, suites*

$265) was built in 1916. Its rooms are poshly decorated, with king-size beds, and service is tops.

Fairmont Hotel *(Map 4, #8; ☎ 529-7111, 800-441-1414;* W *www.fairmont.com; 123 Baronne St; rooms & suites from $300)*, with its majestic, block-long lobby, was the city's elite establishment in days gone by. It opened in 1893, and by the 1930s, when it was called the Roosevelt Hotel, its swanky bar was frequented by governor Huey Long. The Fairmont still has an imposing presence. The curvaceous bar is as stylish as ever, the guest rooms have been tastefully remodeled, and the rooftop swimming pool affords an impressive downtown view. Rates can drop substantially during slow periods.

Hotel Monaco New Orleans *(Map 4, #28; ☎ 561-0010, 866-561-0010;* W *www.monaco-neworleans.com; 333 St Charles Ave; rooms $140-300)* is a swanky designer hotel that largely succeeds in recalling the glory days of steamer-trunk travel. Rooms are somberly lit and jazzed up with updated Art Deco stylings. Service is top-notch. The hip and lively Cobalt restaurant is off the lobby.

Windsor Court Hotel *(Map 4, #32; ☎ 523-6000, 800-237-1236;* W *www.windsorcourt hotel.com; 300 Gravier St; rooms $350, suites from $400)*, with high tea, fine English paintings and antique European furnishings, represents the greatest English invasion of New Orleans since General Pakenham's army. It was founded in 1984 by an honorary British consul who felt that New Orleans needed luxurious accommodations with traditional grand service.

Lower Garden & Garden Districts (Map 5)

The Lower Garden District is a bit scruffier than the Garden District, but it does offer some nice old guesthouses at markedly lower rates than those in its more high-toned neighbor. If you're coming for Mardi Gras, staying along St Charles Ave is not a bad plan, since many parades go down this avenue. There's a cluster of hotels near the corner of Jackson Ave.

For much of its length, St Charles is one of the USA's most attractive thoroughfares, with oak trees arcing across its neutral ground, down which historic streetcars jangle their way Uptown. However, in the Garden District, Prytania St is in some ways the prettier street, with less traffic and just as many trees. Many old homes along Prytania have been converted into guesthouses.

The bargain-basement flops in this neighborhood draw so many complaints from guests that we've stopped recommending them. But this part of town boasts a youth hostel, the Marquette House, that is still good value for budget travelers.

Budget A large Civil War–era building, **St Vincent's Guest House** (Map 5, #22; ☎ 523-3411; W www.stvincentsguesthouse.com; 1507 Magazine St; rooms $59-79) was originally an orphanage. The modernized rooms still have some remnant of that institutional feel, but the place doesn't feel haunted by its former young tenants. The courtyard swimming pool is infrequently cleaned, but its mossy green waters are a pretty centerpiece to the brick courtyard. At times, St Vincent's seems poorly managed, but guests seem mostly satisfied with what they get at this price.

Avenue Garden Hotel (Map 5, #3; ☎ 521-8000, 800-379-5233; W www.avenuegarden hotel.com; 1509 St Charles Ave; rooms $59-199) is a refurbished 19th-century guesthouse with tidy antique-furnished rooms. This is an uncharacteristically drab and treeless block of St Charles Ave, but rates at this hotel are usually very reasonable. Suites can be rented by the week at $500.

Prytania Park Hotel (Map 5, #4; ☎ 524-0427, 800-862-1984; W www.prytaniapark hotel.com; 1525 Prytania St; rooms from $59) is a modern motel adjoined to a restored 1850s guesthouse. It has 49 small but nicely appointed rooms, with refrigerators and microwaves. It's a block from the streetcar line, and the hotel offers a free shuttle to the French Quarter.

Mid-Range On the corner of Prytania St **Josephine Guest House** (Map 5, #25; ☎ 524-6361, 800-779-6361; 1450 Josephine St; rooms $115-165) has many loyal repeat visitors who enjoy the well-maintained old

house and its hospitable environment. The Josephine has just six rooms, but if they're full the proprietors might know of available accommodations nearby.

Garden District Hotel (Map 5, #14; ☎ 566-1200, 800-265-1856; W www.gardendistrict hotel.com; 2203 St Charles Ave; rooms $59-159) is a large, modern Ramada property on the corner of Jackson Ave. Its rooms won't win any interior-design contests, but they are clean and comfortable.

Avenue Plaza Hotel (Map 5, #16; ☎ 566-1212, 800-535-9575; W www.avenueplaza hotel.com; 2111 St Charles Ave; suites $70-550) is a large hotel with a spa (see Gyms in the Things to See & Do chapter). Its smartly furnished rooms have king-size beds and kitchenettes and there's also a courtyard swimming pool at the back.

Maison St Charles (Map 5, #2; ☎ 522-0187, 800-831-1783; W www.maisonstcharles .com; 1319 St Charles Ave; rooms $79-215, suites from $125) is a Quality Inn property with modern rooms.

Terrell Guest House (Map 5, #12; ☎ 524-9859; W www.lacajun.com/terrellhouse.html; 1441 Magazine St; rooms $100-125, suites from $175), an 1858 Georgian-revival house at Euterpe St, offers impressive antique furnishings and marble fireplaces in the main bedrooms. There are also 3rd-floor dorm rooms and rear servants' quarters. All rooms have private bath and include a full breakfast and cocktails.

Top End A large hotel built in 1927, the **Pontchartrain Hotel** (Map 5, #8; ☎ 524-0581, 800-777-6193; W www.pontchartrain hotel.com; 2031 St Charles Ave; rooms $135-185, luxury suites from $235) has been restored to its original splendor and represents a very good value for a full-service hotel.

Sully Mansion B&B (Map 5, #36; ☎ 891-0457, 800-364-2414; W www.sullymansion .com; 2631 Prytania St; rooms $80-175, suites $250) pretty much lives up to everything the Garden District is cracked up to be. It's a beautiful old mansion surrounded by lush gardens and a cast-iron fence. Each of its five guest rooms has a fireplace and elegant, antique, four-poster beds.

Uptown (Map 6)

Uptown is where St Charles Ave really flourishes. It's lined with historic mansions surrounded by carefully manicured gardens. Unfortunately though for visitors, places to stay are few and far between.

Columns Hotel *(Map 6, #38; ☎ 899-9308; 800-445-9308;* W *www.thecolumns.com; 3811 St Charles Ave; rooms $110-180)*, built in 1883, is one of New Orleans' great establishments, with a magnificent mahogany stairwell leading to tidy, unpretentious rooms. Adding to the fun, the downstairs bar and patio is one of the city's most festive gathering spots. On the 2nd and 3rd floors, 20 rooms of various size range from smallish doubles to the two-room 'Pretty Baby Suite' (named for the Louis Malle film shot here in the 1970s). To absorb the late-night revelry take a front room on the 2nd floor; room No 16 has a balcony overlooking the front entry and St Charles Ave.

Lagniappe B&B *(Map 6, #33; ☎ 899-2120, 800-317-2120;* W *www.lanyappe.com; 1925 Peniston St; rooms $99-200)*, in a carefully restored old house, has very stylish rooms, all with high ceilings and private baths. Rates include breakfast, off-street parking and, true to the name (*lagniappe* means 'something extra'), numerous extras ranging from fresh flowers and fruit to complimentary beer, wine and soft drinks. The attentive owners live on site, and treat their guests to a charming and comfortable stay. This is in a transitional area, but only three blocks off St Charles Ave.

Park View Guest House *(Map 6, #25; ☎ 861-7564, 888-533-0746;* W *www.parkview guesthouse.com; 7004 St Charles Ave; rooms with shared bath from $85, rooms with private bath from $115)*, near Audubon Park, was built in 1884 to impress people attending the World Cotton Exchange Exposition the following year. Antique furnishings abound in the lounge and rooms.

Esplanade Ridge (Map 7)

Esplanade Ridge, near City Park and the Fair Grounds, is rife with old and beautiful homes that now accommodate guests looking for some of that Southern grandeur we've all heard about. Of course, this is the ideal area to stay in if you've come for Jazz Fest – the Fair Grounds are just a short walk away. The neighborhood is also home to some of the city's finest dining. It's a couple of miles from this area to the French Quarter, but buses run regularly down Esplanade Ave.

Benachi House *(Map 7, #23; ☎ 525-7040, 800-308-7040;* W *www.nolabb.com; 2257 Bayou Rd; rooms $89-135)*, half a block off Esplanade Ave, is a truly spectacular Greek revival mansion built in 1859. It occupies a spacious lot with landscaped gardens, an ornate cast-iron fence, and the original carriage house and cistern. The restored rooms are handsome indeed, with original details and mahogany furnishings. The house has only four guest rooms, one with private bath. Parking is free. If rooms are not available here, the owners might be able to accommodate you in their other property, the **Esplanade Villa** *(Map 7, #25; ☎ 525-7040, 800-308-7040;* W *www.nolabb.com; 2216 Esplanade Ave; suites from $105)*.

House on Bayou Road *(Map 7, #22; ☎ 945-0992, 800-882-2968;* W *www.houseonbayou road.com; 2275 Bayou Rd; rooms & suites $135-320)* is a very romantic, former Creole plantation home from the late 18th century. It's surrounded by two acres of shaded lawns and gardens. There are rooms and suites in the main house, and a private cottage is also offered. Antique furniture and screened porches cast a Southern spell, while the 'cement pond' adds a touch of Beverly Hills.

Degas House *(Map 7, #24; ☎ 821-5009, 800-755-6730;* W *www.degashouse.com; 2306 Esplanade Ave; rooms $125-250)* is an 1854 Italianate-style house where Edgar Degas, the famed French impressionist, lived when visiting his mother's family in 1873. Rooms recall the painter's stay with reproductions of his work and period furnishings. The more expensive rooms have balconies and fireplaces, while the least expensive are garret rooms, the cramped top-floor quarters that once housed the Degas family's servants. All rooms have private bath. If fully booked, the owners might be able to accommodate you in the nearby **Duvigneaud House** *(Map 7, #19; ☎ 821-5009; 2857 Grand Route St John; suites $135)*.

Mid-City (Map 7)

Most accommodations in Mid-City can be found along Tulane Ave, an automobile-dominated strip where the largest lodging, the city jail (not recommended), contributes to a crummy atmosphere. The only reason to seek lodging here is if you're in town for Jazz Fest and can't find anything in a more desirable part of town. Postwar motels along this route tend to be a bit shabby, but a few acceptable chain outfits dot Tulane Ave. The No 39 Tulane bus provides frequent service along the route from the CBD stop near Canal St at Elk Place.

Quality Inn Midtown *(Map 7, #34; ☎ 486-5541, 800-228-5151;* **w** *www.bigeasy hotels.com; 3900 Tulane Ave; rooms from $49, suites from $99)* has a good reputation.

Best Western Patio Motel *(Map 7, #39; ☎ 822-0200, 800-270-6955;* **w** *www.best western.com/patiodowntownmotel; 2820 Tulane Ave; rooms from $59)* offers comfortable and clean rooms.

The Airport (Map 1)

Hotels near the airport, mostly chains, are a good option for your last night in the city if you have an early flight to catch. The cheapest rooms are available from **Days Inn Airport** *(☎ 469-2531;* **w** *www.daysinn.com; 1300 Veterans Memorial Blvd).*

La Quinta New Orleans Airport *(☎ 466-1401, 800-531-5900; 2610 Williams Blvd; doubles from $67)* has renovated rooms with king-size beds.

New Orleans Airport Hilton *(☎ 469-5000; 901 Airline Hwy)* and **Best Western New Orleans Inn at the Airport** *(☎ 464-1644; 1021 Airline Hwy)* are literally across the street from the airport. The Hilton is pricey and considered a fine standout hotel, but the Best Western can offer rooms as low as $64 for a double. Ask at any of these hotels for discount shuttles to the city.

LONG-TERM RENTALS

Some residents prefer to leave town and rent their homes to visitors when the big events crank up. Such an arrangement can be a good deal for large groups. Another long-term option is a time-share apartment, of which there are many in the French Quarter and Faubourg Marigny. Out-of-towners who buy into these apartments often can't travel to New Orleans as often as they planned, and so they make their time available to travelers.

The best way to seek these out is to search the Web for furnished apartments or long-term accommodations in New Orleans. Check with the B&B brokers (see the 'B&B Madness' boxed text, earlier), who might be able to point you in the right direction.

If you can get your hands on the classified ads in the Sunday edition of the *Times-Picayune* a few months before your trip, look for ads placed by home owners looking to sublet for a week or two. They also advertise in *Gambit Weekly.* Before agreeing to stay at somebody's house, be sure to pinpoint the nearest cross street on a map; homes advertised as 'near the French Quarter' could be either a long taxi ride away or in a dangerous area.

Vacation Rentals On-Line *(***w** *www.vaca tionrentalsonline.com)* has a database of New Orleans' rentals, ranging from condos to houses large enough for seven people. From the homepage, choose 'Property Search' to navigate to its New Orleans' listings.

Oakwood Corporate Housing *(☎ 800-259-6914; $56-97 a day, 30-day minimum)* manages furnished apartments in the CBD and Warehouse District. Facilities include a kitchen, washer and dryer, and parking.

Bonne Chance Bed & Breakfast *(☎ 504-367-0798;* **w** *www.bonne-chance.com; 621 Opelousas Ave),* in Algiers Point, a five-minute ferry ride from the center of New Orleans, has one- and two-bedroom apartments available for extended stays; rates are flexible and negotiable depending on the time of year.

River House *(Map 3, #22; ☎ 945-8142;* **w** *http://corp-apt.hypermart.net; 625 Marigny St; $200 per night, 3-night minimum)* is an apartment in Faubourg Marigny owned by David Lummis and Csaba Lukacs. They've remodeled it, and its floorplan is fairly open and stylish ('loft-like' is how they describe it). It sleeps four people, has a kitchen, and is very conveniently located. Unfortunately, it's also very expensive.

Places to Eat

Food is one of New Orleans' biggest tourist attractions, and some people come to the Big Easy for the sole purpose of eating. (Perhaps it's only coincidence that these are some of New Orleans' biggest visitors.) They plan their entire itinerary around their meals, resigning themselves to the reality that they'll be a few pounds heavier when they get home.

New Orleans has rich and unique culinary traditions that run deeper than those of most North American cities. Beginning with the traditions of French cuisine, the chefs and household cooks of New Orleans created and gradually elevated their own style of cooking. Creole cuisine, one of the USA's most distinctive regional cuisines, originated here. Many venerated 19th-century eateries continue to satisfy the local palate – you can still dine at Antoine's, established in 1840, and experience pretty much the same meal that was served there more than a century ago.

But New Orleans' reputation as a gastronomic paradise doesn't rest solely on tradition. Many contemporary chefs are challenging the city's old culinary habits and winning over loyal new followings. Some have pioneered creative culinary approaches to rival the cutting-edge trends of New York, San Francisco and Los Angeles. Asian, Mexican, Indian and European influences are creeping in, sometimes in surprising combinations. But new trends pass muster only if they appeal to the local population, which takes its food rather seriously and isn't easily impressed. The local audience won't go for food unless, above all else, it tastes great.

FOOD
Creole & Cajun Cuisines
New Orleans' indifference to clear definitions may drive visitors batty if they're trying to figure out the distinctions between these two Louisiana cuisines. Restaurants advertising Creole cuisine often have similar menus to those calling themselves Cajun. Then there are the growing number of Cajun-Creole restaurants.

Extraordinary Eats

One could create a list that goes on and on of all the great restaurants, dives and take-out stands in New Orleans. We've separated out just 10 highlights below, and believe us, it wasn't an easy thing to do. All of these places are listed in greater detail later in the chapter.

Galatoire's (French Quarter) Classic Creole
Central Grocery (French Quarter) Luscious muffulettas
Irene's Cuisine (French Quarter) Romantic Italian
Old Dog New Trick Café (Faubourg Marigny) Hearty vegetarian
Elizabeth's (Bywater) Heapin' breakfast
Uglesich's (Lower Garden District) Superb lunch joint
Commander's Palace (Garden District) Uptown extravaganza
Café Atchafalaya (Uptown) Family dining
Domilise's Po-Boys (Uptown) Po'boy joint
Dante's Kitchen (Riverbend) Sunday brunch

Gumbo, the region's signature soup, offers some insight into the differences between the two cuisines. As a rule, Creoles use okra as a thickener – in fact, 'gombo' derives from an African term for okra – while the Cajuns use filé (ground sassafras leaves). However, when one comes to realize that *no* two gumbos are alike, this broad cultural difference begins to seem less consequential.

The origins of both Creole and Cajun food are quite similar, as both result from adaptations made by European settlers in the unique environment of southern Louisiana. Both the Creoles and the Cajuns began with a basic understanding of French cuisine, and both incorporated American-Indian knowledge of local ingredients. And, of course, they learned from each other. Consequently, the basic elements of Creole and Cajun cuisine are the same: the distinctive *roux* (a thickening agent made from flour browned in butter), which is the backbone of so many of the region's dishes; substitutes for wheat flour, such as okra or filé, that are also used as thickening agents; and all the meats, fish, crustaceans and shellfish that are so abundant in southern Louisiana and along the Gulf Coast.

But traditionally there are some significant differences. Creole cooking is more refined, milder and more subtle than Cajun cooking. It has also benefited more from the contributions of African cooks. Many Creole restaurants in New Orleans today are run by black families.

Over the years, Cajuns developed a reputation for experimentation, the result being versatile dishes like jambalaya that can accommodate just about any added ingredients. It's on the whole an earthier and, some say, livelier cuisine. The use of cayenne and other peppers makes Cajun food hotter. (For the uninitiated, Cajun Country is where that ubiquitous American condiment, Tabasco sauce, comes from.)

Soul Food
Soul food is black Southern food. We're talking fried chicken, chitterlings (or chitluns), collard greens and corn bread. We're talking ham hocks, poke chops (or maybe you call 'em 'pork chops'), beans, and macaroni and cheese. We're talking a dive, without table service, probably somewhere far from the French Quarter. And we're talking cheap. We are not talking health food.

Barbecue is taken pretty seriously here, too, but not in restaurants. Along parade routes and in front of bars in black neighborhoods, you'll sometimes see a customized barbecue cooker, which looks like a converted oil drum, with tantalizing, aromatic smoke puffing from its stovepipe. Jazz trumpeter Kermit Ruffins named his band 'The Barbecue Swingers' as a tribute to his love of barbecue. He often shows up for gigs with a barbecue smoker in the back of his truck, and he'll dish out the 'B-B-Que' to his fans during set breaks.

Po'boys & Muffulettas
New Orleans is rightly proud to have introduced two great sandwiches to the world: the po'boy and the muffuletta.

The po'boy is the more conventional of the two. (A more proper pronunciation would be 'poor boy,' but New Orleanians never say it that way.) In other parts of the country, similar sandwiches are called submarines, heroes

PLACES TO EAT

Pinch da Tail, Suck da Head

Louisiana's official state crustacean is the crawfish, which back home you probably know as crayfish. Cajuns call them *écrevisses*, and many rural folks just call them mudbugs. Peeling and eating their delicate thumb-size tail meat is a Cajun ritual that goes well with drinking beer and telling lies to a crowd around a heaping platter of the miniature swamp lobsters. Some are harvested in the wild; others are farm-raised in rice ponds during the off-season. Local harvests first show up in the spring.

Two keys to tasty crawfish are boiling them live and using a good spicy boil made with red pepper and other seasonings. It takes a 7lb platter to yield about a single pound of tail meat. Real dives even provide tables with a disposal hole in the middle for the wasted head and shell.

A few Cajuns seeking riches search for ways to automate the peeling process; until that happens, the peeling is up to you. First, grab and uncurl the crawfish, snapping the head and body from the tail. Hold the tail with both hands, using your thumb and finger to crack the tail open and pinch out the meat. As an option, you can suck the head to taste the flavorful 'fat' from the orange-colored hepatopancreas organ.

or grinders. The po'boy, so-called since the Depression when you could have a large oyster po'boy for just 25¢, consists of roast beef, ham, fried shrimp, catfish or oysters between slices of New Orleans' soft, spongy brand of French bread. You can order it 'dressed' or not. Dressed means it is served with lettuce, tomato and mayonnaise. Stores and bars selling po'boys pop up all over Uptown along Magazine St and on more remote backstreets, and even upscale French Quarter restaurants include the sandwiches on their lunch menus.

The muffuletta is an unusual New Orleans original. Created in 1906 by Salvatore Lupo, the Sicilian-born proprietor of the Central Grocery on Decatur St, the muffuletta combines ham, salami, provolone and olive relish between slices of flat, round muffuletta bread. The sandwich takes its name from the bread, which is a little like focaccia, but it gets its character from the unique olive relish, made of green and black olives, capers, carrots, garlic, celery, pimentos, bits of cauliflower and olive oil. It is delicious, but digging your chops into one can be a messy business. The Central Grocery (see under the French Quarter, later) is still open for business, and it does a brisk trade in muffulettas and Barq's root beer, which does a right nice job complementing a muffuletta.

Vegetarian Cuisines

Vegetarians often express dismay at finding the inclusion of meat in so many of the region's specialties, and the seeming indifference that many of New Orleans' most popular restaurants have for those who do not eat meat. However, the numerous vegetarians residing in New Orleans are not sentenced to a lifetime of cooking their own meals at home – when dining out, they head for less traditional restaurants, such as Bayona or Peristyle. The chefs in these restaurants are not at a loss when it comes to cooking with greens, and will often feature outstanding meatless dishes on their daily menus.

Of course, it helps to be creative (grazing on meatless appetizers is sometimes the way to go), or at least have a willingness to eat seafood. Few New Orleans restaurants fail to offer wonderful fish dishes, or fresh oysters or crawfish.

For those tiring quickly of the limited selection of meat-free dishes available on most of the city's menus, Old Dog New Trick Café, in Faubourg Marigny, is a strictly vegetarian eatery with a varied, satisfying menu. For many vegetarian visitors, it's a lifesaver.

International Cuisines

Italian – not French – is New Orleans' most popular foreign cuisine. During the early 20th century, the riverfront side of the French Quarter was home to a sizable Sicilian community, and there are still a few family restaurants from that era in the neighborhood. You'll often discover that red sauces are endowed with a distinct Louisianan flavor – that's because zesty Creole tomatoes are frequently used instead of Romas. But the Italian influence extends beyond traditional Italian restaurants. Fine-dining establishments may offer northern Italian specialties such as risotto and seafood dishes, which are readily adapted using local ingredients. Pasta is also common in Creole restaurants.

New Orleans has attracted Vietnamese immigrants in great numbers, and most New Orleanians have a favorite place to go for *pho* (beef noodle soup) or nouveau Vietnamese cuisine. The Vietnamese influence is also evident in some of the city's most prominent restaurants, including Emeril Lagasse's NOLA (see the French Quarter, later). If you are looking for other Asian alternatives to Cajun and Creole food, you can find passable Thai, Indian and Japanese restaurants in the French Quarter and Uptown.

Mexican restaurants are not numerous in New Orleans, but there are some really good places for cheap basics such as burritos and tacos. Some of these are actually owned by Central Americans, and their menus may include tasty items such as yucca and empanadas.

Southern Breakfast (Grits 101)

If you hear a Southern drawl behind the breakfast counter, a serving of grits is probably forthcoming. Grits are coarsely ground hominy and were introduced to European settlers by Native Americans. They are boiled until they have an even, porridge-like consistency, and they taste like whatever they are served with – usually about half a cube of butter. Southerners are rightly particular about their grits – if not prepared properly, they are lumpy or contain hard kernels. If you haven't acquired the taste for them yet, keep trying! And if you do have a hankering for grits, show up early – they don't keep all day, and a lot of restaurants stop serving them at 10am or 11am. A standard New Orleans breakfast also includes fried eggs, meat and a fresh biscuit (sometimes with gravy).

In New Orleans, French toast, called *pain perdu* (lost bread) by Francophiles, is another favorite. You can back up any breakfast with chicory coffee.

Desserts

Like any self-respecting Southern city, New Orleans can gratify your need for a good slice of pie, whether it's key lime pie, sweet potato pie or pecan pie. Pecan pie seems to caramelize more completely and taste better when cooked with a little bourbon.

Pecans also regularly turn up in pralines, those concentrated little doses of sugar, butter and evaporated milk. A popular variant has shredded coconut in place of pecans.

After a day or so on the shelf, stale French bread becomes the basis for bread pudding, and every pastry chef in New Orleans has a favorite recipe for it. It's served with a 'hard sauce' ('hard' refers to its alcoholic content), which is usually rum with butter and sugar.

DRINKS
Alcoholic Drinks

Some visitors come to New Orleans with no plan other than to get thoroughly intoxicated and stay that way until it's time to travel. This is a rather sad approach to travel, but New Orleans is ready to accommodate it.

New Orleans considers itself a pioneer in alcoholic beverages (see the 'Cocktail Cockamamie' boxed text in the Entertainment chapter), and the city boasts a number of original drinks. Probably the best known these days is the Hurricane, a rum-based passionfruit drink invented at Pat O'Brien's.

In the past, drinking in New Orleans was not such a fruity experience. Several of the city's bars served drinks made with absinthe before the supposedly insanity-inducing wormwood-based liqueur was outlawed in 1912. Some of these drinks still exist, albeit in name only. You can't get absinthe in any licensed drinking establishment today. The Sazerac, absinthe Suissesse and absinthe frappé now contain Ojen or Pernod instead.

The gin fizz, created about a century ago by a local barkeep named Henry C Ramos, is also a New Orleans tradition. The concoction of gin, cream, lemon juice, sugar and egg whites was a favorite of Governor Huey Long. Mint juleps, although not a New Orleans original, are equally popular in town.

New Orleans' Dixie beer is drinkable only if chilled till near-frozen. If given a choice between it and Budweiser, go with Bud. The nearby Abita Brewery supplies most New Orleans bars with its passable ambers.

Coffee

As the principal Gulf Coast entrepot for coffee beans from Central and South America, coffee roasters in New Orleans have long supplied the local and national markets. In fact, well before computer programmers began swilling espresso coffees and double lattes in Seattle, New Orleans residents were sipping café au laits. Made with equal parts of steamed milk and coffee, it's usually a blend of coffee beans and chicory. Chicory is a root plant which is used to extend the coffee. The typical mix is 60% coffee beans to 40% chicory. Almost anywhere you find activity in New Orleans, you will also find a café nearby.

FRENCH QUARTER (MAP 2)

Obviously, this is where most visitors to New Orleans eat most of their meals. The French Quarter offers the greatest number and variety of restaurants in town, and some establishments are among the country's most famous eateries. The Quarter is also the most expensive part of New Orleans in which to dine, and during peak seasons reservations at some of the more popular places can be difficult to get.

Budget

Cafés At any of the following places a traveler might drop in for a coffee, a snack, or a light meal.

Café du Monde *(Map 2, #98; ☎ 581-2914; 800 Decatur St; open 24 hrs)* is a New Orleans institution which, despite its fame and prime location opposite Jackson Square, keeps its menu simple and its prices low. Many visitors and locals have weathered sudden showers under du Monde's patio awning while a server delivers café au lait and an order of beignets (light, square-shaped doughnuts dusted with powdered sugar) for $2.50.

Croissant d'Or Patisserie *(Map 2, #37; ☎ 524-4663; 617 Ursulines Ave; meals $3-5; open 7am-5pm daily)* is the place to start your day with the locals. It's between Chartres and Royal Sts. A fluffy individual quiche and one of the extraordinary filled croissants served with juice and coffee costs about $6. Check out the floral ceiling-tile coving.

Royal Blend *(Map 2, #90; ☎ 523-2716; 621 Royal St; meals $4-6; open 7am-midnight daily)* has a pleasant courtyard in which to sip coffee and chew a toasted bagel. They also serve a passable gumbo and light lunch fare. You can log on in the upstairs cybercafe.

Café Beignet *(Map 2, #142; ☎ 524-5530; 334B Royal St; meals $6-8; open 7am-5pm daily)* offers a shaded patio setting and serves small meals over the counter. French-style omelettes stuffed with ham, Belgian waffles and beignets are all a good start to the day, while quiches and sandwiches make up the simple lunch fare.

Restaurants A French Quarter standby that's revered by locals and out-of-towners alike is the **Acme Oyster and Seafood House** *(Map 2, #145; ☎ 522-5973; 724 Iberville St; mains $6-8; open 11am-late daily)*. It first opened in 1910, and it retains some of the casual atmosphere of the old Quarter, but it stands on its reputation for shucking out some of the city's best oysters ($4 for six on the half shell), along with po'boys, red beans and rice, and seafood gumbo. Be warned – the line of people waiting for a table often spills out onto the sidewalk.

Angeli on Decatur *(Map 2, #41; ☎ 566-0077; 1141 Decatur St; breakfast $3-7, mains $6-10; open 10am-4am Sun-Thur, 24 hrs Fri-Sat)* is near several hip and grungy lower Quarter bars so it attracts a young crowd for cheap, late-night sandwiches, pastas and vegie pita rolls. Pizzas ($10 to $16) on thin crusts are a main draw.

Café Maspero *(Map 2, #116; ☎ 523-6250; 601 Decatur St; mains $4-9; open 11am-late daily)* is usually crowded with tourists, but without trying very hard, Maspero's has atmosphere. Its smoky, brick arches make its street-level eating rooms feel underground. Alert waitstaff deliver huge, fried catfish sandwiches or red beans and rice, and offer cold Abita on tap. During the slow season, many locals sneak back in to reclaim an old haunt.

Central Grocery *(Map 2, #68; ☎ 523-1620; 923 Decatur St; open 8am-5:30pm Mon-Sat, 9am-5:30pm Sun)* is the mother church for the muffuletta. The crazy sandwich was invented here in 1906. The grocery is authentic, but swarms of tourists crowd into its narrow aisles on weekends. A whole muffuletta and a Barq's root beer ($9) is a meal for two (solo diners can order half a muffuletta).

Clover Grill *(Map 2, #51; ☎ 598-1010; 900 Bourbon St; meals $3-7; open 24 hrs)* looks much like a '50s diner and serves that kind of food – tasty burgers and fries and other grill fare. The nostalgia stops there, however. A disco-caliber sound system booms out dance music, and the boys serving the food are reputed to get pretty frisky at times. A mixed clientele files through in the early hours, but the Clover gets better as the night goes on.

Coop's Place *(Map 2, #43; ☎ 525-9053; 1109 Decatur St; meals $6-14; open 11am-3am daily)* is as much a neighborhood bar as it is a restaurant. The darkly lit cavern has a full menu, with jambalaya, fried alligator and burgers. It's also a good place to grab a plate of red beans and rice for around $5 and swill it down with beer off the tap.

Felix's Sea Food *(Map 2, #146; ☎ 522-4440; 739 Iberville St; mains $8-15; open 10am-late daily)* is another local favorite just across the street from Acme and its offerings are nearly identical. Felix's dining room and oyster bar are more spacious, so diners rarely have to wait outside.

Johnny's Po-Boys *(Map 2, #126; ☎ 524-8129; 511 St Louis St; meals $4-8; open 8am-4:30pm Mon-Fri, 9am-4pm Sat & Sun)* has been a local favorite since 1950, but the original owner met his maker and the place has declined a bit of late. Still, it's the only traditional po'boy joint in the French Quarter. Breakfast and an assortment of regional dishes are also served.

La Madeleine French Bakery & Café *(Map 2, #85; ☎ 568-9950; 547 St Ann St; mains $6-12; open 7am-9pm daily)* is a convenient stop on Jackson Square, with over-the-counter service and decent quiches, pastas and pizzas. An assortment of fresh-baked pastries and muffins makes this café equally popular for breakfast.

Mona Lisa *(Map 2, #11; ☎ 522-6746; 1212 Royal St; lunch $7-10, dinner $8-12; open 11am-11pm daily)* is in an informal, quiet, local spot in the lower Quarter. Several kooky renditions of da Vinci's familiar subject hang on the walls; she stares impassively (or is there a hint of longing in those dark eyes?) as diners munch on pizzas, pastas and spinach salads. Bring your own wine for a budget candlelight dinner.

Port of Call *(Map 2, #9; ☎ 523-0120; 838 Esplanade Ave; mains $7-21; open 11am-late daily)* is the place locals go for a half-pound burger and a baked potato ($7). (Its burgers are frequently cited as the best in town.) This basic bar and grill also serves up pizzas ($6 to $11) and steaks ($17 to $21). Reservations are not accepted and waiting on the sidewalk is not uncommon.

Verti Marte *(Map 2, #10; ☎ 525-4767; 1201 Royal St; breakfast $2-6, sandwiches $4-6; open 24 hrs daily)* is handy for those who just want to eat a quick, sodium-rich meal on their hotel balcony. The take-out menu seems endless, but stick with basics like po'boys, seafood sandwiches and the daily chef specials and you'll do all right. The main selling points here are the traditional seamy atmosphere and free delivery anywhere in the French Quarter and Faubourg Marigny.

Mid-Range

Café Sbisa *(Map 2, #58; ☎ 522-5565; 1011 Decatur St; starters $6-9, mains $15-25; open 5:30pm-10:30pm daily, 10:30am-3pm Sun brunch)* is a Vieux Carré institution (since 1899) that has a reputation for innovative Creole cuisine. Tasteful restoration of the ancient building, with exposed brick and strikingly decadent art above the long bar, helps make this one of New Orleans' most stylish dining rooms, while New American touches spruce up a solid menu, which includes blackened redfish, garlic-and-honey roasted chicken and pasta jambalaya. Café Sbisa also has a nice brunch on Sunday with a roving 'trad' jazz unit.

Crescent City Brewhouse *(Map 2, #127; ☎ 522-0571; 527 Decatur St; starters $7-10, mains $8-18; open 11am-2am daily)* is a microbrewery that produces passable pilsners and wheat beers. The menu features Louisiana standards, with a seafood emphasis, and there's often live music. It's a lively, upbeat place, and the food is generally good.

Gumbo Shop *(Map 2, #93; ☎ 525-1486; 630 St Peter St; mains $7-17; open 11am-11pm daily)* is not a place locals go to for gumbo. Out-of-towners eat here (in astonishing numbers), and most of them seem to be satisfied. The jambalaya ($9) tastes suspiciously similar to the seafood-okra gumbo ($7), which may indicate why this place doesn't get much respect from New Orleanians.

Irene's Cuisine *(Map 2, #56; ☎ 529-8811; 539 St Philip St; mains $15-20; open 5:30pm-10:30pm daily)* is a French Quarter gem. Its small, romantic dining rooms are conducive to intimate conversation, and the food is hearty. The menu straddles the Italian-French border and includes offerings such as finely seasoned, roasted, rosemary chicken, lamb à la Provençe with an exquisite port-wine glaze and stellar 'duck St Philip,' served with fresh spinach, French mustard and berries. Unfortunately, reservations are not accepted and long waits are the norm.

Louisiana Pizza Kitchen *(Map 2, #33; ☎ 522-9500; 95 French Market Place; pizzas $6-9, meals $11-18; open 11am-10pm Sun-Thur, 11am-11pm Fri & Sat)*, opposite the Old

US Mint, is a popular local chain offering wood-fired, individual pizza crusts that resemble toasted pita bread and are topped with a delicious array of ingredients ($6 to $9). Try a Caesar salad and the pizza with garlic, sundried tomatoes and feta cheese. Pastas and salads round out the menu.

Olivier's *(Map 2, #160; ☎ 525-7734; 204 Decatur St; lunch mains $8-13; dinner mains $14-25; open 11am-3pm & 5pm-10pm daily)* often goes unnoticed because of its quiet location on upper Decatur St. Olivier's has its loyal followers, though, who appreciate authentic, inexpensive Creole food in the French Quarter. Share a gumbo sampler ($9), an education in local cuisine, before digging into regional specialties such as Creole rabbit, crabcakes and broiled catfish. Save room for bourbon-pecan pie.

Top End

Antoine's *(Map 2, #102; ☎ 581-4422; 713 St Louis St; full dinner with wine per person $30-50; open 11:30am-2pm & 5:30pm-9:30pm daily)* is New Orleans' oldest restaurant, having first opened for business in 1840. The dated atmosphere of its dining rooms (a brightly lit room for nonsmokers and a more ambient smoking room) might be just the ticket for a family gathering, particularly if older folks are involved. Dining here is certainly of historical interest, but in general the food here fails to thrill the senses and contemporary palates might find the meat and fish dishes overburdened by staid sauces. Even the oysters Rockefeller, Antoine's own invention, lacks spirit. As a general rule, ask your waiter what's fresh and follow suit. Jackets required, denim prohibited.

Arnaud's *(Map 2, #118; ☎ 523-5433; 813 Bienville St; à la carte entrees $17-29; open 6pm-10pm daily, 10am-2:30pm Sun brunch)* is one of the better places to go for traditional haute Creole cuisine. It was founded in 1918 by 'Count' Arnaud Cazenave, a French immigrant whose extravagant tastes are still evident here. The restaurant is an agglomeration of buildings that take up nearly an entire city block. It's a festive place where locals and tourists go for special occasions and to soak in New Orleans' past.

You can choose to sit in the main dining room, much admired for its stately old-world elegance, or the Richelieu Room, where an acoustic jazz ensemble ($4 music charge) adds class. While it isn't the most scintillating dining, the kitchen surely handles its specialties well; they appear in red type on the menu – shrimp Arnaud, oysters Bienville (an original dish), speckled trout meunière (saved by a rich, gravy-like sauce) and a variety of steaks and fowl dishes.

Bayona *(Map 2, #100; ☎ 525-4455; 430 Dauphine St; starters $5-8, lunch $15-23, dinner before wine $33-50; open 11:30am-2pm Mon-Fri, 6pm-10pm Mon-Thur, 6pm-11pm Fri & Sat)* is one of the city's best all-around dining experiences. It is in a converted Creole cottage, with several former parlors serving as homey dining rooms. On pleasant-weather days, there's also alfresco dining on the back patio. Chef Susan Spicer's menu is always inventive, but rarely shocking. The grilled shrimp with black-bean cake and coriander sauce and the goat-cheese crouton with mushrooms in Madeira cream are elegant starters. Representative entrees include a grilled pork chop with savory semolina pudding and sage *jus* (sauce) and a salmon with sauerkraut and Gewürztraminer sauce. The wine list is extensive and predominantly European, with few choices under $40 a bottle.

Brennan's Restaurant *(Map 2, #122; ☎ 525-9711; 417 Royal St; brunch per person $30-40; open 8am-2:30pm & 6pm-10pm daily)* prides itself on having introduced the luxury breakfast to New Orleans. Indeed, breakfast in one of the restaurant's 12 elegant dining rooms or its lovely courtyard is no *petit déjeuner*: It's a virtual gastronomic extravaganza that could start with an 'eye-opener' (if you can imagine downing a Sazerac cocktail before breakfast), followed by a baked apple or turtle soup, any of about 20 egg dishes, and then dessert (bananas Foster is a Brennan's original). Traditional Creole dinners are served nightly.

Court of Two Sisters *(Map 2, #89; ☎ 522-7261; 613 Royal St; meals per person $30-50; open 9am-3pm & 5:30pm-10pm daily)* has a wonderful ambience but disappointing food.

When it rains, patrons are seated in one of several slightly faded (some are actually drab) indoor dining rooms. The fare is strictly traditional and, unfortunately, uninspired. Considering the Court's high volume – on a warm Sunday, well over 1000 visitors might eat here – the kitchen staff does a commendable job, but you would expect to eat better for the price.

Galatoire's *(Map 2, #140;* ☎ *525-2021; 209 Bourbon St; mains $15-22; open 11:30am-10pm Tues-Sat, noon-10pm Sun)* is a clubby sort of place where the regulars are treated regally and tourists are sometimes dished out surprisingly average food. Local devotees so love this New Orleans establishment that to die here over a plate of, say, grilled pompano with almonds is considered a *belle mort,* or good death. (Fortunately, this doesn't happen very often.) The building has housed a restaurant since 1830 (it was called Victor's before Jean Galatoire bought it in 1905), and history is palpable in the main dining room. Oysters Rockefeller, asparagus salad, 'chicken *clemenceau'* and the to-die-for pompano are good bets off the menu (or ask the waiter what's good on the day). Expect a long wait outside before being seated, especially for lunch on Friday. Reservations are accepted for the new upstairs dining room.

K-Paul's Louisiana Kitchen *(Map 2, #131;* ☎ *596-2530; 416 Chartres St; starters $7-13, mains $26-36)* has lost its edge in recent years, some locals complain. More accurately, this once innovative restaurant just hasn't changed much of late. Chef Paul Prudhomme is no longer active in the day-to-day operation of the kitchen, but the same food he created here in the 1980s is still available. The kitchen eschews shortcuts. The blackened twin beef tenders ($30), a signature dish, come with an incredibly rich 'debris' gravy that's been slowly cooked over a two-day period. You can also get gumbo here ($5 a cup), with hot andouille sausages made on the premises, and turtle soup ($5.50), which has a nice flavorful snap to it. Jambalaya ($12 for lunch) is simmered for hours with jalapeños and is hot indeed. Despite its popularity, K-Paul's retains a no-reservations policy downstairs, but takes reservations for its upstairs tables. For weekday lunches, you might be seated on arrival.

Mr B's Bistro *(Map 2, #148;* ☎ *523-2078; 201 Royal St; lunch mains $10-16, dinner mains $20-26; open 11:30am-3pm Mon-Sat, 10:30am-3pm Sun, 5:30pm-10pm nightly),* run by a branch of the Brennan family, is a clubby, attractively designed restaurant that appeals to a variety of tastes. Creole overtones predominate the menu. The 'gumbo Ya-Ya' with chicken and andouille is excellent, and the 'barbecued' shrimp, sautéed in a delicious buttery sauce, is a fun and messy dish served with a paper bib to protect your shirt. Lunch specials often include less traditional fare, such as blackfin tuna coated in a macadamia-nut crust, while dinner entrees include tried-and-true favorites such as rack of lamb and rib-eye steak.

NOLA *(Map 2, #132;* ☎ *522-6652; 534 St Louis St; lunch mains $15-23, dinner mains $24-32; open 11:30am-2pm Mon-Sat, 6pm-10:30 nightly)* is chef Emeril Lagasse's French Quarter outpost. Lagasse's kitchen staff deftly cull local, Asian and Californian traditions for natural, subtle combinations. Fresh fish parts neatly under your fork, and roasted filet mignon, cooked rare, is so tender you can almost chew it with your eyebrows. NOLA also scores high for its wood-fired pizzas (a good starter for a group) and its 21-page wine list (with many affordable choices). Excessively noisy dining rooms and an energetic staff help make this an exciting place to eat.

Palace Café *(Map 2, #161;* ☎ *523-1661; 605 Canal St; lunch mains $12-18, dinner mains $19-25; open 11:30am-2:30pm Mon-Fri, 10:30-2:30 Sat & Sun, 5:30pm-10pm nightly)* makes a strong first impression, with a striking interior that combines modern and classic designs. When it opened in 1990 in a former music store, the building's original tile floors and interior columns were retained and a corkscrew staircase was added. Businesspeople, conventioneers and office workers seem to have laid claim to the place. The food follows through with modern, nonexperimental approaches to classic Creole standards like catfish pecan meunière. Occasional surprises, such as the herbed gnocchi

Celebrity Chefs

New Orleans is a city of celebrity chefs. Since Paul Prudhomme's days at Commander's Palace in the 1970s, the Crescent City has always had a media sensation at the vanguard of its restaurant scene, and the resulting national attention has proven to be a boon for the city's foodmongers in general. The nonstop parade seems to work like clockwork – once one chef's star is fading, a new one emerges, ensuring that New Orleans stays in the food media spotlight. Here's a rundown of big names on the New Orleans restaurant scene.

Paul Prudhomme

Although he's often mistaken for comedian Dom Deluise, Paul Prudhomme is one of the most recognizable chefs in America. Chef Prudhomme is to Cajun cuisine what Louis Armstrong was to jazz – an innovator and ambassador of New Orleans culture – and his celebrity paved the way for later superchefs like Emeril Lagasse. His greatest contribution to American cuisine is the blackening technique, which he perfected with dishes like blackened redfish at his restaurant K-Paul's.

Susan Spicer

When Susan Spicer opened Bayona in the early 1990s, her nouvelle cuisine definitely went against the grain in traditional New Orleans. Nevertheless, she became one of the city's superchefs for her understated and original cooking, which often displays deft combinations of Asian, European and Indian concepts. As she explains it, her cooking has a lot to do with her upbringing. She's a self-described 'navy brat' who grew up in many countries, and her mother's home cooking often borrowed international techniques, reflecting a curiosity and adaptability that rubbed off on chef Spicer. She consistently challenges local and international traditions in ways that also demonstrate

with wild mushrooms starter served in a smoky chicken stock, add nice twists to the menu. Local products predominate.

Peristyle *(Map 2, #16; ☎ 593-9535; 1041 Dumaine St; starters $8-16, mains $24-27; open 6pm-9pm Tues-Thur, 6pm-10pm Fri & Sat)* at Rampart, is one of the city's more romantic spots for dinner. Chef Anne Kearney, one of New Orleans' rising stars, treats diners to simple yet refined creations in intimate surroundings. Her menu plays on American tastes and French Provençal methods of preparation – it's traditional fare that's sophisticated and attractive. Grilled veal, cooked with the bone, is served in a rich Madeira *jus* atop a bed of polenta, and bass is seared until crispy and served with sautéed capers. After emerging from Chef Kearney's kitchen, dishes like these make tastebuds sing. Reservations are essential.

FAUBOURG MARIGNY & BYWATER (MAP 3)

When the sun goes down, Frenchmen St comes to life. An inviting array of restaurants,

bars and nightclubs along this colorful drag entices many regular customers to keep coming back to the Marigny in the evening. The range of cuisines here is varied enough to keep things interesting on repeated visits.

The Bywater lacks a distinctive cultural strip like Frenchmen St, but a smattering of excellent eateries are to be found along some of its sleepy residential byways.

Budget

Buffa's Bar & Restaurant *(Map 3, #6; ☎ 945-9397; 1001 Esplanade Ave; mains $5-9; kitchen open 11am-8pm daily)* is a bar with an inexpensive menu that has been a neighborhood favorite since 1939. The kitchen churns out greasy burgers and darn reasonable daily specials (usually meat and potatoes and a salad for about $6). It's worth knowing about if you're interested in seeing the neighborhood's down-to-earth side.

Elizabeth's *(Map 3, #39; ☎ 944-9272; 601 Gallier St; breakfast $3-6, lunch $4-8; open 7am-2:30pm Tues-Sat)*, in Bywater, offers one of the best deals in town for breakfast understanding and respect. 'I try not to innovate just for the sake of innovation,' she says, 'and I believe it's important to understand the basic principles of a cuisine before you experiment with it.' She also owns and maintains a daily presence in the Herbsaint and Cobalt restaurants.

Emeril Lagasse

In terms of media exposure, Emeril Lagasse is currently the hottest chef in America, and he appears intent on riding his fame to the fullest extent. A native of Fall River, Massachusetts (his family is French Canadian and Portuguese), chef Lagasse (he pronounces his name 'la-**ga**-see') opened his first restaurant, Emeril's, in the Warehouse District in 1990 and has been soaring ever since. At last count, he owned three restaurants in New Orleans (NOLA, Emeril's and Delmonico), along with one in Orlando, Florida, and another in Las Vegas, Nevada, and his Food Channel TV programmes are filmed in New York. As his empire steadily expands, Lagasse probably finds himself spending more time on airplanes than he does in his New Orleans kitchens, and many say his restaurants have begun to suffer for it.

Anne Kearney

Chef Anne Kearney may well become the next household name out of New Orleans, but her restaurant, Peristyle, remains a modest, romantic little place (it only seats 56), and she proudly describes her food as 'bistro' fare rather than aligning it with more glamorous nouveau and fusion trends. Kearney's career got off to an auspicious start. Since arriving in New Orleans from her native Ohio, she has worked with some high-profile chefs, including the late John Neal (who founded Peristyle) and Emeril Lagasse. Kearney acknowledges that she learned a lot about the business by working with her mentors, but in the kitchen Kearney's style is all her own.

or lunch. No matter what you order from the unassuming menu, it will exceed expectations in quality and quantity. Lulamae's breakfast po'boy, chef Heidi Trull's original combination of smoked sausage, cheesy scrambled eggs and French bread, is as long as a grown man's forearm. Pancakes and waffles come topped with strawberries, and even the basic breakfast ($3.50) is a standout, with eggs, a slab of meat, a biscuit and 'real' grits (none of that instant stuff from Heidi's kitchen). Heaping lunch specials (down-home favorites, deftly handled) and desserts (by Emeril's former pastry chef) will satisfy a king and add to your girth.

The Harbor (Map 3, #10; ☎ 947-1819; 2529 Dauphine St; meals $4-8; open 10am-5pm daily), in the back of a local bar habituated by elderly black men, is a soul-food joint just a few blocks from the Quarter. You won't meet many tourists here, though. It's the real deal, where tasty fried chicken, pork chops, chitterlings, mustard greens and white bread are dished out unceremoniously. The cost for such satisfying fare is surprisingly low.

La Peniche (Map 3, #8; ☎ 943-1460; 1940 Dauphine St; open 24 hrs Thur-Tues) appears at first glance to be an unassuming, little corner restaurant, a few blocks from the Frenchmen St scene. It's open 24 hours, but it tends to get interesting late at night. (For example, on a recent visit we observed a long white limousine pull up in front and discharge an army of hungry sex-industry workers.) Surly waiters serve seafood platters, fried chicken, steaks, chops and po'boys – none of it exceptional, all of it reasonably priced. Red beans and rice costs $6.

Old Dog New Trick Café (Map 3, #31; ☎ 943-6368; 517 Frenchmen St; mains $6-11; open 11am-10pm daily) is an entirely vegetarian restaurant that serves mercifully good food. The Ben burger is a hearty blend of rice, millet, lentils and sunflower seeds, molded into a patty and served in pita bread. Buckwheat soba noodles and udon noodles with tempeh are equally satisfying.

Siam Café (Map 3, #36; ☎ 949-1750; 435 Esplanade Ave; mains $7-13; open 5pm-2am daily) is a dim, narrow den where you can order all the Thai standards, including pad Thai, spicy curries, and many vegetarian dishes. It rises to greater heights with specialties such as the royal hunter's grill. The Siam also offers a nice variety of beers to wash down the spices.

Mid-Range & Top End

Adolfo's (Map 3, #18; ☎ 948-3800; 611 Frenchmen St; starters $4-6, mains $8-16; open 6pm-11pm Mon-Sat) might be just what you came looking for in New Orleans, a romantic little Creole-Italian restaurant hidden away upstairs from the bar. It's rustic and dimly lit, and if the mood strikes him, an unseen dishwasher might be heard singing along to Frank Sinatra tunes on the radio. The hearty pastas with Creole tomato sauces, traditional Italian meat dishes and cheap wines that emerge from the kitchen will surely raise your spirits.

Belle Forché (Map 3, #33; ☎ 940-0722; 1407 Decatur St; café mains $9-14; starters $5-10, mains $17-24; open 5:30pm-10:30pm Tues-Wed & Sun, 5:30pm-2:30am Thur-Sat) has the most stylish dining room in the neighborhood, with dim lighting, an immense fish tank and svelte mermaids painted on the wall. The inventive, contemporary Creole dishes live up to the atmosphere, but so do the prices. Delicious downscale offerings in the adjacent bar-café fetch lower prices. (Try the twice jerked catfish.)

Bywater Barbeque (Map 3, #24; ☎ 944-4445; 3162 Dauphine St; starters $4-7, mains $6-14; open 6am-10pm Mon-Fri, 11am-10pm Sat & Sun), in Bywater, dishes out very good spare ribs, chicken and pulled pork in heaping quantities. On nice evenings, neighborhood regulars congregate on the patio tables out back.

Café Negril (Map 3, #20; ☎ 944-4744; 606 Frenchmen St; starters $4-5, mains $8-13; open 11am-3pm Tues-Fri, 6pm-midnight Tues-Sat) is a large, colorful space featuring the Caribbean creations of Chef Cecil Palmer. The place still manages to fill up with people who love Jamaican jerked fish and West Indian curried goat. A variety of tropical drinks and, of course, Red Stripe beer, make this a fun party spot.

Mandich Restaurant (Map 3, #5; ☎ 947-9553; 3200 St Claude Ave; lunch starters $5-9, mains $10-18; dinner starters $4-10, mains $20-26; open noon-2pm Tues-Fri, 5pm-10pm Fri & Sat) is a Bywater institution that serves authentic Cajun cuisine. Mandich evokes earlier times, with painted brick walls, pebbled linoleum, wood paneling, and food piled high like bouffant hairdos on large platters. Snazzily attired old-timers flock here for lunches comprised of seafood gumbo, crisp catfish topped with smothered crawfish tails, baked oyster platters, and liver and onions. Dinner is served on weekends only. The high prices may come as a shock.

Praline Connection (Map 3, #28; ☎ 943-3934; 542 Frenchmen St; starters $3-8, lunch mains $4-8, dinner mains $9-14; open 11am-10:30pm Sun-Thur, 11am-midnight Fri & Sat) serves up righteous but slightly pricey soul food: fried chicken, Creole gumbo, beans and greens. It's all served up by some of New Orleans' coolest waitstaff (fedoras are de rigueur here).

Santa Fe (Map 3, #9; ☎ 944-6854; 801 Frenchmen St; starters $7-9, mains $10-20; open 5pm-11pm Tues-Sat) is a popular southwestern restaurant that fuels its patrons with potent margaritas to get the scene revved up before chile rellenos (grilled peppers filled with melted cheese), steak tacos and roast duck hit the tables. This is a fun spot.

CBD & WAREHOUSE DISTRICT (MAP 4)

New Orleans' business district is home to some highly acclaimed and expensive restaurants, and in some ways is the city's premier culinary destination. The Central Business District (CBD) and the nearby Warehouse District also have many decent eat-and-run spots for smaller budgets.

Budget

Le Petit Paris (Map 4, #17; ☎ 524-7660; 731 Common St; meals $2.50-6; open 7am-3pm Mon-Fri) is a small café filled with inviting aromas, which offers French pastries, omelettes, roast chicken and a 'croissant la Seine,' with crawfish and béchamel sauce. You can order your meal in French if you like.

Louisiana Products *(Map 4, #54; ☎ 529-1666; 618 Julia St; meals $2-5; open 8am-4pm Mon-Sat)*, on historic Julia Row, has the feel of an old general store, but it's really a deli, with limited seating and inexpensive breakfasts and lunches. If you're headed to a nearby museum, drop in for ham, eggs and cheese on a French roll for breakfast or a mini-muffuletta for lunch.

Mother's *(Map 4, #37; ☎ 523-9656; 401 Poydras St; meals $5-12; open 7am-10pm daily)* is famous for its hearty down-home breakfasts and heaping debris (roast beef drippings) po'boys. Although service is over the counter, everything is cooked to order. Some justifiably complain that the prices are a wee bit too high and that weekend lines are too long, but the loyal following is deserved. Be sure to figure out what you're ordering before you get in line, as the counter people aren't crazy about indecisive patrons.

New City Diner *(Map 4, #12; ☎ 522-8198; 828 Gravier St; meals $3-7; open 7am-2pm Mon-Fri)* is a cafeteria-style place that dishes up full breakfasts and hot lunch specials. It's nothing to write home about, but it's cheap and convenient if you find yourself in the neighborhood.

Red Fye Grill *(Map 4, #62; ☎ 593-9393; 852 S Peters St; meals $5-8; open 11am-late daily)* is a grungy bar in the Warehouse District (for those 21 years and up). This is strictly for greasy burgers and fries served late into the night. It's convenient if you're seeing a show at Howling Wolf.

Vic's Kangaroo Café *(Map 4, #46; ☎ 524-4329; 636 Tchoupitoulas St; meals $5-7; open 11am-2am Mon-Fri, 6pm-2am Sat & Sun)*, in the Warehouse District, is an Australian pub that provides a taste of Down Under by serving savory pies. Lovers of chicken will want to try the chook pie, while herbivores will prefer theirs filled with feta cheese, spinach and tomato.

Mid-Range

Cobalt *(Map 4, #28; ☎ 565-5595; 333 St Charles Ave; starters $5-9, mains $16-22; open 8am-10pm Mon-Sat, 6pm-10pm Sun)*, in the Hotel Monaco, brings a young cosmopolitan crowd to the CBD. The place has swank, and so does its menu. Appetizers include the spectacular duck confit 'debris' biscuit with sweet tomato conserve. A standout entree finds another use for vodka, in a martini sauce dressing grilled salmon. Look sharp.

Liborio Cuban Restaurant *(Map 4, #29; ☎ 581-9680; 322 Magazine St; lunch $7-17, dinner $10-25; open 11am-3pm Mon-Fri, 5:30pm-9pm Tues-Sat)* satisfies Warehouse District lunchers with daily specials such as roast pork with black beans (every Wednesday). Also try the grilled tuna with sweet plantains for $9.

Top End

Bon Ton Café *(Map 4, #36; ☎ 524-3386; 401 Magazine St; mains $15-25; open 11am-2pm & 5pm-9:30pm Mon-Fri)* is an old-style Cajun restaurant. The dining room looks like a pizza parlor, but folks show up dressed to the nines, and meals aren't cheap. This is Cajun food from before Paul Prudhomme came along. Spices are used in tasteful moderation in gumbo, redfish and shrimp étouffée; don't pass on the rum-soaked bread pudding.

Emeril's *(Map 4, #57; ☎ 528-9393; 800 Tchoupitoulas St; mains $20-34; open 11:30am-2pm Mon-Fri, 6pm-10pm Mon-Sat)*, in a converted warehouse in the Warehouse District, is the flagship of chef Emeril Lagasse's restaurant empire. The noise level can be deafening, the service can be aloof, and the chef is rarely in town, but nevertheless Emeril's remains one of New Orleans' finest dining establishments. The kitchen's strengths are best appreciated by ordering the daily specials, although mainstays like shrimp-and-andouille cheesecake with Creole mustard and tomato coulis, or crawfish-stuffed filet mignon with sauce bordelaise are worth a try. The wine list is eclectic and features many sleepers that are well priced.

Herbsaint *(Map 4, #47; ☎ 525-4114; 701 St Charles Ave; lunch mains $8-12, dinner mains $12-18; open 11:30am-2:30pm Mon-Fri, 5:30-10:30 Mon-Sat)*, co-owned by chefs Susan Spicer and Donald Link, is an homage to traditional French bistro fare, but not without strong New Orleanian inflections or subtle, contemporary innovations. Steak frites comes with a zesty pimento aioli, while frog legs are replaced with chicken wings (which, one might suppose, taste just like frog legs). The dining room, understated and warmly lit by windows, is especially pleasant for lunch. Weekend dinner involves a long wait (no reservations).

Lemon Grass (Map 4, #21; ☎ 523-1200; 217 Camp St; lunch mains $7-14, dinner mains $12-20; open 11am-2pm Mon-Fri, 6pm-11pm nightly), in the International House Hotel, is the chic culinary atelier of chef Minh Bui, whose often inspired play on arousing combinations of ingredients and flavors borrows freely from French cuisine as well as the cooking of his own native Vietnam. Main dishes change frequently but may include mirliton (chayote) with shrimp and a buttery French sauce, or ginger chicken and stir-fried vegetables couched in a deep-fried, cracker-like 'bird's nest.' You can also graze on delicious appetizers, such as summer rolls (with a heavenly peanut sauce), deep-fried oysters and shrimp dumplings. Desserts are also exceptional.

Restaurant August (Map 4, #31; ☎ 299-9777; 301 Tchoupitoulas St; lunch starters $4-8, mains $10-18; dinner starters $4-12, mains $18-32; open noon-2pm Mon-Fri, 6pm-10pm Mon-Sat), in a 19th-century tobacco warehouse converted into a very swank upscale dining room, is one of a Warehouse District highlight. The emphasis here is Creole-French, and dishes aim to surprise and satisfy contemporary palates. Dinner standouts include tender pheasant with homemade sauerkraut, seared bass in a rich oxtail *jus* and herb-rubbed, crisp-skinned duck.

Restaurant Cuvée (Map 4, #30; ☎ 587-9001; 322 Magazine St; lunch starters $6-8, mains $10-14; dinner starters $7-11, mains $18-30; open 11:30am-2:30pm Mon-Fri, 6pm-10pm Mon-Sat) is a high-class joint with a menu that switches freely between the French and English languages and jarringly reveals where the mustard greens came from (Morgan City). This is exotic, full-tilt Français-Louisiana cuisine: foie gras and duck *boudin* (sausage) cake set in Creole mustard glaze; millefeuille of panéed eggplant and grilled vegetable quinoa; and sugarcane smoked duck breast with a crispy confit leg.

LOWER GARDEN & GARDEN DISTRICTS (MAP 5)

Food-lovers and hungry people have an interesting array of choices on and off St Charles Ave. Many places in the Lower Garden District are esteemed for their 24-hour breakfasts and late-night fixings, many bars serve decent food, and the Garden District is home to Commander's Palace, one of the most highly acclaimed restaurants in the US.

Budget & Mid-Range

Café Roma (Map 5, #26; ☎ 524-2419; 1901 Sophie Wright Place; meals $7-13, pizzas $10-18; open 11am-1am daily) is a pleasant Lower Garden District restaurant with linen-covered tables next to tall, arched doorways that open out to the street. Pizza is the specialty item here, made in traditional and gourmet varieties (with toppings including shrimp and artichokes). Pastas, chicken dishes and sandwiches round out the menu.

Parasol's (Map 5, #42; ☎ 899-2054; 2533 Constance St; po'boys $6; open 11am-10pm daily), a neighborhood bar and eatery, is an Irish Channel institution. Locals have long insisted that this is one of the best places to get a po'boy sandwich. No argument here. The shredded roast beef po'boys are superb and eating one is a sloppy business. Fine catfish po'boys and other varieties are also available. Nonbarflies (and juniors) can enter a side door into the casual eating room.

Please-U-Restaurant (Map 5, #5; ☎ 525-9131; 1751 St Charles Ave; meals $3-8; open 6am-7pm Mon-Fri, 6am-2pm Sat) is a run-down, old, counter-and-booths establishment that aims to please its customers with cheap, satisfying diner fare. Whether you order steak and eggs, a soft-shell crab sandwich or a po'boy, you won't spend much.

Rue de la Course (Map 5, #23; ☎ 529-1455; 1500 Magazine St • Map 5, #47; ☎ 899-0242; 3128 Magazine St; both open 7:30am-11pm daily), with two locations on Magazine St (plus other branches around town), is a casual and somewhat subdued coffeehouse decked out with pressed tin and wooden tables. You can while away your time over a newspaper (available at the counter) and your choice of coffee and baked goods.

The Trolley Stop *(Map 5, #9; ☎ 523-0090; 1923 St Charles Ave; meals $5-10; open 24 hrs)* has several virtues, none of which is the greasy food. First and foremost, the diner is set in a former gas station, and locals now regard it as a filling station of another sort. New Orleanians of all stripes pull up to this convenient pit-stop along the St Charles Ave corridor for ham and eggs and the usual assortment of sandwiches and burgers. There's always an interesting crowd on hand.

Uglesich's *(Map 5, #1; ☎ 523-8571; 1238 Baronne St; lunch $8-15; open 11am-2pm Mon-Fri)*, a sublime little dive, is the consummate New Orleans lunchtime experience. It's a cherished institution (family run since 1924) that draws suits and blue collars alike to a neglected central neighborhood. The food, with its strong seaward leanings, never fails to amaze newcomers, who nearly always come away feeling they've found what they were looking for in New Orleans. You can get trout, shrimp and crawfish in all sorts of ways, and the menus tacked to the walls don't really indicate what a dish will end up like (some favorites, such as the 'trout muddy waters,' aren't on the menu at all). When you order from the counter, engaging your server in conversation will usually result in your ordering the right thing. A raw-oyster bar makes eating and running a possibility; otherwise, you'll probably wait half an hour or so to be seated (parties of two may be asked to share a table). Cash only.

How Ya Like Dem Ersters?

Hard-core New Orleans oyster bars, such as Casamento's Uptown, can be a little intimidating for neophytes. There's a certain cultishness in the way experienced patrons stand before a cold marble bar top as half a dozen oysters (which some locals pronounce 'ersters') are shucked and laid out on the half-shell. With restrained anticipation, often disguised by an air of ritualism, these oyster fiends dash lemon and a spot of hot sauce or a bit of horseradish onto the first of the oysters. They then slurp down the addictive bivalve, pausing to savor that first oyster's saltiness and to summon up a renewed sense of anticipation before turning their attention to the second one, and this behavioral pattern repeats itself until all six half-shells lie empty on the counter. For many New Orleanians, this entire ritual is completed in about the length of time it takes to fill a tank of gas.

Naturally, people who hold oysters in such high esteem have come to attribute certain health-promoting qualities to them. According to one popular myth, eating oysters can increase a person's sex drive and enhance their sexual prowess. The always contrarian health department, however, insists that people eating raw shellfish only risk food poisoning. After all, oysters are raised in the shallow bottom of the gulf, where toxic debris discharged upstream eventually settle and enter the shells. As a test, with your next half dozen order a large glass of water and dip each plump little oyster in the water and swish it around. Afterward, check out the sediment in the glass and consider whether you would drink it.

Oysters also have a variety of ways of insinuating themselves into a leisurely classic New Orleans meal. In some people's minds, seafood gumbo must include oysters or be called something else. And the list of appetizers on many of the city's menus generally includes several baked-oyster dishes. The most famous local oyster dish, served with a devilish little fork, is oysters Rockefeller, an Antoine's restaurant creation that owes its success as much to an irresistible secret spinach sauce as it does to the well-hidden oysters.

Then, of course, oysters make the classic po'boy. The name, local parlance for 'poor boy', refers to the cheapness of oysters during the Great Depression. An oyster sandwich cost just 20¢ in those days. In some traditional quarters of the city, you can still order an oyster loaf, which as some people may recall was once known as *'la mediatrice'* – the peacemaker – because bringing one home was considered an effective way for a guilty husband to appease an angry wife. The loaf is composed of oysters dipped in cornmeal, deep fried and served on white toast, and it appears to have gone out of fashion as divorces became more popular.

Top End

Commander's Palace *(Map 5, #41; ☎ 899-8221; 1403 Washington Ave; lunch mains $14-25; dinner starters $8-10, mains $22-32)*, in the heart of the Garden District, has long been regarded as one of the USA's great restaurants. Owner Ella Brennan prides her ability to promote her chefs to stardom. (Paul Prudhomme and Emeril Lagasse are among her alumni.) It must be said that Commander's lives up to the hype and still makes its guests feel welcome. The service is impeccable and friendly, the decor tasteful and comfortable, and the food is splendorous. The main dining room is warmly lit through windows during lunch, but at night its artificial lighting is a little stale – try to reserve in the upstairs parlor or in the Garden Room, which looks out over Ella's lovely courtyard. The Creole menu includes regional soup specialties (turtle soup au sherry) and starters such as shrimp *rémoulade* (sauce) and *tasso* (cured, smoked pork) shrimp. Main dishes are where Commander's really sells itself. The Colorado roast rack of lamb is prepared with a Creole mustard crust and an exquisite muscadine lamb sauce. This is obviously a major splurge, but Commander's lunch prices are mercifully reduced. Reservations are required and, for men, so are jackets.

UPTOWN (MAP 6)

There are many reasons to head Uptown for a meal. Great little neighborhood eateries pop up along quiet blocks off the main St Charles Ave and Magazine St arteries. There are a few healthy options up this way, too.

Budget

All Natural Foods & Deli *(Map 6, #46; ☎ 891-2651; 5517 Magazine St; sandwiches $3-7; open 10am-7pm Mon-Thur, 10am-6pm Fri & Sat, 10am-5pm Sun)* has the predictable hippy-dippy feel to it, but it's clean and efficiently run and has a nice selection of organic sandwiches that can be eaten out in the garden patio. Try the albacore tuna melt, or the avocado and cheese sandwich.

Bluebird Café *(Map 6, #39; ☎ 895-7166; 3625 Prytania St; breakfast $3-6, lunch $3-4.50; open 7am-3pm Mon-Fri, 8am-3pm Sat &*

Sun) is often packed with locals and medical students from nearby hospitals. Satisfying breakfasts tend to go a bit beyond traditional Southern eggs and grits combos; *huevos rancheros* are a spicy Mexican repast, and the 'powerhouse eggs' dish contains nutritional yeast, tamari and cheese. The Bluebird is also known for its malted pancakes and Belgian waffles. For lunch, sandwiches (burgers, vegie melts and BLTs) are available. Weekend waits are normal. Cash only.

Café Atchafalaya *(Map 6, #59; ☎ 891-5271; 901 Louisiana Ave; open 11:30-2pm Tues-Sun, 5:30pm-9pm Tues-Sat)* is the kind of place where Southern hospitality and cornbread aren't on the menu, because you get them automatically. The casual dining room here is admirably nondescript, a complement to the down-home Southern cooking that comes out of Atchafalaya's kitchen. Deep South stalwarts, such as fried green tomatoes, crabcakes, fried fish, fried chicken and stuffed pork chops appeal to locals and tourists alike.

Casamento's *(Map 6, #53; ☎ 895-9761; 4330 Magazine St; oysters $1, mains $3-10; open 11:30am-1:30pm & 5:30pm-9pm Tues-Sun)* is where hardcore Uptown oyster fiends go for their fix. Every last detail of the interior, ice box and all, has been impeccably (indeed, surreally) maintained since 1949. Spotless, glowing white-tile floors and walls make it feel more like a laboratory than a family-owned eatery. The oysters are always the freshest and come raw on the half-shell at just $7.50 a dozen. An Italian-inflected gumbo ($7) and oyster loaf (a sandwich of breaded and fried oysters on white bread; $10.50 for a large one) also have faithful followers. Other traditions upheld here include closing during the summer and trading in cash only.

Domilise's Po-Boys *(Map 6, #63; ☎ 899-9126; 5240 Annunciation St; po'boys $7; open 11am-7pm Mon-Sat)*, on a quiet corner near the river, is a bustling little shack that churns out some of the city's best-loved sandwiches. Order a large fried-shrimp po'boy ($7), prepared by the hard-working staff, and sit at the bar, where a friendly old gent draws frosty mugs of draught Dixie. The roast beef is also highly recommended. All in all, it's a most gratifying experience. Cash only.

Dunbar's *(Map 6, #29; ☎ 899-0734; 4927 Freret St; meals $5-10; open 7am-9pm Mon-Sat)* is a clean and basic soul food joint in a sketchy part of town, several blocks from St Charles on the lakeside. A trip here will set you up with a mess of fried chicken and red beans and rice, plus a slab of cornbread. Folks also trek out here for the pork-chop plate and the oyster plate.

Frankie & Johnny's *(Map 6, #61; ☎ 899-9146; 321 Arabella St; starters $3-8, mains $4-14; open 11am-9pm daily)*, near the river, is a friendly neighborhood joint that really drives home the fact that you're in southern Louisiana. Come with a large group and expect to enjoy yourselves. In the spring, when crawfish are in season, order a platter of the boiled critters and a round of beers for your party before choosing from starters like alligator pie and turtle soup, and mains like fried fish.

SnoWizard Sno Ball Stand *(Map 6, #56; ☎ 899-8758; 4001 Magazine St; sno balls $1.50-3; open noon-8pm Sun-Fri, noon-7pm Sat)* is a corner take-out stand worth finding when you've overheated. A shaved-ice 'sno ball,' with 80 different flavors to choose from, will cool you off right away. Cash only.

Tee-Eva's Creole Soul Food *(Map 6, #52; ☎ 899-8350; 4430 Magazine St; snacks $1-3; open 11am-7pm daily)* is another take-out stand that serves snacks to cool you off or satiate a sweet tooth. Sno balls and pralines are the specialties. Owner Tee-Eva used to sing backup vocals in the late, great Ernie K-Doe's Burn K-Doe Burn Band.

Taqueria Corona *(Map 6, #45; ☎ 897-3974; 5932 Magazine St; mains $6-13; open 11:30am-2pm 5pm-9:30pm daily)* draws a regular crowd of students who appreciate inexpensive Mexican fare. A variety of meat and fish tacos prepared on soft, flour tortillas cost around $2 apiece, although it may require two to fill you up. A burrito makes a filling meal for around $6.

Mid-Range & Top End

Kyoto *(Map 6, #42; ☎ 891-3644; 4920 Prytania St; sushi $2-7, starters $4-8, mains $7-15;* open 11:30am-2pm & 5pm-10pm Mon-Fri, noon-10:30pm Sat)*, an undiscovered gem, is a pleasant little sushi bar. Try the spicy shrimp roll.

Pascal's Manale *(Map 6, #32; ☎ 895-4877; 1838 Napoleon Ave; mains $6-11; open 11:30am-10pm Mon-Fri, 4pm-10pm Sat, 4pm-9pm Sun; closed in summer)* is a lively old-time dining establishment (dating to 1913), with walls bedecked with black-and-white photos. Specialties are mostly traditional New Orleans seafood dishes and Italian standards. Pascal's signature dish, called 'barbecue shrimp,' is actually shelled jumbo prawns sautéed in a rich sauce made from butter, garlic and zesty spices. A platter for the table costs $18. The same shrimp can be had in sandwich form ($11) for lunch.

Reginelli's Pizzeria *(Map 6, #44; ☎ 899-1414; 741 State St; sandwiches $6-7, pizzas $10-15; open 11am-11pm Sun-Thur, 11am-midnight Fri & Sat)* is a suitable place for lunch if you've been checking out the Magazine St art galleries and antique shops. Pizzas and focaccia sandwiches get the contemporary treatment, with ingredients such as sundried tomatoes, goat and feta cheeses, artichokes and roasted walnuts making frequent appearances on the tables of this casual and upbeat place.

Upperline Restaurant *(Map 6, #43; ☎ 891-9822; 1413 Upperline St; starters $6-8.50, mains $19-25; open 5:30pm-9:30pm Wed-Sun)* is an excellent choice for contemporary Creole food in romantic surroundings. Owner JoAnn Clevenger enjoys playing the charming host, and makes each guest feel welcome. Start with shrimp *rémoulade* with Creole tomatoes, then have the grilled gulf fish and close out with a slice of delectable key lime pie.

RIVERBEND (MAP 6)

The Riverbend area should not be overlooked for its restaurants. There are some real standouts in this part of town.

Budget

Camellia Grill *(Map 6, #12; ☎ 866-9573; 626 S Carrollton Ave; meals $2-8; open 9am-1am Mon-Thur, 9am-3am Fri, 8am-3am Sat,*

PLACES TO EAT

8am-1am Sun) has enjoyed increasing popularity since it opened in 1946. Its secret? It refuses to change with the times. Well-made American short-order fare (the burgers and omelettes stand out) is served by some of the city's snazziest (in black bow ties) and most entertaining waiters. That this is the South, there is no doubt. The Camellia's fluffy omelettes and addictive pecan waffles have made regulars out of more than a few high-toned Uptowners – the sort of people you don't usually encounter in a diner. (Common folks are comfortable here, too.)

Cooter Brown's Tavern & Oyster Bar *(Map 6, #15; ☎ 866-9104; 509 S Carrollton Ave; sandwiches $4-8, mains $9-13; open 11am-midnight daily)* is a popular place to stop in for oysters on the half-shell and sandwiches (like delicate fried catfish) that generally exceed bar-food standards. While you're here, check out the 'Hall of Foam.' After 8pm, the place turns into a rowdy college hangout. (See the Entertainment chapter for details on Cooter's virtues as a bar.)

Figaro's Pizzerie *(Map 6, #14; ☎ 866-0100; 7900 Maple St; pizzas $6.50-18; open 11:30am-10pm Sun-Thur, 11:30am-11pm Fri & Sat)* has a covered deck, which is a pleasant place to spend a warm evening eating pizza and other Italian-American favorites. Pizza on soft, flavorful crust is the way to go here (the Neapolitan pizzas are particularly tasty) and a pitcher of Abita Amber will make things downright festive. Pasta dishes and specialties such as shrimp scampi ($13) are also available.

Mid-Range & Top End

Brigtsen's Restaurant *(Map 6, #10; ☎ 861-7610; 723 Dante St; mains $14-24; open 5:30pm-10pm Tues-Sat)*, despite all the critical acclaim that has been heaped upon chef Frank Brigtsen, remains a decidedly unpretentious place. Set in a converted double-shotgun building, the restaurant feels homey and inviting. Service is attentive but never oppressive. Brigtsen terms his cooking 'modern Louisiana cuisine,' and those in search of haute Cajun cuisine will not find a better restaurant in the city. Rabbit and duck are among his specialties. Look for the roast duck with dirty rice and honey-pecan gravy, or rabbit tenderloin on a *tasso* parmesan grits cake with Creole mustard sauce. Dinner will cost about $25 per person, not including wine.

Dante's Kitchen *(Map 6, #9; ☎ 861-3121; 736 Dante St; lunch $7-10, dinner starters $5-9, mains $12-21, Sun brunch $7-10; open 11:30am-2:30pm Tues-Sun, 6pm-10pm Tues-Sat)* is only a few paces from the Mississippi River levee, and its patio tables will qualify as front-row seating for the next catastrophic flood. What washes up may well inspire the creative chef. The imaginative food here is by turns basic and refined, and melds French, American and Louisiana traditions. Lunchtime sandwiches are works of art and reasonably priced, and dinner main courses often feature surprise ingredients (falafel-crusted fish, for instance). The Sunday brunch is tops.

Jacques-Imo's Café *(Map 6, #3; ☎ 861-0886; 8324 Oak St; mains $12-18; open 6pm-10pm Mon-Thur, 5:30pm-10:30pm Fri & Sat)* is just a few doors from the famous Maple Leaf Bar, and many people make an evening out of these two spots. Not that you need an excuse to dine at this superb Creole–soul food restaurant. Outward appearances give the impression that it's a dive, but once inside you're led through a kitchen bustling with all the industry of a steamship engine room, before being seated in a comfortable closed-in patio dining room. Chef Austin Leslie's fried chicken is legendary, and there's genuine creativity in the nightly specials, which might include fried trout smothered with jalapeños, pecans and shrimp. Save room for pie. Reservations are not accepted and lines are unavoidable.

Zachary's *(Map 6, #2; ☎ 865-1559; 8400 Oak St; lunch mains $7-13, dinner mains $11-20; open 11am-2:30pm Mon-Fri, 5pm-9:30pm Wed-Sat, 10am-2pm Sun)* preserves the environment that traditional Creole cuisine originally came from – home. Lunch and dinner are served in the capacious dining room of an old house, and people come to enjoy a superb gumbo and subtly seasoned blackened rainbow trout. The lunch menu includes expertly prepared staples like fried chicken and red beans. After dinner, you can walk just half a block to see Louisiana music at the Maple Leaf Bar.

ESPLANADE RIDGE (MAP 7)

Restaurants in the vicinity of the Fair Grounds naturally attract huge crowds for dinner during Jazz Fest. But several places out this way are worth coming to no matter what time of year it is – you can easily combine a meal along Esplanade Ave with a trip to City Park or a stroll along Bayou St John.

During Jazz Fest, many stands in the Fair Grounds purvey great food of all kinds.

Budget

Whole Foods Market *(Map 7, #16; ☎ 943-1626; 3135 Esplanade Ave; sandwiches $4-6; open 8am-9:30pm daily)*, probably the most popular source for a picnic lunch, has quality meats, fresh baked goods and salads. It's just a few blocks from here to City Park.

Liuzza's *(Map 7, #18; ☎ 943-8667; 1518 N Lopez St; sandwiches $3.50-7, mains $4.50-11; open 11am-8:30pm Mon-Fri, 11am-4:30pm Sat)*, a corner bar near the Fair Grounds, is a convenient stop on the way to Jazz Fest or the ponies. It's primarily a sandwich joint known for its oyster and garlic po'boys and meats roasted on the premises, but daily specials (red beans and rice, filet mignon, 'comfortable' pork chops, and the like) are always up to scratch.

Mid-Range & Top End

Café Degas *(Map 7, #17; ☎ 945-5635; 3127 Esplanade Ave; lunch mains $8-12; dinner starters $4-9, mains $10-20; open 11:30am-2:30pm Tues-Fri, 11:30am-3pm Sat, 10:30am-3pm Sun, 6pm-10pm nightly)* is a congenial and romantic little spot that warms the heart with first-rate French bistro fare. Diners are seated in a large enclosed deck featuring a fully grown tree thrusting through the floor and roof, and the casual atmosphere is accentuated by the mildly eccentric waitstaff. Savory meat dishes are Degas' forte, but you can also order a healthy lunch, such as salad niçoise with grilled tuna. Lamb shanks are cooked to perfection with a delicate but assertive Dijon sauce and, natch, are arranged beautifully on the plate.

Lola's *(Map 7, #14; ☎ 488-6946; 3312 Esplanade Ave; starters $4-7, mains $10-19, paellas $8-14; open 6pm-10pm nightly)* is an energetic and fun little place serving good, inexpensive Spanish food. Cool, soothing gazpacho ($3) is a smart way to start. Elaborate paellas and *fideuas* (an angel-hair pasta variation on the rice-based paella) are specialties here – they're feasts for the eyes as well as the stomach, and great for sharing. Fish, meats and stews are also good and reasonably priced. Lola's takes no reservations, and lines are almost inevitable. It's BYO, so get a bottle of wine at Whole Foods across the street, have it uncorked and make the most of the wait.

Gabrielle *(Map 7, #15; ☎ 948-6233; 3201 Esplanade Ave; fixed-priced lunch $17, dinner mains $18-32; open 11:30am-2pm Fri, 5:30pm-10pm Tues-Sat)* is a modest-looking spot where chef Greg Sonnier captures the attention of both locals and a national audience with his innovative Creole and Cajun dishes. Save room for dessert, as Greg's wife, Mary, creates outstanding pastries.

Restaurant Indigo *(Map 7, #21; ☎ 947-0123; 2285 Bayou Rd; starters $7-12, mains $18-31; open 11:30am-2:30pm Fri, 6pm-10pm Mon-Sun, 11am-2:30pm Sun)* is a beautiful restaurant in a wonderful setting, with windows opening up to a lush tropical garden. The contemporary regional cuisine is polished and expensive. Pan-roasted Chilean sea bass is served with sautéed crawfish, and the grits and grillades turns out to be macarpone grits and veal osso bucco. Most diners here agree that the space outshines the food.

MID-CITY (MAP 7)

Mid-City is known for its down-to-earth neighborhood eateries and, surprisingly, some of the best Vietnamese food in town. A number of good restaurants are within a block of the intersection of N Carrollton Ave and Canal St – convenient for Mid-City Carnival parade watchers and not so far out of the way if you're in town for Jazz Fest.

Budget

Angelo Brocato's *(Map 7, #26; ☎ 486-0078; 214 N Carrollton Ave; ice cream $2; open*

PLACES TO EAT

9:30am-10pm daily) is a New Orleans institution, a traditional family-run establishment that specializes in homemade ice
cream, Italian spumoni and pastries.

Betsy's Pancake House *(Map 7, #38;
☎ 822-0213; 2542 Canal St; breakfast $3-6,
lunch $3-9; open 5:30am-3pm Mon-Fri,
5:30am-2pm Sat & Sun)* is a sedate neighborhood spot where blue-collar locals chow
down hearty breakfasts and straightforward
lunch fare.

Mandina's Restaurant *(Map 7, #29;
☎ 482-9179; 3800 Canal St; starters $3.50-8,
sandwiches $4-7, mains $8-17; open 11am-
10:30pm Mon-Sat, noon-9pm Sun)* is a
bustling old-time Creole-Italian restaurant
where many local families prefer to dine.
Classics such as shrimp Creole are joined
by seafood, steaks and chops either broiled,
grilled or deep fried.

Mid-Range

Café Indo *(Map 7, #27; ☎ 488-0444; 216 N
Carrollton Ave; starters $5-10, mains $9-20;
open 6pm-9:30pm daily)* is a French-Asian
bistro where the inventive multicultural

cooking quickly earned a loyal following.
It's a slick, modern sort of place where diners can start with spring rolls and fried nutty
tempura-crusted oysters before digging into
pan-roasted ribeye served with sizzling
marrow butter.

Dooky Chase Restaurant *(Map 7, #31;
☎ 821-0600; 2301 Orleans Ave; mains $10-
25; open 11:30am-10pm Sun-Thur, 11:30am-
midnight Fri & Sat)*, opposite a downtrodden
housing project, is a historic gathering place
that has gained national renown on the
strength of chefs Leah and Dooky Chase
Jr's inspired Creole-soul cuisine. It has an
illustrious past, and Civil Rights activists
and touring jazz musicians (Duke Ellington,
Nat 'King' Cole – the list goes on) frequently gathered here. The main dining
room has all the atmosphere of a hotel conference room, but if you want to soak in the
historic vibe, request a table in the more
convivial original Gold Room. In the same
building, but through a different entrance,
Dooky's down-home take-out counter and
bar offers the same fried chicken and
gumbo at considerably lower prices.

PLACES TO EAT

Entertainment

You will be entertained in New Orleans. It doesn't matter what time of year it is, what your budget is, or how early you go to bed, because New Orleans keeps its carnival atmosphere stoked pretty much round-the-clock, year-round, and its nonstop music spills out of clubs and bars, hoping to draw passers-bys in for just one more drink.

Your best sources for upcoming performances and reviews are the free monthly entertainment guide *Offbeat* and the weekly *Gambit*. The *Times-Picayune* entertainment section, 'Lagniappe,' is published on Friday. Tune into radio station WWOZ (90.7 FM) for a round-the-clock education on southern Louisiana music, or call the station's events hotline, the **Second Line** (☎ 840-4040), for a daily listing of shows.

Large venues for concerts and plays tend to have their own box offices, where tickets can be purchased in advance. Additionally, **TicketMaster** (☎ 522-5555) has information on, and sells tickets to, just about any major event in the city. You can reserve tickets over the phone with a credit card and pick them up at the venue or at a TicketMaster outlet including **Tower Records** (*Map 2, #138; ☎ 529-4411; 408 N Peters St*) in the Quarter.

BARS & CLUBS
French Quarter (Map 2)
Live Music A humble joint, which happens to be the premier brass-band club in the city, is **Donna's Bar & Grill** (*Map 2, #20; ☎ 596-6914; 800 N Rampart St*). All the best local brass musicians are booked here, and when they aren't on the bill they drop in to jam. Artists stretch out and the music tends to be jazzier than the funkier, more raucous sounds that accompany your average parade, but things tend to really get cooking nonetheless. There's always a diverse crowd on hand, and on some nights free barbecue is served.

El Matador (*Map 2, #14; ☎ 569-8361; 504 Esplanade Ave; admission free-$5; open 9pm-late Tues & Wed, 5pm-late Thur-Mon*), a cornerstone of the hip and edgy lower Decatur

Real Live Musicians

When in New Orleans, try to catch some of the following musicians in action:

Astral Project An all-star modern jazz combo.

John Boutte An entertaining R&B singer known for his forays into honky-tonk country.

Henry Butler A versatile powerhouse on the piano.

Davell Crawford An R&B pianist in the New Orleans tradition.

Joe Krown A groovy Hammond B3 organ impresario.

Los Hombres Calientes A hot Latin jazz ensemble, starring young trumpeter Irvin Mayfield and veteran percussionist Bill Summers.

Shannon Powell A smart jazz drummer who presides some of the city's best jazz jams.

Rebirth Brass Band A funky brass band with a contemporary street edge.

Herlin Reilley A snazzy trap-drummer who makes it look so easy.

Kermit Ruffins A cool trumpet-playing showman who fronts some of the city's best jam sessions at Vaughan's.

Tremé Brass Band A traditional second-line brass band starring Lionel Batiste on the big bass drum.

St scene, is a large, coolly stylized bar with a high stage. The nightly music bill varies, with Django-inspired swing taking turns with neo-rockabilly and 'Nawlins' R&B, and the acts generally fall into the 'undiscovered talent' category. Happy-hour shows get things rolling early some nights, and the always fashionable young crowd is usually willing to loosen its collective collar once the grooves and high-octane cocktails take effect.

Funky Butt on Congo Square (*Map 2, #49; ☎ 558-0872; 225 N Rampart St; admission $5-15; open 8pm-3am nightly*) is a swanky place with a sexy, Jazz Age atmosphere. There's

ENTERTAINMENT

almost always something interesting going on here, usually modern jazz, although on occasion a Mardi Gras Indian gang will set the Butt on fire. The Funky Butt isn't a particularly old establishment, but in name it claims a little piece of New Orleans history. Owner Richard Rochester says the late guitarist Danny Barker suggested that he name his club in honor of Buddy Bolden's raunchy 'Funky Butt' theme song. During Bolden's reign as the cornet king of New Orleans, the song lent its name to a hall where Bolden often played. Appropriately, the current Funky Butt stands opposite Congo Square, the throbbing heart of African culture during the mid-19th century.

House of Blues (HoB; Map 2, #156; ☎ 529-2583; 255 Decatur St; tickets $7-25; open 8pm-2am nightly; gospel brunch 9:30am-4pm Sun) caused some locals to grumble when Dan Akroyd and a pack of out-of-town investors opened it, but the full calendar of headliner acts (from the hottest local talent to major touring bands) and the congenial space quickly won people over. There's no denying that HoB is one of the best live-music venues in the city for rock, alt-rock and alt-country. After hours the club turns into a popular disco. On Sunday morning, HoB's Gospel Brunch will fortify your soul. A few doors up, HoB's small auxiliary club, **The Parish** (Map 2, #155; ☎ 529-2583; 229 Decatur St), features mostly local acts.

Margaritaville Café (Map 2, #45; ☎ 592-2560; 1104 Decatur St; admission free; open 11am-midnight daily) is Jimmy Buffett's club and banks primarily on its owner's cheesy 'Parrothead' appeal. If you can stand that, you'll appreciate the club's policy of booking as many as three shows daily (usually blues or R&B) and not charging a cover.

Palm Court Jazz Café (Map 2, #35; ☎ 525-0200; 1204 Decatur St; admission $5; open 7pm-11pm Wed-Sun), traditional jazz fans will want to know, is a noteworthy alternative to Preservation Hall. It lacks the rustic patina of Preservation Hall, but it is roomier and has a bar and a full menu, and guests can expect chairs and a table. Palm Court has an excellent music calendar, too, with a regular lineup of local legends. Shows start at 8pm.

Preservation Hall (Map 2, #78; ☎ 522-2841; 726 St Peter St; admission $5; open 8pm-midnight nightly) always pleases large crowds (mostly tourists) with traditional jazz in a picturesque, historic setting. The white-haired grandpas who raise the roof here every night are clearly jazzed by what they're doing, and fans cram into the worn-out hall and sit on the floor to watch 'em play 'When the Saints Go Marching In' and other classics. Barbara Reid and Grayson 'Ken' Mills formed the Society for the Preservation of New Orleans Jazz in 1961, at a time when Louis Armstrong's generation was already getting on in years. When it's warm enough to leave the window shutters open, you can join the crowd on the sidewalk to listen to the sets. Get in line early. No booze or snacks are served in the club.

Shim Sham Club (Map 2, #107; ☎ 299-0666; 615 Toulouse St; admission $5-15; open 2pm-6am daily) is a devilishly hip retro nightclub that seems in denial of its location in the heart of the tourist zone. Headliner punk, post-punk, rockabilly and rock and roll legends perform several nights a week. (A recent week featured Mike Watt, the post-Jello Dead Kennedys, and white-trash thrasher Hasil Adkins on different nights.) DJ's fill out the weekly agenda. Every Sunday night, Shim Sham also has its own Shim Sham Revue, a strip-tease-o-rama straight outta Betty Page's book.

Bars One fine local dive, **The Abbey** (Map 2, #42; ☎ 523-7150; 1123 Decatur St; open 24 hrs) is a cut above the numerous grungy taverns that predominate on lower Decatur. The jukebox is a kick in the pants, the regulars are an interesting mix of eternally transient hipsters and down-at-heels locals, and some of the female bartenders are wickedly quick-witted. Getting stewed in such colorfully run-down environs just seems like a very New Orleans thing to do.

The Hideout (Map 2, #31; ☎ 529-7119; 1207 Decatur St; open 24 hrs) is notorious for the brawls that spill out onto the sidewalk from time to time. Legend has it Marilyn Manson was beat up here, and Shane MacGowan supposedly lost a few teeth out

Bourbon Street's Blathering Boozeoisie

You don't need a guidebook to tell you about Bourbon St, the main stem of New Orleans' round-the-clock tourist bacchanalia. The street's reputation as a haven of delirium precedes itself. Most tourists end up on Bourbon St, and some never seem to find their way out.

Bourbon St is undeniably unique. Where else in America can you find eight historic blocks closed to traffic so tourists and conventioneers can get loaded, spill beer on each other, flash their breasts from cast-iron balconies, yell their heads off, leave trash all over the place and even vomit on the buildings?

New Orleans relies on the tourist dollar, and judging by the nightly scene on Bourbon St, the city effortlessly succeeds in showing visitors a good time. It isn't a bad arrangement between the city and the tourists who are hell-bent on waking up with a major hangover. To New Orleans' credit, Bourbon St has a certain 'Big Easy' panache that's rare among tourist traps. But if you're looking for genuine local color, Bourbon St will only disappoint. Locals rarely go to Bourbon St unless they're regulars at Galatoire's or have jobs in its bars and shops.

front. (Probably the number of bars in the world making a similar claim outnumber the teeth McGowan originally had.) It's always dark, rarely inviting, and on many an evening the drunk bikers and runaway punks nodding off at the bar leave little room for feisty fighters. Still, visitors can't be blamed for taking an interest in the place.

Jean Lafitte's Old Absinthe House *(Map 2, #141; ☎ 523-3181; 240 Bourbon St; open 10am-4am)* is one of many bars in New Orleans that served absinthe, the notorious wormwood potion, until it was outlawed in 1914. At the beginning of the 20th century many Western governments concluded that absinthe destroyed the central nervous system and drove its enthusiasts mad, and while that hasn't been scientifically proven, it hasn't been disproved either. (Today, Pernod is a relatively safe, 90-proof stand-in for absinthe-based drinks.) This is a historic spot, having opened in 1807, but the crowd is generally of the bottom-shelf Bourbon St variety.

Kerry Irish Pub *(Map 2, #154; ☎ 527-5954; 331 Decatur St; open 2pm-4am daily)* attracts a local crowd with pool, darts and Guinness. (It should be mentioned, however, that New Orleans' climate is a poor complement for Guinness.) At night, live folk and acoustic shows, often starring up-and-coming talent, draw large crowds (no cover charge, but there's a one-drink minimum).

Lafitte's Blacksmith Shop *(Map 2, #24; ☎ 523-0066; 941 Bourbon St; admission free; open noon-late daily)* is an atmospheric haunt, lit entirely by tabletop candles, that has a back-room piano bar. If you're in a particular mood, hearing tourists sing along to Fats Domino and Otis Redding tunes can be entertaining. Local lore maintains that Jean Lafitte and his brother Pierre, New Orleans' legendary pirates, ran a blacksmith shop in the building as a cover for their illegal trade in slaves, but historians don't buy it.

Molly's at the Market *(Map 2, #44; ☎ 525-5169; 1107 Decatur St; open 10am-6am daily)* is the unofficial Irish cultural center of the French Quarter. Owner Jim Monaghan inaugurated the wild St Patrick's Day Parade that starts at Molly's. Molly's is not strictly for the shamrock crowd though, and a diverse mix of locals and tourists congregate here. Pub food is served in the back courtyard.

Napoleon House *(Map 2, #124; ☎ 524-9752; 500 Chartres St; open 11am-midnight Tues-Thur, 11am-1am Fri & Sat, 11am-7pm Sun)* is another ancient bar, having opened its doors in 1797. It's a particularly attractive example of what Walker Percy termed 'vital decay.' By all appearances, its stuccoed walls haven't received so much as a dab of paint in over two centuries, and the diffuse glow pouring through the open doors and windows in the afternoon draws out the room's gorgeous patina. The back courtyard is also pleasant, day or night. Locals and tourists agree that this is one happening place for cocktails and a quick bite to eat, but would Napoleon himself

ENTERTAINMENT

have appreciated these surroundings? When the deposed emperor was banished to St Helena, a band of loyal New Orleanians, including former mayor Nicholas Girod and the pirate Jean Lafitte, reputedly plotted to snatch him and set him up in this building's 3rd-floor digs. But Napoleon died before the alleged plan was carried out.

Pat O'Brien's *(Map 2, #79; ☎ 525-4823, 800-597-4823; 718 St Peter St; open 10am-4am daily)* is where a labyrinth series of alcoves links Bourbon St and St Peter St with a grand courtyard patio lit by flaming fountains. You haven't completed the tourist rounds until you've had a Hurricane or mint julep at Pat O'Brien's. You can join trendy, young professionals who cruise the scene at this continuous party, and then buy bar souvenirs at the gift shop. Needless to say, Pat O'Brien's has its cynical detractors. 'Have Fun!' is a registered trademark owned by the bar, as is the Hurricane, a 29oz concoction of rum, orange juice, pineapple juice and grenadine ($6 plus $3 refundable deposit on the souvenir glass). Don't forget to get your deposit before you leave, unless you want to keep the glass as a souvenir.

Rawhide 2010 *(Map 2, #50; ☎ 525-8106; 740 Burgundy St; open 24 hrs)* is – surprise! – a gay leather bar.

Dance Clubs In New Orleans it is permissible to shake your booty pretty much anywhere, any time, but the Crescent City completely lacks a cosmopolitan Euro-trash club scene.

Gay bars are the primary destinations for club-hoppers looking for a rug to cut. Foremost are the twin sentinels of pulsing sounds: **Oz** *(Map 2, #62; ☎ 593-9491; 800 Bourbon St; admission free-$5; open 24 hrs)* and **Bourbon Pub and Parade Disco** *(Map 2, #61; ☎ 529-2107; 801 Bourbon St; admission $2-5; open 24 hrs)*. Both are open to straights who want to dance nonstop and don't have a problem mingling with guys in G-strings.

House of Blues *(Map 2, #156; ☎ 529-2583; 255 Decatur St; admission $5; club open 2am-dawn Mon & Thur-Sat)* turns into New Orleans' largest dance club after the nightly music shows end (see Live Music, earlier).

Tremé District (Map 2)

The Tremé, the historic black neighborhood on the other side of Rampart St from the French Quarter, has always had great little bars where musicians love to perform. Visitors venturing this way after dark should take the usual inner-city precautions.

Cocktail Cockamamie

It should come as no surprise that New Orleans claims to have invented the whole concept of having a drink for the hell of it – that is, having a cocktail. As always, the Crescent City backs up the claim with a good story that may well explain the origin of the word 'cocktail'.

It all begins with a man named Peychaud, who settled in New Orleans after fleeing the 18th-century slave uprisings in Hispaniola. He opened an apothecary on Royal St, where, we are told, he developed a penchant for drinking brandy in an eggcup. The concept appealed to the people of New Orleans, and Peychaud began serving drinks in this fashion at his shop. (One might wonder why people were so willing to drink from an eggcup, but read on....)

The eggcup, of course, was not called an eggcup in French-speaking New Orleans. It was called a *coquetier*; well it was called that until Peychaud's inebriated patrons began mispronouncing it. The term evolved – much as the word Acadian turned into Cajun – from 'coquetier' to 'cock-tay' to 'cocktail'. In time, the eggcup was disposed of in favor of a regular glass, and other liquors came to be more popular than brandy, but the name stuck.

On another booze-related historical note: in the mid-19th century, a French brandy manufacturer, Sazerac-du-Forge, lent its name to a brandy cocktail, called the Sazerac, that evolved into an absinthe-based drink, which eventually featured whiskey instead of brandy. And today, the Sazerac cocktail includes no absinthe, either, because too many 19th-century enthusiasts of the wormwood-based liquor went out of their minds, and the beverage was outlawed in many countries, including the US. You can still order a Sazerac in just about any New Orleans bar, but don't expect great things from the syrupy beverage.

Joe's Cozy Corner *(Map 2, #4;* ☎ *581-4676; 1030 N Robertson St)* has a regular show on Sunday night, featuring Kermit Ruffins and the Rebirth Brass Band. The small neighborhood hang-out gets extremely crowded, with a mix of older folks, slick inner-city operators and, of late, a greater number of Uptown college students who cab to the Tremé. Because this is a neighborhood gig, musicians from around town are always likely to drop by and sit in.

Ernie K-Doe Mother-In-Law Lounge *(*☎ *947-1078; 1500 N Claiborne Ave; open 5pm-2am daily)* was opened by R&B recording artist Ernie K-Doe just a few years before his death in 2001. K-Doe's widow, Antoinette, keeps the bar open as a homage to her late, great husband, and fans of the eccentric singer still flock here to listen to K-Doe's hits on the jukebox.

Faubourg Marigny & Bywater (Map 3)

Blue Nile *(Map 3, #29;* ☎ *948-2583; 534 Frenchmen St; admission free; open 6pm-4am nightly)* has a certain bluesy charm, despite its poor acoustics. Nightly shows feature local talent, mostly with a blues bent, and drinks are reasonably priced.

Café Brasil *(Map 3, #30;* ☎ *947-9386; 2100 Chartres St; admission $5; open 6pm-2am Sun-Thur, 6pm-4am Fri & Sat)* is a hip, bohemian space with a colorful Caribbean vibe. The club often features the city's best Latin jazz and brass artists. When there's no live music, the space seems too expansive for the smattering of locals sitting at the bar, but this sort of minimalism also has its appeal.

d.b.a. *(Map 3, #19;* ☎ *942-3731; 618 Frenchmen St; admission free; open 5pm-4am daily)* is one of New Orleans' most sophisticated bars, with an impressive selection of international beers and live music on most nights. Hip, young professionals (who don't think of themselves as young professionals) predominate, and drink prices are high, but by virtue of strong entertainment bookings and no cover charge this is one of the neighborhood's top fun spots.

Hi-Ho Lounge *(Map 3, #1;* ☎ *947-9344; 2239 St Claude Ave)* is a friendly, bohemian

dive that in some ways verges on cliche – fire-sale furniture, cheap booze and a barrage of young eccentrics donning outlandish outfits. It is sort of like a slow-moving caboose carrying the would-be avant-garde. The club does have an interesting musical calendar, however, offering a steady diet of convention-defying artists.

Igor's Checkpoint Charlie *(Map 3, #32;* ☎ *947-0979; 501 Esplanade Ave; admission free; open 24 hrs)* is a grungy bar where you can order greasy grill food, do laundry, shoot a game of pool and hear live music. Don't expect to see any headliners among the loud rock and R&B groups that perform here.

R Bar *(Map 3, #14;* ☎ *948-7499; 1431 Royal St; admission free; open 3pm-late daily)* is an idiosyncratic local with a pool table and a good jukebox. The decor tries a bit too hard, but the real attraction is the mixed gay and straight crowd that never seems to lose the Mardi Gras spirit.

Saturn Bar *(Map 3, #3;* ☎ *949-7532; 3067 St Claude Ave; admission free; open 3pm-midnight daily)* is indeed saturnine. It feels more like a junk store than a bar, and the back room appears a bit creaky. (Be careful not to bump into that old Frigidaire on your way in.) Light comes only from two cosmic neon lamps (a surreal touch) and there does not seem to be a comfortable seat in the place. The mummy hanging from the ceiling looks like somebody actually dug it up – and some of the grouchy characters who spend time here look like they might have done it. Late at night, hipsters are drawn to the Saturn, but they haven't quite succeeded in colonizing it. All in all, a great bar.

Snug Harbor *(Map 3, #17;* ☎ *949-0696; 626 Frenchmen St; admission $5-25; open 5pm-3am daily)*, New Orleans' premier contemporary jazz venue, regularly books headliner talent. There really isn't a bad seat in the place, upstairs or down, and the room's acoustics are unparalleled in town. Performers who regularly appear here include pianist Ellis Marsalis and R&B singer Charmaine Neville. The main floor serves as a restaurant with a menu featuring burgers and steaks.

Spotted Cat *(Map 3, #16;* ☎ *943-3887; 623 Frenchmen St; admission free; open 4pm-late* *daily*) manages to squeeze bands into its friendly little space every night. Shows often start early here (6pm or 8pm), making this a convenient link between dinner and visiting the clubs on Frenchmen St.

Vaughan's *(Map 3, #26; ☎ 947-5562; 800 Lesseps St; admission $7-10; open 11am-3am daily, shows at 11pm Thur)*, on Thursday night, is as good as New Orleans gets. That's the night trumpeter Kermit Ruffins raises the roof here. The weekly gig regularly features Ruffins' band, the Barbecue Swingers, and drummer Shannon Powell, who is an amazing performer. Anyone might show up to sit in – Wynton Marsalis has dropped by, and when pianist Henry Butler shows up, the bar's poor little upright piano darn near explodes. The crowds spill out onto the street, and between sets Kerm often dishes out barbecue from the smoker on the back of his pickup truck. The rest of the week, Vaughan's quietly serves the neighborhood well.

CBD & Warehouse District (Map 4)

Circle Bar *(Map 4, #71; ☎ 588-2616; 1032 St Charles Ave; admission free; open 4pm-late daily, shows at 11pm)*, right on Lee Circle, is a stylish, dimly lit tavern with small rooms which are suitable for an intimate party. Young professionals gather here for cocktails and live jazz.

Howlin' Wolf *(Map 4, #60; ☎ 522-9653; 828 S Peters St; admission $5-15; open 3am-late Mon-Fri)* is one of New Orleans' best live-music venues. Blues are naturally part of the tradition, but touring rock bands and a wide range of local acts also appear at this first-rate club. This is where alternative artists such as Cracker and Frank Black might perform when in town. Local funk bassist George Porter Jr also makes frequent appearances.

Le Chat Noir *(Map 4, #48; ☎ 581-5812; 715 St Charles Ave; admission free-$20; open 4pm-2am Tues-Sat, shows at 8pm)* is a smartly accoutred bar and cabaret, where the beverage of choice is the martini and the entertainment ranges from Edith Piaf reincarnations to comic monologists. Central Business District (CBD) office workers

prevail during 'happy hour' (4pm to 8pm), and a well-heeled mature audience turns out for the evening shows.

New Orleans is not Cajun Country, but the city does have a pair of Cajun supper clubs that don't quite live up to the real thing: **Michaul's** *(Map 4, #55; ☎ 522-5517; 840 St Charles Ave; admission free; open 6pm-late Mon-Sat)* and **Mulate's** *(Map 4, #53; ☎ 767-4794; 201 Julia St; admission free; open 6pm-late daily)*. Both of these places offer the *fais-do-do* (a Cajun house dance) experience, with complete meals, a dance floor and live Cajun music, and both rely strictly on the tourist trade. If given the choice, go with Mulate's.

Pete Fountain's *(Map 4, #42; ☎ 523-4374; 2 Poydras St; irregular hours)*, in the Hilton Riverside Hotel, features the famed clarinetist whenever he's in town (call for show times). Fountain has become one of the city's musical elder statesmen, although he was never regarded as a particularly significant musician. He first made his mark nationally as a performer on the Lawrence Welk show in the late 1950s, and for many years he operated a more famous club on Bourbon St.

Vic's Kangaroo Café *(Map 4, #46; ☎ 524-4329; 636 Tchoupitoulas St; admission free; open 11:30am-4am daily)* is among the most popular after-work spots, where Australian hospitality, hearty beers on tap and cheap food attract a sizable crowd to the bar's narrow confines. Local blues bands play several nights a week.

Lower Garden & Garden Districts (Map 5)

Balcony Bar & Café *(Map 5, #46; ☎ 895-1600; 3201 Magazine St; admission free; open 5pm-late daily)* is a low-key neighborhood spot with two levels and a balcony overlooking Magazine St.

The Bulldog *(Map 5, #49; ☎ 891-1516; 3236 Magazine St; admission free; open noon-2am daily)* entices beer aficionados, particularly those of the post-college set, with a wide array of import and domestic microbrews on draft and in bottles.

Half Moon *(Map 5, #27; ☎ 522-7313; 1125 St Mary St; admission free; open 11am-4am*

ENTERTAINMENT

The imposing St Louis Cathedral (top) is the very heart of the French Quarter. New Orleans' architecture, with its lacy details and colorful facades, is a myriad of styles (bottom left & right).

RICHARD CUMMINS

RICHARD CUMMINS

JERRY ALEXANDER

New Orleans has strong culinary traditions. Whether you're nibbling on a beignet and sipping a café au lait (top left), digging your chops into a po'boy (top right) or chowing down on fresh crabs (bottom), eating in this town is serious business.

daily) is where Uptown bar-hopping trend-setters typically drop in, but you might stay and play at the best pool tables in the area.

Igor's Lounge *(Map 5, #15; ☎ 522-2145; 2133 St Charles Ave; admission free; open 24 hrs)* is a good old joint, with a greasy grill, pool tables and washing machines. This is the best of the Igor's chain scattered round town, and its constant rotation of characters makes it a good place to end up if you're staying nearby.

Red Room *(Map 5, #17; ☎ 528-9759; 2040 St Charles Ave; admission free; open 5pm-2am Mon-Sat)*, in a scrap-heap removed from the Eiffel Tower, certainly stands out. (Local detractors refer to it as the 'Awful Tower;' the restaurant was actually part of the Eiffel Tower before it was dismantled and sold to the highest bidder.) Inside, it's a swank supper club with a decidedly upscale take on the swing era. Dinner and drinks are expensive, and the clientele is well heeled, but people come here to cut a rug and have a good time. Late at night a DJ draws a younger crowd.

Uptown (Map 6)

Columns Hotel *(Map 6, #38; ☎ 899-9308; 3811 St Charles Ave; admission free; open 3pm-midnight Mon-Thur, 3pm-2am Fri, 11am-2am Sat, 11am-midnight Sun)* provides Uptown society with its most dignified drinking environs in its Victorian Lounge and on its broad front porch. It's a see-and-be-seen locus for local professionals, and suits and gowns abound. Ordinary out-of-town folk won't feel unwelcome, although men might want to don a jacket. Over the clinking glasses filled with gin fizzes, the murmur of the crowd grows louder as the night goes on.

Le Bon Temps Roulé *(Map 6, #49; ☎ 895-8117; 4801 Magazine St; admission free; 11am-3am daily)* is a neighborhood bar – a very good one at that – with a mostly college and post-college crowd drawn by two pool tables and a commendable beer selection. Late at night, high-caliber blues, zydeco or jazz rocks the joint's little back room. Any time you can catch an extraordinary talent like Henry Butler in such close quarters, don't miss it.

Neutral Ground Coffee House *(Map 6, #31; ☎ 891-3381; 5110 Danneel St; admission free; open 7pm-1am Tues-Sun)* is a non-profit organization dedicated to keeping live folk music alive. Acoustic performers of just about every genre regularly play here. Most nights showcase three or more performers, and a few nights each month are reserved for nonsmokers.

Tipitina's *(Map 6, #64; ☎ 895-8477, concert line ☎ 897-3943; 501 Napoleon Ave; admission $8-20; open 5pm-late daily)* is the legendary nightclub, where in the 1970s the Neville Brothers and the Meters regularly rocked the city till dawn. 'Tips,' as locals refer to it, remains a mecca and a shrine to the great Professor Longhair, whose 1953 hit 'Tipitina' inspired the club's name. With the emergence of several newer medium-sized venues in the Quarter, Tips no longer stands head and shoulders above the competition, but outstanding music from the local talent pool still packs 'em in year-round. The joint really jumps in the weeks prior to Mardi Gras and during Jazz Fest, when Dr John and a bevy of Fess-inspired piano players takes over.

Riverbend (Map 6)

Maple Leaf Bar *(Map 6, #4; ☎ 866-9359; 8316 Oak St; admission $5-10; open 3pm-4am daily)* is the prime nighttime destination in the Riverbend area. It has a solid musical calendar, and its dimly lit, pressed-tin caverns are the kind of environs you'd expect from a New Orleans juke joint. Scenes from the film *Angel Heart*, in which the late, great blues man Brownie McGhee starred, were shot here. You can regularly catch performances by local stars such as Walter 'Wolfman' Washington, Rockin' Dopsie Jr and the Zydeco Twisters, and the Rebirth Brass Band. Slide guitarist John Mooney also plays here often, and on Monday night (when there's no cover charge) a traditional piano player sets the tone. You can choose to work up a sweat on the small dance floor directly in front of the stage or to relax at the bar in the next room. There's also a nice back patio in which to cool your heels. The crowd is a healthy mix of college students, tourists and music lovers of all stripes.

ENTERTAINMENT

Rounding out the Riverbend area club-hopping scene are two clubs on Willow St that feature live dance music and a young party atmosphere: **Carrollton Station** *(Map 6, #6; ☎ 865-9190; 8140 Willow St; admission $5-10; open 3pm-3am daily)* and **Jimmy's** *(Map 6, #5; ☎ 861-8200; 8200 Willow St; admission free-$15; open 8pm-3am Tues-Sat)*.

Cooter Brown's Tavern & Oyster Bar *(Map 6, #15; ☎ 866-9104; 509 S Carrollton Ave; admission free; open 11am-late daily)*, near St Charles Ave, is an Uptown local that takes its beer seriously, serving over 40 draft brews and hundreds of international bottled brews. What really makes this place unique in its love of suds is its 'Beersoleum & Hall of Foam' – a gallery of 100 plaster bas-relief statuettes of everybody from Liberace to Chairman Mao, each holding a bottle of beer (Albert Einstein, Mother Theresa and Andy Warhol also appear). This curious, still-growing exhibit is the work of the uniquely talented Scott Connery, a former New Orleanian who now sends additions for the gallery from his Las Vegas home.

Rivershack Tavern *(Off Map 6; ☎ 834-4938; 3449 River Rd; admission free; open 11am-midnight Mon-Thur, 11am-3am Fri & Sat)*, in Jefferson, upstream from Riverbend beside the levee, is an advertisement-adorned roadhouse, which probably hit its prime in the 1940s. The old hand-painted signs were discovered when the asbestos shingles were removed. It's packed with students and older bikers and has a good selection of beers on tap. If you're hungry, the lunch specials are pretty good. Don't miss the clever legs on the bar stools.

Mid-City (Map 7)

Mid-City Rock & Bowl *(Map 7, #32; ☎ 482-3133; 4133 S Carrollton Ave; admission $5-10; open noon-2am daily, shows usually at 10pm)* is one of the more incredible music venues in town. What we have here is the unlikely marriage of live music and a bustling bowling alley. The clincher is that owner John Blancher consistently books quality artists from around southern Louisiana. Two-stepping to the sounds of a hot zydeco ensemble accompanied by the crash of bowling pins is an unreal experience. (Other musical styles include rockabilly, R&B and blues.) Add to this a perky teenage bar staff and unusual side acts (lip-synching black Elvis impersonators, anyone?), and you begin to get the idea that Blancher (who *looks* fairly normal) is a genius of the absurd. He claims he was on the road to visit a religious shrine when he had an epiphany to buy the bowling alley. With two stages (upstairs and down) and a cast of musical characters you'd never expect to see in this type of setting, Rock & Bowl is not to be missed.

Lion's Den *(Map 7, #41; ☎ 821-3745; 544 S Broad St, shows at 10pm)* is a neighborhood bar on the ragged edge of the CBD that generally goes unnoticed. During Jazz Fest the place draws outsiders by the cab load by booking Irma Thomas, the 'Soul Queen' of New Orleans, for several nights running. Seeing Irma sing here before friends and devoted fans is an intimate, unforgettable experience. Call for show times and this year's cover price. Enter off the club's Gravier St parking lot.

Dixie Taverne *(Map 7, #35; ☎ 822-8268; 3340 Canal St; admission free; open 4pm-2am daily)* is where backpacking lodgers from the India House Hostel congregate.

ARENAS & AUDITORIUMS

Entertainment in New Orleans is meant to be an intimate experience, where shows are enhanced by interaction between the performers and the audience. Large venues such as basketball arenas are not conducive to such an experience, but some touring performers and shows passing through town are just too big for small nightclubs and theaters. Hence, New Orleans, like everywhere else, offers regular stadium rock concerts, traveling Broadway shows and other major entertainment extravaganzas.

University of New Orleans (UNO) Kiefer Lakefront Arena *(Map 1; information ☎ 286-7222)* seats 6000 in its basketball-arena grandstand. Touring headliners such as Bob Dylan and Paul Simon play here when they pass through town.

Louisiana Superdome *(Map 4; ☎ 587-3810; Sugar Bowl Dr)*, built with football games in mind, is where stadium-rock acts like the Rolling Stones play; it's also home to the annual Essence Festival.

Mahalia Jackson Theater (Map 2; ☎ 565-7470), in Louis Armstrong Park, hosts a variety of events, particularly during the holiday season. The theater was dedicated to the powerful, late gospel singer, who was born in New Orleans in 1911 and moved to Chicago in 1927, where her career blossomed.

New Orleans Arena (Map 4; tickets ☎ 58/3824, information ☎ 846-5959; 1500 Poydras St) was built for the local hockey team, and is frequently used for larger-than-life touring rock shows.

Saenger Theatre (Map 2, #111; box office ☎ 524-2490; 143 N Rampart St) is the most intimate of New Orleans' large concert venues. It was built with performing arts rather than professional sports in mind, so the sound quality is superior as well. Still, it is a voluminous space, and the cheapest, highest seats seem clouds away from the stage.

THEATER

New Orleans has a strong theatrical bent. The city has numerous local theater companies, and a few large theatrical venues for touring productions.

Contemporary Arts Center (Map 4, #64; ☎ 523-1216; W www.cacno.org; 900 Camp St), in the Warehouse District, stages some of New Orleans' most cutting-edge and interesting performances.

Le Petit Théâtre du Vieux Carré (Map 2, #109; ☎ 522-2081; 616 St Peter St), just off Jackson Square in the French Quarter, is one of the oldest theater groups in the US. The troupe offers an interesting repertory, with a proclivity for Southern dramas, as well as special children's programming.

Saenger Theatre (Map 2, #111; ☎ 524-2490; 143 N Rampart St) is New Orleans' premier site for major touring troupes. It's worth the admission just to see the ornate interior of this fine 1927 theater.

Southern Repertory Theater (Map 2, #15; ☎ 861-8163; 333 Canal Place, 3rd floor), founded in 1986, performs classically Southern plays that deal with relationships, crisis and humor in an intimate 150-seat theater.

True Brew Theater (Map 4, #59; ☎ 524-8440; 200 Julia St), in the Warehouse District, is an added feature of the popular coffee shop. The group performs seasonal classics such as Dickens' *Christmas Carol* along with original works, which typically explore local themes with a sharp satirical sensibility.

Student plays are frequently performed at the **UNO Performing Arts Center** (☎ 286-7469) and Tulane University's **Lupin Theatre** (Map 6, #19; ☎ 865-5105).

CLASSICAL MUSIC

New Orleans' concert-goers are very proud of the **Louisiana Philharmonic Orchestra** (Map 4, #11; ☎ 523-6530; W www.lpomusic.com; box office 305 Baronne St, 6th floor; tickets $11-36), led by music director Klauspeter Seibel. When the New Orleans Symphony financially collapsed in 1990, the musicians invested their own money to create one of only two musician-owned symphonies in the world. From September through May, the symphony performs at the richly ornamented **Orpheum Theater** (Map 4, #7; 129 University Place), downtown.

CINEMAS

Canal Place Cinemas (Map 2; ☎ 581-5400; 333 Canal St, 3rd floor) is New Orleans' best all-around multiplex in a convenient downtown location. The cinema features first-run art and mainstream movies.

Entergy IMAX Theater (Map 2, #163; ☎ 581-4629; Canal St; adult/child $6.50/4.50) is part of the Audubon Institute complex at the foot of Canal St. IMAX stands for 'image maximum,' and its films are shown on a 74ft by 54ft screen. It's all about the size of the image, and indeed cinematography at this scale can be very impressive. Films such as *The Living Sea* and *Antarctica* are guaranteed to capture your attention. Shows begin on the hour between 10am and 8pm.

Movie Pitchers (Map 7, #28; ☎ 488-8881; 3941 Bienville Ave) in Mid-City, runs an eclectic programme of films that wouldn't otherwise get exposure in New Orleans.

Prytania Theatre (Map 6, #41; ☎ 891-2787; 5339 Prytania St) is an old movie hous (since the 1920s) that screens independent and art films.

FREE & OUTDOOR EVENTS

'Free' events often have a catch. Having a good time at such a thing usually requires filling your gullet with overpriced vittles and beer. The joy of it is that the cost of the entertainment depends mostly on how hungry and thirsty you are.

If your travel plans include Mardi Gras, you're in for beaucoup free and outdoor entertainment. See the special section 'Mardi Gras' for more details. Of course, you pay for it all when you shell out for your exorbitant hotel bill.

For the annual French Quarter Festival, in early April (see Public Holidays & Special Events in the Facts for the Visitor chapter), the city sets up stages in Jackson Square and Woldenberg Park and books artists for three days of all-day live music. The entertainment is entirely free.

Many of New Orleans' nightclubs (see listings earlier in this chapter) feature free indoor entertainment nightly. The logic behind this, of course, is that the club will cover its losses in booze sales. Sound logic. Once inside one of these places, it is indeed difficult to lay off the liquor, and very quickly what started out as an enticingly good deal turns out to be an expensive night out.

New Orleans Jazz National Historic Park
(Map 2, #46; ☎ 877-520-0677; 916 N Peters St; admission free; open 9am-5pm daily) puts on free afternoon shows nearly every day. These tend to have an educational nature, but often feature local musical stars. The events are government sponsored, so there's no catch; for more information, see the Things to See & Do chapter.

Jackson Square *(Map 2)* in the Quarter is the locus of free outdoor entertainment year-round. Street performers passing the hat around the park's periphery include solo saxophonists, blues artists and complete brass bands. Local celebrity Tuba Fats can often be found among a makeshift swing combo near the Cabildo. Mimes, tarot-card readers, artists and other street performers are also part of the passing show.

Nearby, on Royal St, a bevy of talented buskers claim nearly every street corner. Roslyn and David, an elderly husband-and-wife street act, set up along the street nearly every day.

Elsewhere around town, the black New Orleans 'second-line' tradition is still going strong. In Uptown and Mid-City, often in some of New Orleans' most impoverished neighborhoods, foot parades several-thousand people strong, following one or several brass bands, stream through the streets, pausing at pre-selected bars. Sounds of a sousaphone and brass instruments are like an open invitation to join the party.

SPECTATOR SPORTS

New Orleans is a football town. The city is home to a National Football League (NFL) team, and every few years its formidable football stadium, the Superdome, is the site of the NFL championship game, the Super Bowl. The NCAA (college) Sugar Bowl game is also a major sporting event held in the Superdome each January 1.

New Orleans has no major league baseball team or NBA basketball team. The town does have minor league baseball and (strangely enough) hockey teams that play full schedules in and around town. Gambling on horse races is probably the city's second-biggest sport.

Football

Louisiana Superdome *(Map 4; ☎ 587-3810; Sugar Bowl Dr; tickets $22-50)*, with 60,000 seats, is home to the NFL's New Orleans Saints. Barring postseason play, the Saints play nine home games from August through December, and seats are generally available.

The hottest college football ticket is the New Year's Sugar Bowl contest, featuring the Southeastern Conference champions. Out-of-town fans keep the demand high for Superdome tickets, which cost $60 to $100.

Horse Racing

Fair Grounds Race Track *(Map 7; ☎ 944-5515; 1751 Gentilly Blvd)*, opened in 1872, is the third-oldest track in the nation. The handsome gatehouse entryway was designed by

James Gallier in 1859 for an agricultural fair, and the stands were rebuilt following a disastrous fire in 1993. Buried in the infield here are derby winners from an era when New Orleans was one of the premier tracks in the country. The racing season runs from November to March on Wednesday through Sunday, with a 1:30pm post time.

Baseball

With 72 home games from April to September, you can catch the minor league New Orleans Zephyrs at **Zephyr Field** *(Map 1; ☎ 734-5155, 282-6777; 6000 Airline Hwy; general admission $5, reserved seats adult/ senior/child $7/6/5)*, at the junction with Hickory Ave. Games between the Zephyrs (a Milwaukee Brewers affiliate) and other Triple-A clubs in the Southern League begin at 7:05pm, except on Sunday, when games begin at 6:05pm.

College Sports

College football, basketball and baseball games get plenty of attention; local teams tend to rank highly nationally and contribute stars to the professional ranks. Attending college games is quite inexpensive (plus refreshments are usually very cheap), and you can often catch a glimpse of the nation's up-and-coming players.

The Tulane Green Wave plays NCAA Division I football at the Superdome. The best and most exciting Tulane game is a battle with long-standing rival Louisiana State University (LSU) from Baton Rouge.

The University of New Orleans Privateers basketball team is quite good; games are played at the **UNO Kiefer Lakefront Arena** *(Map 1; ☎ 280-6100)*. At Tulane, women's and men's games are played at the small but very lively **Avron B Fogelman Arena** *(Map 6, #23; ☎ 865-5000)* on campus.

Tulane and UNO baseball games are worth spending a lazy afternoon watching. Tulane plays on campus, while UNO games take place in the larger **Privateer Park** *(Map 1)* on the lakefront. In late February, baseball teams from Louisiana face off against Mississippi teams in the Winn-Dixie Showdown, a three-day series of triple-headers in the Superdome.

Shopping

Souvenir shopping in New Orleans presents a bit of a puzzle for the curious traveler. Many shops are devoted to selling items that would have no market elsewhere, because the items simply have no use *anywhere* – the obvious case in point being the multitude of shellacked alligator heads available at the Farmer's Market. Where else would you be tempted to buy an alligator head if not in New Orleans? On the other hand, some popular New Orleans souvenirs are ubiquitous elsewhere. Why do so many people feel compelled to buy Tabasco sauce in New Orleans, when the stuff is available in every single supermarket in America? (OK, some people do buy Tabasco to take home to Europe or Australia.)

All that aside, New Orleans does offer travelers with some genuinely attractive money-spending opportunities.

Naturally, this is a great city in which to hunt down music recordings (whether you like CDs, LPs, 45s, or 78s), as well as rare posters and photographs of musicians past and present. Lovers of art, antiques, antiquarian books and vintage clothing will also delight in bountiful shopping strips such as Royal, Chartres, lower Decatur and Magazine Sts. If you're a voodoo practitioner, or just intrigued by the religion's colorful paraphernalia, New Orleans is probably the best city in the US in which to stock up on supplies. The availability of Mardi Gras costumes and masks often inspires the out-of-town visitor to start planning ahead for their next Halloween party back home. As is often the case with interesting places, the stores in New Orleans just tend to be selling interesting things. Of course, ordinary shopping of the all-American shopping-mall variety can also be done here, but you won't find it exceptional unless you're coming from the boondocks.

Independently owned shops are often the most interesting, but these also tend to keep odd hours. Small shops typically open up to an hour later than the sign out front indicates, and stay closed on the odd day or two every week. Common shop hours are Tuesday through Saturday from 10am or 11am until 5pm or 6pm. Bookstores are an exception: many are open daily, and booksellers tend to sleep in and keep later hours in the evening. Of course, most tourist-oriented shops (where cheesy T-shirts and the like are sold) are also open daily.

Merchants participating in the Louisiana Tax Free Shopping (LTFS) programme provide tax-refund vouchers to passport carriers at the time of purchase, which is similar to the European value-added tax (VAT) refund programme (see Taxes & Refunds in the Facts for the Visitor chapter).

WHAT TO BUY
Music
New Orleans, being a musical sort of place, is naturally a good city in which to buy records, CDs and musical instruments – and many music-mad tourists do just that.

Records & CDs A multitude of independently owned record stores serve the discriminating local audience. Most of these stores are also good sources for information about Louisiana music.

Jim Russell Rare Records (Map 5, #28; ☎ 522-2602; 1837 Magazine St) is a dense emporium of used 45s, with some highly rare, collectable and expensive disks featuring all the blues, R&B and soul stars of the past. (Collecting Johnny Adams' singles? This is the place.) The used LPs have mostly given way to CDs, with an uneven selection available. Turntables make it possible to assess the quality of your purchases before you lay down the crisp greenbacks.

Louisiana Music Factory (Map 2, #159; ☎ 586-1094; 210 Decatur St) is a great shop for new and used CDs, specializing in the music of Louisiana. Get your Cajun and zydeco here, along with sacks of CDs by New Orleans' bottomless talent pool. The listening stations are a great way to familiarize yourself with local artists. Upstairs is a small selection of used LPs, and there's also a nice selection of cool T-shirts that you won't find elsewhere. Live performances on Saturday afternoons really rock the joint.

Magic Bus Records (Map 2, #135; ☎ 522-0530; 527 Conti St) mostly sells used LPs, but the used CD bins are also worth a look.

Metropolis Music (Map 6, #51; ☎ 899-4532; 4532 Magazine St) is a small Uptown shop that specializes in alternative and underground rock, along with a smattering of local releases.

Rock & Roll Collectibles (Map 2, #34; ☎ 561-5683; 1214 Decatur St) has a large selection of rock, blues and R&B on vinyl. The shop walls are covered with vintage concert posters that are for sale.

Musical Instruments You would think New Orleans would be the perfect place to find an inexpensive old tuba or something else to make your carry-on luggage more interesting, but the city's music shops are on the whole disappointing. If looking for a guitar, a horn, or a Cajun accordion, there are a few shops worth stopping at.

International Vintage Guitars (Map 4, #72; ☎ 524-4557; 1011 Magazine St), in the Warehouse District, is a small shop specializing in used guitars and amps. The collection usually features a few showpieces, but its stock is generally nothing to get excited about.

New Orleans Music Exchange (Map 5, #50; ☎ 891-7670; 3342 Magazine St), Uptown, is always worth a look for used, reasonably priced guitars, amps, and brass and woodwind instruments.

Werlein's for Music (Map 2, #158; ☎ 883-5080; 214 Decatur St) has a large French Quarter showroom that is regrettably understocked. There's usually a beautiful vintage National guitar in the window, and some nice accordions and zydeco rubboards (*frottoirs*, they're called), but all in all Werlein's in the Quarter is not a reliable source for real musicians. **Werlein's Superstore** (☎ 883-5060; 3750 Veteran's Blvd, Metairie), miles from downtown New Orleans, is more like it.

For your basic Guitar Center, you'll have to leave town. The nearest one is in Jefferson.

Books

New Orleans is home to many writers and literati, so naturally book lovers will find plenty of good independent bookstores. Most of the stores selling used books also carry a small stock of new titles and guides about New Orleans.

General Books One place offering a good New Orleans selection, plus a large stock of foreign-language books, travel guides and fiction, is **Beaucoup Books** (Map 6, #48; ☎ 895-2663; 5414 Magazine St).

Bookstar (Map 2, #136; ☎ 523-6411; 414 N Peters St), in the French Quarter, is a local superstore with a wide variety of new-release books and magazines. Bookstar also features a commendable selection of works by local authors.

Garden District Bookshop (Map 5, #35; ☎ 895-2266; 2727 Prytania St), in The Rink, offers a select collection of first-edition works and also books on the region, among mostly new titles.

Maple Street Bookstore (Map 6, #16; ☎ 866-4916; 7529 Maple St) is where shopkeeper Rhonda Kellog Faust advocates for the antiracism group Erace and she is a storehouse of local knowledge. The business, which includes a children's bookstore, was founded by her mother and aunt more than 30 years ago.

Tower Records (Map 2, #138; ☎ 529-4411; 408 N Peters St) has underground comics, magazines and obscure publications.

Specialty Books The South's oldest gay bookstore, **Faubourg Marigny Book Store** (Map 3, #21; ☎ 943-9875; 600 Frenchmen St) is a good place to learn about the local scene.

Faulkner House Bookstore (Map 2, #94; ☎ 524-2940; 624 Pirate's Alley), both a bookstore and a literary attraction, offers a good selection of new titles and first editions, with a particularly strong collection of books by local and Southern authors. As expected, William Faulkner is a staple, and a literary group works out of the shop (see the French Quarter in the Things to See & Do chapter).

Historic New Orleans Collection (Map 2, #104; ☎ 598-7147; 533 Royal St) has a little gift shop with a small collection of new and used books on the region's history and politics.

Old Children's Books (Map 2, #82; ☎ 525-3655; 734 Royal St) offers well-preserved antique books for children – and, come to think of it, for 'old children.'

Starling Books & Crafts (Map 2, #36; ☎ 595-6777; 1022 Royal St) is where voodoo and occult works are available.

Community Book Center & Neighborhood Gallery (Map 7, #37; ☎ 822-2665; 217 N Broad Ave) is the place to head to for books written by or for African Americans.

Antiquarian & Used Books New Orleans offers bibliophiles a variety of stores with small- to medium-sized collections around the French Quarter and Uptown.

Arcadian Books & Art Prints (Map 2, #71; ☎ 523-4138; 714 Orleans Ave), in the French Quarter, is a small, crowded little shop that's filled with Southern literature and history, as well as many volumes in French. Owner Russell Desmond speaks French fluently and is a wonderful, yet cynical, ambassador to New Orleans.

Beckham's Bookstore (Map 2, #157; ☎ 522-9875; 228 Decatur St), in the French Quarter, has two floors of used books that make for good browsing. The store also sells used classical LPs.

Crescent City Books (Map 2, #152; ☎ 524-4997; 204 Chartres St) is another two-story shop in the French Quarter offering a variety of used works at reasonable prices plus a few new titles.

Kaboom Books (Map 2, #8; ☎ 529-5780; 915 Barracks St), in the far reaches of the lower Quarter, is a worthwhile store to visit for its large and varied collection.

Librairie Books (Map 2, #73; ☎ 525-4837; 823 Chartres St) is where you must be able to tolerate a smoke-filled room if you wish to peruse very old volumes of New Orleans material and items of more general interest. The shop also specializes in scholarly texts.

Art & Photography
New Orleans can be a very hospitable city to artistic types, and in walking around Jackson

Square and along the gates surrounding St Anthony's Garden on Royal St, you are likely to come across some very unconventional material by unknown local artists. The best local work is available in galleries.

628 Gallery (Map 4, #39; ☎ 529-3306; 628 Baronne St), a Warehouse District gallery that shouldn't be missed, is where Young Artists/ Young Aspirations (YA/YA), founded by painter Jana Napoli, shows its work. YA/YA is an exemplary arts programme that works with at-risk teens. Sponsors such as Swatch, the UN General Assembly and film director Spike Lee have commissioned the teens of YA/YA to apply their creative talents.

A Gallery for Fine Photography (Map 2, #150; ☎ 568-1313; 241 Chartres St) sells historical prints such as William Henry Jackson's early-20th-century views of New Orleans and EJ Belloq's rare images of Storyville prostitutes. Mind you, these are first-generation prints, from the original glass plates. The gallery also regularly features Herman Leonard's shots of Duke Ellington and other jazz legends, as well as the occasional Cartier-Bresson enlargement (available at second-mortgage prices). Don't miss the stunning exhibits upstairs.

Community Book Center & Neighborhood Gallery (Map 7, #37; ☎ 822-2665; 217 N Broad Ave), in Mid-City, is where African-American art and literature are featured. In addition to exhibition space dedicated to local artists, the gallery also includes an area for performing-arts events such as storytelling, African dancing, music and poetry.

Jean Bragg Antiques (Map 6, #57; ☎ 895-7375; 3901 Magazine St), at General Taylor St, is a good source for the Arts and Crafts–style Newcomb Pottery, which originated at New Orleans' own Newcomb College. Bragg also deals in old art by local painters.

Johnny Donnels (Map 2, #92; ☎ 525-6438; 634 St Peter St) is the gallery of a fine local photographer. The collection is anchored by some touchingly beautiful shots of the French Quarter.

Kurt E Schon Ltd Gallery (Map 2, #103; ☎ 524-5462; 523 Royal St) is a six-floor gallery that purveys fine 19th-century paintings dolled up in ornate gold-leaf frames.

Naturally, everything costs a bomb here, and none of it would look at home in a humble walk-up apartment.

La Belle Galerie (*Map 2, #143; ☎ 529-3080; 309 Chartres St*) is a gallery specializing in limited-edition prints, particularly by African-American artists. Among its art-filled rooms you'll find vintage Jazz Fest posters and rare prints of Ernest Barnes' distinctive paintings.

New Orleans Conservation Guild (*Map 3, #38; ☎ 994-7900; 3301 Chartres St*), in Bywater, is principally an art-restoration business, but the shop also sells restored vintage frames. On the third Saturday of each month it holds an outdoor art fair where you can purchase paintings, pottery, photography and sculpture by local artists.

New Orleans School of Glassworks (*☎ 529-7277; 727 Magazine St*) also focuses on works by youths. The school's gallery sells the artisans' wares at reasonable prices.

Photo Works (*Map 2, #75; ☎ 593-9090; 839 Chartres*) is a polished showroom for the accomplished photographer Louis Sahuc, who has been shooting New Orleans for years and years.

Porché West Gallery (*Map 3, #11; ☎ 947-3880; e porche@communique.net; cnr Burgundy & Louise Sts*), in Bywater, is the rustic shop and studio of photographer Christopher Porché West. Pathos defines Porché West's black-and-white images of the people of New Orleans, and his photos of the Mardi Gras Indians are among the best. Call for an appointment.

Stone and Press (*Map 2, #151; ☎ 561-8555; 238 Chartres St*) is a French Quarter shop that specializes in fine-art lithographs, mezzotints and etchings by 20th-century American artists.

Antiques & Interesting Junk

New Orleans rewards the shopper who appreciates that a surprising number of things just get better with age, including old lamps, ashtrays, toys and the kind of bric-a-brac that once was considered worthless. And even if you're looking for those things that don't get better with age (plaid polyester love seats come to mind), you're still in luck.

When it comes to home furnishings, New Orleanians pride themselves on having exquisite taste. A peek inside an opulent Garden District mansion generally reveals greater extravagance inside than out, while shotgun shacks in the Marigny are often decked out with a panache that far exceeds expectation. It follows then that the local market for antiques is not particularly accommodating to the bargain hunter.

You'll find antique shops along Royal, Chartres, lower Decatur and Magazine Sts.

David's (*Map 2, #13; ☎ 568-1197; 1319 Decatur*) is a rummage shop that is filled with found objects, collectibles, funky lamps, swanky duds, bar accoutrements, jewelry and other odds and ends.

The Garage (*Map 2, #32; 1234 Decatur St*) is, well, pretty much just a garage filled with interesting stuff to sift through. The wares include odd clothing items, furniture and the objets d'arts of yesteryear.

James H Cohen & Sons (*Map 2, #114; ☎ 522-3305; 437 Royal St*) sells museum-quality antique weapons (flintlocks, colts etc). Some display cases offer Confederate money and, oddly, jewelry.

Magazine Arcade (*Map 5, #43; ☎ 895-5451; 3017 Magazine St*) houses an assortment of independent stalls in which dealers peddle an intriguing and varied range of antique bric-a-brac.

Migon Faget's boutique (*Map 6, #11; ☎ 865-7361; 710 Dublin St*), the shop of the celebrated jewelry designer, is one block from the streetcar line. Faget is a Newcomb College alumnus who carries on the Newcomb art tradition with highly regarded jewelry designs – some of which are specifically created for the alumnae association.

Modell's Restoration (*Map 6, #50; ☎ 895-5267; 4600 Magazine St*) is the place to go for cool old lamps.

Santa's Quarters (*Map 2, #57; ☎ 581-5820; 1025 Decatur St*) does its best to keep the Christmas spirit alive year-round. The shop carries classic holiday ornaments, lights and cards.

Wirthmore Antiques (*Map 6, #58; ☎ 899-3811; 3900 Magazine St*) sells rustic French-provincial furnishings.

Costumes & Masks

Mardi Gras and Halloween give New Orleanians two excuses to disguise themselves, but the preponderance of shops specializing in duds for such occasions suggests that the locals are playing dress up more often than that. Out-of-towners can get with the programme right quickly in a single fun-filled shopping excursion.

Little Shop of Fantasy (Map 2, #125; ☎ 529-4243; 515 St Louis St) deals in unique hand-crafted masks and party attire. The exquisite pieces by mask makers from around the USA include some really macabre clowns and traditional Venetian styles.

Royal Rags (Map 2, #66; ☎ 566-7247; 627 Dumaine St) sells everything women and drag queens need for a fun night out. The shop is stuffed with costumes, masks, feather boas and other Mardi Gras essentials.

Uptown Costume & Dancewear (Map 6, #54; ☎ 895-7969; 4326 Magazine St) is filled from floor to ceiling with flashy Mardi Gras attire (boas, tiaras, wigs, masks etc) and ballerina tutus and Capezio shoes. A smaller, more central store (Map 2, #69) is on St Ann St in the French Quarter.

Tattoos

Getting tattooed in New Orleans is pretty much perfect.

Electric Ladyland (Map 3, #17; ☎ 947-8286; 610 Frenchmen St) is a clean, brightly lit spot where young tattoo artists can set you up with a classic set of dice ('born to lose'), a growling wolf or a naked woman sashaying beneath a coconut palm. Customized designs can also be arranged.

Vintage Clothing

When it comes to second-hand clothing, this town ain't too shabby. Magazine St Uptown and lower Decatur St in the Quarter are interspersed with antique stores, some of which have a clothing rack or two.

Funky Monkey (Map 5, #45; ☎ 899-5587; 3127 Magazine St) sells vintage attire for cute club-hopping types, hipster types and Goth types.

Meyer the Hatter (Map 4, #18; ☎ 525-1048; 120 St Charles Ave), in the CBD, features an inventory of truly world-class head-gear. Biltmore, Dobbs, Stetson and Borsalino are just a few of the countless hatmakers represented in this overcrowded shop. Meyer's only flaw is its springtime emphasis on straw hats favored by Southern dandies.

Thrift City (Map 7, #33; ☎ 482-0736; 4125 S Carrollton Ave), in Mid-City, has a large floor lined with well-organized racks. The stock is uneven, as can be expected from a thrift store, but patient sifting is almost always rewarded here. Baggy suits, snazzy shirts and a range of intriguing accessories are just waiting to be found.

Risqué Clothing

New Orleans is still a very risqué, French sort of place, so naturally many visitors to the city start to feel a little frisky. The city has a variety of shops to help you get your get-up together.

Bourbon Strip Tease (Map 2, #139; ☎ 581-6633; 205 Bourbon St) has all manner of things to put on before you take 'em off, starting with lacy lingerie and progressing to edible undies and sleazy toys.

Trashy Diva (Map 2, #74; ☎ 581-4555; 829 Chartres St) is not really as trashy as it pretends to be. The specialty at this place is sassy Victorian-style undergarments – lots of corsets and lacy, frilly stuff for both ladies and gentlemen who enjoy those drawn-out undressing rituals.

Voodoo & Occult

If you're not feeling well, try some gris-gris worn in a sachet. Dried frog gris-gris is useful if you want to practice a little black magic on a bad neighbor. Or maybe you just need some love potion No 9?

Reverend Zombie's House of Voodoo (Map 2, #80; ☎ 897-2030; 723 St Peter St) is where you can take your pick of potions. You'll also find a large selection of books on the occult, as well as carved wooden masks from Mexico and Africa. If you don't find what you're looking for here, try **Marie Laveau's House of Voodoo** (Map 2, #60; ☎ 581-3751; 739 Bourbon St), which carries similar stock. Shipping is available from either store.

Starling Books & Crafts (Map 2, #36; ☎ 595-6777; 1022 Royal St) is a serious, scholarly shop that sells books, potions and voodoo dolls.

Foodstuffs

Granted, customs won't always allow you to take sacks of groceries back home with you, and generally there's little point in doing that anyway. But New Orleans does offer the gourmand many tempting and unique edibles that make nice gifts for the loved ones back home. Also, while in town, you may need to dash out for some beer or bottled water, right?

By the way, local parlance for grocery shopping is 'making groceries.' As you stroll the aisles of a store, be sure to tell everyone you meet that this is what you're doing.

Groceries Smack in the heart of the French Quarter, **A&P Market** (Map 2, #91; ☎ 523-1353; 701 Royal St) is convenient for beer, bottled water and snacks, along with various sundry items. It's open 23 hours a day (closing at 3am for just an hour of cleaning and restocking). A&P is also a fine place to go to stock up on Cajun spices and pepper sauces at lower prices than those at the Farmer's Market.

Central Grocery (Map 2, #68; ☎ 523-1620; 923 Decatur St) is a hyper-busy store offering cooking ingredients typically found in Louisiana kitchens: Zatarain's Creole Seasoning and Crab Boil (even Chef Emeril uses it), McIlhenny Tabasco or Crystal hot sauce, chicory coffee and filé, for making filé gumbo.

Uncle Wilbur's Emporium (Map 2, #67; ☎ 581-2914; 1039 Decatur St) is a purveyor of Café du Monde products. Chicory coffee and beignet mix are the signature items, but the shop also carries a selection of pepper sauces and coffee mugs.

Vieux Carré Wine & Spirits (Map 2, #129; ☎ 568-9463; 422 Chartres St) is a densely stocked shop run by two Italian-born brothers who can often be found socializing at a table near the front door. It has an impressive selection of wines from California, Australia, France and Italy, and a commendable choice

of international beers. If you're really serious about wine, and willing to pay good money for it, ask to see the back room, where the rare vintages are kept.

Pralines A natural use of the abundant Louisiana sugar crop is to mix it with some butter and pecans to make pralines. Freshness really counts.

Southern Candy Makers (Map 2, #144; ☎ 523-5544; 334 Decatur St) is a local favorite for a sugar fix.

Tee-Eva's Creole Soul Food (Map 6, #52; ☎ 899-8350; 4430 Magazine St) is an Uptown snack shack that deals in pralines, among other sweets.

Crawfish If you really have a thing for crawfish and they're hard to come by in your hometown, it might make sense to buy some in New Orleans and ship them back home. (Weird as it may sound, out-of-state crawfish fiends do this all the time.)

Big Fisherman Seafood (Map 5, #48; ☎ 897-9907; 3301 Magazine St), at Toledano St, will pack and ship crawfish to anywhere in the USA.

St Roch Seafood Market (Map 3, #2; ☎ 943-6666; 2381 St Claude St), located in a

---

Alligator Heads

As a souvenir from your trip to New Orleans, you can purchase a shellacked alligator head – something to toss into the trunk of the car, where it will probably add new meaning to the expression, 'heads will roll.' This is how New Orleans caters to tourists – in characteristic eccentric fashion.

But seriously, folks, the trade in alligator heads really should not be encouraged. If the fad catches on, it could conceivably spell the end for the species. We are told that most of the alligator heads are byproducts of legitimate game control sanctioned by the Louisiana Department of Wildlife & Fisheries. Although in recent years the alligator has made a comeback from near extinction, poachers could readily decimate the population again if the demand for gator heads rises.

handsome Work's Progress Administration marketplace on the edge of the Faubourg Marigny, is one of the best spots for crawfish during the spring.

Coins
Coin shops in New Orleans tend to carry everything from Confederate currency to Mardi Gras doubloons and old musket balls.

The Civil War Store (Map 2, #153; ☎ 522-3328; 212 Chartres St) is a tiny shop that sells Confederate currency and old 'Dix' bills.

James H Cohen & Sons (Map 2, #114; ☎ 522-3305; 437 Royal St) is the place to try for a wide selection of coins and other collectibles, such as political campaign buttons.

Old US Mint (Map 2, #15; ☎ 523-6468; 400 Esplanade Ave) has a Coin Vault with a very knowledgeable staff.

WHERE TO SHOP
French Quarter (Map 2)
The Quarter is lined with great strips that are well suited to window shopping and sticking your nose into people's businesses.

Royal St Many regard Royal St as the 'Main Street' of the French Quarter. Portions of Royal St are closed to automobiles during daytime shopping hours.

Between Iberville and St Ann Sts, visitors will find a number of distinguished galleries and specialty shops. These shops inhabit buildings that have been prominent commercial addresses since before the 1803 Louisiana Purchase.

More recently, clothing boutiques and other small shops have extended the Royal St shopping area into the lower Quarter to St Philip St. Many shops are gay- and lesbian-owned.

Chartres St In shopping terms, Chartres St is Royal St's equal. It's lined with interesting small shops dealing in antiques, art and expensive curiosities.

Decatur St Upper Decatur St is where all the T-shirt shops and cheap tourist bric-a-brac is sold. About the only worthwhile thing sold in these stores are plastic snow domes that

bring together charming incongruities such as alligators and snow.

Lower Decatur, below Governor Nichols St, is another matter altogether. The street is lined with interesting antique and junk shops, boutiques, and some good bars where you can get loaded after shopping.

French Market (Map 2, #59)
Truth be told, the French Market is a bit of a disappointment. It's split in two sections – a produce market and a flea market – and neither is particularly special. In a pinch, the French Market will supply the visitor with cheap gimcracks to give away back home, but for quality shopping you'll have to look somewhere else.

Farmer's Market (Map 2, #47) Only a vestige of former market activity remains at the Farmer's Market, where large freezer trucks have replaced the small trucks of farmers. Still, you might occasionally see a beat-up pickup truck on sagging springs heading from the market to sell a load of fresh produce on the streets of an outer district. (Many restaurateurs and residents now rely on the Saturday morning Green Market in the Warehouse District at Girod and Magazine Sts – where real farmers sell to those out 'makin' groceries.')

Merchants in the Farmer's Market offer fresh fruit and vegetables, including green beans, mangos, papaya, bananas, plantains, peaches, strawberries, watermelon, apples and pecans, as well as cold drinks. In addition, there are lots of kitchen supplies, spices (including a large selection of hot sauces), garlic and chili strings, and cookbooks for the tourist trade.

Flea Market (Map 2, #48) Shoppers can pick up some unique southern Louisiana products here any day of the week. There is a motley assortment of T-shirt and sunglasses vendors, as well as African art (obviously mass-produced), inexpensive silver jewelry, chintzy Mardi Gras masks and dolls, musical tapes and CDs of dubious origin, and enough preserved alligator heads to populate a swamp.

Canal St (Map 2 & 4)

Beginning in the 1830s, businesses began a gradual shift from the Creole French Quarter to Canal St and the American sector above it. Although the street was never a canal, its broad neutral ground separated the Creole and American sectors. Now this neutral ground is a bus corridor. Mingling with the multitude of tax-free camera shops and drugstores are a few remnants from the days when shopping downtown was popular with the elite of the city.

Rubenstein Bros *(Map 4, #19;* ☎ *581-6666; 102 St Charles Ave)* offers upscale men's clothes, and each customer gets personalized service immediately after entering the two-story haberdashery – the shop can afford it by selling designer shirts for $200.

Warehouse District (Map 4)

In the Warehouse District, anchored by the nearby **Contemporary Arts Center** *(Map 4, #64;* ☎ *528-3805; 900 Camp St),* artists have created a vibrant community of galleries on Julia St between Commerce and Baronne Sts. Drop by the Contemporary Art Center or any gallery to pick up a comprehensive guide to the area's art dealers. See the Things to See & Do chapter for more information about the Contemporary Arts Center.

Garden District & Uptown (Maps 5 & 6)

The Rink *(Map 5, #35),* opposite Lafayette Cemetery No 1 at Prytania St and Washington Ave in the heart of the Garden District, houses a small group of upscale shops, including a bookstore and coffee shop.

Riverside Market Shopping Center *(Map 6, #62; cnr Jefferson Ave & Tchoupitoulas St)* is a modern surprise that primarily serves the locals' grocery, video rental, liquor and drugstore needs. The No 10 Tchoupitoulas bus goes there from downtown.

Magazine St (Maps 5 & 6)

Coursing along the riverside edge of the Garden District and Uptown, Magazine St is miles long, and for much of its length is lined with small shops that sell antiques, art, vintage clothing and other odds and ends.

No one shop stands out, and businesses seem to come and go, but on any given Saturday the street will keep any shopaholic busy all day.

Riverbend (Map 6)

An interesting area here is the fashionable shops and restaurants fronting a small square on Dublin St near S Carrollton Ave where it meets St Charles Ave. To get there, take the St Charles Ave streetcar to the Riverbend near Camellia Grill.

Student-oriented shopping is centered on Maple St, which is also accessible by the St Charles Ave streetcar line. Here, bookstores, coffee shops and restaurants make for a happening district.

On the riverside of S Carrollton, Oak St is an older neighborhood commercial zone intersecting with the streetcar line. It is reasonably compact for pedestrian strolls and offers a few interesting businesses, such as a vibrant fresh-fish market, along with a few restaurants and the stellar Maple Leaf Bar (check out the Entertainment chapter for more information).

Shopping Malls

If you get invited to a masquerade ball and didn't happen to pack a gown or tuxedo in your backpack, just head over to the fashionable air-conditioned shops at **Canal Place** *(Map 2; 333 Canal St).* The upscale mall is anchored by a Saks Fifth Avenue store; supporting roles are played by Kenneth Cole, Ann Taylor, Laura Ashley, Brooks Brothers and Banana Republic. A multiplex cinema and a performing-arts theater are on the 3rd floor (see the Entertainment chapter). The mall parking lot is convenient and has reasonable rates.

Jackson Brewery *(Map 2, #117;* ☎ *566-7245; 600 Decatur St)* has been redeveloped into a small shopping mall that's best known for its convenient ATM and public restrooms. You have to wonder about a brewery that couldn't survive in New Orleans though.

New Orleans Centre *(Map 4;* ☎ *568-0000),* adjoining the Superdome at La Salle St and Poydras St, is yet another downtown air-conditioned shopping emporium. It has got a Lord & Taylor, a Macy's department store and a wide selection of favorite mall shops, as well as a food court.

Riverwalk Mall *(Map 4; ☎ 522-1555; open 10am-9pm Mon-Thur, 10am-10pm Fri & Sat, 10am-7pm Sun)*, an unappealing byproduct of the 1984 New Orleans World's Fair, provides a sanitized, air-conditioned alternative to the Quarter's shops and restaurants. In fact, many Quarter shops have outlets in the mall or its food court – perhaps to keep the cash flowing during heat waves and thunderstorms. The mall lacks an anchor store but does have branches of Banana Republic, Sharper Image and other mall standards. Many stores have shorter operating hours than the mall. If you don't want to walk there, take the Riverfront streetcar.

Excursions

New Orleans is a beguiling, but exhausting city. When you reach the point that you can't face another plate of shrimp *rémoulade* (sauce), and the thought of one more Sazerac cocktail sets your stomach churning, head for the hinterlands. Most excursions are an hour or so away, but Cajun Country destinations will take a couple of hours or more.

Here are a few options: Drive north and browse through the hip antique stores across Lake Pontchartrain in Covington; drive south to paddle a canoe through the swamp at the Jean Lafitte National Historic Park; head southwest to the Cajun Wetlands, and come face to face with a gator on a swamp tour; or wend your way upriver toward Baton Rouge to get a glimpse of antebellum opulence along the River Rd.

Although Cajun Country is a bit farther away, it's the epicenter of Louisiana's festival circuit, where weekend celebrations of everything from zydeco music to jambalaya are feted with a street party. But don't wait for a festival. Almost any weekend you can stop off at a cinder-block roadhouse, where the beer is ice cold, the accordion music is hot, and the boiled crawfish or crabs are so spicy you'll into break into a sweat.

NORTH SHORE
There was a time when the northern shore of Lake Pontchartrain was a resort destination for New Orleans residents. They came – first by boat, then train and finally, in 1956 with the completion of the 24mi causeway, by car – to enjoy the lake breezes and calm atmosphere. Today these North Shore communities are less resort destinations than they are bedroom communities for New Orleans.

Of the towns on the North Shore, the jewels are undoubtedly Covington and Abita Springs, with Hammond, Madisonville and Slidell, having little to offer beyond comparatively economical overnight accommodations. Mandeville is the site of a lovely state park and camping grounds, as well as a trio of good restaurants. The **St Tammany Parish**

Tourist & Convention Commission (☎ 985-892-0520; 68099 Hwy 59, Mandeville, LA 70471) is located off I-12 at exit 65.

Fontainebleau State Park
This 2700-acre park, sprawling along the north shore of Lake Pontchartrain, has nature trails, the ruins of a plantation brickyard and sugar mill, a beach, a **swimming pool** (open in summer), a camping ground and picnic areas. It's bordered by Bayou Cane and Bayou Castine, and is an excellent spot for bird- and wildlife-watching. The Tammany Trace (see following) passes through here.

The **camping ground** (☎ 985-624-4443; camp sites $10-12) has well-spaced, shaded sites with picnic tables and grills. Some sites have clean bathhouses and restrooms and a public phone. For groups, there's a separate camping area and a lodge that sleeps nine to 13 people ($90). To get there from I-12, take exit 65, go south 3½mi and turn left onto Hwy 190; then travel another 2½mi and turn right. From New Orleans, take the Lake Pontchartrain Causeway and exit at Hwy 190 east; continue 5mi to the entrance.

Tammany Trace
An old railroad track was converted into this 32mi trail for **biking**, **hiking** and **in-line skating**, which stretches from Mandeville to Abita Springs, including a section through Fontainebleau State Park. Parallel to the trace is an unpaved **equestrian trail**.

Abita Springs
North of Mandeville along Hwy 59, is the bucolic village of Abita Springs, popular in the late 1800s as a spot to bask in what were thought to be curative waters.

Today, the spring water still flows from a **fountain** in the center of the village, but the primary liquid attraction here is the **Abita Brewery** (☎ 985-893-3143; 21084 Hwy 36), just a mile or so west of town. Abita was the first microbrewery in the southeast, and its popular Turbo Dog, Purple Haze and Amber

EXCURSIONS

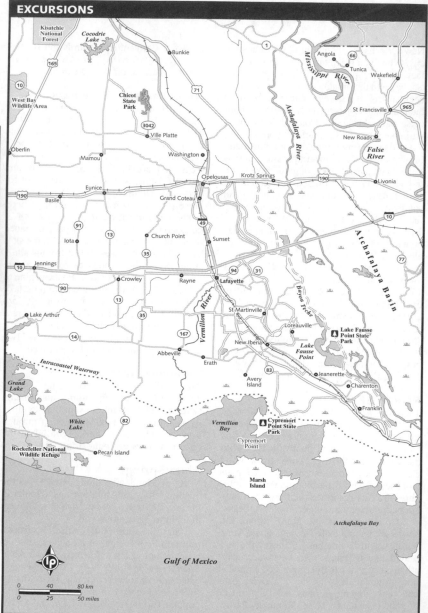

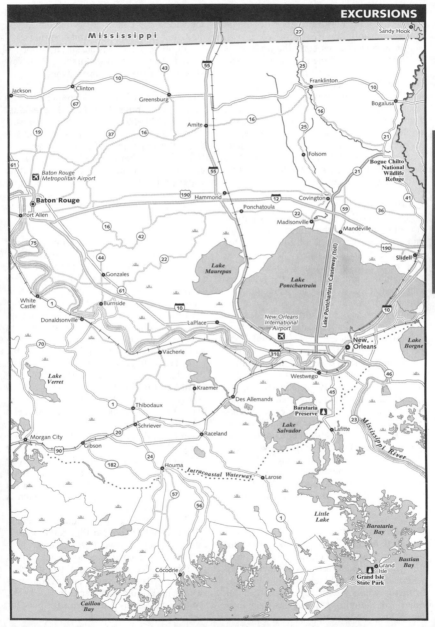

beers are top sellers throughout the state. Housed in a jumble of prefabricated metal and block buildings, with an overgrown auto-repair shop at its core, the brewery is not picturesque, but the personalized tours are charming and idiosyncratic, and positive proof that beer making is not just the province of multinational conglomerates. Tours of the brewery are free and offered at 1pm and 3pm on Saturday, and infrequently on Sunday. Other times may be arranged by appointment. On your way home, you may want to stop off at the **Abita Brew Pub** (see Places to Eat, later) for a more formal tasting of the brewery's beers.

Covington

Founded in 1816, Covington was a port of some importance on the Bogue Falaya River and emerged as the seat of government for St Tammany Parish in 1819. The city served as a center of commerce for North Shore communities until 1956, when the causeway was completed across Lake Pontchartrain. Covington then became a bedroom community for nearby New Orleans.

Long the haunt of artists and writers, Covington was home to the revered 20th-century author Walker Percy, whose novels examining what he termed the 'modern malaise' – *The Moviegoer, Lancelot, Love in the Ruins* – won wide acclaim. Today, the quaint little town is enjoying a renaissance, as artists and writers are joined by entrepreneurs in remaking the brick storefronts in the downtown area into a shop and gallery district reminiscent of New Orleans' Magazine St corridor. The gentrification makes for interesting juxtapositions: Ray's Knives and Archery ('Bow Hunting Spoken Here') is just round the corner from Earthsavers Relaxation Spa.

Places to Stay

Although intended as a day-trip destination, the North Shore is so close to New Orleans that you may want to consider staying here when New Orleans hotels are booked to the brim, or when your budget calls out for relief. For camping grounds, see Fontaine-bleau State Park, earlier. For motels, the Hwy 190 corridor offers the most choices at the widest range of prices. No matter if you stay in Mandeville or Abita Springs, all North Shore attractions are just a 10- or 15-minute drive from one another. And New Orleans is a 40-minute drive away.

Abita Springs There are a couple of B&Bs downtown. **Trail's End Bed & Breakfast** (☎ 985-867-9899; 71648 Maple St; singles/doubles $75/85, plus supplement Sat & Sun $20), the most appealing of the springs' B&Bs, is a charming Victorian cottage close to the Tammany Trace and well within walking distance of two of the town's popular restaurants and the town springs. Breakfast at the Abita Springs Café (see Places to Eat, later) is included.

Covington Another North Shore camping ground on the bank of the Tchefuncte River is in the **Fairview-Riverside State Park** (☎ 845-3318; camp sites $10-12). It offers 80-plus sites, all with electricity and water, on a first-come, first-served basis. During the 19th century, the site was a lumber camp. Now the river and woodlands are recovering only to be assaulted by encroaching suburban development near the margins of the park. The state park is 3mi west of the Lake Pontchartrain Causeway on Hwy 22.

Mt Vernon Motel (☎ 985-892-1041; 1110 N Hwy 190; singles & doubles $45) is a spiffy little 30-room property, which has been recently renovated.

Green Springs Motel (☎ 985-892-4686; 72533 Hwy 21; singles/doubles $45/50), just a mile or so north along Hwy 21, on the edge of Covington, is a single-story brick motel tucked into a neighborhood of beautiful homes. There is a nice pool here, which is open in summer only.

Closer to the I-12 are a number of chain motels. **Best Western Northpark Inn** (☎ 985-892-2681; 625 N Hwy 190; singles/doubles $65/75) is the best. Among the amenities are a better-than-average continental breakfast, a heated outdoor pool, and an adjoining restaurant, Dakota (see Places to Eat, later), which rivals many New Orleans spots for elegant, sophisticated food.

Places to Eat

Mandeville The local favorite for breakfast, **Mande's Restaurant** (☎ 985-626-9047; 340 N Causeway; open 7am-6pm daily) serves bounteous platters of grits and eggs ($4) along with plate lunches ($6), which are rib-sticking if not inspired.

Rag's Po-Boys (☎ 985-845-3327; 4960 Hwy 22; open lunch & dinner Mon-Sat), just west of town, is the purveyor of the best po'boys in town. Get your roast beef sandwich ($4) 'dressed' (with mayonnaise, lettuce, tomatoes and a dab of mustard) and eat it quickly before the gravy soaks through the loaf.

Trey Yuen (☎ 985-626-4476; 600 Causeway Blvd; lunch from $10, dinner from $20; open lunch Wed-Fri & Sun, dinner 6pm-10pm daily) is a revelation: a well-appointed, even fashionable, Chinese restaurant serving inventive cuisine. Among the perennial favorites are pot stickers, shrimp in a cloud and a velvety-rich lobster in black-bean sauce.

Abita Springs While savoring the seafood, salads, sandwiches and steaks at **Abita Brew Pub** (☎ 985-892-5837; 72011 Holly St; open 11am-9pm Mon-Thur, 11am-10pm Fri & Sat, 11am-8pm Sun) you can gaze at the vats full of beer. Try the seafood muffuletta ($8). The brew sampler ($4.50) features five 4oz glasses of different beers.

Abita Springs Café (☎ 985-867-9950; 22132 Level St; open 8am-2pm Tues-Sun) is better yet. Try the seafood omelette ($6), a po'boy ($5) or the daily soup such as crawfish and corn ($3 a cup).

Artesia (☎ 985-892-1662; 21516 Hwy 36; lunch $10-15; open lunch Wed-Fri, dinner Wed-Sat) is the choice for haute cuisine in a refined setting. Chef Gerard Maras rules the roost at this subdued restaurant, set in a restored Victorian home. Dishes such as oyster and eggplant soup ($6.50) and pan-roasted veal tenderloin ($27) draw crowds from New Orleans, as well as the surrounding suburbs.

Covington The spot for pastries and sandwiches is **Coffee Rani** (☎ 985-893-6158; 226 Lee Lane; open 8am-5:30pm daily). The café exhibits work by local artists, and the staff are a font of information on what's going on in town.

Alavolasiti's Courthouse Café (☎ 985-893-9030; 323 New Hampshire St; open 6:30am-2pm Mon-Fri), a simple box of a place, features $5 plate lunches of white or red beans and rice.

Acme Oyster Bar (☎ 985-898-0667) on Boston St, is a boisterous outpost of a New Orleans standby.

Etoile (☎ 985-892-4578; 407 N Columbia St; lunch $7-10, dinner $13-16; open 11am-7pm Mon-Sat), near Acme, is an antique-accented bar and restaurant, connected to a retail wine shop. Daily grilled fish specials and innovative sandwiches are the draws at this vibrantly funky place.

Dakota (☎ 985-892-3712; 628 N Hwy 190; open lunch Mon-Fri, dinner Mon-Sat, brunch Sun), adjoining the Best Western Northpark Inn, may well be the best restaurant on the North Shore. At dinner, try the sweet-potato nachos with ground lamb in a tomato-currant chutney and topped with Roquefort cheese ($7) for an appetizer. Dakota has an excellent wine list and attentive but not overbearing staff.

Entertainment

Most locals head to New Orleans for a night on the town, but, as is the case in most of southern Louisiana, you can always count on restaurants having an adjacent bar that is more than an afterthought. For live entertainment, try the **Abita Brew Pub**, in Abita Springs, or **Etoile**, in Covington (see Places to Eat, previous), although your best bet is Covington's **Columbia St Tap Room** (☎ 985-898-0899; 434 N Columbia St), which hosts rock and blues acts most Thursday through Saturday nights. It stays open until 2am on the weekends.

Getting There & Away

A car or motorbike is almost essential for exploring the North Shore. The most direct access from New Orleans is via the Lake Pontchartrain Causeway. However, if the thought of a 24mi-long trip across Lake Pontchartrain on a four-lane ribbon of concrete is not enticing, take I-10 west to I-55

EXCURSIONS

north toward Hammond, or I-10 east toward Slidell and then I-12 west; the Slidell detour should add another 25 or so minutes of driving time, the Hammond route, maybe an extra 35. Beware: Traffic in and around Covington seems to be always clogged.

SOUTHWARD TO THE SWAMP

Below New Orleans, the Mississippi River flows 90mi to the bird's foot–shaped delta, where river pilots board ships entering from the gulf. Rather than drive for hours to Venice, the farthest downstream point accessible by automobile, you can satisfy the same desire to travel to the end of the road at Barataria Preserve, Lafitte or Westwego, each less than an hour's drive from New Orleans. For those in search of a wetlands adventure, the Barataria Preserve beckons. In the little fishing village of Lafitte, about 10mi or so south of Barataria down Hwy 45, you will find a wonderful country inn and two great seafood shacks in a setting more reminiscent of the Mosquito Coast than suburban New Orleans. A bit farther west from the Hwy 45 turnoff, but more easily accessible, is the little town of Westwego, home to one of the state's best swamp tours.

Barataria Preserve

The Barataria Preserve, a unit of southern Louisiana's **Jean Lafitte National Historic Park** is set in an area originally settled by Isleños (Canary Islanders) in 1779. It offers hiking and canoe trips into the swamp and a good introduction to the wetlands environment. It is not a pristine wilderness, as canals and other structures offer evidence of human activity, yet wild animals and plants are abundant. Even a brief walk on the boardwalks that wend their way through the swamp will yield sightings of gators and egrets.

The best place to start is the **National Park Service Visitors Center** (☎ 504-589-2330; Hwy 3134; open 9am-5pm daily), 1mi west of Hwy 45, where you can pick up a map of the 8mi of hiking trails and 9mi of dedicated canoe routes, which are all closed to motorized boats. A 25-minute introductory nature film, *Jambalaya: A Delta Almanac*, is also shown at the center.

Trails in the preserve are open daily from 7am to 5pm, with extended hours during daylight-saving time. Ranger-led walks around Bayou Coquille are offered daily at 2pm. Other activities, which require reservations, include a guided canoe trek on Sundays at 8:30am. On evenings around a full moon, moonlight canoe treks are offered.

Jean Lafitte Inn (☎ 504-689-3271; cnr Hwy 45 & Hwy 3134) rents canoes for use in the preserve; $25 gets you a canoe seating up to three people plus a drop-off and pick-up service in the preserve. Check-in is at the adjacent Earl's Bar, a welcoming joint frequented mostly by locals with dirt-cheap ice-cold beer. Cabins at the inn are convenient to the preserve, but, at $75, are a bit overpriced.

Bayou Barn (☎ 504-689-2663; open Tues-Sun) also rents canoes ($15 for two hours). It's on the Bayou de Familles just outside the park, and is a pleasantly funky restaurant compound of tin-topped weather-beaten buildings on the opposite side of the intersection. Cajun or zydeco bands play to lively local crowds at the dances ($5) held most Sundays from noon to 6pm.

Restaurant de Familles (☎ 504-689-7834; meals $7-15; open Tues-Sun), behind Bayou Barn, offers upscale dining. It's a reward for a day of hiking and paddling. The formal dining room, which overlooks the bayou, features soft-shell crabs (when they're in season) smothered in an artichoke sauce.

Lafitte

After you cross the high-rise bridge and double back onto Hwy 45 heading south, you will first come to the little town of **Jean Lafitte**. Quaint and remote though it may be, it has nothing on the little fishing village of Lafitte, some 8mi farther down the road. Soon the road narrows and you can almost feel the swamplands closing in around you. Due to frequent flooding, even the mobile homes down this way are set on stilts, and the Spanish moss hangs heavy – like green streamers tossed pell-mell onto the boughs of the live oak trees. This was once the province of the pirate Jean Lafitte and is now home to a hardy camp of commercial fishers. Around these parts, 90% of the locals still make their

Drinks on the Tickfaw & Catfish at the Roadhouse of Your Dreams

West of I-55 and south of I-12, just 10mi or so beyond Ponchatoula on Hwy 22, is the little town of **Springfield**, epicenter of an odd waterborne phenomenon. Arrayed along the Tickfaw River, which runs parallel to I-55 south from Mississippi and into Louisiana before pouring forth into Lake Maurepas and finally Lake Pontchartrain, are a collection of bars, many of which are only accessible by boat. Rather than being little dives, these bars are behemoths, sprawling out over the water, offering ample deck space for sunning and ample bar space for quaffing cocktails.

One bar that is accessible by car is **Tin Lizzies** (☎ 985-695-6787; 29592 Hwy 22), open Friday to Sunday only and closed during the late fall and winter. From a perch on the deck, you can watch cigarette boats ply the waters and you may be able to hitch a ride to one of the bars, such as the **Prop Stop**, which are only accessible by water.

During the spring and summer, boat parades and poker runs are infrequently held – the latter is a floating game of five-card stud, where the players are dealt one card at each bar they stop in, and the winning hand is announced around dusk. For those in search of an adventure, these hinterland hideaways promise drinking and debauchery, far from the maddening tourist milieu.

Many of the bars on the river offer decent to good food, but for an excellent meal, head to - **Middendorf's** (☎ 985-386-6666; open 10:30am to 9pm Tues-Sun), at exit 15 off I-55, a gussied-up roadhouse hard by Lake Maurepas. In business since 1934, Middendorf's is famous for its thin-cut catfish fillets ($7 for an ample small order served with green-onion flecked hushpuppies and forgettable fries), which are cooked to a crisp – fried so crisp, in fact, that they resemble more of a fish-flavored potato chip than a traditional fillet. That said, they are delicious, as is the oyster stew ($4.50) and the Italian salad ($5), an oily morass of lettuce, olives and parmesan cheese. But the real treat to behold is the timeless wood-paneled interior, where waitresses with beehive hairdos trundle back and forth bearing platters piled high with deftly fried seafood and icy beers. Middendorf's is open every day but Monday.

WENDY YANAGIHARA

EXCURSIONS

living from the waters, and life owes its design to the patterns of the seasons and the sea. Although there are no typical tourist attractions to visit, the abundant waterside funk is worthy of an hour or so of wandering.

Cochiara's Marina (☎ 504-689-3701), on the left coming into town and hard by the Goose Bayou Bridge, is where you can buy a fan belt for your car, Miracle-Gro for your garden and a cold beer from the bar. 'Folks around here like to tell their wife they're going to the hardware store,' says the proprietor, his face creased by a sly smile. 'Where else can you go shopping and catch a buzz?'

Farther south along the ever-narrowing roadway, you pass the turnoff for the Victorian Inn, Lafitte's de facto tourism office, where the innkeepers will help you secure reservations for swamp tours and the like.

Cattycorner from Boutte's is the **home of folk artist JP Scott**, who has constructed a fleet of ships with the detritus he salvaged from around town. Although most of his vessels have been sold to museums and galleries, you can still catch a glimpse of a few of his works from the road.

Need a place to stay? Only a 45-minute trip from the French Quarter, the following unconventional accommodations can also serve as a base for exploring New Orleans to the north and the Cajun Wetlands to the west.

Cochiara's Marina (☎ 504-689-3701; rooms from $55), at Goose Bayou Bridge, rents out motel rooms bordering on the bayou. Although the rooms lack charm, they are right on the waterfront.

Victorian Inn (☎ 504-689-4757; rooms from $100), on the southern side of the bridge, offers 14 rooms in two West Indies–style plantation homes surrounded by gardens. And just over the levee looms a lake, known locally as 'The Pen,' complete with a private dock. The rooms can be a bit cramped for the price, but the innkeepers are welcoming and extremely knowledgeable about the area, and the surroundings are sure to please guests in search of a respite from cookie-cutter motels.

Boutte's Restaurant (☎ 504-689-7978; open 11am-10pm Tues-Sun), a mile or so farther south of the Victorian Inn, is a comfortable local joint with a great rooftop deck overlooking the Intracoastal Waterway. A half-shrimp, half-oyster po'boy costs just $5 and is sure to satisfy. Turtle soup at $3.50 a cup is damn near perfect. Steaks and chicken are also available, but why would you want to order them when the fishing boats dock just a block or two away?

Continuing south down Hwy 45, just before the road ends, you will see the turnoff for **Voleo's Seafood** (☎ 504-689-3889; open 11am-9pm Wed-Mon, 11am-3pm Tues), which is set in a ramshackle building fronted by a German-inspired beer garden. Local favorites include seafood-stuffed eggplant, and trout topped with a crawfish and cream sauce for about $10.

Westwego

At Highway 90 and Louisiana Ave is a site you're not likely to see outside Louisiana, a huge **open-air fish market** (open dawn-dusk daily). There are 20 little shacks clustered in a horseshoe fashion around a gravel parking lot selling fresh-off-the-boat shrimp, crawfish and crabs at such rock-bottom prices. At last pass, large shrimp were selling for around $3.50 a pound. It's the perfect spot to pick up a sack or two of live crawfish for boiling later, or to just take a gander at the bounty of the sea.

Chacahoula Swamp Tours (☎ 504-436-2640; 422 Louisiana St), a family-owned business run by Jerry Dupre and his wife, offers a far more intimate swamp experience than larger operators. Boats seat about 12, rather than 50, and the narration is not amplified. Instead, you float along amid the stillness of the swamps and bayous as Captain Jerry

points out the flora and fauna, and coaxes an alligator to the side of the boat for the viewing pleasure of his passengers. Most tours last two hours and are a bargain at $25 per person. For an extra $13, the Dupre family will pick up passengers from New Orleans hotels. To get there, make the turn south onto Louisiana St. A block later the pavement gives way to dirt, and soon you are pulling up in front of the charmingly ramshackle home of this operation. Of late, Chacahoula has cut back to one morning tour per day at 10am in warm weather and at noon when it's cold. An alternative tour is **Cajun Critters** (☎ 504-431-7238).

The Westwego area is home to two outstanding restaurants, each perched at the opposite end of the scale of affordability.

Mo's Pizza (☎ 504-341-9650; 1112 Ave H; open 10am-10pm Mon-Sat) is just a mile or so east of Louisiana St, off Hwy 90. Here you will find one of the metropolitan area's best muffulettas ($4) as well as wonderful pizzas, sausage rolls, po'boys and spaghetti with meatballs, all served at ridiculously low prices. At press time Mo's was rebuilding after a fire, and should be reopened by the time you read this.

Mosca's (☎ 504-436-9942; 4137 Hwy 90; open 5pm-10pm Tues-Sat) is another 3mi west from Mo's Pizza, in Waggman. Once a hang out for mafiosos (the original chef is rumored to have worked for Al Capone), it's now a favorite of slumming suburbanites and New Orleans swells, who make the trip to this dilapidated roadhouse for Italian oysters ($25), drowning in oil and garlic, and a crab salad ($11) fat with lump meat that everyone seems to love. Portions are huge – a single entree easily feeds two – and the wine list is reasonable if uninspired. No credit cards are accepted.

Getting There & Away

From New Orleans, motorists heading to the Barataria Preserve should take Business Hwy 90 across the Greater New Orleans Bridge to the Westbank Expressway and turn south on Barataria Blvd (Hwy 45) to Hwy 3134, which leads to the national park entrance. The trip takes about 30 minutes.

Infrequent bus services to and from New Orleans are also available.

To reach Lafitte, continue south on Hwy 45 past the turnoff for the park. Take a switchback turn on a high-rise bridge and then pass through the town of Jean Lafitte before reaching land's end at Lafitte. Total travel time is 45 minutes or so.

Thirty minutes from New Orleans, Westwego is just off the Westbank Expressway (Hwy 90), west of Marrero.

CAJUN WETLANDS

In 1755, *le Grande Dérangement*, the British expulsion of the rural French settlers from Acadia, created a homeless population of Acadians who searched for decades for a place to settle. In 1785, seven boatloads of exiles arrived in New Orleans. By the early 19th century, some 3000 to 4000 Acadians, or Cajuns as they became known, had arrived in Louisiana to occupy the swamplands southwest of New Orleans. Here, they eked out a living based upon fishing and trapping and developed a culture substantially different from the Cajuns who settled farther inland in the prairie region, where animal husbandry and farming were the primary vocations. Early German peasant farmers also produced crops for the New Orleans market in the vicinity of Thibodaux. About 1780 Isleños arrived on the upper Bayou Lafourche. By 1800, Acadians and Americans extended down the bayou to Thibodaux. Today the entire polyglot mix has a tendency to proudly call themselves Cajuns. The largest towns in the area are Thibodaux and Houma.

Thibodaux

Positioned at the confluence of Bayou Lafourche and Bayou Terrebonne, Thibodaux (pronounced **ti**-buh-dough) was, at the time when water travel was preeminent, the most important town between New Orleans and Bayou Teche. It has been the Lafourche Parish seat since 1820. The copper-domed **courthouse** *(cnr 2nd & Green Sts)*, was built in 1855 and remains a testament to Thibodaux's glory days. Today, the town is home to a population of approximately 15,000. Stop by the **Thibodaux Chamber of Commerce**

(☎ 985-446-1187; 1048 E Canal St) for maps and information on local events.

The **Wetlands Cajun Cultural Center** *(☎ 985-448-1375; 314 St Mary St; open 9am-8pm Mon, 8am-5pm Tues-Fri, 9am-5pm Sat & Sun)* is a spacious museum and gallery operated by the National Park Service (NPS). Exhibits cover virtually every aspect of Cajun life in the wetlands, from music to the environmental impacts of trapping and oil exploration. Visitors learn about 'the time of shame,' from 1916 to 1968, when the Louisiana Board of Education discouraged speakers of Cajun-French. Cajun musicians jam at the center from 6pm to 8pm on Monday evenings.

About 2mi east of town on Hwy 308 down Bayou Lafourche, **Laurel Valley Village** *(☎ 985-446-7456)*, established in 1785, is one of the best-preserved assemblages of plantation slave structures in the state. Hard by the highway, a nonprofit group operates the **General Store** *(open 10am-3pm Tues-Fri, noon-3pm Sat & Sun)*, which houses numerous displays about the now-abandoned settlement. You'll also find pirogues, vintage farm equipment and livestock. But the real reason to visit is to take a gander at the surviving slave quarters – 70 tumble-down tar-paper shacks, that seem to sway in the slightest breeze. The quarters can be viewed from the road, but a $5 donation might be enough to get a volunteer at the store to take you on a tour.

Places to Eat For breakfast, **Rob's Donuts** *(☎ 985-447-4080; cnr St Mary & Tiger Sts; open 24 hrs daily)* is the place to try for praline-stuffed pastries (two for $1) oozing with pecans and syrup.

Bubba's II *(☎ 985-446-5171; 764 Bayou Rd; open 11am-2pm Mon-Fri, 5pm-9:30pm Mon-Sat)*, a raucous sports bar, is your best bet for $5 po'boys overstuffed with shrimp or roast beef.

Fremin's *(☎ 985-449-0633; 402 W Third St; open 11am-2pm Mon-Fri, 5pm-11pm Wed-Sat)* serves innovative cuisine – Cobb salad with crab instead of ham ($9), crawfish-stuffed pork chop glazed with cane syrup ($16) – in a refurbished pharmacy.

But to eat really well, and cheaply, you'll have to do a bit of work, first stopping off at one of the Rouse's Grocery Stores (there are numerous locations dotting the town) for a few picnic fixings – some potato salad, French bread, mustard and, for dessert, one of their famous *tarte à la bouille* (a custard pie with a lattice-crust top) – and then head south on Hwy 24 toward Schriever.

Bourgeois Meat Market (☎ 985-447-7128; *519 Schriever Hwy*), at about the 3mi mark on Hwy 24, is one of the few remaining markets that operates its own slaughterhouse. Open since 1891, this is one of the best spots to sample links of andouille sausages. Then find a shady spot, slap a link of andouille on that French bread, smear it with mustard, heft a spoonful of potato salad to your plate and you have the makings of a fine lunch. Their beef jerky is justly celebrated as the smokehouse equivalent of shrunken sirloin.

Gros Place (☎ 985-446-6623; *710 St Patrick St; open 9am-about midnight daily*) is a popular spot, set in an old service station, where locals gather to shoot pool and quaff beer after beer. Stop by on a Friday evening and you're likely to get a chance to sample some deep-fried turkey, which the proprietor cooks for the crowd.

Getting There & Away Thibodaux is 60mi west of New Orleans, best reached by taking I-10 to the I-310 crossing of the Mississippi River, and then following Hwy 90 to Hwy 1, which parallels Bayou Lafourche for 17mi to Thibodaux.

Houma

Named for the Houma tribe of Native Americans, who were displaced in the mid-19th century by the Acadians, this town of 30,000 is the economic hub of the Cajun Wetlands region. Driving into town, up and over the many bridges that crisscross the numerous bodies of water wending their way through the city center (Bayou Black, Little Bayou Black, the Intracoastal Waterway and Bayou Terrebonne) you come to appreciate Houma's self-styled moniker, Venice of America. That said, the city itself offers little of interest to visitors, save functioning as

a way station for travelers on their way to the docks just west of town, from where two of the area's best swamp tours depart. The local tourist commission operates a **visitor center** (☎ 985-868-2732; *Hwy 90 at St Charles St*) west of town.

Organized Tours Locals vouch that the following two operators offer the best swamp tours. Both tours last two hours and are offered year-round on schedules that vary according to the season. Call for reservations. If both tours are booked out, check with the folks at the Bayou Delight Restaurant (see Places to Eat, following) for alternate suggestions. The restaurant seems to serve as a sort of de facto clubhouse for swamp-tour operators.

Alligator Annie Miller's Swamp Tours (☎ 985-879-3934; *Hwy 90; adult/child $15/ 10*), 8mi west of Houma, has been feeding chicken drumsticks to the alligator babies for so long that they're now trained to respond to the sound of her approaching motor and rise from the muck to take a bite. No matter if you take advantage of the moment as a photo opportunity or plunge headlong for the opposite side of the boat, it's great fun. More recently, **Annie Miller's Son's Swamp and Marsh Tours** (☎ 985-868-4758) got into the act, and may soon be the primary family provider.

Cajun Man's Swamp Cruise (☎ 985-868-4625; *Hwy 90; adult/child $15/10*), 10mi west of Houma, is run by Black Guidry, who serenades his passengers with a bit of accordion music, while piloting them through a scenic slice of swamp, his trusty dog Gator Bait at his side.

Places to Eat Looking and feeling like an old country store is **A-Bear's Café** (☎ 985-872-6306; *809 Bayou Black Dr; open 7am-5pm Mon-Thur, 7am-10pm Fri, 7am-2pm Sat*). Although it caters to the tourist trade, you'll find a good measure of locals inside, tucking into plates of red beans and rice, po'boys and plate lunch specials, topped off with a slice of icebox pie, all for about $10. And on most Friday nights, there's a live Cajun band.

Bayou Delight Restaurant (☎ 985-876-4879; Hwy 90; open 11am-10pm daily), about 7mi west of Houma, may display shellacked alligator snouts in the showcase by the register, but don't let that dissuade you; it's not really a tourist trap. Start with homemade onion rings ($2), followed by a plate of white beans and rice with fried catfish ($9). Most Friday and Saturday nights, it offers live Cajun or country music.

Getting There & Away Houma is 60mi west of New Orleans. Take I-10 west to I-310, cross the Mississippi River and follow Hwy 90 south into town. Thibodaux is just 20mi northwest of Houma by way of Hwy 20.

RIVER ROAD RAMBLE

Elaborate plantation homes line the banks of the Mississippi River between New Orleans and Baton Rouge along the 'River Rd.' Here, relatively simple French-Creole plantation homes, like those found at Vacherie, stand in stark contrast with the Greek-revival mansions built by American settlers after the Louisiana Purchase in 1803.

No matter what the architectural style on the River Rd, the stories of plantation slave society get short shrift. Instead, the emphasis is on the glory of days past, when black men and women of bondage labored at the behest of white masters. Save for the ascendant, but struggling, African American Museum at the Tezcuco Plantation and the Laura Plantation tours, you will get a feel for what life was like for the master and missus, but rarely will you catch a glimpse of life out the back of the big house, where slaves made the bricks, raised the roofs, tended the fires and worked the fields. Instead, expect costumed guides leading interior tours of 45 to 60 minutes, which focus on the lovely architecture, ornate gardens and genteel lifestyle of antebellum Louisiana. Most plantation houses have a gift shop, and daily hours of 9am or 10am to 4pm or 5pm. Admission usually includes a guided tour of the main house and self-guided tours of the grounds with their enormous moss-draped live oaks.

To understand the area, you must know a bit about agriculture. Throughout the time of French colonial stewardship, rice and indigo were the principal plantation crops. But, in 1795, with the introduction of the open-kettle process, which enabled sugar to be reduced to more easily transportable crystals, the agricultural economy was transformed. Sugarcane planting expanded exponentially during the antebellum period – as did slave ownership. Financial success led to the proliferation of grand plantation homes for which River Rd is now known. On the eve of the Civil War in 1861, Louisiana had 1200 plantations producing 95% of the sugar in the US.

Following the war, less than 200 plantations remained. Blacks and whites alike left the plantations in droves, heading north and west, in search of jobs. Today, many of the grand homes are open to the public, although the setting is far different than it once was. Where once stretched mile after mile of sugarcane fields, now sit myriad chemical plants and refineries, belching sulfurous clouds of smoke morning, noon and night – suffocating the surrounding countryside in a wet blanket of industrial fog. It's a truly surreal juxtaposition of old and new, of beauty and the beast.

Orientation

Looking at a map, the East Bank is the area above the Mississippi River, while the West Bank is the area below the river. 'Downriver' means heading southeastward, as the river flows toward New Orleans. 'Upriver' means northwestward, against the river's flow, toward Baton Rouge. River Rd is a name given, not to one particular road, but to the various routes that follow the sinuous levees. As an example, traveling upriver on the east bank, River Rd will show up on a map as Hwy 48, then Hwy 44 and then Hwy 942, yet few of the towns you pass through will display any signage to indicate the change in highway numbers.

Sound confusing? It isn't. Just keep the river in sight, and remember that ferry crossings are offered frequently. Should you stop to ask directions, memorize the difference between upriver and downriver, East Bank and West Bank before you ask.

EXCURSIONS

Along the East Bank

Only 12mi from New Orleans International Airport, **Destrehan Plantation** (☎ 985-764-9315; 13034 Hwy 48; open 9:30am-4pm daily), downriver from I-310, is the oldest plantation home remaining in the lower Mississippi Valley. Indigo was the principal crop in 1787 when Antoine Robert Robin DeLongy hired a mulatto builder to construct the original French colonial–style mansion, using *bousillage* (mud- and straw-filled) walls supported by cypress timbers. The house features a distinctive African-style hipped roof – no doubt a tip of the hat to the builder's ancestry. When DeLongy's daughter, Celeste, married Jean Noel Destrehan, they added the present Greek-revival facade. Tours by costumed guides cost $10 for adults, $5 for teens and $3 for children.

The stunning 'steamboat Gothic' **San Francisco Plantation** (☎ 985-535-2341; Hwy 44; open 10am-4pm daily), 20mi upriver from I-310, is on a 1700-acre site purchased in 1830 by Edmond B Marmillion from Elisee Rillieux, a free person of color. With $100,000 and 100 slaves, Marmillion's son, Valsin, built a grand sugar plantation. Today, only the architectural confection of the house and metal-domed cisterns remain. The surrounding fields where sugarcane once grew now sprout smokestacks. Tours of the ornately furnished interior are $10 for adults, $5 for teens and $3 for children.

One mile upriver from the Sunshine toll bridge, **Tezcuco Plantation** (☎ 225-562-3929; 3138 Hwy 44), a Greek-revival raised cottage, is no more grand than any number of grand homes downriver in New Orleans. But the onsite **African American Museum & Gallery** (☎ 225-562-7703; admission $3; open Mon-Fri by appointment, 1pm-5pm Sat & Sun) is worth a detour. Started by Kathe Hambrick (a local African-American woman who, after visiting Tezcuco several years ago, decided that someone needed to tell the story of the slaves), this humble museum details thehistory of escape and resistance during the time of slavery, as well as its aftermath. Typical of the displays is a facsimile of the container in which Henry 'Box' Brown escaped from slavery by 'shipping'

himself from Richmond, Virginia to Philadelphia, Pennsylvania.

Upriver from Tezcuco is a succession of three plantation homes worthy of a peek from the road. **Houmas House** (☎ 225-473-7841; 40136 Hwy 942; adult/teen/child $10/6/3; open 10am-5pm Feb-Oct, 10am-4pm Nov-Jan), 4mi upriver from the Sunshine Bridge, was named for the Native-American tribe that once inhabited the area. It offers a postcard image of the great Greek-revival plantation home that has long been associated with Louisiana. The original structure, built in the 1790s, now forms the back end of the main house, which was built in 1840. It's open for tours.

Upriver another 2mi and 3mi are two private antebellum homes: **Bocage Plantation House**, built in 1801 and remodeled in 1840, and the **Hermitage Plantation House**, built in 1812 by Marius Bringier, a Haitian builder responsible for many of the region's homes, including Whitehall, Tezcuco and Bocage. Its impressive Tuscan brick columns were added in 1838.

The **Ascension Parish Tourist Center** (☎ 225-675-6550) in the purposefully quaint **Cajun Village** (cnr Hwys 22 & 70), near I-10 exit 182, offers state and local maps and information. Also on the premises is **Southern Tangent Gallery** (☎ 225-675-6550) featuring works by more than 100 self-taught artists, including color-saturated images painted by Alvin Batiste of nearby Donaldsonville (see Along the West Bank, later), as well as the Coffee House (see Places to Eat, following).

Places to Eat For the widest variety of choices and the best prices, cross the Sunshine Bridge to the town of Donaldsonville (see Along the West Bank, following). That said, there are a number of convenient East Bank eateries also worth a try.

Don's Market (☎ 985-536-2275; 388 Central Ave; open 7am-7pm Mon-Sat, 8am-noon Sun), in Reserve, is the place to pack a picnic lunch. Try their housemade hogshead cheese and andouille sausage.

Airline Motors Restaurant (☎ 985-652-9181; 221 E Airline (Hwy 61); open 4am-10pm Mon-Thur, 24 hrs Fri-Sun) in La Place, is a rough-edged Art Deco palace, embellished with enough glass blocks, chrome and neon to send you reeling. Grab a seat at the counter and take it all in while enjoying a cup of surprisingly good chicken-andouille gumbo ($3), or a BLT.

Coffee House *(☎ 225-473-8236; cnr Hwys 70 & 22)* in Cajun Village, serves a heaping plate of crusty brown, powdered-sugar crowned beignets (doughnuts) for $1.50. Skip the rest of the menu.

Tut's Place *(☎ 225-675-8629; 3408 Hwy 70; open 6am-late daily)*, 4mi farther down Hwy 22 from the Coffee House, is a no-frills local favorite of a bar where the welcome is warm and the beers are cold. Most Fridays somebody is in the kitchen cooking for 'the hell of it.' The proprietor is Mama Tut.

Hymel's Seafood *(☎ 225-562-7031; 8740 Hwy 44; lunch specials around $5; open 11-2:30 Tues-Fri, dinner 11pm-10pm Fri & Sat, 11am-8pm Sun)* has been a local favorite for 40-plus years, and is 4mi downriver from the Sunshine Bridge. This former filling station now serves a fine platter of soft-shell crab ($8), as well as 'turtle sauce piquant' ($7) and weekday lunch specials.

Cabin Restaurant *(☎ 225-473-3007; cnr Hwys 44 & 22; open 11am-9pm Tues-Sat,* *11am-6pm Sun, 11am-3pm Mon)*, 2mi from the River Rd, is set in a collection of slave dwellings and other dependencies rescued from the demolished Monroe, Welham and Helvetia plantations. The interior walls are papered with old newspapers in the same manner that slaves once insulated the rough-sawn walls of their cabins. Besides po'boys you can get dishes such as red beans and rice with sausage for about $5, or an omelette filled with crawfish étouffée ($7). Broiled or fried seafood plates cost around $10. Even though the restaurant is geared toward serving the tourist crowds, the food is actually pretty good.

Along the West Bank

Laura Plantation *(☎ 225-265-7690; 2247 Hwy 18; open daily)* at Vacherie, is a comparatively unassuming West Indies–style plantation home, built in 1805 by Guillaume Duparc and named for his granddaughter, Laura Locoul. Rather than a pristine showplace, Laura Plantation is a work in progress, an ongoing historical experiment, wherein visitors are invited to imagine life as it existed for both slave and master. Here, thanks to the ongoing restoration efforts that give you a carpenter's-eye view of repairs,

---

Houseboat Heaven in Henderson

One of the most distinctive overnight experiences you can find anywhere is a night aboard a houseboat in the Atchafalaya Basin. Doug Sebatier and his wife Diane run **Houseboat Adventures** *(☎ 33/-228-7484)* and will 'push you out' from their landing in Jennings into a protected cove for a stay aboard a comfortably cozy, modern houseboat, which sleeps four to six in futons or twin bunks. The boats are equipped with generators to power the TV, VCR, lights and air-conditioning. Or you can skip the noise and go natural, with candles for light, the breeze off the water for cooling and the sounds of the birds, bugs and frogs (and maybe even an alligator's roar in mating season) for entertainment. Boats have two-burner ranges and some have mini-refrigerators. All have porch swings for rocking away the afternoon.

Bring your own food and drinking water, as well as an ice chest if you plan on drinking more than a 12-pack of beer or soft drinks over the course of your stay. Judging from guestbook accounts, beer drinking is a favorite pastime. A flashlight will also come in handy, as will insect repellent, and, of course, pack your fishing gear. The Sebatiers provide linens and towels, dishware, candles, matches and simple generator-operating lessons. They'll even throw in a pirogue or motorized skiff so you can row around, or motor back and forth to shore and nearby restaurants.

Advance reservations are essential. The peak rate, from March to October, is $145 a night (two-night minimum on weekends) plus a $25 towing fee. (A larger boat is available for $175.) Discounts are available for three or more nights. Henderson is about 40mi west of Baton Rouge, just off I-10.

EXCURSIONS

you will come to understand how these monstrous homes were constructed, and what back-breaking labor was required for their upkeep. Tours give equal weight to the grand architecture and mundane ephemera such as period clothing and even toiletries. Guided tours cost $10 for adults and $5 for children.

Just upriver of Laura Plantation, **Oak Alley Plantation** (☎ 225-265-2151; 3645 Hwy 18; adult/child $10/5; open 9am-5pm daily) features the most dramatic approach of all the plantations: a quarter-mile canopy of majestic live oaks running from the River Rd to the house. The 28 trees, 14 on each side of the driveway, predate the house by 100 years. More symmetry awaits at the plantation house, which is built in Greek-revival style: 28 columns, each 8ft in diameter, frame the scene. Tours are offered daily.

Donaldsonville is – surprise! – not a plantation, but a pleasant little town with a surprising collection of good restaurants (see Places to Eat, following). It's also home to the **Historic Donaldsonville Museum** (☎ 225-746-0004; cnr Railroad & Mississippi Sts; open 10am-4pm Tues, Thur & Sat), a charming paean to small-town life set in a majestic, white masonry building that was once home to the Lemann Department Store – at the time of its closing, it was the oldest family-owned department store in the state.

But the premier attraction in town, indeed one of the premier attractions on the River Rd, is **Rossie's Custom Framing** (☎ 225-473-8536; 510 Railroad Ave; open daily), where the works of folk artist Alvin Batiste are on display. His depictions of life in his home-town will take your breath away. And the prices are more than reasonable, with most pieces falling between the $100 to $500 range. Most days, he sets up his easel in the shops window, so he can watch the street life passing by. Hours vary, but afternoons are the best time to catch him in.

For sheer size, **Nottoway Plantation** (☎ 225-545-2730; Hwy 1; adult/child $10/4; open 9am-5pm daily), 2mi north of White Castle, built between 1849 and 1859 by Virginian sugar planter John Hampton Randolph, is the finest on the river. The largest

plantation house in the South, it has 64 rooms covering 53,000 sq ft. Guides don't wear costumes and don't deliver any drama, yet the tours are rich in personal history. The house has original furnishings and period pieces. Wide galleries with rocking chairs are accessible to visitors who wish to sit and gaze out upon the river.

Places to Eat For those on a River Rd ramble, Donaldsonville is by far the best place to stop for a meal. Set at the base of the Sunshine Bridge, it is an easy drive from most attractions.

First & Last Chance Café (☎ 225-473-8236; 812 Railroad Ave; open 9am-midnight Mon-Sat) is a relic of the time when this trackside joint was the only place to grab a drink on the rail trip from New Orleans to Baton Rouge. Great burgers ($2.50) and toothsome steaks smothered in garlic sauce (from $15) are the best bets.

Railroad Café (☎ 225-474-8513; 212 Railroad Ave; meals $5-7; open 10am-2pm Mon-Wed, 10am-7:30pm Thur-Sat), set in an old grocery store, is just the spot for an oyster po'boy. The cooks care, going so far as to ask whether you want your oysters fried 'soft, medium or crisp?' Plate lunches are also offered here.

Ruggiero's (☎ 225-473-8476; 206 Railroad Ave; open lunch 11am-1pm Tues-Fri, dinner 5pm-9pm Tues-Sat) is a creaky old bar and restaurant serving a wide range of foods, the best of which are the garlicky shrimp and pasta dishes ($12).

Lafitte's Landing at Bittersweet Plantation (☎ 225-473-1232; Railroad St) may well be the best haute cuisine restaurant between New Orleans and Lafayette. Although the setting is not as grand as the original Lafitte's Landing (it burned down in 1998), the executive chef, John Folse, has won a large following for his Cajun-influenced cuisine such as quail eggs in toasted brioche. Prices are steep at approximately $40 per person.

B&C Seafood Market & Cajun Deli (☎ 225-265-8356; 2155 Hwy 18; open 9am-6pm Mon-Sat), in Vacherie, is convenient to Laura Plantation, and if you stick to fried seafood po'boys, you'll eat well here for around $6.

Getting There & Away Travel times between destinations vary widely, depending upon whether you drive the interstate most of the way or prefer to take to the winding roads that hug the levee. It's best to budget the better part of a day for your trip, especially if you want to view more than one plantation. But don't despair if you're still on the road at 6pm and have 8pm dinner reservations in New Orleans. Even the distant upriver plantations are not much more than a one-hour drive from the city via I-10.

Between New Orleans and Baton Rouge, I-10 provides motorists with the quickest access to the winding, river-levee roads. Alternately, parallel to I-10, Hwy 61, once the primary artery north, offers a glimpse of the US roadside past. Ferries still outnumber bridges across the Mississippi River. A few motorists and all bicyclists use the state-operated ferries ($1 toll traveling westward, free eastward) to cross the river. Traveling upriver from New Orleans, you will come upon the following bridges in succession: the Huey Long Bridge (Hwy 90); I-310, which connects with Hwy 90, farther upriver; the Grammercy-Wallace Bridge (Hwy 641); and the Sunshine toll bridge (Hwy 70) at Donaldsonville.

BATON ROUGE

This industrial Mississippi River town is the home of the state's two largest universities – Louisiana State University (better known as LSU) and Southern University – as well as the nation's tallest capitol. You have to work a little harder to find something interesting to do hereabouts, but it can be done. Oh, in case you were wondering, the city's name, which translates from the French as 'red stick,' is said to derive from a Native-American practice of painting cypress poles with blood to mark off the boundaries of hunting territories.

Orientation

The new and old state capitols, casinos and a riverfront entertainment complex are downtown, off I-110. LSU is in the southwest quadrant of the city, off I-10. The neighboring streets are home to parks, inexpensive restaurants, nightclubs, movie theaters and shops. Highland Rd is the main college thoroughfare.

Things to See & Do

The **Louisiana Capitol** (☎ 225-342-7317), an Art Deco skyscraper built during the height of the Great Depression at a cost of more than $5 million, is populist Governor Huey Long's most visible legacy. Today, the 34-story capitol, a towering palace of marble, is a beauty to behold. On the 27th floor there is an **observation tower** offering sweeping views of the city, as well as a wonderful vantage point from which to watch the barges chugging by on the river.

Facing the capitol is a massive **bronze** of Long. His left hand rests on a marble replica of the capitol as if it were a scepter. His body is buried beneath. The inscription on the sculpture boasts that he was 'an unconquered friend of the poor who dreamed of the day when the wealth of the land would be spread among the people.'

A few blocks away you'll find the **Old State Capitol** (☎ 225-342-0500; 100 North Blvd; open 10am-4pm Tues-Sat, noon-4pm Sun). The imposing Gothic structure now serves as the Center for Political & Governmental History. Worth a look is a 20-minute film bolstered by interactive exhibits, the best of which allows you to stand at a lectern, call up a speech by Huey Long, and then watch and listen as the performance is projected on a screen in front of you while the text scrolls by on a teleprompter.

Louisiana State University sits on a 650-acre plateau southwest of town and is reached by way of Highland Rd. For visitor information, call ☎ 225-388-5030; for a fall football schedule and tickets, call ☎ 225-388-2184.

Also southwest of downtown is the **Rural Life Museum** (☎ 225-765-2437; 4600 Essen Lane; adult/senior/child $5/4/3; open 8:30am-5pm daily). The focus here is everyday life in the 19th century. View a collection of rural buildings typically found on sugar plantations, including slave cottages, a commissary, shotgun-style and dogtrot houses, an overseer's home and a sugar house with a 'Jamaica train' of open kettles. The oddest 'attraction' is the controversial sculpture known as 'Uncle Jack,' a tribute to the 'good darkies of Louisiana,' which was originally cast in 1927 and is now on display at the museum's entrance. You may view the sculpture without paying an entrance fee.

Places to Stay
Many of the chain motels, with rooms costing from $35 to $45, can be found just west of town on I-10 at exit 151 in Port Allen. More expensive at $55 to $85 are the hotels at I-10 exit 158, near College Dr. But if you plan to spend any time on or near LSU, you should book a room on campus at **Pleasant Hall** (☎ 225-387-0297). Basic rooms are $50.

Places to Eat
Poor Boy Loyd's (☎ 225-387-2271; 205 Florida St; open 7am-2pm Mon-Fri) is chockablock with political memorabilia, and the chicken and dumplings ($5), not to mention the po'boys, are good.

Arzi's Café (☎ 225-927-2111; 5219 Government St; meals from $10; open lunch & dinner) offers great vegie fare. Falafel, *baba ganoush* (eggplant dip), *dolmades* (stuffed vine leaves) and *spanakopita* (spinach and cheese pie) are offered; the best deal being a mix of appetizers to share for $18. Lamb, beef and chicken dishes are also on the menu.

Fleur-De-Lis Cocktail Lounge (☎ 225-924-2904; 5655 Government St; open 10am-10pm Tues-Sat) is a funky Baton Rouge favorite that's been in business since the 1940s. The Pepto Bismo–pink exterior and Art Deco–tinged interior are a kick, and the 'Roman' pizzas are tasty.

Silver Moon (☎ 225-387-3345; 206 W Chimes St), across the tracks from LSU, serves white beans and rice, smothered pork chops and turnip greens by the bowlful.

Louisiana Pizza Kitchen (☎ 225-763-9100; 7951 One Calais Ave; open 11am-10pm Sun-Thur, 11am-11pm Fri & Sat), the closest spot to the Rural Life Museum, serves new-wave pizzas and pastas ($8).

Getting There & Away
Traveling from New Orleans I-12 merges into I-10 on the eastern periphery of Baton Rouge, at which point I-10 continues westward toward Lafayette. Travel time from New Orleans is one to 1¼ hours.

CAJUN COUNTRY
Cajun Country encompasses a 22-parish region of southern Louisiana: a triangle bound by the Mississippi River Delta and the wetlands south of New Orleans, the uplands near Ville Platte and the Texan borderlands west of Lake Charles. Home to the largest French-speaking minority in the US, the region is named for the French settlers from L'Acadie (now Nova Scotia) who were exiled by the British in 1755, and almost 10 years later began seeking refuge in the bayou country.

Cajun Country consists of three distinct subregions. At the core is Lafayette, the self-proclaimed capital of French Louisiana. South of Lafayette, swinging east in an arc below New Orleans, is a maze of bayous and swamps where the first Cajuns settled. Northwest of Lafayette is the Cajun prairie, an area of cattle ranches and rice and crawfish farms settled by Acadians and Creoles; today, it's a center of Cajun and zydeco music.

Although much of Cajun Country is beyond the traditional driving distance (two hours) for a day trip, the sights, sounds and smells are so compelling that we couldn't leave the region out. Here's a very selective sampling of the best spots in the region.

Lafayette
Known as the 'Hub City,' Lafayette, with a population of 115,000, is best treated as a base from which you can explore the rural Cajun communities. But it becomes a destination in itself when one of the city's two great music festivals are staged. This is not an easy town to navigate, so here's a primer: I-10 traverses the north side of town; Evangeline Thruway bisects I-10 along parallel one-way streets. A mile south of I-10 on the Evangeline Thruway is the main **visitor center** (☎ 318-232-3737).

Things to See & Do The leading NPS museum in Cajun Country is the **Acadian Cultural Center** (☎ 337-232-0789; 501 Fisher Rd; admission free). Interactive displays –

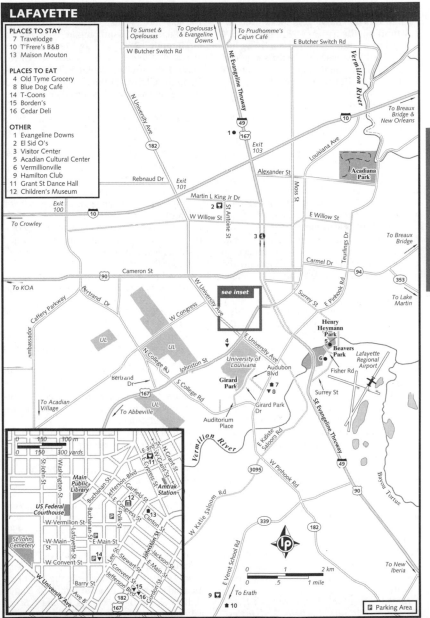

LAFAYETTE

PLACES TO STAY
7 Travelodge
10 T'Frere's B&B
13 Maison Mouton

PLACES TO EAT
4 Old Tyme Grocery
8 Blue Dog Café
14 T-Coons
15 Borden's
16 Cedar Deli

OTHER
1 Evangeline Downs
2 El Sid O's
3 Visitor Center
5 Acadian Cultural Center
9 Vermillionville
9 Hamilton Club
11 Grant St Dance Hall
12 Children's Museum

EXCURSIONS

P Parking Area

like a Cajun joke-telling booth – give life to local folkways. The rangers speak French.

Vermilionville (☎ *337-233-4077; 1600 Surrey St; adult/student $8/5*) is a living history and folklife museum. Docents in period costumes guide you through a 19th-century Cajun village. Bands perform shows daily in the barn, and there are daily cooking demonstrations and tastings.

Acadian Village (☎ *337-981-2364; 200 Greenleaf Dr; adult/child $6.50/2*) is less glitzy than Vermilionville and is favored by locals. Follow a brick path around a rippling bayou to restored houses, craft shops and a church. And be sure to check out the display dedicated to Dudley LeBlanc, the man behind Hadacol, an infamous patent medicine peddled as a quack's cure to gullible folks.

The **Children's Museum** (☎ *337-232-8500; 201 E Congress St; admission $5*) is of the hands-on variety. Kids are encouraged to explore an operating room, a TV studio and – this is Louisiana – an Acadian-style cottage.

Special Events In late February or early March, Lafayette hosts Mardi Gras parades, a **Courir de Mardi Gras** at Vermilionville, and a five-day festival leading up to Fat Tuesday; for information call ☎ 337-235-2471 or ☎ 800-346-1958. Better yet, for six days at the end of April, the free **Festival Internationale de Louisiane** (☎ *337-232-8086;* W *www.festivalinternational.com*) pulls 150,000 people to listen to music from the French-speaking world. In mid-September, the **Festivals Acadiens** (☎ *337 232-3737, 800-346-1958*) celebrates Acadian music, food and folklife.

Places to Stay Lafayette offers nearly 4000 hotel and 60 B&B rooms. All the usual chains are present at or near exits 101 and 103, off I-10. Budget rates are around $35 to $45 for doubles.

Travelodge (☎ *337-234-7402, 800-578-7878, fax 337-234-7404; 1101 W Pinhook Rd; singles/doubles $48/52*) is a bit south of downtown, but well located for exploring the city.

Maison Mouton (☎ *337-234-4661, fax 337-235-6755; 402 Garfield St; singles/*

doubles $59/89) is a B&B in a centrally located spot, which, although handsome, could use a bit of sprucing up.

T'Frere's B&B (☎/fax *337-984-9347,* ☎ *800-984-9347; 1905 E Verot School Rd; rooms $95*) is within walking distance of the Hamilton Club and offers six rooms, all with private bath. Breakfast is served on the porch.

Places to Eat The local favorite for $5 crawfish omelettes in the morning and $6 plates of smothered rabbit or jambalaya for lunch is **T-Coons** (☎ *337-232-3803; 740 Jefferson Blvd*).

Old Tyme Grocery (☎ *337-235-8165; 218 W St Mary St*), for $5 shrimp or roast beef po'boys at lunch or dinner, is the best in town.

Creole Lunch House (☎ *337-232-9929; 713 13th St*) serves a $6 lunch of savory pastry stuffed with sausage and cheese and good stewed cabbage.

Cedar Deli (☎ *337-233-5460; 1115 Jefferson Blvd*) is a Syrian-owned deli, that serves falafel, as well as vegie and meat muffulettas for $4 to $6.

Borden's (☎ *337-235-9291; 1103 Jefferson Blvd*), next door to Cedar Deli, dishes up fountain treats and milkshakes. Take a seat in a red-vinyl booth beneath Elsie the Cow's wide-eyed gaze.

Blue Dog Café (☎ *337-237-0005; 1211 W Pinhook Rd; entrees $13-21*), a Cajun-fusion restaurant decorated with 'blue dog' paintings by George Rodrique, is good to try for a splurge at dinner.

Prudhomme's Cajun Café (☎*337-896-7964; I-49 exit 7*), 7mi north of I-10 on I-49, is better yet. Here Paul Prudhomme's sister, serves $15 eggplant 'pirogue' stuffed with shrimp and crawfish.

Entertainment To find out who's playing in the clubs, look for the free, weekly *Times*. For zydeco, try **El Sid O's** (☎ *337-237-1959; 1523 Martin Luther King Dr*) at St Antoine St, a big and welcoming cinder-block joint, or **Hamilton Club** (☎ *337-991-0783; 1808 Verot School Rd*). For a more eclectic menu of musical offerings, head to **Grant St Dance Hall** (☎ *337-237-2255; 113 W Grant St*), a cavernous warehouse of a place.

When you're tired, hot and need to quench your thirst after a hard day's shopping at one of the city's many galleries (top left & right), cool down with a shaved-ice sno ball (bottom).

Stately oaks line the entrance to Oak Alley Plantation

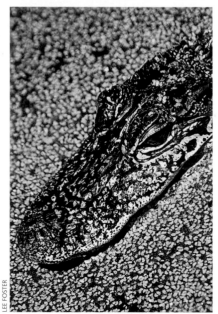

Lurking in the depths of the swamp

The lush, green bayou

Want to play the horses? **Evangeline Downs** (☎ 337-896-7223) is a mile north of I-10. Listen out for the announcer's call at the start of each race, '*Ils sont partis!*' ('They're off!').

Getting There & Away Lafayette is an hour west of Baton Rouge and two hours west of New Orleans by way of I-10. **Greyhound** (☎ 337-235-1541; cnr Clinton & Lee Sts) offers 11 buses a day running from New Orleans ($17.50 one way).

St Martinville

Massive **Evangeline Oak**, poised along Bayou Teche just off Main St, has become a lodestar for those seeking a connection to the Acadians deposed during *le Grand Dérangement* – the expulsion of French men and women from Canada's Acadie. Thanks goes, in large part, to Henry Wadsworth Longfellow's 1847 epic poem *Evangeline*, which recounts the story of star-crossed French lovers Evangeline and Gabriel.

This is picture-postcard beautiful town, worthy of an hour or two of ambling about. Facing Main St is the graceful **St Martin de Tours Church** (☎ 337-394-7334; open daily). Even though the church was built c. 1844, the congregation dates back to 1765. To gain a deeper understanding of the events that compelled Longfellow to write his ode, and grasp how African Americans have made this region their own, visit the **Museum of the Acadian Memorial and African American Museum** (☎ 337-394-2258; open daily 10am-4pm), which is alongside Evangeline Oak.

A mile north of town on Hwy 31 is **Longfellow-Evangeline State Historical Site** (☎ 337-394-3754; admission $2; open 9am-5pm daily), a former sugar plantation. Today the lush grounds boast huge moss-draped trees, a narrow bayou, and a restored, raised Creole cottage (1815), which is open for tours. Occasional living-history programmes shed light on 19th-century life.

Feeling a bit hungry? For breakfast try a pastry and coffee ($2) at **Poupart's Bakery** (☎ 337-394-5366; 207 E Bridge St), while a lunch of $5 stewed shrimp over rice is best

at **Josephine's Creole Restaurant** (☎ 337-394-8030; 830 S Main St). For dinner, drive 10mi south to New Iberia (see following).

St Martinville is about 15mi southeast of Lafayette. Driving from New Orleans, take Hwy 31 south 12mi from Breaux Bridge. Travel time from New Orleans is a little more than two hours.

New Iberia

Named for the Iberian Peninsula, New Iberia was settled by the Spanish in 1779. The town prospered on the sugarcane of surrounding plantations. Today, the town's best-known native son may well be mystery writer James Lee Burke, whose novels often take place in and around New Iberia and feature Detective Dave Robicheaux.

Want to wander about? Look for a poster emblazoned with a proposed walking tour on the front of the now closed Evangeline Theater on E Main St. Any walk should start at **Shadows on the Teche** (☎ 337-365-5213; 317 E Main St; adult/child $6/3), a grand, Greek-revival plantation house set on the bank of Bayou Teche. End your tour in the City Park along the bayou.

Estorage-Norton House (☎ 337-365-7603; 446 E Main St; rooms $60-90), across the street from Shadows, is a comfortable 100-plus-year-old home. Prices for one of the four rooms include a full breakfast.

Teche Hotel (☎ 337-369-3756; 1030 E Main St; rooms about $40), east of town, is a retro cottage-style place on the cheaper side.

Bon Creole (☎ 337-367-6181; 1409 E St Peter), is the place to try for $5 po'boys overstuffed with shrimp. While at **Brenda's Diner** (☎ 337-367-0868; 409 W Pershing St) $6 plate lunches of chicken fricassee and amazing smothered okra are best.

There are also a couple of upscale dining spots in town; the best among them are **Clementine's** (☎ 337-560-1007; 113 E Main St) and **Le Rosier** (☎ 337-367-5306; 314 E Main St).

Guiding Star (☎ 337-365-9113) is a great place for $15 trays of boiled crawfish and crabs seasoned with Tabasco dregs. Located a few miles north of town along Hwy 90, it's on the east side of the road near a truck stop.

Avery Island

Drive southwest of New Iberia along Hwy 329 through cane fields to Avery Island, home of McIlhenny Tabasco factory and a wildlife sanctuary. The island is actually a salt dome that extends 8mi below the surface. The salt mined here goes into the sauce, as do the locally grown peppers. The peppers and salt mixture ferments in oak barrels before it is mixed with vinegar, strained and bottled.

McIlhenny Tabasco (☎ 337-365-8173) tours run from 9am to 4pm daily and are a touchstone for many travelers, but most visitors no longer enter the factory itself. One way to beat the system: Order a bag of the 'Tabasco dregs,' which are the lees strained when making the sauce, and you'll gain a fine seasoning mix and get a back-door tour to boot.

At nearby **Jungle Gardens** (☎ 337-365-8173; adult/child $5.75/4; open 8am-4:30pm daily) drive or walk through 250 acres of subtropical jungle flora. View an amazing array of waterbirds (especially snowy egrets, which nest here), turtles and even alligators. Watch for turtles and peacocks crossing the road.

New Iberia is 30 minutes southeast of Lafayette by way of Hwy 90. Travel time from New Orleans is approximately 2½ hours.

Eunice

Eunice is the family oriented flip side to smaller and more decadent Mamou (see later). Thanks to the Prairie Acadian Cultural Center and the Liberty Theater it's also the unofficial capital of prairie Cajun heritage. The best day to visit is Saturday, when the Liberty Theater is open. The **Chamber of Commerce** (☎ 337-457-2565, 800-222-2342) operates a **visitor center** (Hwy 13), which is downtown.

The **Prairie Acadian Cultural Center** (☎ 337-457-8490; cnr Third St & Park Ave), adjacent to the Liberty Theater, is part of Jean Lafitte National Historic Park and Preserve. The displays at the cultural center introduce visitors to Acadian heritage, as well as mapping the immigration of French men and women to Louisiana. The gift shop has a good selection of books.

The **Liberty Theater** (☎ 337-457-7389; cnr S Second St & Park Ave), c. 1924, is best known for its **Rendez-vous des Cajuns** (admission $3, child under 12 free), which is a Saturday-night performance broadcast on local radio stations. The Rendez-vous des Cajuns features traditional Cajun music in a variety-show format. Tickets go on sale at 4pm, and the show runs from 6pm to 8pm. Also worth a peek is the **Cajun Music Hall of Fame** (☎ 337-457-6534; 240 First St) which showcases Cajun instruments and other musical memorabilia.

Three miles east of town is **Savoy Music Center** (☎ 337-457-9563), which houses the accordion factory of musician Marc Savoy. On most Saturday mornings, Savoy hosts a Cajun-music jam session happens here from around 10am to noon; his wife, Ann, a guitarist, often joins him (her book *Cajun Music: A Reflection of a People* is a must for serious aficionados). Look for the huge Savoy Music Company sign west of the Cajun Campground.

Places to Stay Surrounded by woods, **Cajun Campground** (☎ 337-457-5753; Hwy 190; tent/RV sites $10/16, cabins $55) has a pool, small store, playground and small lake. The seven cabins also have kitchenettes.

Howard's Inn (☎ 337-457-2066; 3789 Hwy 190; singles/doubles $40/50), a bit closer to town, has clean rooms.

Best Western (☎ 337-457-2800, 800-962-8423; 1531 W Laurel Ave; singles/doubles $65/75), west of downtown, has a pool.

Places to Eat Considered by many to be the best purveyor of *boudin* (sausage) in the state is **Johnson's Grocery** (☎ 337-457-9314; 700 E Maple Ave).

Ruby's Café (221 W Walnut Ave), in business since 1958, is the place to head to for a lunch of stewed shrimp atop rice.

Mama's Fried Chicken (☎ 337-457-9978; 1640 W Laurel/Hwy 190) serves good fried birds, but better yet is their crawfish *étouffée*, served by the bowl, or ladled into a hotdog bun and dubbed a 'crawdog.'

Getting There & Away Eunice is 20mi west of Opelousas on Hwy 190 and about 20mi north of I-10 exit 80 at Crowley. Travel time from New Orleans is approximately 2½ hours.

Mamou

Mamou is a rough-and-tumble prairie town that has seen better days. The main drag, 6th St, is a ragtag collection of sleepy businesses and boarded storefronts. Visit any day other than Saturday, and you'll never know that this little village hosts two of the wildest celebrations in Louisiana.

In 1950, Mamou citizens revived the traditional **Courir de Mardi Gras**, where, instead of tossing beads from floats, celebrants mount horses and tear off through the countryside, often collecting the ingredients for a gumbo from nearby farmers. The garb worn (colorful suits, spooky wire-mesh masks) adds to the mystique. Mamou hosts a street party on the Monday night of Mardi Gras, and sends its riders out at 7am Tuesday morning, welcoming drunken celebrants back to 6th St at around 3pm that afternoon.

The other great Mamou event takes place not once a year, but each Saturday morning. Welcome to **Fred's Lounge** (☎ 337-468-5411; 420 6th St): Tanté Sue, a grandmotherly looking woman, her face framed by a halo of gray curls, is taking healthy swigs from a bottle of cinnamon-flavored schnapps, squeezing her chest in time to the music as if playing an anthropomorphic accordion. A gaggle of middle-aged couples waltz a wide arc around the band. Not an uncommon sight for Louisiana, you say? Check the clock. It's only 9:30 in the morning, and Fred's is at full tilt. It's like this every Saturday at Fred's. And for those lucky enough to squeeze through the front door, it may well be the best free show in Louisiana. From 9am to 1pm, Wayne Thibodaux and Cajun Fever broadcast live from the bar over KVPI 92.5 FM.

Your best bet is to enjoy a little dining and dancing in Opelousas or Eunice on Friday night, and then bed down, rising early for the drive to Mamou. Or, from New Orleans,

take I-10 west to Baton Rouge, then Hwy 190 west through Opelousas to Eunice. Turn north on Hwy 13 to Mamou. Total travel time from New Orleans: 2½ hours; Eunice is 15 minutes away, and Opelousas 25 minutes.

Opelousas

Opelousas is the epicenter of Louisiana zydeco club culture. You haven't really experienced this music until you've made the trek to Slim's Y-Ki-Ki or Richard's Club, two of the most venerable venues in the state. These are the kinds of bars where if you clap at the close of a song, you're immediately branded an interloper, for in the clubs of southwest Louisiana, if you like the music, you dance.

Both **Slim's Y-Ki-Ki** (☎ 337-942-9980; Hwy 167 N) and **Richard's Club** (☎ 337-543-6596; Hwy 190 W) are family run bars that welcome outlanders with open arms. Although it might be best to call ahead, you can almost be assured that, on the weekends, these wobbly wood-frame buildings will be featuring local acts of international renown.

If you're keen on learning a bit more about zydeco, stop by the **Opelousas Museum and Interpretive Center** (☎ 337-948-2589; 315 N Main St) where they house a collection of recordings made at the annual **Southwest Louisiana Zydeco Festival** (☎ 337-942-2392; w www.zydeco.org). The festival is held the Saturday before Labor Day in a bean field north of town near Plaisance. It's, arguably, the best music festival in the state.

The **Town House Motel** (☎ 337-948-4488; 343 W Landry St; singles/doubles $35/40) has simple rooms, while the **Quality Inn** (☎ 337-948-9500; Hwy 190 at I-49; singles/doubles $65/70), has all the accustomed amenities including an outdoor pool. A worthwhile splurge is the **Estorge-Norton House** (☎ 337-942-8151; 446 E Main St; rooms $60-90), an opulent 1827 home that's just a few blocks off the square.

The **Palace Café** (☎ 337-942-2142; Hwy 190) is a downtown institution, which has been in business since 1954 and is famous for onion rings and fried chicken. Lunch and dinner run at about $7 to $10. Just want a little something? Try **Billy's and Ray's Boudin and Cracklins** (☎ *337-942-9150; 904 Short Vine St)* where $1 gets you a link of sausage and a four crackers. Look for the sign: a pistol-packing sausage sporting a cowboy hat.

To get to Opelousas from New Orleans, take I-10 west 70mi to Baton Rouge, and then Hwy 190 northwest for 45mi. Total travel time is two hours.

Glossary

andouille – (ahn-**doo**-we) a French sausage made with tripe; Creole versions are made from ground pork in casings of smoked pig intestines; also known as chitterlings

arpent – a French unit of measurement equal to 0.85 acres

banquette – diminutive form of 'banc' meaning bench, applied to early wooden boardwalks; today it's sometimes used to refer to sidewalks

bayou – a canal of sluggish and marshy water removed from the main river channel

beignet – (ben-**yea**) a deep-fried pastry, which is New Orleans' version of the doughnut; typically covered with powdered sugar and sweet, although savory variations also exist

boudin – *Cajun* sausage usually filled with pork, pork liver and rice

briquette entre poteaux – similar to English half-timber construction, except that bricks are used to fill the intervening wall space between posts

café au lait – mixture of coffee and steamed milk

Cajun – a corruption of the word Acadian; the term refers to a Louisianan descended from French-speaking Acadia, but may also apply to other rural settlers that live amid Cajuns; also relating to food and music

carpetbagger – a derogatory name given to itinerant financial or political opportunists, particularly Northerners in the reconstructed South, who moved in with their possessions in heavy cloth satchels; their Southern accomplices were branded 'scalawags'

chicory – a root plant related to endive; *Creole* coffee is a blend of roasted coffee beans (60%) and chicory (40%)

Code Noir – the 'Black Code' adopted by the French administration in 1724 that governed the conduct of free people of color and prescribed how masters should treat slaves and under what conditions freedom should be granted; free people of color were accorded the rights of full citizenship except that they could neither vote, hold public office nor marry a white person

Creole – a free person of French, Spanish or African descent born in Spanish America; during the 19th century whites of French or Spanish descent used Creole to exclusively refer to whites; however, following the Civil War the term also came to encompass the free Creoles of color; its definition has shifted with time – now persons descended from any of the above cultures are regarded as Creole (from the Spanish 'criollo,' meaning native to the locality); also relating to food and music

dirty rice – small quantities of giblets or ground pork, along with green onions, peppers and celery, fried with rice

dressed – a 'dressed' *po'boy* sandwich comes with mayonnaise, mustard, lettuce and tomato

entresol – mezzanine-like area of low rooms between the ground floor and the 1st floor; in many French Quarter buildings the entresol was used for storage

étouffée – (ay-too-**fay**) literally 'smothered,' in French; a spicy, tomato-based stew that typically includes either crawfish, shrimp or chicken, served with rice

fais-do-do – *Cajun* house dance

filé – ground sassafras leaves used to thicken sauces; a Native-American contribution to Louisiana cuisine

frottoir – a metal rubboard used for percussion, especially in *zydeco* music

gallery – a balcony or roofed promenade

gens de couleur libre – French phrase for the 'free people of color' during the antebellum period; after the Civil War they were known as *Creole*s of color

go cup – a plastic container provided for patrons so that they can transfer an alcoholic beverage from a bottle or glass as they leave a bar; it is legal to drink alcoholic beverages in the street; however, it's illegal to carry an open glass container

Grand Dérangement – literally 'forced migration;' used to describe the great dispersal of Acadians; following the 18th-century colonial wars between England and France, 10,000 Acadians were deported from Nova Scotia by the English in 1755

gris-gris – magical objects used in voodoo, which have curative, protective or evil powers

grits – coarsely ground hominy prepared as a mush; served throughout the South it picks up the flavor of whatever is ladled over it, often butter or gravy

gumbo – traditionally an African soup thickened with okra and containing seafood or chicken; *Cajun* gumbos substitute a *filé* powder for okra

icebox pie – a cold, often creamy, pie

jambalaya – one-dish meal of rice cooked with onions, peppers and celery along with ham; Louisiana chefs waste nothing – any leftovers go into this dish

jus – sauce

krewes – clubs that sponsor Mardi Gras parades and events; ersatz Old English spelling for 'crews'

Ku Klux Klan – KKK; an organization begun in 1866 that espouses white supremacy; although outlawed by the federal government in 1870, it has secretly conducted a campaign of violence against blacks and others whom they accuse of betraying the white race

lagniappe – literally 'a little something extra'; small gift from a merchant or resident

levee – a French word meaning 'raised' or 'elevated' that applies to the natural or artificial riverbanks that guard the floodplain

meunière – (muhn-**yair**) food, usually fish, seasoned, coated lightly in flour and pan-fried in butter; served with a lemon-butter sauce

mirliton – an indigenous pear-shaped vegetable with a hard shell that is cooked like squash and stuffed with either ham or shrimp and spicy dressing; known as 'chayote' in Spanish-speaking parts of the world

muffuletta – Italian dock workers were once sustained with this enormous sandwich of ham, hard salami, provolone and olive salad piled onto a round loaf of Italian bread and liberally sprinkled with olive oil and vinegar

mulatto – the child of a black and a white parent

neutral ground – a median; the Canal St median served as a neutral meeting space dividing the *Creole* and American communities

NPS – National Park Service

picayune – used to refer to something of little value; also a coin formerly used by the Spanish in the South

pirogue – a dugout canoe that was traditionally carved by burning the center of a log and scraping out the embers; modern pirogues are shallow-draft vessels that can be made from plywood

po'boy – a submarine-style sandwich served on fresh French bread; fried oysters, soft-shell crabs, catfish or deli meats are offered as fillings

praline – a dessert made from pecans, sugar and butter

quadroon – a person who is one-quarter black; the term was used to refer to light-skinned free women of color in the 18th and 19th centuries

red beans and rice – spicy bean stew made with peppers, many seasonings and a hunk of salt pork, or *tasso*, often served over white rice with *andouille* sausage

rémoulade – (reh-moo-**laud**) mayonnaise-based sauce with a variety of ingredients such as pickles, herbs, capers and mustard; crawfish or shrimp rémoulade is often a cold noodle salad

réveillon – a traditional *Creole* Christmas Eve dinner

R&B – abbreviation of rhythm & blues; a musical style developed by African Americans that combines blues and jazz

roux – a mixture of flour and oil or butter that is heated slowly until it browns; used as a thickener in *Cajun* soups and sauces

second line – the partying group that follows parading musicians

swamp – a permanently waterlogged area that often supports trees

tasso – a highly spiced cured pork that's smoked for two days; small quantities are used to flavor many dishes

'trad' jazz – traditional jazz, as it was played before the Swing era

Vieux Carré – French for 'old square;' it refers to the French Quarter; original walled city of New Orleans bounded by Canal St, N Rampart St, Esplanade Ave and the Mississippi River

zydeco – fast, syncopated *Creole* dance music, which is influenced by *Cajun*, African-American and Afro-Caribbean cultures; often a combination of *R&B* and *Cajun* with French lyrics; bands typically feature guitar, accordion and *frottoir*

Index

Abbreviations

MG – Mardi Gras color section between 48 & 49

Text

A

A&P Market 155
Abita Brewery 159-62
Abita Springs 159-62
Acadian Cultural Center 174-6
Acadians, see Cajuns
accommodations 109-19
    apartments 119
    B&Bs 115
    Bywater 114-15
    camping 110, 159, 162, 178
    Central Business District
        115-16
    Esplanade Ridge 118
    Faubourg Marigny 114-15
    for Mardi Gras & Jazz Fest
        111
    French Quarter 111-13
    Garden District 116-17
    hostels 110-11
    hotels & guesthouses 52,
        111-19
    houseboats 171
    Lower Garden District 116-17
    Mid-City 119
    rates 109-10
    reservations 109
    tipping 42
    Tremé District 113-14
    Uptown 118
    Warehouse District 115-16
    see also Places to Stay index
        for listings
activities, see specific activities,
    eg, jogging
Adams, Johnny 29
African American Museum &
    Gallery 170
African Americans
    books 46
    Carnival MG6-8
    exhibits 85, 86, 97, 170
    festivals 55
    history 12, 17-18
    soul food 121
    special events 54-7
    tours 69

AIDS 50
air pollution 21
air travel 58-60, 63
    airline offices 60-2
    New Orleans International
        Airport 60, 63, 119
    overseas travel 59-60
    to/from the airport 63-4
    travel within the USA 58-9
airport, see New Orleans
    International Airport
alligators 21, 155, 168
Almonaster y Roxas, Don
    Andrés 75-6
Amistad Research Center 52,
    53, 97-108
Andrews, James 31-2
animals 21, 46-7, 88, 96-7,
    106, 178
antiques 153
Antoine's 126
apartments 119
Aquarium of the Americas
    87-8
Archibald Boulware House 93
architecture 22-3, 71, see also
    historic buildings
area codes 43-4
arenas & auditoriums 146-7
Armstrong, Louis 26-7, 32, 47,
    84-5, 87
arts 22-34, 90-1, 152-3
ATMs 41
Audubon Institute 87, 96, 106-7
Audubon Louisiana Nature
    Center 51, 106-7
Audubon Park 100
Audubon Zoological Gardens
    96
Avart-Peretti House 73
Avery Island 178

B

B&Bs 115
Backstreet Museum 85
Bank of Louisiana 74

banks 40-1
Barataria Preserve 164
Barbarin, Paul 27-8
Barbecue Swingers 31, 144
bargaining 42
Barker, Blue Lu 28
Barker, Danny 27-8
bars
    in New Orleans 139-46
    outside New Orleans 163,
        165, 176
    tipping 42
    see also entertainment
Bartholomew, Dave 28-9
baseball 149
basketball 149
Baton Rouge 61, 173-5
Battle of New Orleans 15, 54
Bayou St John 36, 101-3, **102**,
    Map 7 (color)
    walking tour 101-3
Beauregard, PGT 72, 82-3,
    103, 106
Beauregard-Keyes House 72,
    82
Bechet, Sidney 27, 32
bicycles, see cycling
Bienville, Jean-Baptiste Le
    Moyne, Sieur de 12, 19
Bigard, Barney 27
Black Code, see Code Noir
blues 28
boats 62, 67, 88, 89, 97
Bocage Plantation House 170
Bolden, Buddy 25-6, 47
Bonaparte, Napolean 14, 75
Booker, James 28
books 23-33, 45-8, 151-2,
    see also literature
bookstores 50-1, 73, 151-2
Botanical Gardens 104
Bourbon St 141
Bourgeois Meat Market 168
brass bands 30-1
Brown, Henry 170
Buckner House 94
bus travel 61, 63-4

184

Bold indicates maps.

Places to Stay

Places to Eat

Boxed Text

New Orleans Map Section

MAP 1 – NEW ORLEANS

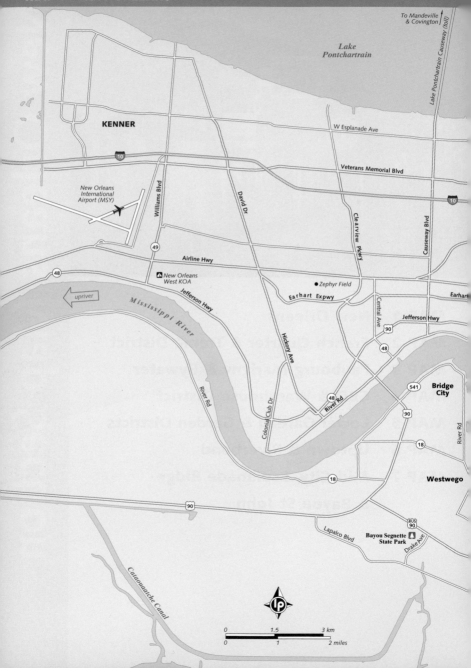

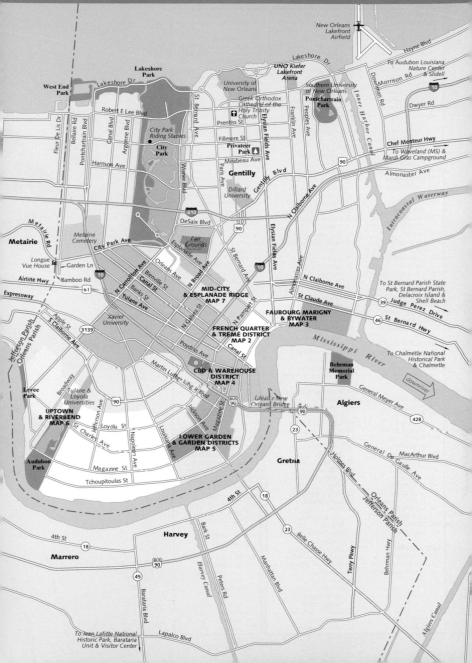

MAP 2 – FRENCH QUARTER & TREMÉ DISTRICT

FRENCH QUARTER

PLACES TO STAY
12 Le Richelieu
18 Hotel St Pierre
21 Gentry House
22 The Creole House Hotel
25 Lafitte Guest House
27 Ursuline Guest House
30 Soniat House
38 Hotel Villa Convento
52 Cornstalk Hotel
53 Andrew Jackson Hotel
54 Chateau Hotel
55 Hotel Provincial
70 Bourbon Orleans Hotel
72 Place d'Armes Hotel
115 Omni Royal Orleans
119 Royal Sonesta
149 Hotel Monteleone

PLACES TO EAT
9 Port of Call
10 Verti Marte
11 Mona Lisa
16 Peristyle
33 Louisiana Pizza Kitchen
37 Croissant d'Or Patisserie
41 Angeli on Decatur
43 Coop's Place
51 Clover Grill
56 Irene's Cuisine
58 Café Sbisa
68 Central Grocery
85 La Madeleine French Bakery & Café
89 Court of Two Sisters
90 Royal Blend; Royal Access
93 Gumbo Shop
98 Café du Monde
100 Bayona
102 Antoine's
116 Café Maspero
118 Arnaud's
122 Brennan's Restaurant
126 Johnny's Po-Boys
127 Crescent City Brewhouse
131 K-Paul's Louisiana Kitchen
132 NOLA
140 Galatoire's
142 Café Beignet
145 Acme Oyster and Seafood House
146 Felix's Sea Food
148 Mr B's Bistro
160 Olivier's
161 Palace Café

BARS & CLUBS
14 El Matador
20 Donna's Bar & Grill
24 Lafitte's Blacksmith Shop
31 The Hideout
35 Palm Court Jazz Café
42 The Abbey
44 Molly's at the Market
45 Margaritaville Café
49 Funky Butt on Congo Square
50 Rawhide 2010
61 Bourbon Pub and Parade Disco
62 Oz
78 Preservation Hall
79 Pat O'Brien's
107 Shim Sham Club
124 Napoleon House
141 Jean Lafitte's Old Absinthe House
154 Kerry Irish Pub
155 The Parish
156 House of Blues

OTHER
8 Kaboom Books
13 David's
15 Old US Mint; New Orleans Jazz Exhibit; Houma Indian Arts Museum; Southern Repertory Theater
17 Hula Mae's Laundry
19 Voodoo Spiritual Temple
23 Alternatives Shop
26 French Quarter Postal Emporium
28 Royal Pharmacy
29 Gallier House & Museum
32 The Garage
34 Rock & Roll Collectibles
36 Starling Books & Crafts
39 Beauregard-Keyes House
40 Ursuline Convent
46 New Orleans Jazz National Historic Park
47 Farmer's Market
48 Flea Market
57 Santa's Quarters
59 French Market; Public Restrooms
60 Marie Laveau's House of Voodoo
63 Historic Voodoo Museum
64 Royal Mail Service
65 Madame John's Legacy
66 Royal Rags
67 Uncle Wilbur's Emporium
69 Uptown Costumes & Dancewear
71 Arcadian Books & Art Prints
73 Librairie Books
74 Trashy Diva
75 Photo Works
76 French Quarter Bicycles
80 Reverend Zombie's House of Voodoo
81 Labranche Buildings
82 Old Children's Books
83 St Anthony's Garden
84 Presbytère
86 New Orleans Welcome Center
87 1850 House & Museum Store
88 Court of Two Lions
91 A&P Market
92 Johnny Donnel's
94 Faulkner House Bookstore
95 Cabildo
96 St Louis Cathedral
97 Jackson Monument
99 Musée Conti Historical Wax Museum
101 Hermann-Grima House
103 Kurt E Schon Gallery
104 Historic New Orleans Collection; Merieult House
105 Brulatour Courtyard
106 Le Monde Creole
108 Bastille Computer Café
109 Le Petit Théâtre du Vieux Carré
112 Post Office
113 Louisiana State Bank; New Orleans Police Department; Tourist Information Center
114 James H Cohen & Sons
117 Jackson Brewery; Virgin Megastore; Public Restrooms
120 Rillieux-Waldhorn House
121 Louisiana State Bank
123 Maspero's Exchange
125 Little Shop of Fantasy
128 ATM
129 Vieux Carré Wine & Spirits
130 Williams Research Center
133 New Orleans School of Cooking
134 Jean Lafitte National Historic Park NPS Visitor Center
135 Magic Bus Records
136 Bookstar
137 ATM
138 Tower Records
139 Bourbon Strip Tease
143 La Belle Galerie
144 Southern Candy Makers
147 U-Park Garage
150 A Gallery for Fine Photography
151 Stone and Press
152 Crescent City Books
153 Civil War Store
157 Beckham's Bookstore
158 Werlein's for Music
159 Louisiana Music Factory
162 US Custom House
163 Entergy IMAX Theater

TREMÉ DISTRICT

PLACES TO STAY
1 Maison Esplanade
2 Hotel Storyville
3 Rathbone Inn

BARS & CLUBS
4 Joe's Cozy Corner

OTHER
5 New Orleans African American Museum
6 St Augustine's Church
7 Backstreet Museum
110 Mortuary Chapel
110 Budget Rent-A-Car
111 Saenger Theatre

TREMÉ
DISTRICT

FAUBOURG
MARIGNY

Washington
Square
Park

Police
Station

Radio
Station

Perseverance
Hall

Louis
Armstrong
Park

Louis
Armstrong
Statue

Municipal
Auditorium

Congo
Square

FRENCH
QUARTER

Jackson
Square

Pontalba
Buildings

State
Supreme
Court

Steamboat Natchez
(Riverboat)

Mississippi River

ALGIERS

Woldenberg
Park

John James Audubon
(Riverboat Zoo Cruise)

Ferry to Algiers

Canal
Place

Harrah's
Casino

Aquarium
of the
Americas

Cajun Queen
(Riverboat)

Canal St Ferry

see MAP 3
Faubourg Marigny
& Bywater

0   150   300 m
0   150   300 yards

MAP 3 – FAUBOURG MARIGNY & BYWATER

N Rocheblave St
N Tonti St
Allen St
Annette
N Anthony St
Pauger St
Touro
Frenchmen St
Marigny St
Mandeville St
Spain St
N Roch Ave
Music St
Arts St
Painters St
AP Tureaud Ave
New Orleans St
Franklin Ave
N Miro St
N Galvez St
Elysian Fields Ave

I-10

N Johnson St

St Roch Park

N Prieur St

N Roman St

St Roch Cemetery

N Derbigny St

39

N Claiborne Ave

N Robertson St

39

Roman St

N Villere St

Derbigny St

Urquhart St

I-10

3021

N Claiborne Ave

Marais St

N Robertson St

St Claude Ave   46   ■ 1   ● 2

N Villere St

Kerlerec St

N Rampart St

N Peters St

Marais St

Burgundy St

N Rampart St
Marigny St
Mandeville St
Spain St
N Roch Ave
Music St

TREMÉ DISTRICT

St Aloysius ♦

6
● 7

8 ▼

Washington Square Park
▼ 9

Dauphine St

10 ▼

FAUBOURG MARIGNY

St Augustine's Church ♦

Treme St

Burgundy St

Esplanade Ave

♦ 12

13 14

● 15

17 ▼ 16
19 ▼ 18
21 ▼ 20

Royal St

Chartres St

● 22   23 ■

Louis Armstrong Park

St Claude Ave

Governor Nicholls St

Barracks St

27 ●

28 ▼ 30
29 ▼ 31

Decatur St

Louis Armstrong Statue

St Philip St

Ursulines Ave

32 33
■ 34
■ 35
■ 36   37 ■

N Peters St

see MAP 2 French Quarter & Tremé District

Dauphine St

Bourbon St

Royal St

Chartres St

Old US Mint

Port St

N Peters St

Esplanade

Elysian Fields Ave

📮 Post Office

FRENCH QUARTER

Dumaine St

St Ann St

Orleans St

St Peter St

Troulouse St

Ursuline Convent

French Market Pl

Decatur St

Riverfront Streetcar

N Peters St

⊞ Ursulines

French Market

Madison

Dumaine

Moonwalk

St Louis Cathedral

Jackson Square

Pontalba Buildings

Mississippi River

upriver →

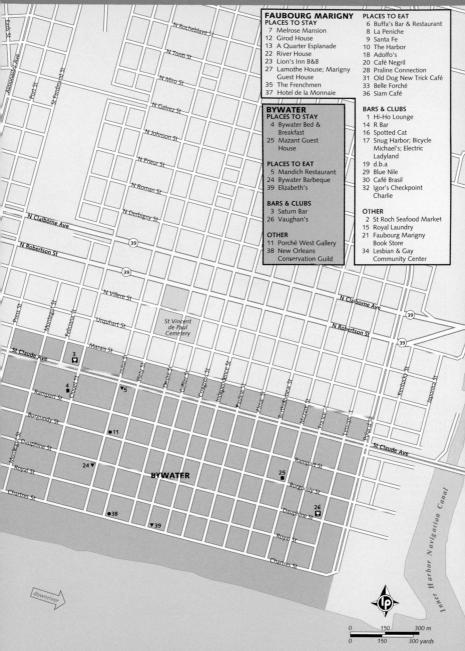

FAUBOURG MARIGNY
PLACES TO STAY
7 Melrose Mansion
12 Girod House
13 A Quarter Esplanade
22 River House
23 Lion's Inn B&B
27 Lamothe House; Marigny Guest House
35 The Frenchmen
37 Hotel de la Monnaie

BYWATER
PLACES TO STAY
4 Bywater Bed & Breakfast
25 Mazant Guest House

PLACES TO EAT
5 Mandich Restaurant
24 Bywater Barbeque
39 Elizabeth's

BARS & CLUBS
3 Saturn Bar
26 Vaughan's

OTHER
11 Porché West Gallery
38 New Orleans Conservation Guild

PLACES TO EAT
6 Buffa's Bar & Restaurant
8 La Peniche
9 Santa Fe
10 The Harbor
18 Adolfo's
20 Café Negril
28 Praline Connection
31 Old Dog New Trick Café
33 Belle Forché
36 Siam Café

BARS & CLUBS
1 Hi-Ho Lounge
14 R Bar
16 Spotted Cat
17 Snug Harbor; Bicycle Michael's; Electric Ladyland
19 d.b.a
29 Blue Nile
30 Café Brasil
32 Igor's Checkpoint Charlie

OTHER
2 St Roch Seafood Market
15 Royal Laundry
21 Faubourg Marigny Book Store
34 Lesbian & Gay Community Center

MAP 4 – CBD & WAREHOUSE DISTRICT

St Louis
Cemetery
No 2

■ 1

■ 2

● 3

4 ✛

■ 5

New Orleans
Public Library

*see MAP 7
Mid-City &
Esplanade Ridge*

MID-CITY

S Claiborne Ave

Cleveland St

Palmyra St

Tulane Ave

S Robertson St

S Villere St

Tulane Ave

Gravier St

New Orleans
Public Library

Gravier St

S Rocheblave St

S Tonti St

S Galvez St

S Johnson St

S Prieur St

S Roman St

Bertrand St

S Dorgenois St

S Miro St

Poydras St

Sugar Bowl Dr

Perdido St

City
Hall

**Louisiana
Superdome**

New Orleans
Arena

New
Orleans
Centre

Hyatt
Regency

Girod St

S Loyola Ave

■ 38

Earhart Blvd

90

Union
Passenger
Terminal

Main
Post
Office

Immigration &
Naturalization
Service

S Loyola Ave

Tulane Ave

Clio St

Erato St

Thalia St

90
BUS

Clio St

Erato St

Thalia St

S Liberty St

S Saratoga St

Simon Bolivar Ave

S Rampart St

S Robertson St

O'Keefe Ave

Julia St

Martin Luther King Jr Blvd

Carondelet St

Baronne St

*See MAP 5
Lower Garden &
Garden Districts*

Felicity St

Euterpe St

Terpsichore St

Melpomene St

S Saratoga St

Josephine St

Jackson Ave

Oretha Castle Haley Blvd

Polymnia St

Dryades St

Baronne St

Camp St

PLACES TO STAY

1 Days Inn
2 Radisson Hotel
5 Ramada Inn & Suites
  Downtown Superdome
8 Fairmont Hotel;
  American Airlines
  Office
10 Holiday Inn
  Downtown Superdome
15 Hampton Inn
22 Comfort Suites
  Downtown
28 Hotel Monaco; Cobalt
32 Windsor Court Hotel;
  Grill Room
35 Le Pavillion
44 Lafayette Hotel
69 Holiday Inn Select

PLACES TO EAT

12 New City Diner
17 Le Petit Paris
21 Lemon Grass
29 Liborio Cuban
  Restaurant
30 Restaurant Cuvée
31 Restaurant August
36 Bon Ton Café
37 Mother's
40 Vic's Kangaroo Café
47 Herbsaint
54 Louisiana Products
57 Emeril's
61 Taqueria Corona
62 Red Eye Grill

BARS & CLUBS

6 &
42 Pete Fountain's
48 Le Chat Noir
53 Mulate's
55 Michaul's
60 Howlin' Wolf
71 Circle Bar

OTHER

3 Tulane University Hospital
4 Medical Center of Louisiana
7 Orpheum Theater
9 Walgreens Pharmacy
11 Louisiana Philharmonic
  Orchestra Box Office
13 Hibernia National Bank
14 New Orleans Cotton Exchange
16 Indian Consulate
18 Meyer the Hatter
19 Rubenstein Bros
20 Whitney National Bank
23 UK, Danish & Korean Consulate
24 Liberty Camera Center
25 Factors Row
26 United Fruit Company
27 Downtown Fast Foto
33 Dominican Republic, Mexican
  & Spanish Consulate
34 World Trade Center; Post Office
38 Japanese Consulate
39 628 Gallery
40 Gallier Hall
41 French Consulate
43 Cookin' Cajun
45 Post Office
49 Kinko's Copy Center
50 Lighthouse
51 St Patrick's Church
52 Accent on Children's
  Arrangements
56 Louisiana Children's Museum
58 Thai Consulate
59 True Brew Theater
63 YMCA
64 Contemporary Arts Center
65 Robert E Lee Monument
66 Ogden Museum of Southern
  Art
67 Civil War Museum
68 National D-Day Museum
70 K&B Plaza
72 International Vintage Guitars
73 Hertz

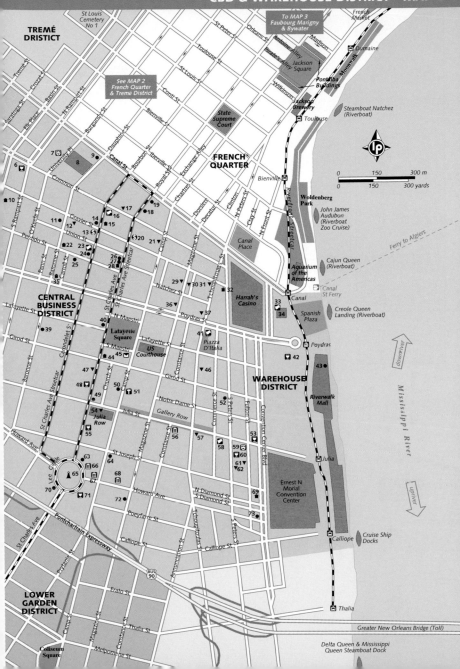

St Louis
Cemetery
No 1

**TREMÉ
DRISTICT**

To MAP 3
Faubourg Marigny
& Bywater

French
Market

Antoine Alley
Pirate Alley
Madison

Dumaine

St Peter St
Orleans St

Toulouse St

Jackson
Square

Pontalba
Buildings

**See MAP 2
French Quarter
& Tremé District**

St Louis St

Wilkinson

Jackson
Brewery

State
Supreme
Court

Conti St

Toulouse

Steamboat Natchez
(Riverboat)

Bienville St

**FRENCH
QUARTER**

7

8

9

Canal St

Bienville

6

Common St

Woldenberg
Park

10

John James
Audubon
(Riverboat)
Zoo Cruise)

Gravier St

14

17

16

15

11

12

Union St

13

20

18

19

21

22

23

24

25

26
27
28

Natchez St

29

30 31

32

**Harrah's
Casino**

Cajun Queen
(Riverboat)

Ferry to Algiers

**Aquarium
of the
Americas**

**Canal
Place**

35

36

37

**CENTRAL
BUSINESS
DISTRICT**

Lafayette St

Poydras

33

34

Canal

**Spanish
Plaza**

Canal
St Ferry

Creole Queen
Landing (Riverboat)

39

40

**Lafayette
Square**

N Maestri

41

Piazza
D'Italia

Poydras

Girod St

N Maestri

**US
Courthouse**

Lafayette St

45

44

46

Poydras

42

43

**WAREHOUSE
DISTRICT**

**Riverwalk
Mall**

47

48

49

50

51

Girod St

Mississippi River

downriver

upriver

Notre Dame St

Gallery Row

52

Julia

54 **Julia
Row**

55

56

57

58

53

59
60

61
62

Julia

**Ernest N
Morial
Convention
Center**

Calliope

Cruise Ship
Docks

St Joseph

63

64

65

66

68

67

69

70

71

72

73

Howard Ave

N Diamond St
S Diamond St

Poeyfarre St

**LOWER
GARDEN
DISTRICT**

Pontchartrain Expressway

Calliope St

Calliope St

BUS
90

Erato St

Thalia St

Thalia

Greater New Orleans Bridge (Toll)

**Coliseum
Square**

Melpomene St

Delta Queen & Mississippi
Queen Steamboat Dock

MAP 5 – LOWER GARDEN & GARDEN DISTRICTS

LOWER GARDEN DISTRICT

PLACES TO STAY
2 Maison St Charles
3 Avenue Garden Hotel
4 Prytania Park Hotel
8 Pontchartrain Hotel
12 Terrell Guest House
13 HI Marquette House Hostel
14 Garden District Hotel
16 Avenue Plaza Hotel; Mackie Shilstone Spa
22 St Vincent's Guest House
25 Josephine Guest House

PLACES TO EAT
1 Uglesich's
5 Please-U Restaurant
9 The Trolley Stop
23 Rue de la Course
26 Café Roma

BARS & CLUBS
15 Igor's Lounge
17 Red Room
27 Half Moon

OTHER
6 John Thornhill House
7 Goodrich-Stanley House
10 ATM
18 1328 Felicity St
19 John McGinty House
20 John T Moore House
21 Archibald Boulware House
24 Alliance Française
28 Jim Russell Rare Records
33 Southern Fossil & Mineral Exchange

GARDEN DISTRICT

PLACES TO STAY
36 Sully Mansion B&B

PLACES TO EAT
41 Commander's Palace
42 Parasol's
47 Rue de la Course

BARS & CLUBS
46 Balcony Bar & Cafe
49 The Bulldog

OTHER
29 Charles Briggs House
30 Chapel of Our Lady of Perpetual Help
31 Louise S McGehee School
32 Buckner House
34 Swiss Consulate
35 The Rink; Garden District Bookshop
37 Colonel Short's Villa
38 1315 First St
39 Anne Rice's House
40 1238 Philip St
43 Magazine Arcade
44 Ah-Ha
45 Funky Monkey
48 Big Fisherman Seafood
50 New Orleans Music Exchange

WAREHOUSE
DISTRICT

Ernest N
Morial
Convention
Center

Cruise
Ship
Docks

Calliope

See MAP 4
CBD & Warehouse
District

Pontchartrain Expressway

Poeyfarre St
Howard Ave
S Diamond St

Clio St
Erato St

BUS
90

Thalia St
Calliope St

Thalia
Greater New Orleans Bridge (toll)

Greater New Orleans Bridge (toll)

Delta Queen &
Mississippi Queen
Steamboat Dock

Erato St

Terpsichore St

Melpomene St

Coliseum
Square

Euterpe St

Race St

Annunciation
Center

Orange St

Richard St

LOWER
GARDEN
DISTRICT

Market St

St James St

Felicity St

New Orleans
General Hospital

Jackson Ave

Tchoupitoulas St

Mississippi River

downriver

upriver

GRETNA

First St

Jackson Ave Ferry

To Gretna

MAP 6 – UPTOWN & RIVERBEND

To Rivershack Tavern

River Rd

Oak Street Shopping Area

Joliet St

Carrollton Ave

Dante St

Dublin St

Hickory St

Green St

Cohn St

Birch St

Jeannette St

Willow St

Adams St

Plum St

Carrollton Cemetery

Spruce St

Hampson St

Oak St

Maple St

Zimpel St

Levee Park

Panola St

Short St

French St

Fern St

Broadway

Lowerline St

Pine St

Audubon Blvd

Audubon Blvd

Versailles Blvd

RIVERBEND

Park

Maple Street Shopping Area

Cherokee St

Hampson St

Maple St

Cambronne St

Burthe St

Ursuline College & Convent

State St

Teale Ave

St Charles Ave Streetcar

St Charles Ave

Pine St

Newcomb College

McAlister Dr

Calhoun St

Palmer Ave

Birdie St

Adams St

Hilary St

Dominican St

Millaudon St

Newcomb Blvd

Tulane University

Loyola St

Tulane University

Benjamin St

Hurst St

Audubon Pl (Private)

Loyola University

Nashville Ave

State St

Joseph St

Octavia St

St Charles Ave

Broadway

Broadway

Hillary St

Benjamin St

Garfield St

Pitt St

Audubon St

Walnut St

West Dr

Exposition Blvd

International Dr

Nashville

St Charles Ave

Jefferson Ave

Golf Course

Audubon Park

Benjamin St

Garfield St

Pitt St

Prytania St

Perrier St

Coliseum

Theodore St

Nashville Ave

Arabella St

Joseph St

Octavia St

Leontine St

Upperline St

Valmont St

Belfast St

State St

De Paul

Henry Clay Ave

Chestnut St

Camp St

Constance St

Magazine St

Patton St

Laurel St

North St

South St

Zoo Ave

Audubon Zoological Gardens

Riverview Dr

Whitney Ave

Magazine St

Patton St

Laurel St

Annunciation St

Tchoupitoulas St

Mississippi River

upriver

downriver

Bike Path

Bike Path

Children's Hospital

US Marine Hospital

Jefferson Ave

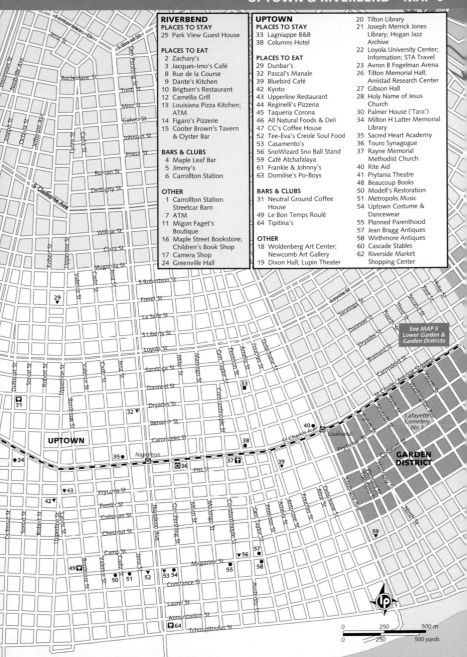

RIVERBEND
PLACES TO STAY
25 Park View Guest House

PLACES TO EAT
2 Zachary's
3 Jacques-Imo's Café
8 Rue de la Course
9 Dante's Kitchen
10 Brigtsen's Restaurant
12 Camellia Grill
13 Louisiana Pizza Kitchen;
   ATM
14 Figaro's Pizzerie
15 Cooter Brown's Tavern
   & Oyster Bar

BARS & CLUBS
4 Maple Leaf Bar
5 Jimmy's
6 Carrollton Station

OTHER
1 Carrollton Station
   Streetcar Barn
7 ATM
11 Migon Faget's
   Boutique
16 Maple Street Bookstore;
   Children's Book Shop
17 Camera Shop
24 Greenville Hall

UPTOWN
PLACES TO STAY
33 Lagniappe B&B
38 Columns Hotel

PLACES TO EAT
29 Dunbar's
32 Pascal's Manale
39 Bluebird Café
42 Kyoto
43 Upperline Restaurant
44 Reginelli's Pizzeria
45 Taqueria Corona
46 All Natural Foods & Deli
47 CC's Coffee House
52 Tee-Eva's Creole Soul Food
53 Casamento's
56 SnoWizard Sno Ball Stand
59 Café Atchafalaya
61 Frankie & Johnny's
63 Domilise's Po-Boys

BARS & CLUBS
31 Neutral Ground Coffee
   House
49 Le Bon Temps Roulé
64 Tipitina's

OTHER
18 Woldenberg Art Center;
   Newcomb Art Gallery
19 Dixon Hall; Lupin Theater

20 Tilton Library
21 Joseph Merrick Jones
   Library; Hogan Jazz
   Archive
22 Loyola University Center;
   Information; STA Travel
23 Avron B Fogelman Arena
26 Tilton Memorial Hall;
   Amistad Research Center
27 Gibson Hall
28 Holy Name of Jesus
   Church
30 Palmer House ('Tara')
34 Milton H Latter Memorial
   Library
35 Sacred Heart Academy
36 Touro Synagogue
37 Rayne Memorial
   Methodist Church
40 Rite Aid
41 Prytania Theatre
48 Beaucoup Books
50 Modell's Restoration
51 Metropolis Music
54 Uptown Costume &
   Dancewear
55 Planned Parenthood
57 Jean Bragg Antiques
58 Wirthmore Antiques
60 Cascade Stables
62 Riverside Market
   Shopping Center

MAP 7 – MID-CITY, ESPLANADE RIDGE & BAYOU ST JOHN

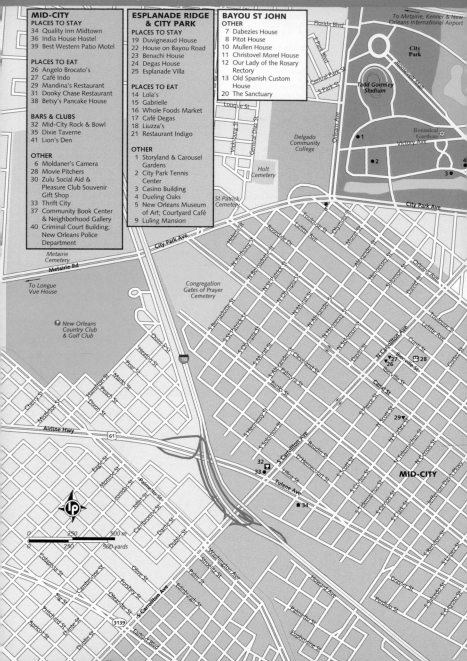

MID-CITY

PLACES TO STAY
- 34 Quality Inn Midtown
- 36 India House Hostel
- 39 Best Western Patio Motel

PLACES TO EAT
- 26 Angelo Brocato's
- 27 Café Indo
- 29 Mandina's Restaurant
- 31 Dooky Chase Restaurant
- 38 Betsy's Pancake House

BARS & CLUBS
- 32 Mid-City Rock & Bowl
- 35 Dixie Taverne
- 41 Lion's Den

OTHER
- 6 Moldaner's Camera
- 28 Movie Pitchers
- 30 Zulu Social Aid & Pleasure Club Souvenir Gift Shop
- 33 Thrift City
- 37 Community Book Center & Neighborhood Gallery
- 40 Criminal Court Building; New Orleans Police Department

ESPLANADE RIDGE & CITY PARK

PLACES TO STAY
- 19 Duvigneaud House
- 22 House on Bayou Road
- 23 Benachi House
- 24 Degas House
- 25 Esplanade Villa

PLACES TO EAT
- 14 Lola's
- 15 Gabrielle
- 16 Whole Foods Market
- 17 Café Degas
- 18 Liuzza's
- 21 Restaurant Indigo

OTHER
- 1 Storyland & Carousel Gardens
- 2 City Park Tennis Center
- 3 Casino Building
- 4 Dueling Oaks
- 5 New Orleans Museum of Art; Courtyard Café
- 9 Luling Mansion

BAYOU ST JOHN

OTHER
- 7 Dabezies House
- 8 Pitot House
- 10 Mullen House
- 11 Christovel Morel House
- 12 Our Lady of the Rosary Rectory
- 13 Old Spanish Custom House
- 20 The Sanctuary

To Lakeshore Park &
Lake Pontchartrain

To Dilliard
University

610

Sere St

Sere St

Lafreniere St

Pleasure St

Bayou Oaks
South Golf
Course

Florida Ave

Roger Williams St

DeSaix Blvd

Gentilly Blvd

Treasure St

Abundance St

Trafalgar

Derby Place
Castiglione
Belfort

Agriculture St

Industry St

Duels St

Fredericks Dr
Collins Diboll
Circle

LeLong Dr

St Louis
Cemetery
NO 3

Fair Grounds
Race Track

90

Beauregard
Monument

Moss St

Delgado Dr

7 🏛 1

🏛 8

Esplanade Ave

🏛 10

Magnolia
Bridge

12 🏛

13
🏛

🏛 5
9

14 ▼

15

🏛 11

BAYOU
ST JOHN

Fortin St

16 ▼

Maurepas St

17
▼

▼ 18

90

Aubry St

D'Abadie St

Onzaga St

Lapeyrouse St

19

Ponce de Leon St

Grande Route St John

DeSoto St

Le Page

● 20

Bell St

ESPLANADE
RIDGE

Kerlerec St

La Harpe St

Columbus St

N Dorgenois St

N Broad Ave

Paul Morphy St

Roger St

Gayoso St

Dupre St

N Lopez St

N Salcedo St

N Galvez St

N White St

21

22
23

St Bernard Ave

Barracks St

Governor Nicholls St

Ursulines Ave

St Philip St

Dumaine St

Jeans Ave

St Ann St

St Peter St

● 30

Esplanade Ave

24

25 ●

Bayou Rd

N Tonti St

N Rocheblave St

N Dorgenois St

N Prieur St

N Johnson St

N Galvez St

Kerlerec St

Bayou Rd

31

Orleans Ave

N Rocheblave St

N Dorgenois St

N Broad Ave

N White St

N Prieur St

N Johnson St

N Galvez St

● 36

37 ●

Bienville St

Iberville St

Canal St

90

N Rendon St

N Lopez St

N Salcedo St

N Galvez St

N Dupre St

N White St

▼
38

Toulouse St

N Miro St

N Tonti St

N Rocheblave St

N Dorgenois St

Cleveland St

Palmyra St

Banks St

40 ☒

Tulane Ave

☒ 41

90

S Broad Ave

S White St

St Louis St

Conti St

Lafitte Ave

Lafitte Ave

N Robertson St

N Claiborne Ave

N Derbigny St

N Roman St

N Prieur St

N Johnson St

10

Dumaine St

St Philip St

St Peter St

Toulouse St

Louis
Armstrong
Park

Municipal
Auditorium

TREMÉ
DISTRICT

Governor Nicholls St

N Villere St

N Robertson St

N Claiborne Ave

St Ann St

N Derbigny St

N Roman St

N Prieur St

London Outfall Canal

Park Ave

St Bernard Ave

Havana St

April St

Arts St

N St Bernard Ave

Treasure St

N Rocheblave St

N Tonti St

N Miro St

N Galvez St

N Prieur St

N Johnson St

Pleasure St

Desire St

Pauger St

N Roman St

Derbigny St

Roman St

N Robertson St

N Villere St

N Prieur St

N Derbigny St

St Philip St

Dumaine St

St Ann St

Treme St

MAP LEGEND

ROUTES

City	Regional	
		Freeway
		Toll Freeway
		Primary Road
		Secondary Road
		Tertiary Road
		Dirt Road

Pedestrian Mall
Steps
Tunnel
Walking Tour
Trail, Bike Trail
Path

TRANSPORTATION

Train
Streetcar
Bus Route
Ferry

ROUTE SHIELDS

Interstate Freeway (80)
US Highway (101)
State Highway (95)

HYDROGRAPHY

River; Creek
Canal
Water
Spring; Rapids
Waterfalls
Dry Lake

BOUNDARIES

International
State
County

AREAS

Beach
Building
Campus
Cemetery
Forest
Garden; Zoo
Golf Course
Park
Plaza
Reservation
Sports Field
Swamp; Mangrove

POPULATION SYMBOLS

○ NATIONAL CAPITAL .... National Capital
◉ STATE CAPITAL .... State Capital
● Large City .... Large City
● Medium City .... Medium City
● Small City .... Small City
○ Town; Village .... Town; Village

MAP SYMBOLS

● .... Place to Stay
▼ .... Place to Eat
● .... Point of Interest

Airfield	Cinema	Mountain
Airport	Dive Site	Museum
Archeological Site; Ruin	Embassy; Consulate	Observatory
Bank	Ferry Terminal	Park
Baseball Stadium	Footbridge	Parking Area
Battlefield	Fountain	Pass
Beach	Gas Station	Picnic Area
Border Crossing	Hindu Temple	Police Station
Buddhist Temple	Hospital	Pool
Bus Terminal	Information	Post Office
Cable Car; Chairlift	Internet Café	Pub; Bar
Campground	Lighthouse	Pueblo
Castle	Lookout	RV Park
Cathedral; Church	Mine	Shipwreck
Cave	Mission	Shopping Mall
Church; Cathedral	Monument	Skiing - Cross Country

Skiing - Downhill
Stately Home
Surfing
Synagogue
Taoist Temple
Taxi
Telephone
Theater
Toilet - Public
Tomb
Trailhead
Tram Stop
Transportation
Volcano
Windsurfing
Winery

Note: Not all symbols displayed above appear in this book.

LONELY PLANET OFFICES

Australia
Locked Bag 1, Footscray, Victoria 3011
☎ 03 8379 8000 fax 03 8379 8111
email: talk2us@lonelyplanet.com.au

USA
150 Linden St, Oakland, CA 94607
☎ 510 893 8555 TOLL FREE: 800 275 8555
fax 510 893 8572
email: info@lonelyplanet.com

UK
10a Spring Place, London NW5 3BH
☎ 020 7428 4800 fax 020 7428 4828
email: go@lonelyplanet.co.uk

France
1 rue du Dahomey, 75011 Paris
☎ 01 55 25 33 00 fax 01 55 25 33 01
email: bip@lonelyplanet.fr
www.lonelyplanet.fr

World Wide Web: www.lonelyplanet.com *or* AOL keyword: lp
Lonely Planet Images: www.lonelyplanetimages.com